The Pocket Hawaiian Dictionary
with a Concise Hawaiian Grammar

MARY KAWENA PUKUI
SAMUEL H. ELBERT
ESTHER T. MOOKINI

The University Press of Hawaii
Honolulu

First printing 1975
Second printing 1977
Third printing 1978

Copyright © 1975 by The University Press of Hawaii

Manufactured in the United States of America

Book design by Roger J. Eggers

Library of Congress Cataloging in Publication Data

Pukui, Mary Wiggin, 1895–
    The pocket Hawaiian dictionary, with a concise Hawaiian grammar.

    Bibliography: p.
    1. Hawaiian language—Dictionaries—English.
2. English language—Dictionaries—Hawaiian.   I. Elbert,
Samuel H., 1907—   joint author.   II. Mookini, Esther
K., joint author.   III. Title.
PL6446.P84 1975   499.4   74–78865
ISBN 0-8248-0307-8

The Pocket Hawaiian Dictionary

Contents

Preface

The Hawaiian Pocket Dictionary is intended for residents of the Islands and visitors who are interested in the Hawaiian language, and, more particularly, for beginning students of Hawaiian and for students of comparative Polynesian languages. Advanced students desiring to translate Hawaiian legends, historical documents, chants, and songs will need to consult Pukui and Elbert's *Hawaiian Dictionary,* which served as the source of the entries for the present volume and for the definitions and glosses. Words to be included in this book were chosen on the basis of frequency of use in the contemporary Hawaiian scene. Words traced back to ancestral forms were also included even though a few of them are not in common use today. About 6,000 Hawaiian words are entered in this book, and, in the English-Hawaiian section, about 4,800 English words. These totals represent about 23 percent of the 26,000 Hawaiian entries in the Pukui and Elbert dictionary, and nearly 40 percent of the 12,500 English entries.

About 1,300 words in the Hawaiian-English section are labeled as inherited from ancestral Polynesian forms, Proto Polynesian and its less remote daughter languages. The methods used in tracing these words are briefly explained in section 11 of the grammar included in this volume. The Pukui and Elbert dictionary, in contrast, traced back only about 239 words, but to a greater antiquity.

In the English-Hawaiian section, as well as in the Pukui and Elbert prototype, Hawaiian glosses for any given word are arranged in approximate order of frequency of usage. Not every Hawaiian word appearing here will be found in the Hawaiian-English section, but all will be found in the

Pukui and Elbert dictionary. Not all derivatives of a given English base are entered. For example *observe* is included but not *observation*, *abortion* but not *abort*, *happy* but not *happiness*. In general, Hawaiian verbs are made into nouns by the addition of *'ana* to the base; comparatives are made by addition of *a'e* to the Hawaiian base.

The careful student will note a few changes in spelling in this volume, especially in the assignment of macrons. We believe the present rendition to be the more accurate, and the one that should be used by modern students. Study of a language for several decades is bound to result in refinements of analysis. A very few other changes have been made; particularly in updating the scientific names of plants and animals. The grammar section was read in manuscript by Andrew Pawley and Albert J. Schütz. Dr. Pawley also checked reconstructed ancestral forms. We are grateful also to Elizabeth Bushnell for her helpful criticisms. While we have attempted to take advantage of the many wise suggestions offered by these friends, none of them can be held responsible for our shortcomings!

Pronunciation of Hawaiian

Consonants

p, k about as in English but with less aspiration.

h, l, m, n about as in English.

w after *i* and *e* usually like *v;* after *u* and *o* usually like *w;* initially and after *a* like *v* or *w*.

' a glottal stop, similar to the sound between the *oh's* in English *oh-oh*.

Vowels

Unstressed

> **a** like *a* in above
> **e** like *e* in bet
> **i** like *y* in city
> **o** like *o* in sole
> **u** like *oo* in moon

but without off-glides.

Stressed

> **a, ā** like *a* in far
> **e** like *e* in bet
> **ē** like *ay* in play
> **i, ī** like *ee* in see
> **o, ō** like *o* in sole
> **u, ū** like *oo* in moon

but without off-glides; vowels marked with macrons are somewhat longer than other vowels.

Diphthongs

ei, eu, oi, ou, ai, ae, ao, au   these are always stressed on the first member, but the two members are not as closely joined as in English.

Stress (or Accent)

On all vowels marked with macrons: ā, ē, ī, ō, ū.
Otherwise on the next-to-last syllable and alternating preceding syllables of words, except that words containing five syllables without macrons are stressed on the first and fourth syllables. Final stress in a word (') is usually louder than preceding stress or stresses ('): *hále, maká'u, hòlohólo, 'èlemakúle*.

For more details see section 2 of the Grammar.

Abbreviations used in the dictionary

Cap.	beginning with a capital letter
Cf.	compare
Eng.	of English origin
Fig.	figuratively
Lit.	literally
PEP	Proto Eastern Polynesian reconstruction (see Grammar, section 11)
PNP	Proto Nuclear Polynesian reconstruction (see Grammar, section 11)
PPN	Proto Polynesian reconstruction (see Grammar, section 11)
Redup.	reduplication
Var.	variant

Hawaiian-English

A

a. 1. Of. PPN (')*a.* 2. Like, in the manner of. 3. When, until, as far as. 4. And.

-a. Passive/imperative suffix. PPN *-a.*

ā. Jaw. PEP *aa.*

'a. Oh! Well! Ah!

'ā. Fiery, burning. ho'ā. To set on fire, to light. PNP *kaa.*

'ā-. In the nature of. See *'āhina.*

a'a Small root, vein, nerve, tendon. PPN *aka.*

'a'a. 1. To dare, challenge. 2. To gird, tie on. 3. Bag, pocket; fiber from coconut husk. PPN *kaka.*

'a'ā. 1. To burn; glowing. hō-'a'ā. To kindle, light. PPN *kakaha.* 2. *Aa* lava; stony, abounding with rough *aa* lava.

'ā'ā. 1. Dumbness; to stutter, stammer. 2. Dwarf, small person. 3. Demented, panic-stricken. hō'ā'ā. To look about in confusion. 4. Male 'ō'ō bird. PPN *kakaa.* PEP *kaakaa.*

'a'ahu. Clothing in general; to put on or wear clothing. See *'ahu.*

'a'ahuwā. To speak reproachfully; jealous challenge.

'a'ai. 1. Redup. of *'ai, 1;* eating, spreading, increasing (as a sore). 2. Bright, as of contrasting colors.

'a'aiole. Inferior, weak. *Fig.,* of persons dying before their time.

'a'aka. Surly, cranky, roiled.

'a'aki. Redup. of *'aki, 1;* to nip repeatedly. *Fig.,* thick, obscure, dark, penetrating.

a'a koko. Vein, blood vessel.

a'a kūkūkū. Varicose veins. *Lit.,* raised veins.

'a'ala. Fragrant, sweet-smelling. *Fig.,* of high rank, royal. PPN *kakala.*

'a'ala-'ula. A branching, velvety-green, succulent-appearing seaweed (*Codium edule*).

a'alele. Pulse. *Lit.,* leaping vein.

'a'ali. Redup. of *'ali, 1;* scarred, marked, grooved.

'a'ali'i. Native hardwood shrubs or trees (*Dodonaea,* all species).

'a'aiina. 1. Scarred. 2. Large, fat, weak.

'a'alo. Redup. of *'alo, 1, 2.*

'a'a lole. Coconut cloth, European cloth.

a'alolo. Nerve. *Lit.,* brain vein.

'a'alu. Ravine, small stream, valley.

'a'ama. 1. A large, black, edible crab (*Grapsus grapsus tenuicrustatus*) that runs over shore rocks. PPN *kamakama.* 2. To spread and relax, as the fingers.

'a'ā maka. To stare with wide-open eyes, as in desire, fear, or intent to frighten. hō'a'ā maka. To stare.

'a'amo'o. Young coconut cloth; gauze. *Lit.,* lizard coconut cloth.

'a'ana. To use abusive language, revile.

'a'anema. To criticize maliciously.

'a'a niu. Coconut cloth.

'a'ano. Overbearing, arrogant, daring. hō'a'ano. To act the bully, boast of courage that is lacking; to challenge, dare.

'a'api. Warped, curved.

'a'apo. To learn quickly.

'a'apu. Coconut-shell cup; cuplike. hō'a'apu. To form a cup of the hollow of the hand; to fold a leaf into a cup.

'a'apūhaka. Girdle, belt. *Lit.,* loin belt.

'a'ā pu'upu'u. Sharp or water-worn, coarse gravel or rock.

'a'au. To move here and there, rove.

'ā'aua. Coarse, as wrinkled or blotched skin.

'a'awa. Wrasse fishes, including hogfish (*Bodianus bilunulatus*). PPN *kawakawa*.

a'e. 1. Several native trees, soapberry (*Sapindus saponaria*). PPN *ake.* **2.** (*Cap.*) Northeast trade wind. Cf. *Moa'e.* **3.** To, upward, obliquely, sideways; next; then (directional particle). PPN *hake.* **4.** Sign of the comparative degree.

'ae. 1. Yes; to say yes, consent, agree, approve. PEP (')a(a)e. **2.** Sap wrung from seaweed or leaves of plants such as taro; saliva, drooling of the mouth. **3.** Fine, smooth. **hō-'ae.** To make fine, soft, etc. **4.** To rise (of the tide).

'a'e. To step over, get on top of, tread upon, trespass. *Fig.*, oppressed. PPN *kake.*

aea. To rise up; to raise the head; to come up from under water.

'ae'a. Wandering, shiftless, unstable, to wander. **hō'ae'a.** To cause to wander; to wander.

aeae. A prolonged sound, wail. **ho'āeāe.** A style of chanting with prolonged vowels and fairly short phrases.

a'ea'e. Mixing of a dark or brilliant color with a lighter one, as feathers in a lei.

'ae'ae. Redup. of *ae, 3.*

'a'e'a'e. Redup. of *'a'e.*

'ae'a-hauka'e. Vagrant person, trespasser; to trespass.

'ae kai. Place where sea and land meet; water's edge.

'aeko, aeto. 1. Eagle. **2.** Alto. *Eng.*

'aeko-kula. Golden eagle.

'aelike. Agreement, contract, truce.

āelo. Rotten (of eggs that do not hatch due to infertility). *Fig.*, spoiled, worthless. PPN *'elo.*

a'e nei. Just now, lately; nearby, not far; ordinary.

āe'o. 1. Stilts. **2.** Hawaiian stilt (bird).

āewa. 1. Thin, spindly; to weave to and fro, as seaweed. **2.** Possessing a family or lineage.

aha. Why? What? For what reason? To do what? *He aha kēlā?* What's that? *No ke aha?* Why? PEP *afa.*

āhā. Aha (exclamation of surprise).

'aha. 1. Meeting, assembly, gathering, court. **2.** Sennit; cord braided of coconut husk or human hair; string for a musical instrument; measurement of an edge or border. **hō'aha.** To make or braid *'aha.* PPN *kafa.*

'ahā. Four (usually in counting in a series); four times. *Pō-'ahā,* Thursday.

ahaaha. To pant, to breathe hard with heat, as a dog.

'aha'aha. 1. Cordage. **2.** To sit with back stiff and upright, arms akimbo, head up, as with haughty air of superiority. PPN *kafa.*

'aha'aina. Feast, banquet; to feast. *Lit.*, meal gathering.

'aha'aina a ka Haku. Holy Communion; feast of the Lord.

'aha'aina ho'ola'a. Feast of consecration or dedication, as of a house, church, canoe, or fish net.

'aha'aina ho'omana'o. Commemorative or anniversary feast.

'aha'aina komo. Initiation feast.

'aha'aina laulima. Feast held after completion of a joint project or cooperative undertaking, especially harvest.

'aha'aina make. Funeral feast, intended to comfort the mourners.

'aha'aina male (mare). Wedding feast or reception.

'aha'aina māwaewae. Feast given shortly after the birth of the first child, intended to clear the way (māwaewae) of misfortune for that child and for all others to follow.

'aha'aina mōliaola. Feast of the Passover.

'aha'aina pelena (berena). Holy Communion. Lit., feast of bread.

'aha'aina piha makahiki. Feast on the first birthday of a child, or to celebrate any anniversary. Lit., feast for completion of the year.

'aha'aina puka. Graduation feast.

'aha'aina 'ūniki. Graduation feast, as for hula dancing.

'aha 'āpana. District court.

'aha 'elele. Convention of delegates; name for American presidential conventions.

ahahana. Syllables repeated in chants; a taunting singsong teasing phrase, used especially by children.

'aha hāwele. Cord support for gourd water bottles.

'aha hīmeni. Song festival, concert.

'aha hō'ike makahiki. Annual meeting of Sunday schools, as of Congregationalists.

'aha ho'okolokolo. General name for court assembly.

'aha ho'okolokolo 'āpana. District court.

'aha ho'okolokolo ho'omalu. Police court.

'aha ho'okolokolo ka'apuni. Circuit court.

'aha ho'okolokolo ki'eki'e. Supreme court.

'aha ho'okolokolo koa. Military court.

'aha ho'okolokolo ko'iko'i. Superior court.

'aha ho'omalu. Administrative body, assembly.

'aha ho'oponopono i ka noho-na. Court of domestic relations.

'ahahui. Society, club, association.

'Ahahui Hō'ikaika Kalikiano. Christian Endeavor Society.

'ahahui hō'ole wai 'ona. Temperance union.

'Ahahui Kanu Kō Hawai'i. Hawaiian Sugar Planters' Association.

'ahahui kula Kāpaki (Sabati). Sunday school association.

'Ahahui Māmakakaua. Sons and Daughters of Hawaiian Warriors. Lit., warriors' society.

'Ahahui Mo'olelo Hawai'i. Hawaiian Historical Society.

'āha'i. To carry off, chase, rout; to flee, run away.

'āha'iha'i. Redup. of 'āha'i.

'aha iki. Small gathering for private conversation; small or secret council.

'aha'ilono. Reporter, messenger, bringer of news; to tell the news.

'aha inu. Drinking party.

'āha'i 'ōlelo. Messenger; to carry word.

'aha ka'apuni. Circuit court.

'aha kākau. Court of records.

'aha kau kānāwai. Session of the legislature.

'aha ki'eki'e. Supreme court.

'ahakū. Cord used for measuring.

'aha kuhina. Cabinet, assembly of ministers.

'aha kūkā. Council meeting, discussion meeting, conference.

'ahalualike. Rectangle. Lit., two equal sides.

'aha lunakahiko. Meeting of elders.

'aha lunakānāwai. Judiciary session, meeting of judges.

'aha maha. Place or assembly for practice of athletic games. Lit., assembly for relaxation.

'aha mele. Concert, song concert, song festival.

'aha mokupuni. Island conference, with representatives from a single island, especially of Congregationalists.

ahana. Same as ahahana.

'aha'ōlelo. Legislature, assembly; to hold such meetings.

'aha'ōlelo kau kānāwai. Legislature, law-making body.

'aha'ōlelo lāhui. Congress of the United States; national assembly.

'aha'ōlelo nui. Congress.

'aha o nā lunakānāwai 'āpana. District court.

'aha pae'āina. Convention of delegates from all the islands, especially one held by the Hawaiian Evangelical Association of Congregational Christian Churches.

'aha pule. Congregation, prayer assembly.

ahe. Breeze; to blow or breathe gently.

'ahē. A hacking cough; to cough.

'āhē. Timid, shy.

ahea. When (interrogative, future).

aheahe. Redup. of ahe; soft, gentle in sound.

'āheahea. To wilt, as a plant; warm, insipid.

'āhewa. To condemn, blame. **ho'āhewa.** To find guilty.

ahi. Fire, match; to burn in a fire, destroy by fire. PPN *afi*.

'ahi. Hawaiian tuna fishes, especially the yellowfin tuna (*Thunnus albacares*).

'ahia. How many (interrogative).

ahiahi. Evening; to become evening. PPN *afiafi*.

Ahiahi Kalikimaka. Christmas Eve.

Ahiahi Makahiki Hou. New Year's Eve.

'āhihi. Any plant with long runners or creepers.

'ahiku. Seven (especially in counting in a series); seven times.

'āhina. Gray, gray- or white-haired. See *hina, 2.*

'āhinahina. 1. Same as 'āhina. 2. The silversword (*Argyroxiphium sandwicense*), a native plant found only at altitudes of 6,000 feet or more on Maui and Hawai'i.

ahipele. Match.

'āhiu. Wild, untamed, as animals.

'āhiwa. Dark, somber, dusky.

aho. 1. Line, cord, lashing fishing line. PPN *afo*. 2. Breath; to breathe. *Fig.*, patience. **ho-'āho.** A narrow escape. PEP *a(f, s)o*. 3. It is better (always used after *e*). *E aho ia*, that's better.

'aho. Thatch purlin and rafter. PPN *kaso*.

āhole. A fish (*Kuhlia sandvicensis*).

āholehole. Young stage of the *āhole* fish.

ahona. Better, well, improved.

ahonui. Patience; patient, enduring. *Lit.*, great breath.

ahu. Heap, pile; altar, shrine. **ho'āhu.** To pile or heap up; to lay away. PPN *afu*.

'ahu. Garment or covering for the upper part of the body and shoulders, as a cape, shirt, coat; to put on or wear such. PPN *kafu*.

āhua. To swell, as a wave; heap, mound. **ho'āhua.** To pile up.

ahuahu. Healthy, vigorous; strength and vigor; to grow rapidly.

ahu 'ai. To overeat, waste food.

'āhui. Bunch or cluster, as of bananas.

'āhui hala. Pandanus fruit.

ahu lā'ī. Ti-leaf raincoat or cape.

ahulau. Pestilence, epidemic.

ahuli'u. Overheated; white-hot.

ahulu. Overdone, overcooked.

'**āhuluhulu.** Young of the *kūmū* fish. PNP *'afulu.*

ahupua'a. Land division usually extending from the uplands to the sea.

'**ahu'ula.** Feather cloak or cape.

ahu waiwai. Storehouse, heap of goods.

ai. 1. Who. PPN *hai.* 2. Short for *aia,* there. Cf. *ai hea, ai lalo, ai loa.* 3. To have sexual relations. PPN *ha'i.* 4. Linking or anaphoric particle. PPN *ai.*

aī. Interjection of surprise.

-a'i. Verbal suffix. See *lua'i, luma'i.* Cf. *Kaua'i, kaula'i.* PPN *-'aki.*

'**ai.** 1. Food or food plant, especially vegetable food; to eat, rule. **hō'ai.** To feed, give food to. PPN *kai.* 2. Score, points in a game; stake, wager. PPN *kai.*

'**ā'ī.** Neck. PNP *ka(a)kii.*

aia. 1. There, there it is. 2. Depending on, only if. *Aia nō ia iā'oe,* depending on you; it's up to you.

'**aiā.** Ungodly, wicked. PPN *kaiha'a.*

aia ho'i. Behold!

a'ia'i. Bright, as moonlight; fair, shining.

aia kā. There now!

aia lā. There!

'**aialo.** Attendant or intimate of a chief.

'**aiana.** Clothes iron; to iron, press, as clothes. *Eng.*

aia na'e. But, furthermore.

'**ai'ē.** Debt: to owe. **hō'ai'ē.** To loan; to borrow.

'**aiea.** All species of the genus *Nothocestrum,* soft-wooded shrubs and trees.

ai hea, aia i hea. Where?

'**aihue.** To steal, rob; thief.

'**aihue kanaka.** To kidnap; kidnapper.

'**ā'ī kala.** Collar. *Lit.,* neck collar (*Eng.*)

'**aikalima.** Ice cream. *Eng.*

'**ai kanaka.** Cannibal; maneater.

aikāne. Friend; friendly.

'**ai kapu.** To eat under taboo; to observe eating taboos.

'**ai kepa.** To cut or tear obliquely, as with teeth or edged instrument.

'**ai kepakepa.** Redup. of '*ai kepa;* to snap the jaws; to speak rapidly.

'**aikola.** Interjection of scorn or derision. **hō'aikola.** To treat contemptuously. Perhaps PEP *kaitoa.*

ai lā. Short for *aia lā.*

'**aila.** Any oil, grease; to oil, grease. *Eng.*

'**ai lā.** Scorched by the sun.

'**ailahonua.** Kerosene. *Lit.,* earth oil.

'**aila ho'omalo'o pena.** Turpentine. *Lit.,* oil for drying paint.

'**aila ho'onahā.** Castor oil. *Lit.,* purge oil.

ai laila, aia i laila. There, to be there.

'**aila koka (koda).** Cod-liver oil.

'**aila kolī.** Castor oil. *Lit.,* castor-bean oil.

ai lalo, aia i lalo. Down there.

'**aila mahu.** Kerosene. *Lit.,* steam oil.

'**ailana.** Island. *Eng.*

'**aila palai.** Frying oil. *Eng.*

'**aila pua'a.** Lard, pork grease.

'**ailea.** Gasoline (contraction of '*aila,* oil, and *ea,* air).

ai loa, aia i loa. Away off in the distance.

'**ailolo.** Ceremony marking the end of training.

-'ailona. hō'ailona. Sign, symbol, emblem, mark; trophy, emblem of victory.

ai luna, aia i luna. Up there.

'**ai māmā.** Light meal, snack.

'**ai moku.** Ruler of a *moku* (district or island).

'**aina.** Meal.

'āina. Land, earth. PPN *kaainga.*

'aina ahiahi. Evening meal, supper, dinner.

'aina awakea. Noon meal, lunch.

'āina 'ē. Foreign land.

'āina hānau. Land of one's birth, native land, homeland.

'aina kakahiaka. Morning meal, breakfast.

'ainakini. Navy blue cotton cloth.

'āina kō. Cane trash, bagasse.

'āina kū'ai. Land purchased or for sale; land in fee simple.

'āina lei ali'i. Crown lands.

'āina makua. Fatherland.

'ai noa. To eat without observance of taboos.

ai'ole. Or.

'ai pa'a. Cooked taro pounded into a hard mass not mixed with water, sometimes preserved in ti-leaf bundles. *Fig.,* a difficult problem. *Lit.,* hard *poi.*

'ā'ī-pahāha. Mumps. *Lit.,* swollen neck.

'aipuni. To encircle, go around.

'ā'īpu'upu'u. Steward.

aīwa. Same as āīwaīwa. Kapua-aīwa (name of Ka-mehameha V), mysterious taboo.

'aīwa. Nine (usually in counting in a series); nine times.

'ai waiū. To suckle, nurse. *Lit.,* to eat milk.

aīwaīwa. Inexplicable, mysterious. ho'āīwaīwa. Mystifying, causing wonder.

aka. Shadow, reflection, image. ho'oaka. To cast a shadow or reflection. PPN *'ata.*

aka-. Carefully, slowly. PEP *ata-.*

akā. But, however, nevertheless, on the other hand.

'aka. To laugh, laughter. PPN *kata.*

akaaka, akaka. Clear, luminous; distinct. ho'ākaaka. To clarify, explain. PEP *ataata.*

'aka'aka. To laugh, ridicule; laughter, merriment. hō'aka-'aka. To cause laughter, create mirth.

'aka'akai. 1. The great bulrush (*Scirpus validus*). 2. Onion.

'aka'akai-pilau. Garlic.

'aka'akai-pūpū. Garlic. *Lit.,* bunched onion.

akahai. Modest, gentle, meek.

akahele. Slow in doing anything; cautious, careful.

'akahi. 1. One (especially in counting in a series). 2. For the first time, never before.

akahoe. To paddle carefully, silently.

akaholo. To sail or run cautiously.

ākai. By the sea.

akakē. Spry, quick, especially about getting into people's way.

akakū. Vision; reflection, as in a mirror.

akaku'u. Lessened; grow calm; quieted.

'ākala. 1. Pink. 2. Two endemic raspberries (*Rubus hawaiensis* and *R. macraei*) and the thimbleberry (*R. rosaefolius*).

akamai. Smart, clever. PPN *'atamai.*

'Akamu, Adamu. Adam. *Eng.*

'ākau. 1. Right (not left). PEP *katau.* Cf. PPN *mata'u.* 2. North.

aka'ula. Red sunset. *Lit.,* red shadow.

ake. 1. Liver. PPN *'ate.* 2. To desire, yearn.

ākea. Broad, wide, public, at large. *Fig.,* liberal. PPN *'aatea.*

'ākea. Starboard or outer hull of a double canoe. PPN *katea.*

'āke'ake'a. To block, hinder; obstruction.

ake maka. Raw liver, as eaten after cleaning and salting.

akemāmā. Lung. *Lit.*, light liver.

akena. To boast, brag.

ākepakepa. Unkempt, as hair; oblique.

'akeu. Active, lively; pleasant.

'aki. 1. To take a nip and let go; to nibble; to bite off the bark of sugarcane; to heal, as a wound; sharp recurring pain. *Fig.*, to attack, snap at. PNP *kati.* 2. Height, tip, top (preceded by *ke*). 3. Pillow.

'aki'aki. Redup. of *'aki, 1;* to nibble, as a fish.

'aki'aki-haole. Buffalo grass (*Stenotaphrum secundatum*).

'akiki. Dwarfed; dwarf.

'aki-lolo. A wrasse fish of the *hīnālea* type (*Gomphosus varius*).

'akimalala, adimarala. Admiral. *Eng.*

'akiu. To search, seek, probe.

ako. Thatching; to thatch. PPN *'ato.*

'ako. 1. To cut, shear, clip, trim, as hair. PEP *kato.* 2. Itch, throat irritation. *Fig.*, lust.

'ako'ako. 1. Redup. of *'ako, 1, 2.* 2. Crest of a wave; to break or swell, as waves.

ākoakoa. To assemble; assembled, collected. **ho'ākoakoa.** To assemble, congregate. PPN *kaatoa.*

'āko'ako'a. Coral in general.

'akolo. To creep; to put out small roots, as potatoes.

'akolu. Three (as in counting in a series); three times.

aku. 1. Skipjack (*Katsuwonus pelamis*); to run, of *aku* fish. PPN *'atu.* 2. Particle expressing direction away from the speaker, and time either past (with *nei*) or future. PPN *atu.*

akua. God, goddess, spirit, image, idol; divine, supernatural, godly. **ho'ākua.** To deify, make a god of; godlike. PPN *'atua.*

akua kahikolu. Holy trinity.

akua lapu. Ghost, apparition.

akua loa. A tall image, especially an image of Lono carried on a circuit of the island during the *makahiki*, harvest festival.

akua pā'ani. God of sports that accompanied the *akua loa* on its circuit, to preside at the sport festivals.

akua poko. God of the *makahiki* that went only as far as the border of a district.

'āku'iku'i. 1. To pound. See *ku'i, 1.* 2. A long fish net; to drive fish into the net by striking the water with sticks.

'akūkū. Tossing; jolting, as a vehicle on a rough road.

akule. Bigeye or goggle-eyed scad fish (*Trachurops crumenophthalmus*). PPN *'atule.*

'ākulikuli. General name for succulent plants. PEP *katuli.*

'ākulikuli-lei. The ice plant (*Mesembryanthemum*), from Africa, a low succulent with thick, narrow leaves and pink, rose, or orange flowers (used for leis).

'akumu. Broken or cut off; blunt, stumpy.

aku nei. A while ago. See *aku, 2.*

ala. 1. Path, road, trail. PPN *hala.* 2. To waken; awake. PPN *'ara.* **ho'āla.** To awaken someone. 3. To rise up, come forward. *Ala hou*, resurrection. **ho'āla.** To arouse, stir up.

'ala. Fragrant, perfumed; fragrance (preceded by *ke*). *Fig.*, esteemed, chiefly. **hō-'ala.** To perfume.

'alā. Dense waterworn volcanic stone, as used for *poi* pounders, adzes, hula stones. PPN *kalaa.*

'āla'a. A large tree (*Pouteria*

sandwicensis). PPN *kalaka*.

'ala'ala-wai-nui. All species of *Peperomia*, small native succulent forest herbs, related to *'awa*.

'alae. Mudhen or Hawaiian gallinule (*Gallinula chloropus sandvicensis*); a cry of this bird, believed a bad omen. PPN *kalae*.

'alaea. Water-soluble colloidal ocherous earth, used for coloring salt, for medicine, for dye.

'alae-kea. Hawaiian coot (*Fulica americana alai*), a marsh and pond bird.

'alae-'ula. Hawaiian gallinule or mudhen (*Gallinula chloropus sandvicensis*).

alahaka. Plank bridge; rough road over ravines or chasms.

alahaki. Mountain ladder or steps cut into a cliff.

alahao. Railway, railroad track. *Lit.*, iron road.

alahe'e-haole. Mock orange (*Murraya paniculata*).

ala hele. Pathway, route, road, way to go, means of transportation.

ala hele wāwae. Pedestrian's road, sidewalk.

alahia. Passive/imperative of *ala*, 2. PPN *'arafia*.

ala hou. Resurrection; to rise again.

alahula. A frequented and well-known path.

ālai. Obstruction; to hinder, oppose. PEP *aala'i*.

'ala'ihi. Various species of squirrelfishes of the genus *Holocentrus*.

a laila. See *laila*.

ala kai. Sea course, as of canoe or ship; path where one must swim around a projecting cliff or bluff.

alaka'i. To lead, direct; leader, conductor.

alakō. To drag.

'alalā. 1. To bawl, cry, caw, scream. 2. Hawaiian crow (*Corvus tropicus*).

alaloa. Highway, main road, belt road around an island.

'alamihi. A common black crab (*Metopograpsus messor*). PPN *kalamisi*.

alamimo. Quick.

ala muku. Cut-off or unfinished road, dead-end road.

alana. Awakening, rising. See *ala*, 2, 3.

'ālana. 1. Offering, especially a free-will offering. 2. Light, buoyant.

alani. Brown seaweeds (*Dictyota* spp.), regularly divided into narrow segments, and very bitter to the taste.

'alani. Any kind of orange, both fruit and tree.

'alani-Pākē. Tangerine (*Citrus nobilis* var. *deliciosa*). *Lit.*, Chinese orange.

alanui. Street, road, highway. *Lit.*, large path.

alanui hele wāwae. Sidewalk.

ala 'ololī. Narrow path, lane.

'ālapa. Athletic, active; athlete.

'alapahi. Slander, falsehood; to defame.

alapi'i. Stairs, steps, ladder.

alapi'i kū. Steep road or path.

alapi'i mele. Musical scale.

alapine. 1. Quick. 2. Frequent, often.

alaula. Light of early dawn, sunset glow. *Lit.*, flaming road.

ala'ula. Red dust in a road.

ala'ume. To draw, pull, attract.

'alawa. To glance.

alawai. Channel, canal.

alawī. To shriek; shrill.

alawiki. To hurry; quick.

ale. To swallow, gulp.

'ale. Wave, crest of a wave; to form waves; to well, as tears in the eyes. PPN *kale*.

'ale'ale. Redup. of *'ale*; stirring, moving, rippling.

alelo. 1. Tongue, language. PPN *'alelo.* 2. Concave curve of the lower portion of the *lei palaoa,* whaletooth pendant, suggestive of a tongue.

'alemanaka. Almanac, calendar. *Eng.*

'ale'o. Tower, high lookout; towering.

'alepapeka, alepabeta. Alphabet. *Eng.*

'āleuleu. Old, worn out, as tapa, mats, clothing.

'ālewa. Same as *'ālewalewa.*

'ālewalewa. Buoyant, floating.

'ali. 1. Scar, depression, groove. 2. To dig. PNP *kali.*

alia. To wait, stop; usually as a command: Stop!

ālia. Salt bed, salt-encrusted area; salty. PNP *aalia.*

aliali. Crystal clear, white. PPN *'ali.*

'alihi. 1. Cords or fine ropes threaded through marginal meshes of upper and lower edges of nets, to which were attached floats and sinkers. PEP *kalifi.* 2. Horizon.

'alihikaua. General, commander in battle.

ali'i. Chief, chiefess, king, queen, noble; royal, kingly; to rule or act as a chief. *Fig.,* kind. PPN *'ariki.*

ali'i 'ai moku. Chief who rules a *moku* (district).

ali'ikoa. Military officer, officer of army or navy.

'ālikalika. Clammy, sticky, tenacious. *Fig.,* stingy.

'ālike, ālike. Alike.

'alima. Five (especially in counting in a series); five times.

'alimakika, arimatika. Arithmetic. *Eng.*

'ālina. Scar, blemish, maimed. *Fig.,* low, disgraced.

alo. Front, face, presence; upper surface. PPN *'aro.*

'alo. 1. To dodge, evade, avoid.

PPN *kalo.* 2. To be with, go with, attend.

aloali'i. In the presence of chiefs; royal court.

aloalo. All kinds of hibiscus.

'aloe. Aloe, any plant of the genus *Aloe.*

aloha. Aloha, love, mercy, compassion, pity; greeting; loved one; to love; to greet, hail. Greetings! Good-by! Common greetings follow: *Aloha 'oe,* may you be loved, or greetings (to one person). *Aloha kāua,* may there be friendship between us, greetings (to one person). *Aloha kākou,* same as above, but to more than one person. *Ke aloha nō!* Aloha! Greetings! *Aloha ali'i,* royalist. *Aloha 'āina,* love of the land. *Aloha 'ino!* What a pity! *Aloha akua,* love of god. *Me ke aloha o Kawena,* with the love (or greeting) of Kawena. *'O wau iho no me ke aloha,* I remain, with very best regards. The following greetings were introduced by the missionaries: *Aloha ahiahi,* good evening. *Aloha kakahiaka,* good morning. PPN *'alofa.*

aloha kakahiaka. See *aloha.*

ālohaloha. Redup. of *aloha.* **hō'ālohaloha.** To make love; to give thanks.

aloha 'oe. See *aloha.*

aloha 'ole. Pitiless, without love.

'alohi. To shine, sparkle; bright, brilliant. PEP *kalo (f, s)i.*

'ālohilohi. Redup. of *'alohi.*

alolua. Two-sided, two-faced; facing one another, as cliffs on opposite sides of a valley.

alu. Combined, acting together; to cooperate, act together.

'alu. Depression, ravine; descent, as of trail or road; to bend, stoop. **hō'alu.** To slacken; depression. PPN *kalu.*

'alua. Two, twice.

alualu. To follow, pursue; to run, as for political office.

'alu'alu. Loose, flabby; wrinkled, uneven. **hō'alu'alu.** To slacken; to make gathers, as in a skirt.

'ālualua. Rough, bumpy, pitted with holes.

'āluna. Descent, loosening. See *'alu.*

'āluna ahiahi. Late afternoon or early evening.

'āluna awakea. Early afternoon.

'ālunu. Greedy.

ama. Outrigger float. PPN *hama.*

'ama. 1. Light, bright. PEP *kama.* **2.** Talkative. PEP *kama.*

'ama'ama. Mullet (*Mugil cephalus*), a very choice fish. PEP *kamakama.*

'āma'amau. In rapid succession.

'amakihi. Small Hawaiian honeycreepers (*Loxops virens*).

'āmama. Finished, of a pre-Christian prayer.

'āmana. Y-shaped crosspiece at the end of a pole; branches of a tree in the form of a Y; gallows; T-shaped.

'ama'u. All species of an endemic genus of ferns (*Sadleria*).

'āma'uma'u. Plural of *'ama'u;* many *'ama'u* ferns, ferny.

a me. And. Cf. *me.*

'Amelika, America. America; American. *Eng.*

'Amelika-'ākau. North America.

'Amelika-hema. South America.

'Amelika-hui-pū-'ia. United States of America.

'āmene. Amen.

'ami. 1. Hinge. **2.** A hula step with hip revolutions; to do this step.

'ami'ami. Redup. of *'ami, 1, 2.*

āmio. Narrow channel, as to a sea pool; to pass in and out.

Fig., to die. Cf. *mio.* PPN *'a(a)mio.*

amo. To carry a burden on the shoulders; a burden. *Fig.,* responsibility. Cf. *'auamo.* PPN *'amo.*

'amo. Wink, sparkle; to wink. PPN *kamo.*

amu. To curse, revile. Cf. *kūamuamu.* PNP *amuamu.*

amuamu. Redup. of *amu.*

'āmuku. To cut off.

ana. 1. To measure; pattern. **ho'oana.** To make measurements. PPN *hanga.* **2.** To have enough or too much, satisfied. **3.** Cave, grotto. PPN *'ana.* **4.** Larynx. **5.** Particle after *e* (verb). See *e* (verb) *ana.* **6.** Particle after words with meaning "there," or "then," and often used as indicative of the future.

āna. His, her, hers, its (zero-class, *a*-class). PNP *ana.*

'ana. 1. Nominalizing particle. PNP *kanga.* **2.** Pumice, used for rubbing. PPN *kana.*

ana 'āina. Land surveying.

'anā'anā. Black magic, evil sorcery.

'anae. Full-sized *'ama'ama* mullet fish. PPN *kanahe.*

anahonua. Geometry.

ana honua. Surveying; to measure the surface of the earth.

anahulu. Period of ten days; for ten days. PPN *hangafulu.*

anaina. Congregation, audience; to assemble.

anaina ho'olewa. Funeral wake or gathering.

anaina ho'omana. Congregation for worship.

'anakā. Anchor. *Eng.*

'anakala. Uncle. *Eng.*

'anakē, anate. Aunt, auntie. *Eng.*

'anali'i. 1. Wee, stunted. **2.** A native fern (*Asplenium lobulatum*).

ana loa. Measurement of length.

anana. Fathom.

ananū. Turnip.

ana 'ole. Without equal.

'anapa. To shine, gleam, glitter. PEP *kanapa.*

ana paona. Scales, balance. *Lit.,* pound (*Eng.*) measure.

'anapau. To leap, frisk, frolic; frisky.

ana piwa. Thermometer. *Lit.,* fever (*Eng.*) measure.

anapuni. Boundary, perimeter; to go around.

anawaena. Diameter. *Lit.,* middle measure.

ana wai. Water meter.

ana waina. Liquid measure.

ana wela. Thermometer; to measure heat.

ane. A dermestid beetle; to be insect eaten. PPN *ane.*

ānea. 1. Insipid, tasteless. **2.** Vibration caused by heat. **3.** Passive/imperative of *ane*; moth-eaten. PPN *anea.* **4.** Bare, leafless.

'ane'ane. Nearly, almost, scarcely.

'āne'e. To move along by jerks.

'āne'e ali'i. Parasite or sponger on a chief.

ānehe. To come upon quietly, move stealthily.

anei. Particle, following a word, indicating that a question may be answered by yes or no.

'ane'i. 1. Here (usually after *ma-, i,* or *kō*). **2.** Doubtful (used idiomatically).

'ānela. Angel.

'anemoku. Peninsula. *Lit.,* near island.

ani. To beckon, wave. **ho'āni.** To beckon, wave; to blow softly. PPN *angi.*

aniani. 1. Mirror, glass; clear, transparent. **2.** Cool; to blow softly. PEP *angiangi.* **3.** To travel swiftly.

aniani ho'onui 'ike. Magnifying glass. *Lit.,* glass to enlarge vision.

aniani kilohi. Mirror, looking glass.

aniani kū. Standing mirror.

aniani kukui uila. Electric-light bulb. *Lit.,* electric-light glass.

aniani pa'a lima. Hand mirror.

ani pe'ahi. To wave or beckon, as with the hand.

ano. Awe, reverence; weird solitude; awestruck. **ho'āno.** Holy, hallowed.

'ano. 1. Kind, nature, character (preceded by *ke*). PNP *kano.* **2.** Somewhat, rather; to show signs of.

'ānō. Now; present.

'ano'ai. 1. Greeting. **2.** Unexpected. **3.** Perhaps.

anoano. Redup. of *ano.*

'ano'ano. Seed, kernel. PNP *kano.*

'ano 'ē. Strange, odd, unusual.

'ano hou. New variety or kind; new.

'ano'i. Desire; desired one; beloved.

'ano like. Resembling; of similar nature or type.

'ano nui. Important.

'ano 'ole. Insignificant, trivial.

anu. 1. Cool, cold. **ho'ānu.** To cool. PEP *anu.* **2.** Cold; to have a cold.

anuanu. Redup. of *anu,* cold.

ānuenue. Rainbow. PNP *aanuanua.*

'anuhe. Caterpillar. PPN *'anufe.*

anuhea. Cool, soft fragrance.

'anu'u. 1. Stairs, terrace. **2.** Tower in ancient *heiau.*

ao. 1. Light, daylight; to dawn. **ho'āo.** To marry. PPN *'aho.* **2.** Any kind of cloud. PPN *'ao.* **3.** World, earth.

a'o. Instruction, learning; to teach, advise. **ho'ā'o.** To test, try, taste. PPN *ako.*

'ao. 1. A new shoot, leaf or bud, especially of taro. PEP *kao.* **2.** Dried baked taro or sweet potato. PEP *kao.*

'aoa. To bark, as a dog; to howl. PEP *aoa.*

'ao'ao. 1. Side, boundary. PPN *kaokao.* 2. Group; party, as a political party. 3. Page. 4. Way, mode of living.

'ao'ao kālai'āina. Political party.

'ao'ao kū'ē. Opposition, opponent, as in a trial.

'ao'ao kūpale. Defense, as in a trial.

'a'ohe. None; no, not; to have none.

a'o heluhelu. Reader, primer; to learn or teach to read.

a'o hōkū. Astronomy; to teach or learn astronomy.

aokanaka. To think or behave reasonably.

a'o kepela (sepela). Spelling book.

a'o kiko. Manual of punctuation.

'a'ole. No, not; to have none. *'A'ole loa!* Certainly not! Not at all! Never.

'aōno. Six (especially in counting in a series); six times.

a'o palapala. Instruction, education; to teach or learn writing.

a'o pili'ōlelo. Grammar, instruction in grammar.

aoūli. Firmament, sky.

'apa. To delay, waste time, keep others waiting.

'āpala. Apple. *Eng.*

'āpana. Piece, portion, section, land division.

'āpani. To block, shut.

'apapane. A Hawaiian honeycreeper (*Himatione sanguinea*).

apau. All, entirely.

'ape. Large taro-like plants (*Alocasia macrorrhiza, Xanthosoma robustum*). PPN *kape.*

'ā pele. Volcanic rock of any kind.

'Apelika, Aferika. Africa; African. *Eng.*

'Apelila, Aperila. April. *Eng.*

'api. 1. Soft spot in the temples. 2. To palpitate, throb. 3. Fish gills. 4. Surgeonfish. PPN *hapi.*

'api'api. 1. Redup. of *'api, 2*; elastic, springy; short of breath.

'āpi'i. Curly.

'āpi'ipi'i. Wavy, kinky, very curly.

'āpiki. Crafty, mischievous; trickery, treachery.

'āpikipiki. 1. Troubled, agitated, as the sea. 2. Fold, pleat; to fold. PNP *kapiti.*

apo. Circle, hoop, belt, ring; embrace.

'apo. To catch, grasp; acceptance. PEP *kapo.*

'āpo'ipo'i. To pounce.

apo kula (gula). Gold bracelet.

apo lima. Bracelet.

'āpona. Embracing.

'āpono. To approve, accept. ho'āpono. To approve, find not guilty in a trial.

'apōpō. Tomorrow.

'apu. Coconut shell cup. PPN *kapu.*

'āpu'epu'e. Difficulty; to struggle.

'āpuka. To swindle, cheat; forgery.

'āpulu. Worn out, as a garment; to show wear and tear.

au. 1. Period of time, age, era; the passing of time. 2. Current (of water). PPN *'au.* 3. Movement, eddy, tide. 4. Gall, bile. PPN *'ahu.* 5. Also wau. I. PPN *au.*

āu. Your, yours (singular, zero-class, *a*-class).

a'u. 1. Swordfish, sailfish, marlin. PPN *haku.* 2. Me (used after *e* and *me* and fusing with *iā* to form ia'u). *'Ai 'ia e a'u,* eaten by me. *Hā'awi mai ia'u,* give to me. 3. My, mine (zero-class, *a*-class). PNP *aku.*

-a'u. Me (see ia'u). PNP *aku.*

'au. 1. To swim, travel by sea. hō'au. To teach to swim, learn to swim. PPN *kau.* 2.

Handle, staff, stem. PPN *kau*. 3. Group. PPN *kau*.

'au'a. Stingy; to withhold, detain, refuse to part with.

'auamo. Pole or stick used for carrying burdens across the shoulders; yoke, palanquin. *Lit.,* carrying handle.

'auana, 'auwana. To wander, drift, go from place to place.

auane'i. 1. Soon, by and by; probably, merely. 2. Probably not, possibly, doubtful.

'au'au. To bathe. **hō'au'au.** To give a bath. PPN *kaukau*.

auē. Var. spelling of *auwē*.

'auhau. Tax, assessment, levy; to levy a tax, tax.

'auhea. 1. Where (in questions). 2. Listen (usually in commands).

'auhea ho'i. Where indeed (with implication of neglect or indifference)?

'auhe'e. To flee from danger.

auhele. To go looking from place to place without any definite course, to drift or sail aimlessly.

'auhuhu. A slender, shrubby legume (*Tephrosia purpurea*), formerly used for poisoning fish.

'aui. 1. To turn aside, pass by. 2. To swell and roll, as the sea. 3. A hula step.

'auina, auwina. Bending, sloping; descent.

'auinalā. Afternoon. *Lit.,* declining sun.

'aukā. Bar, as of soap or gold.

'aukai. To travel or swim by sea; seafaring; sailor.

'Aukake. August. *Eng.*

'aukā kopa. Bar of soap. *Lit.,* bar soap (*Eng.*).

'au ko'i. Axe handle.

'au kolo. Crawl (swimming); to swim thus.

'auku'u. Black-crowned night heron (*Nycticorax nycticorax hoactli*).

aulama. To light with a torch.

aulau. To gather leaves to wrap fish in for cooking.

'aulau. Leaves strung on lines at ends of seines, as ti leaves.

aulele. To fly, as a frightened flock of birds.

aulike. 1. Even, smooth, as timber. 2. To treat kindly.

'aulima. 1. Bone of arm below elbow. 2. Fire-plow. See *'aunaki*.

'aumakua. Family or personal god.

'aumākua. Plural of *'aumakua*.

'aumoana. To travel on the open sea; sailor.

aumoe. Late at nigh as about midnight. *Lit.,* time to sleep. **hō'aumoe.** To pass the night.

'au moku. Fleet of ships.

'aunaki. 1. Stick in which the *'aulima* is rubbed in obtaining fire by friction. PPN *kaunatu*, PEP *kaunati*. 2. Also *'aunake, auneki*. Ounce. *Eng.*

aupuni. Government, kingdom, nation; national.

'au umauma. Breast stroke (swimming); to swim thus.

'au wa'a. Canoe fleet.

'auwae. Chin. *Fig.,* indifferent, scornful. **hō'auwae.** To show no interest. PPN *kau'ahe*.

'auwaepa'a. Firmly opposed, set against. *Lit.,* firm chin.

'auwae-pahāha. Mumps. *Lit.,* puffed chin.

'auwai. Ditch.

'auwai papa. Flume.

'auwana. Var. spelling of *'auana*, to wander.

auwē. Oh! O dear! Alas! Too bad! (much used to express wonder, fear, scorn, pity, affection); to groan, moan, grieve. *Auwe noho'i e!* Goodness! Alas! Oh! PPN *auee*.

auwī. Ouch! (expression of pain).

'auwina. Var. spelling of *'auina*.

awa. 1. Port, harbor; channel or passage, as through a reef.

PPN *awa*. **2.** Milkfish (*Chanos çhanos*). PPN *'awa*.

'awa. 1. The kava (*Piper methysticum*). PPN *kawa*. **2.** Sour, bitter. **hō'awa.** To make bitter. PPN *kawa*. **3.** Cold mountain rain; to rain or mist. *Fig.*, tragic misfortune.

'awa'awa. 1. Redup. of *'awa, 2*; bitter, sour. **hō'awa'awa.** To embitter; bitter tasting. **2.** Redup. of *'awa, 3*.

awakea. Noon; to be at noon; to become noon.

awa kū moku. Ship harbor or anchorage.

'ā wale. To burn for no particular reason; spontaneous combustion; overcooked.

'awalu. Eight (usually in counting in a series).

'awapuhi. Wild ginger (*Zingiber zerumbet*). PNP *kawapu(s)i*.

'awapuhi-'ai. Same as *'awapuhi-Pākē*. *Lit.*, edible ginger.

'awapuhi ke'oke'o. White ginger (*Hedychium coronarium*).

'awapuhi ko'oko'o. Torch ginger (*Phaeomeria magnifica*). *Lit.*, walking-stick ginger.

'awapuhi-luheluhe. Shell ginger (*Alpinia speciosa*). *Lit.*, drooping ginger.

'awapuhi-melemele. Yellow ginger (*Hedychium flavescens*).

'awapuhi-Pākē. Ginger (*Zingiber officinale*). *Lit.*, Chinese ginger. Also called *'awapuhi-'ai*.

'awapuhi-'ula'ula. Red ginger (*Alpinia purpurata*).

awāwa. Valley, gulch. **ho'āwāwa.** To make a groove.

awe. 1. Strand, thread, tentacle. PPN *kawe*. **2.** Wake of a ship.

'awe. 1. Pack, knapsack carried on the back. Cf. *'auamo, hā-'awe*. PPN *kawe*. **2.** Tentacle. PPN *kawe*.

'awe'awe. Redup. of *'awe, 1*.

'āwe'awe'a. Faint trace, glimpse; faint, faded, dim.

'aweoweo. Various Hawaiian species of *Priacanthus*, red fishes, sometimes called bigeye.

'āwihi. To wink, ogle.

'āwiki. To hurry, be quick.

'āwikiwiki. Redup. of *'āwiki*.

'āwili. To mix, interweave, entwine. PEP *kaawili*.

'awini. Sharp, bold, forward.

'āwīwī. To hurry; quick, fast.

E

e. 1. Particle marking imperative/exhortative mood. **E hele!** Go! PEP *e*. **2.** Particle marking the vocative. *E Pua*, oh Pua. PNP *'e*. **3.** By, by means of. *'Ai 'ia ka poi e a'u*, the poi was eaten by me. PNP *e*.

'e-. Prefix to numbers. PPN *'e-*.

'ē. 1. Different, foreign, strange. PPN *kehe*. **2.** Away, off. *Hele ma kāhi 'ē*, go away. **3.** Beforehand, already. **4.** Yes. **5.** The letter "e."

ea. 1. Sovereignty, rule, independence. **2.** Life, breath, vapor, air, spirit. **3.** To rise, go up. PPN *'ea*.

'ea. 1. Coated tongue; the thrush disease of children, infectious disease. PEP *kea*. **2.** Is that so? Isn't it? **3.** Hawkbill turtle. PNP *kea*.

'ē a'e. Different, other.

eā eā. Particle at end of verses in songs and chants that maintains rhythm and affords pleasure.

e (verb) **ai.** Particles indicating incompleted aspect or future tense and accompanying subordinate verbs.

e (verb) **ala.** Same as *e* (verb) *lā.*

e (verb) **ana.** Particle indicating incompleted action and future tense. PEP *e* (verb) *ana.*

'e'e. 1. To climb on, mount, go aboard; one who mounts, boards. **hō'e'e.** To rise or swell, as surf; to mount, as a surfer mounts a wave. PPN *heke.* **2.** Armpit. PEP *keekee.*

'e'ehi. Same as *hehi*, to step on.

'e'ehia. Overcome with fearful reverence; awe-inspiring; fear.

'e'e kuahiwi. To climb mountains; mountain climber.

'e'e moku. To board a ship; ship passenger; immigrant.

'e'epa. Extraordinary, incomprehensible, as persons with miraculous powers; such persons.

'eha. Hurt, in pain, aching, pained; injury, suffering; to cause suffering. **hō'eha.** To inflict pain or punishment.

'ehā. Four; four times.

'eha'eha. Redup. of *'eha*; great pain.

'ēheu. Wing, as of bird, kite, or airplane; winged.

'ehia. How many (usually in questions); how much, what price.

'ehiku. Seven; seven times.

'eho. Stone pile especially as used to mark land boundaries; stone image; heap of stones under water. PEP *keho.*

'ehu. 1. Spray, foam (formerly *ehu*). PPN *efu.* **2.** Reddish tinge in hair, of Polynesians and not of Caucasians; one with *'ehu* hair. PPN *kefu.*

'ehu kai. Sea spray, foam. Formerly, *ehu kai.*

'ehu pua. Flower pollen.

eia. 1. Here, here is, here are, present (as response to roll call). **2.** This place.

eia a'e. Here close by, here approaching.

eia aku. Approaching, nearby, soon.

eia ala. Here, here it is; you over there, you.

eia ho'i. And, finally, behold.

eia iho. Wait a moment.

eia kā. So at last, then.

eia lā. Same as *eia ala.*

eia nei. You, you there; the one here (sometimes affectionate).

eia (no) na'e. But, furthermore.

ei nei. Same as *eia nei.*

'eiwa. Nine; nine times.

'eka. 1. Dirty; filth. **2.** Acre. *Eng.*

'ekaha. Birds-nest fern (*Asplenium nidus*).

'ekahi. One; once.

'ekālekia, ekalesia. Church (the organization, not the building).

'eke. Sack, pocket, bag; scrotum. PPN *kete.*

'eke huluhulu. Gunny sack. *Lit.*, hairy sack.

'ekeke'i. Short, as a dress.

'eke leka (leta). Mail pouch, mailbag.

'ekemu. To answer briefly.

'eke pa'a lima, 'eke'eke pa'a lima. Handbag, brief case.

'eki. Ace. *Eng.*

'ekolu. Three; three times.

'eku. To root, as a pig. *Fig.*, prow of a canoe. PEP *ketu.*

e (verb) **lā.** Similar to *e* (verb) *nei*, except that *lā* indicates action away.

'ēlau. 1. Tip, point, end. **2.** Bayonet, spear point, short spear.

'ēlau alelo. Tongue tip.

'ele. Black. PEP *kele.*

'ele'ele. 1. Black, dark; the black color of Hawaiian eyes. **hō'ele'ele.** To blacken, darken; to become dark. **2.**

Long, green, edible seaweeds (*Enteromorpha* spp.).

'elekū. 1. Coarse vesicular basalt. **2.** Entirely black, said jokingly of dark people, including Blacks.

'elele. Messenger, delegate; any diplomatic representative. PEP *kelele*.

elelo. Same as *alelo*, tongue.

'elelū. Cockroaches (Blattidae).

'elemakule. Old man; to become an old man; old (of males).

'elepaio. A species of flycatcher with subspecies on Hawai'i (*Chasiempis sandwichensis sandwichensis*), Kaua'i (*C. sandwichensis sclateri*), and O'ahu (*C. sandwichensis gayi*).

'elepani, elepani. Elephant. *Eng.*

'eleu. Active, alert, lively. **hō-'eleu.** To animate, stir into action.

'eli. To dig, excavate. PPN *keli*.

'elima. Five; five times.

'elua. Two; twice.

emi. 1. To diminish, reduce; to droop, lower. **ho'ēmi.** To reduce, lessen. PEP *emi*. **2.** Cheap. **ho'ēmi.** To lower the price.

'emo. A waiting, delay.

'emo 'ole. Without delay, immediately, suddenly.

'ena. Red-hot, glowing. *Fig.*, raging, angry.

'ena'ena. Redup. of *'ena;* glowing, red-hot, raging.

e (verb) **nei.** Particles indicating incompleted aspect and future tense and accompanying subordinate verbs. The *nei* indicates action here or now.

'enemi. Enemy; to feel enmity; to be an enemy. *Eng.*

'enuhe. Caterpillar, as of hawk or sphinx moths (Sphingidae). Also, *nuhe*.

eo. To win; winning.

eō. 1. Yes, I am here (in answer to a call by name). **2.** Call; to call, answer.

'eono. Six; six times.

'epa. Tricky, mischievous.

'eu. Mischievous, naughty. **hō-'eu.** To stir up, incite, encourage. PPN *keu*.

'euanelio. Evangelical; gospel.

'eu'eu. Exciting, rousing, alert, aroused. **hō'eu'eu.** To encourage, stir; spirited.

'Eulopa, Europa. Europe; European. *Eng.*

ewa. Unstable, wandering. PPN *'ewa*.

'ewa. 1. Crooked, out of shape, imperfect. **2.** (*Cap.*) Place name for area west of Honolulu, used as a direction term.

'ewalu. Eight; eight times.

ewanelio. Var. spelling of *'euanelio*.

ēwe. 1. Sprout; lineage kin; birthplace; family trait. **2.** Navel string. **3.** Same as *'iēwe*, afterbirth. PEP *ewe*.

F

Loan words from English sometimes spelled with initial *f-* are entered under *p-*. For example: *falu*, see *palū*, flu; *fea*, see *pea*, fair; *fiku*, see *piku*, fig; *fila*, see *pila*, fiddle; *fiwa*, see *pīwa*, fever.

G

Loan words from English sometimes spelled with initial g- are entered under k-. For example: *gita*, see *kikā*, guitar; *gula*, see *kula*, gold.

H

hā. 1. Four, fourth. PPN *faa*. 2. To breathe, exhale. 3. Hoarse. PPN *faa*. 4. Stalk. PPN *fa'a*. 5. Trough, ditch, sluice.

hā-. Same as *ha'a-*. PEP *faa-*.

ha'a. 1. Low; dwarf. PNP *saka*. 2. A dance with bent knees. PPN *saka*.

ha'a-. Prefix similar to *ho'o-*. PPN *faka-*.

hā'ae. Saliva, spittle; to slobber, drool.

ha'aha'a. Redup of *ha'a, 1;* low, lowly, humble, meek, modest. **ho'oha'aha'a.** To lower, debase, humiliate.

ha'aheo. Proud, haughty; to strut; to cherish with pride. **ho'oha'aheo.** To act haughty.

ha'alele. To leave, desert, abandon, quit, give up, reject.

ha'alele loa. To abandon permanently or completely; extremely.

ha'alulu. To shake, quake, tremble.

ha'anui. To boast, brag, exaggerate, gloat.

hā'awe. To carry a burden on the back; a bundle or burden so carried.

hā'awi. To give, grant; to offer.

ha'awina. Lesson, task, portion, appropriation.

ha'awina ho'i hope. Review lesson. *Lit.,* lesson going backward.

hā'awina hō'ike. Examination, test. *Lit.,* showing lesson.

hae. 1. Wild, furious, ferocious. **ho'ohae.** To make wild or savage; to provoke, tease.

PNP *sae*. 2. To bark, growl, of a dog; to chirp noisily or scold, as a mynah bird. **ho-'ohae.** To cause to bark, growl. 3. To tear. PPN *sae*. 4. Flag, banner.

hae-Hawai'i. 1. Hibiscus. *Lit.,* Hawaiian flag, from having red petals striped with white. 2. Carnation (*Dianthus caryophyllus*) having petals red with white stripes. 3. A variety of plumeria.

haele. To go, come (dual or plural). PPN *sa'ele*.

haha. 1. Redup. of *hā, 2;* to breathe hard. 2. Same as *haha kā 'upena*, net gauge or spacer. Probably PEP *'afa*.

hāhā. To grope, feel. PPN *faafaa*.

-hāhā. **ho'ohāhā.** To beat, pound. PPN *sasa*.

hahae. To strip, as pandanus leaves for plaiting; to tear.

hahai. To follow, pursue, hunt; to go with.

haha'i. To break into pieces; to break off.

hahaki. Redup. of *haki*, to break.

hahana. Warm, hot. **ho'ohahana.** To create heat; to rouse to fury.

hahao. To insert, put in. PPN *fafa'o*.

hāhāpa'akai. Salt bed or pool; to gather salt. **ho'ohāhāpa-'akai.** To gather salt.

hahau. To strike, thrash; to throw down a playing card with force; to play, as a card or *kōnane* pebble.

hahu. To clear; to purge. PPN *safu.*

hai. 1. Offering, sacrifice; to sacrifice. PPN *fai.* **2.** To follow. PEP *fai.*

ha'i. 1. To break, as a stick; fracture. PPN *faki.* **2.** To say, tell. PEP (*f,s*)*aki.* **3.** Another, someone else (not used with the articles).

hāiki (in fast speech, *haiki*). Narrow, pinched; restriction.

ha'ikū. Kāhili flower (*Grevillea banksii*).

haili. Same as *hāli'a.*

hailepo. Stingray. PPN *hai.*

ha'ilono. To tell the news, to spread a report.

hailuku. To stone.

ha'i mana'o. To state an opinion, testify.

ha'i manawa. To tell of the times.

haina. Offering, sacrifice.

hainā. Cruel.

ha'ina. Saying, statement, song refrain, riddle answer. *Ha'ina 'ia mai ana ka puana,* tell the refrain.

ha'ina hou. Repeat the *ha'ina* of a song.

hainakā. Handkerchief. *Eng.*

ha'i'ōlelo. Speech, address; to preach; speaker.

haipule. Religious.

ha'i waha. Word-of-mouth, verbal; to tell verbally.

haka. 1. Shelf, perch, platform; roost as for chickens. PPN *fata.* **2.** Medium, one possessed. **3.** Vacancy; empty, full of holes or spaces.

hakahaka. Redup. of *haka, 3;* vacant space; blanks, as in a questionnaire; thin, emaciated. PEP *fatafata.*

hakakā. To fight, quarrel; a fight.

hakakā-a-moa. Cockfight.

haki. Same as *ha'i, 1.* PPN *fati.*

hāki'i. To tie, bind.

hākikili. Peal of thunder. PNP *fatitili.*

hākilo. To observe closely, spy on, eavesdrop.

hakina. Broken piece, remnant, portion; fraction, as in arithmetic.

hakina maoli. Common fraction.

hakina 'ōlelo. Portion of a word, syllable.

hākōkō. Wrestling; to wrestle.

haku. 1. Lord, master, employer, owner. **ho'ohaku.** To act as *haku;* to rule others. PEP *fatu.* **2.** To compose, arrange. PPN *fatu.* **3.** Stone. PPN *fatu.*

haku 'āina. Landowner; landlord.

hakuhaku. To fold. PPN *fatu.*

haku hale. Landlord, house owner, host, hostess.

haku hana. Overseer, superintendent, employer.

hākuma. Pockmarked, as by smallpox; ravaged, as by leprosy.

haku mele. Poet, composer; to compose song or chant.

haku mo'olelo. Author, story writer.

haku nui. Manager, as of a plantation or firm.

hala. 1. Sin, error, offense; to sin. **ho'ohala.** To cause to sin, lead astray. PPN *sala.* **2.** To pass, as time; to pass by; to die. **ho'ohala.** To pass, as time. *Ho'ohala manawa,* to pass the time. **3.** The pandanus or screw pine (*Pandanus odoratissimus*). PPN *fara.*

halahala. Redup. of *hala, 1;* correction, criticism, complaint. **ho'ohalahala.** To criticize, complain, find fault.

hala-kahiki. Pineapple (*Ananas comosus*). Lit., foreign *hala.*

hālala. To bend low. PPN *falala.*

hala loa. Gone a long distance or time; far.

halalū. 1. Young of the *akule*, a fish. 2. To rumble.

hālau. Long house, as for canoes or hula instruction. PPN *folau*.

hālawa. Same as *kālawa*.

hālāwai. Meeting; to meet. **ho-ʻohālāwai.** To arrange a meeting.

hale. House, building; to have a house. **hoʻohale.** To lodge in a house; to receive in a house. PPN *fale*.

hale ʻaina. Restaurant, cafe, eating house.

hale aliʻi. Chief's house, royal residence, palace.

hale aupuni. Capitol building, government building.

hale ʻauʻau. Bathhouse.

hale ʻauhau. House where taxes are paid; tax building.

hale hālāwai. Meetinghouse, synagogue.

hale hōʻikeʻike. Exhibition hall, museum, art academy. *Hale Hōʻikeʻike o Ka-mehameha*, Bishop Museum.

hale hōʻikeʻike iʻa. Aquarium.

hale hoʻokipa. Guesthouse, lodging house.

hale hoʻokolokolo. Courthouse.

hale hoʻolewa. Funeral parlor, undertaker's establishment.

hale hoʻomaha. Rest house.

hale hoʻomalu. Quarantine house or station.

hale hoʻoponopono. Administrative building.

hale inu pia. Beer parlor.

hale ipukukui. Lighthouse.

hale kaʻa. Garage.

hale keaka. Theater.

hale kinai ahi. Fire station.

hale kipa. 1. Guesthouse, inn, house of hospitality. 2. Hospitable friend.

hale koa. Armory, barracks.

hale kūʻai. Store, shop.

hale kūʻai lāʻau. Drugstore, pharmacy.

hale kūʻai lole. Clothing store, dry goods store.

hale kūʻai meaʻai. Grocery store.

hale kūʻai palaoa. Bakery.

hale kuke (dute). Customhouse.

hale kula. Schoolhouse.

hale leka. Post office. *Lit.*, letter (*Eng.*) house.

halelū. Psalm, in the Bible; to sing psalms.

hale maʻi. Hospital.

hale mākaʻi. Police station.

hale noho. Dwelling house, residence.

halepā. Cupboard, safe. *Lit.*, dish house.

hale paʻahana. Workshop, tool house.

hale paʻahao. Jail, prison.

hale paʻi. Publishing house, printing establishment.

hale peʻa. Menstrual house.

hale pili. House thatched with *pili* grass.

hale puhi kō. Sugar mill; boiling house of a sugar mill. *Lit.*, cane cooking house.

hale pule. Church, chapel. *Lit.*, prayer house.

hāleu. Toilet paper; to wipe, as with toilet paper. PPN *faʻelu*.

hale wili kō. Sugar mill.

hāliʻa. Sudden remembrance.

hāliʻi. A covering, spread; to spread, as a sheet. PPN *faaliki*.

hāliʻi moe. Bedspread or sheet.

hālike. Alike, similar. **hoʻohā-like.** To compare, make alike.

hālikelike. Redup. of *hālike*. **hoʻohālikelike.** Redup. of *hoʻohālike*.

hālili. Sundial shell (*Architectonica* sp. or *Philippia* sp.). Also called *pūlewa*.

haliu. To turn, look, hearken. PPN *fa(a)liu*.

halo. Motion of the fins or

hands in swimming; motion of rubbing. PPN *sa'alo*.

hālō. To peer, as with the hands shading the eyes.

hāloa. Far-reaching, long.

hālo'i. To well with tears.

haluku. To clatter, bang, rattle.

halulu. To roar, thunder; loud noise, racket.

hāmale, hamare. Hammer; to hammer. *Eng.*

hāmama. Open, as a door or obstruction; to open, gape. **ho'ohāmama.** To open, expose.

hāmau. Silent, silence. **ho'ohāmau.** To silence, hush.

hame. Ham. *Eng.*

hamo. 1. Anointed, smeared; to rub, as with oil; to fondle, caress. 2. To spread, as butter.

hamo puna. Plasterer; plaster; to plaster.

hamu. To eat scraps. PPN *samu*.

hana. 1. Work, labor, job, duty, office; activity of any kind, act, deed; to develop, as a picture. **ho'ohana.** To use, employ, cause to work, carry out; use, employment, management, administration. PNP *sanga*. 2. Same as *hahana*, warm. PPN *fana*. 3. Notch. PPN *kausanga*.

Hana-. Bay, valley, as in *Hanalei, Hanauma.* PPN *fanga*.

-hana. Nominalizing suffix similar to *'ana.* PPN *-fanga, -sanga.*

hana aloha. Love magic; to make such.

hana ho'ohiwahiwa. Celebration, as to honor an individual.

hana ho'onanea. Pleasant pastime, hobby, avocation.

hana hou. To do again; repeat; encore.

hānai. 1. Foster child, adopted child; foster, adopted. 2. To raise, feed, nourish, sustain; provider. PPN *faangai*.

hana 'ino. To mistreat, abuse, treat cruelly; cruel.

hana kīwila. Civil service.

hana kolohe. Mischief; to do mischief.

hana lepo. Dirty work; excrement; to excrete.

hana lima. Handmade, manual; to work with the hands.

hana ma'i. Sexual intercourse. *Lit.*, genital activity.

hana make. Thing of destruction, as a weapon; to kill, destroy.

hana pa'a. 1. To make secure, fasten. 2. Steady employment.

hanapēpē. To bruise, crush.

hana pipi. To work with cattle, especially as a cowboy.

hana punahele. Favorite pastime, hobby.

hānau. 1. To give birth; to lay (an egg); born; offspring, childbirth. **ho'ohānau.** To act as midwife, deliver a baby. PPN *faanau*. 2. Happy birthday (as in toasts).

hānau hope. Younger brother or sister; the last-born.

hānau hou. Reborn; baptism.

hānau mua. First-born child.

hanauna. Generation; ancestry, birth.

hanawai. 1. Irrigation; to irrigate. 2. Menstruation; to menstruate. 3. Urine; to urinate.

hanele, haneri. Hundred. *Eng.*

hani. To step or move lightly or softly; to touch.

hanini. To overflow, pour out; to pour down as rain.

hano. 1. Hoarse. PEP *fango.* 2. Nose flute.

hānō. Asthma; to wheeze.

hanohano. Glorious, honored, dignified; pomp, glory. **ho'ohanohano.** To honor, exalt, glorify.

hanu. To breathe, smell; respiration. **ho'ohanu.** To cause to breathe, resuscitate. PPN *fangu.*

hanu pau. Last breath or gasp.

hao. 1. Iron; brand, as on a horse. PPN *fa'o.* 2. All native species of a genus of small trees (*Rauvolfia*). PPN *fao.* 3. To come with force, as wind or rain; to do with force and energy.

hao hakahaka. Grill, as for broiling. *Lit.,* iron with spaces.

ha'oha'o. Strange, puzzling; astonished, puzzled; to wonder. **ho'oha'oha'o.** To arouse wonder, surprise, puzzlement.

haole. White person; formerly any foreigner; foreign, introduced, of foreign origin. **ho-'ohaole.** To act like a white person, to ape the white people, or assume airs of superiority (often said disparagingly, especially of half-whites). **Ho'ohaole 'ia.** Europeanized, Americanized, to have become like a white man, to have adopted the ways of a white man.

hao makēneki (mageneti). Magnet.

hao waha. Bit of a bridle. *Lit.,* mouth iron.

hapa. 1. Portion, fragment, part; to be a portion, less. (*Eng.,* half.) 2. Of mixed blood; person of mixed blood.

hapahā. One fourth, one quarter, quarter, twenty-five cents; quarterly. *Lit.,* fourth part.

hapa haole. Part-white person; of part-white blood; part white and part Hawaiian, as an individual or phenomenon.

hāpai. 1. To carry, lift, raise. PPN *sa(a)pai.* 2. Pregnant. **ho'ohāpai.** To cause conception.

hapaipū. Heavy breathing, as of one with asthma; to breathe heavily; to carry or raise in unison.

hapakolu. Third; one third.

hapaku'e. Crooked, deformed, crippled; to speak with an impediment, as one who has had a stroke; crippling.

hāpala. To daub, blot, besmear, spread, as butter on bread.

hapalima. Fifth; one fifth.

hapalua. Half; half dollar; in two portions.

hapa makahiki. Semiannual.

hapa nui. Majority, most; greatest or largest portion.

hapa'umi. Tenth part; five cents.

hapa 'u'uku. Minority, small portion; less.

hapawalu. One eighth; eighth part.

hape. Incorrect, faulty. PPN *sape.*

hapenūīa, hapenuia. Happy New Year. *Eng.*

hāpuna. 1. Spring, pool. 2. Harpoon. *Eng.*

hāpu'u. 1. An endemic tree fern (*Cibotium splendens*) common in many forests of Hawai'i, as at Kīlauea Volcano, and now frequently cultivated. 2. Grouper, a fish (*Epinephelus quernus*). PPN *faapuku.*

hāpu'upu'u. Young *hāpu'u* ferns that have not yet developed trunks.

hau. 1. A lowland tree (*Hibiscus tiliaceus*), PPN *fau.* 2. Cool, iced; ice, dew, snow; to blow, of a cool breeze. PPN *sau.* 3. Same as *hahau;* to hit, smite. PPN *fa'u, sau.*

hau-. 1. Intensifying prefix. See examples below. PPN *fau-.* 2. (*Cap.*). Prefix to names of goddesses. Perhaps a reflex of PPN *sau,* to rule.

hau'eka. Defiled, filthy, smutty.

hauhana. Lashing. PNP *fausanga.*

hauhia. To hit. PNP *fausia.*

hauka'e. Stained, smeared, smudged; to stain; defiled, as taboo food. ho'okauka'e. To spoil, as a ballot.

haukalima. Ice cream. Lit., creamed (Eng.) ice.

haukapila. Hospital. Eng.

hā'uke. To search for lice. PPN sakule, PNP saakule.

hau kea. White snow, snow.

hā'uke'uke. An edible variety of sea urchin (Colobocentrotus atrata).

hā'ule. To fall, drop; dropped. ho'ohā'ule. To cause to fall.

hā'ule lau. Fall, autumn. Lit., leaf falling.

haumana, haumāna. Student, pupil, apprentice. Perhaps lit., to lay before one a ball of masticated food (māna); to feed masticated food. ho'ohaumana. To act as a pupil, become a pupil.

haumia. Uncleanliness, defilement; contaminated. ho'ohaumia. To pollute, defile.

hauna. Unpleasant odor, as of spoiling fish or meat. ho'ohauna. To cause an offensive odor. PNP saunga.

haunāele. Panic, commotion, riot. ho'ohaunāele. To provoke panic, riot.

hau'oli. Happy, glad, joyful; happiness, joy. Hau'oli makahiki hou, happy new year. Hau'oli lā hānau, happy birthday. ho'ohau'oli. To cause happiness, gaiety, joy.

haupia. Pudding made from coconut cream, formerly thickened with arrowroot, now usually with cornstarch.

hā'upu. To recall, recollect, remember.

hauwala'au. To gossip, chatter.

hawa. Defiled, filthy. PNP sawa.

hāwa'e. A sea urchin (Tripneustes gratilla). PNP saawak(e,i).

Hawai'i. Hawai'i (both the island and the group of islands); Hawaiian person; Hawaiian. PPN Sawaiki.

hāwanawana. To whisper; whispering.

hāwāwā. Unskilled, awkward; blunder, incompetence.

he. Indefinite article, usually at the beginning of a phrase: a, to be a, have (with a possessive). He Hawai'i au, I am a Hawaiian.

hē. 1. General name for caterpillar. PEP fee. 2. To rub. 3. The letter "h."

hea. 1. To call, name; to sing or recite a name chant; to give a name to. 2. Which (in questions and after other words). Ka mea hea? Which thing? 3. Where (in questions, and after ai, 'au-, i, mamai, no, 'o). PNP fea.

he aha, heaha. See aha.

heahea. To call frequently; to call hospitably.

hea inoa. To give a name; to chant a name chant; to call the roll.

heana. Corpse, victim. PEP (f,s)eana.

he'e. 1. Squid, octopus (Polypus spp.). PPN feke. 2. To slide, surf, flee. ho'ohe'e. To cause to slide; to put to flight. PPN seke. 3. To hang down, sag, as fruit.

he'ehe'e. Breast disease with caking during lactation. Probably PPN fekefeke.

he'e nalu. To ride a surfboard; surfing; surf rider. Lit., wave sliding.

he'e-pū-loa. Ornated octopus (Polypus ornatus). Lit., long-headed he'e.

he'e umauma. Body surfing.

heha. Lazy, indolent, drowzy.

hehena. Insane, raving, mad, crazy, possessed; insanity, lunatic.

hehi. To stamp, tread, step on.

hei. 1. Net, snare; to ensnare,

catch in a net. **hoʻohei.** To snare, tangle. **2.** String figure, cat's cradle; to make string figures. PEP *fai*.

hēʻī. Same as *mīkana*, papaya. Perhaps PEP *feekii*.

heiau. Pre-Christian place of worship. PPN *fai*.

heiau hoʻōla. *Heiau* for treating the sick.

heiau hoʻoūlu ʻai. *Heiau* where first fruits were offered to insure further growth. *Lit.*, *heiau* for the increase of food crops.

heiau hoʻoūlu iʻa. *Heiau* where fish were offered to insure good fishing.

heiau hoʻoūlu ua. *Heiau* where offerings were made to insure rain.

heiau poʻo kanaka. *Heiau* where human sacrifices were offered.

heihei. Race, as foot race, canoe race; to race. **hoʻoheihei.** To run swiftly, take part in a race.

hekau. Anchor, stone anchor, towline; to anchor, make fast.

heke. **1.** Best. **2.** Top gourd in a gourd hula drum.

hekili. Thunder; to thunder. PNP *fatitili*.

hela. To spread, as the arms. PPN *fela*.

hele. **1.** To go, come, walk; to move, as in a game; going, moving. *Hele mai*, come. **hoʻohele.** To cause to move. PPN *saʻele*, PEP *sele*. **2.** Everywhere, here and there, continuously. *Holo hele*, run here and there. **3.** To tie, bind, snare. PPN *sele*. **4.** To cut. PPN *sele*.

helehelena. Features, face.

hele hewa. To go wrong, take the wrong path, to go astray.

helei. Pulled down, as an eyelid. PEP *felei*.

heleleʻi, helelei. Falling; scattered, as rain, tears; crumb-

ling, as the earth. **hoʻoheleleʻi.** To scatter, sow.

hele loa. To go or come far; to go with no hope of returning.

hele malihini. To go to a place for the first time or as a stranger.

hele mauna. To travel in the mountains; mountain climber.

hele pēlā. Get out! Go away!

hele wale. To go naked; to go without fixed purpose, or far and wide; to go empty-handed.

hele wāwae. To walk, go on foot; pedestrian.

helo. Red, as *ʻōhelo* berries. Probably PPN *felo*.

helu. **1.** To count, number, list; to assess, as taxes; to chant a list of names as of genealogy; census, figure, inventory. **2.** Arithmetic, score; serial, numbered. **3.** To scratch the earth, as a hen. PPN *salu*.

heluhelu. To read, count.

heluna. Number, count, total sum; grade (evaluation).

heluna papa. Grade or mark, as given in school; number of a school grade (class).

helu nui. Large number; plural number.

helu pāloka (balota). To count ballots; election teller.

helu papa. To count in order or consecutively.

helu waiwai. Inventory.

hema. **1.** Left; left side. PPN *sema*. **2.** South.

hemahema. Awkward, clumsy, unskilled, inexpert; to not know well.

hemo. Loose, separated; discharged, divorced, opened; taken off, as clothes. **hoʻohemo.** To loosen, undo, unfasten, free.

hemolele. Perfect, faultless, holy; perfection, virtue, holiness; angel, person without fault.

henehene. To laugh at, ridicule, giggle. **ho'ohenehene.** To tease, laugh at.

heno. Same as *henoheno.* **ho'oheno.** To cherish, love, caress; expression of affection.

henoheno. Lovable, sweet.

hepa. Imbecilic; idiot.

hepekoma, hebedoma. Week; seven years. *Greek.*

Hepekoma Hemolele. Holy Week.

heu. Down or fine hair, fuzz, loose fibers on certain fruits or leaves. PEP *feu.*

hewa. Mistake, fault, error, sin, guilt; wrong, incorrect, wicked, sinful, to err. **ho'ohewa.** To cause one to do wrong, cause or feign a mistake; to blame, condemn.

hī. 1. To cast or troll, as for bonito. PPN *sii.* 2. Dysentery, diarrhea; to flow, hiss.

hia. To desire. PPN *fia.*

-hia. 1. How many? How much? PPN *fiha.* 2. Passive/imperative. PPN *-fia, -sia.*

hi'a. 1. To make fire with the fire-plow. PPN *sika.* 2. Needle for making nets. PPN *sika.*

hia'ai'ono. Pleased with, delighted with; appetite. PPN *fiakai.*

hiamoe. Sleep, to sleep, fall asleep. **ho'ohiamoe.** To put to sleep, lull to sleep. PPN *fiamohe.*

hiamoe iki. A little sleep, nap; to take a nap.

hiamoe loa. To oversleep, sleep deeply; death, eternal sleep.

hiapo. First-born child; first born.

hie. Attractive, distinguished. **ho'ohie.** Stately, delightful.

hiehie. Redup. of *hie.* **ho'ohiehie.** To beautify, make distinctive, beautiful.

hihi. To entangle, intertwine,

entanglement. **ho'ohihi.** To cause entanglement; to entwine. PEP *fifi.*

hīhī. Redup. of *hī,* 2; to hiss. PNP *si(i)sii.*

hihia. 1. Entangled, interwoven; snarl, problem, trouble. **ho'ohihia.** To get into difficulties, entangle. 2. A lawsuit or case before the court.

hihia kalaima. Criminal case.

hīhīmanu. 1. Various stringrays (Dasyatidae) and eagle rays (Myliobatidae). PPN *faimanu.* 2. Lavish, magnificent, elegant.

hihiu. Wild, untamed.

hi'i. To hold or carry in the arms, as a child. PPN *siki.*

hi'ikua. To carry on the back, as children.

hi'ilawe. To lift, carry.

hi'imo'opuna. To bear a grandchild in the arms; to be a grandparent (a term of pride and affection).

hi'ipoi. To tend, feed, cherish, as a child.

hiki. 1. Can, to be able. 2. All right, O.K. (in sense of "able to do"). 3. To get to or reach a place, arrive. PPN *fiti.* 4. Next.

-hiki. ho'ohiki. To vow, swear, take an oath.

hikie'e. Large immovable Hawaiian couch. See *pūne'e.*

hīki'i. Binding; to tie, make fast. PEP *fiitiki.*

hiki'iki'i. Redup. of *hīki'i.*

hikilele. To jump or start from shock; shock.

hikina. 1. East. 2. Coming.

hikina 'ākau. Northeast.

hikina hema. Southeast.

hiki nō. All right, O.K.

hiki 'ole. Impossible.

hikiwale. 1. Easy. 2. To come accidentally.

hikiwawe. Quickly; possible to do quickly. **ho'ohikiwawe.** To accelerate, hurry.

hiku. Seven; seventh (usually

preceded by the numeral prefix ʻe). PPN *fitu*.

hila. 1. Same as *hilahila*. 2. Heel. *Eng. Hila ʻauliʻi*, high heels.

hilahila. Bashful, shy, embarrassed. **hoʻohilahila.** To make ashamed, humiliate; shameful, bashful.

hili. 1. To braid, plait, string, as flowers for a lei or candlenuts for a torch. PPN *firi*. 2. To turn, wander, stray. PPN *fili*. 3. To whip, bat; batter, as in baseball.

hilinaʻi. To believe, trust; to rely on.

hilo. 1. To twist, braid; threadlike; faint streak of light. PPN *filo*. 2. (*Cap.*) First night of the new moon. PEP *filo*. 3. (*Cap.*) Name of a famous Polynesian navigator.

hilu. Various species of reef fishes of the genus *Coris*.

hiluhilu. Elegant, beautiful.

hīmeni. Hymn, any song not used for hulas; to sing a *hīmeni*. *Eng.*

hina. 1. To fall over or from an upright position; to throw down. PPN *singa*. 2. Gray- or white-haired; gray. PPN *sina*. 3. (*Cap.*) Name of a goddess. PPN *Sina*.

hinahina. 1. The silversword (*Argyroxiphium sandwicense*). See *ʻāhinahina*, 2. 2. Spanish or Florida moss (*Tillandsia usneoides*), an air plant, growing on tree branches and hanging baskets.

hīnaʻi. A kind of basket fish trap. PPN *fīnaki*.

hinakā. Handkerchief. *Eng.*

hīnālea. Small- to moderate-sized, brightly colored wrasses. Varieties include *hīnālea-lauwili* (*Thalassoma duperreyi*), *hīnālea-luahine* (*T. ballieui*), and *hīnālea-nukuʻiʻiwi* (*Gomphosus varius*).

hīnano. Male pandanus blossom. PPN *singano*.

-hine. Female, feminine. PPN *fine*.

hinihini. Indistinct. PEP (*f, s*)*ini*.

hinu. Oil, grease; oily; smooth and polished, lustrous. PPN *sinu*.

hinuhinu. Intensification of *hinu*; bright, glittering, as of polished stones or shells. **hoʻohinuhinu.** To shine, polish.

hio. To blow in gusts. PEP *fio*.

hiʻohio. 1. To whistle softly; to blow softly. 2. Gibberish.

hiolo. To tumble down, collapse; overthrown; landslide. **hoʻohiolo.** To overthrow, demolish.

hiʻona. General appearance, as of a person.

hipa. Sheep. *Eng.*

hipahipa. Hip, hip, hurrah! Cheers! (*Eng.*, hip.) *ʻEkolu hipahipa no ka mōʻī*, three cheers for the king!

hipa kāne. Ram. *Lit.*, male sheep.

hipa keiki. Lamb.

hiu. To fling. PEP *fiu*.

hiʻu. 1. Hind part or tail section of a fish. PPN *siku*. 2. Caudal fin.

hiwa. 1. Entirely black, as of pigs offered to the gods. PEP *siwa*. 2. Choice. See *hiwahiwa*.

hiwahiwa. Precious, beloved, esteemed; favorite. **hoʻohiwahiwa.** To honor, adorn; to display, as the flag; to treat as a favorite.

hiwi. Ridge. PEP *siwi*.

hō. 1. To give, transfer, go (followed by directionals). PPN *soo*. 2. Hoe; to hoe. *Eng.*

hō-, hoʻ-, hō'-. Same as *hoʻo-*.

hoa. 1. Companion, friend, associate, partner. **hoʻohoa.** To make friends. PPN *soa*. 2. To tie, lash. 3. To strike. PPN *foa*.

hōʻā. 1. To set on fire, burn,

ignite. See '*ā*. 2. To drive, as
cattle.

hō'ā ahi. To kindle fire.

hoa hana. Fellow worker, col-
league, partner.

hoahānau. Cousin; brother or
sister, as a church member.

hoa hele. Traveling companion,
fellow traveler.

ho'āhewa. To blame, condemn.
See '*āhewa*.

hō'ai. To feed. See '*ai*, food.

hō'ailona. See '*ailona*.

hoaka. 1. Crescent, arch; crest,
as on a helmet. 2. (*Cap.*)
Second day of the month.
PEP *soata*. 3. Brightness; to
glitter, shine. PEP *soata*.

hō'aka'aka. See '*aka'aka*, to
laugh.

hoa kamali'i. Childhood playmate.

hoa kanaka. Fellow man.

ho'ākoakoa. See '*ākoakoa*.

hoa kūkā, hoa kūkākūkā. Con-
sultant, adviser, one with
whom one confers and de-
liberates.

hoa kula. Schoolmate.

ho'āla. See *ala*, to waken, rise
up.

hō'ala. See '*ala*, fragrant.

hoalauna. Neighbor, close associate or friend.

hoa lawehana. Fellow laborer
or worker, helper.

hoa like. Companion or contemporary of equal status.

hoaloha. Friend. *Lit.*, beloved
companion. Cf. *aloha*. **ho-
'ohoaloha.** To make friends,
be friendly.

hō'alu. See '*alu*, depression.

hō'alu'alu. See '*alu'alu*, loose.

hoa lumi. Roommate.

hoa moe. Sleeping companion,
bedfellow.

hoana. Hone, whetstone, grindstone; to rub, grind.

ho'āna. See *ana*, to measure.

hoana ka'a. Grindstone, rolling
grindstone.

ho'āni. See *ani*, to beckon.

hoa noho. Neighbor, one who
lives with or near another.

ho'ānu. See *anu*, cool.

ho'āo. Marriage. See *ao, 1,*
light.

ho'ā'o. To try, taste. See *a'o,*
instruction.

hoa pa'ahana. Fellow worker.

hoa paio. Opponent, antagonist,
enemy.

hoa pili. Close, intimate, or personal friend.

ho'āpono. To approve. See
'*āpono*.

hō'au. See '*au*, to swim.

hō'auana, ho'oauwana. See
'*auana*, to wander.

hō'au'au. See '*au'au*, to bathe.

hoe. 1. Paddle, oar; to paddle,
row. *Fig.*, to travel, get to
work, continue working. *Hoe
aku i ka wa'a*, paddle ahead
the canoe (do your share;
continue; keep going). PPN
fohe. 2. To draw in the breath
and expel it with a whistling
sound, as when tired.

hō'ea. To arrive.

hō'ele'ele. To blacken. See '*ele-
ele*.

ho'ēmi. To reduce, diminish,
cheapen. See *emi, 1, 2.*

hoene. A soft sweet sound, as
of song; to sound softly.

hō'ewa. See '*ewa*, crooked.

hoe wa'a. Oarsman, paddler; to
paddle a canoe.

hohola. To spread out, unfold.

hohono. Unpleasant acrid odor,
body odor; to smell thus.

hohonu. Deep, profound. PEP
fofonu, PPN *fonu*.

hoi. Bitter yam (*Dioscorea
bulbifera*). PPN *soi*.

ho'i. 1. To leave, go or come
back; to cause to come back.
PPN *foki*. 2. Intensifying
particle. *Maika'i ho'i*, fairly
good. See *auwe noho'i, noho'i*. 3. Also, besides. *'A'ole
ho'i*, neither. PPN *foki*. 4.
Particle expressing doubt, un-

certainty. *Pehea hoʻi,* how indeed, I don't know.

hoʻihā. Intensive of *hoʻi,* 2. *E hele hoʻihā kāua,* well, let's go then.

hoihoi. Pleased, happy, joyful, entertaining, interesting; pleasure, interest. **hoʻohoihoi.** To entertain, charm, please.

hoʻihoʻi. To return, send back, restore.

hoʻi hope. To go back, return, revert, backslide.

hoʻi hou. To go or come back, return.

hōʻikaika. See *ikaika,* strong.

hōʻike. To show, exhibit. See *ʻike.*

Hōʻike ʻAna. Revelation (Biblical).

hōʻikeʻike. Display. See *ʻikeʻike.*

hoʻili. See *ili,* 1, 2.

hoʻilo. See *hoʻoilo.*

hoka. 1. Disappointed, baffled; frustration. **hoʻohoka.** To cause disappointment, to thwart. 2. To squeeze. PPN *fota.*

hōkā. Same as *hoʻokā.* See *kā, 1.*

hokahoka. Redup. of *hōkai.*

hōkai. To confuse; to blunder along; bother, disorder.

hōkake. To interfere, as would a child. See *kake, 1.*

hōkana, hosana. Hosanna.

hōkele, hotele. Hotel. *Eng.*

hōkeo. Large gourd calabash.

hoki. 1. Mule, ass. *(Eng.,* horse.) 2. Barren, of a woman. *Modern.*

hōkio. A small gourd whistle, musical pipe; to whistle.

hōkiokio. Gourd whistle, musical pipe; to whistle.

Hoku. Night of the full moon. PEP *fotu.*

hōkū. Star. PPN *fetuʻu.*

hōkū-ʻaeʻa. Planet. *Lit.,* wandering star.

Hōkū-ao. Morning star, Venus when seen in the morning.

Hōkū-keʻa. Southern Cross. *Lit.,* cross star.

hōkū-lele. Shooting star, meteor, any moving star.

hōkū-lewa. Moving star, planet.

Hōkū-paʻa. North Star. *Lit.,* immovable star.

hōkū-welowelo. Shooting star, comet. *Lit.,* streaming star.

hola. 1. Hour, time, o'clock, *Eng. Hola ʻehia kēia?* What time is it? 2. Same as *hohola,* to spread. PPN *fola.*

holahia. Passive/imperative of *hola,* 2. PNP *folasia.*

Hōlani. 1. Name of a mythical place. 2. Holland; Dutch. *Eng.*

hole. To skin, peel; to strip, as sugarcane leaves from the stalk. PEP *sole.*

holi. To sprout, as plants or a youth's beard.

holina. Immature and inferior, as breadfruit falling prematurely.

hōlina. Haul in. *Eng.*

holo. 1. To run, sail, ride, go; to flow, as water; to run, as for political office; to slide, as an avalanche; fleet, fast. **hoʻoholo.** To sail, run; to cause to run, sail, run free, as a horse; to add water, as to *poi;* to flush as a toilet. PPN *solo.* 2. Decided, agreed upon, passed, enacted. **hoʻoholo.** To decide, determine, settle, conclude; decision. 3. Hall. *Eng.*

holo a iʻa. To swim like a fish; to get the bends; to drown.

holoʻanai. To gallop.

holohau. To ice skate, ski. *Lit.,* ice run.

holo hele. To run to and fro; bustle.

holohiʻa. To dart this way and that, as children at play.

holoholo. 1. To go for a walk, ride, or sail; to go out for pleasure. **hoʻoholoholo.** To take someone out for a drive;

to escort. **2.** Basting; to baste, sew. **ho'oholoholo.** To make large running stitches. PPN *solosolo*.

holoholo ka'a. To go for a drive, ride.

holoholona. Animal, beast.

holoholo'ōlelo. To gossip, slander; tattler, spreader of gossip.

holo hōlua. Course for *hōlua*, sledding.

holoi. To wash, clean; washing, erasure. **ho'oholoi.** To have washed, cleaned. PPN *solo(i)*.

holo i mua, holoimua. To progress, advance; successful. Also *holomua*.

holo ka'a. To ride in a car or carriage.

holokahiki. Sailor; to sail to foreign lands.

holokai. Seaman, seafarer; to sail on the sea.

holokē. To run here and there; helter-skelter.

holo kikī. To run or sail swiftly; headlong.

holokū. A long, one-piece dress, usually fitted and with a train and a yoke, patterned after the Mother Hubbards of the missionaries.

holo kūkū. To trot, as a horse.

holo lio. To ride horseback; horseman, rider.

holomakani. Breezy, airy. *Lit.*, wind running.

holo mana'o. To decide, determine.

holomoku. Sailor, passenger, anyone who sails; to take a sail or ocean trip.

holomū. A long, fitted dress, a combination of *holokū* (without a train) and *mu'umu'u*. *Modern*.

holomua. Same as *holo i mua;* improvement, progress.

holo'oko'a. Whole, entire, all; entirely, paramount.

holo pahe'e. To skate, skid.

holopeki. To trot. *Lit.*, pace (*Eng.*) run.

holopono. To pass off successfully, succeed; success.

holopuni. To sail or travel around, circumnavigate.

holo pūpule. Reckless, mad running; to speed recklessly, as an auto.

holowai. Water ditch; to run in such courses; watery.

holu. Springy, pliable, resilient, as a mattress; to sway, as palm fronds; to ripple, as waves; bumpy, as an airplane ride. PPN *soru*.

hōlua. Sled, especially the ancient sled used on grassy slopes; the sled course.

holunape. To sway.

home. Home. *Eng.*

home ho'opa'a. Detention home.

hone. 1. Sweet and soft, as music; sweetly appealing, as perfume or a memory of love; to tease, mischievous. **2.** Honey. *Eng.*

honekakala. Honeysuckle.

hōnēnē. To attract.

honi. 1. To kiss; formerly to touch noses on the side in greeting. **2.** To smell, sniff; a scent. PPN *songi*.

honi lima. To throw a kiss; such a kiss.

hono. 1. To stitch, sew, mend; a joining, as of mountains. PPN *fono*. **2.** Back of the neck. **3.** Gathering of chiefs; group of islands in a circle. PPN *fono*.

Hono-. Bay, gulch, valley (as a part of place names such as Honolulu, Honokōhau, Honoli'i, Honomanu). PPN *fanga*.

honohono. Short for *honohonokukui*. See also *'okika-honohono*.

honohono-kukui. Basket grass (*Oplismenus hirtellus*).

Honolulu. Name of the capital

city in the Hawaiian Islands. *Lit.*, sheltered bay.

honu. General name for turtle and tortoise. PPN *fonu.*

honua. Land, earth; background, as of quilt designs; basic, at the foundation, fundamental. PPN *fanua.*

honua-ʻula. A variety of sugarcane, a dark brown-red mutant of *manu-lele*, with purple leaf sheaths and leaves.

honu-ʻea. Hawkbill turtle (*Chelonia*); the shell of this turtle was used as medicine for the disease called ʻea, and was also used for combs and fans.

hoʻo-. A very active former of causative/simulative derivatives. *Hoʻo-* usually precedes stems beginning with the vowels *i-* and *u-* and all the consonants except the glottal stop. Important meanings are: (1) Causation and transitivization, as *pono*, correct; *hoʻoponopono*, to correct. (2) Pretense, as *kuli*, deaf; *hoʻokuli*, to feign deafness. (3) Similarity, as *kamaliʻi*, children; *hoʻokamaliʻi*, childish. (4) No meaning, as *kāholoholo*, to hurry; *hoʻokāholoholo*, to hurry. The meanings of some *hoʻo-* derivatives are quite different from the meanings of the stems, as *maikaʻi*, good; *hoʻomaikaʻi*, to congratulate. *Hoʻo-* derivatives are defined under the stems. Delete *hoʻo-* and see the stems. PPN *faka-.*

hoʻohaʻahaʻa. See *haʻahaʻa*, low, humble.

hoʻohaʻaheo. See *haʻaheo*, proud.

hoʻohae. See *hae*, wild, and *hae*, to bark.

hoʻohahana. See *hahana*, warm.

hoʻohaku. See *haku*, lord.

hoʻohala. See *hala*, to sin, and *hala*, to pass.

hoʻohalahala. See *halahala.*

hoʻohala manawa. To pass the time.

hoʻohālike. See *hālike*, alike.

hoʻohāmama. See *hāmama*, open.

hoʻohanohano. See *hanohano*, glorious.

hoʻohaʻohaʻo. See *haʻohaʻo*, puzzling.

hoʻohaukaʻe. See *haukaʻe*, stained.

hoʻohāʻule. See *hāʻule*, to fall.

hoʻohaumia. See *haumia*, defilement.

hoʻohaunāele. See *haunāele*, panic.

hoʻoheʻe. See *heʻe*, to slide.

hoʻohei. See *hei*, snare.

hoʻoheihei. See *heihei*, race.

hoʻohele. See *hele*, 1.

hoʻoheleleʻi. See *heleleʻi*, falling.

hoʻohemo. See *hemo*, loose.

hoʻohenehene. See *henehene.*

hoʻoheno. To cherish. See *heno.*

hoʻohewa. See *hewa*, mistake.

hoʻohiamoe. See *hiamoe*, sleep.

hoʻohie. See *hie*, attractive.

hoʻohihia. See *hihia*, entangled.

hoʻohiki. See *-hiki.*

hoʻohilahila. See *hilahila*, bashful.

hoʻohinuhinu. See *hinuhinu.*

hoʻohiwahiwa. See *hiwahiwa*, precious.

hoʻōho. See *oho*, to call.

hoʻohoa. See *hoa*, companion, and *-hoa.*

hoʻohoihoi. See *hoihoi*, pleased.

hoʻohoka. See *hoka*, disappointed.

hoʻoholo. See *holo*, to run, and *holo*, decided.

hoʻohopohopo. See *hopohopo*, anxiety.

hoʻohū. See *hū*, to swell.

hoʻohua. See *hua*, fruit.

hoʻohuhū. See *huhū*, angry.

hoʻohuhuki. See *huhuki*, to pull.

hoʻohui. See *hui*, club, and *hui*, to join.

hoʻohuʻihuʻi. See *huʻihuʻi*, cold.

ho'ohuikau. See *huikau*, mixed.

ho'ohuki. See *huki*, to pull.

ho'ohuli. See *huli*, to turn, and *huli*, to look for.

ho'ohulu. See *hulu*, esteemed.

ho'ohūnā. See *hūnā*, to hide.

hō'oia. See *oia*, truth.

hō'oiā'i'o. See *oiā'i'o*, true.

ho'oiki. See *iki*, small.

ho'oili. See *ili*, stranded, and *ili*, inheritance.

ho'oilina. See *ilina*, recipient.

ho'oilo. Winter, rainy season.

ho'oinu. See *inu*, to drink.

ho'okā. See *kā*, 1.

ho'oka'a. See *ka'a*, 1, 3.

ho'oka'awale. See *ka'awale*.

ho'okae. See *kae*.

ho'okahe. See *kahe*, to flow.

ho'okahi. See *kahi*, 1.

ho'okahua. See *kahua*.

ho'okahuli. See *kahuli*, overthrow.

ho'okala. See *kala*, 1, 3.

ho'okali. See *kali*, to wait.

ho'okamakama. See *-kamakama*.

ho'okamani. See *kamani*, 2.

ho'okani. See *kani*, sound.

ho'okano. See *-kano*.

ho'okaulike. See *kaulike*, equality.

ho'okē. See *kē*, 1.

ho'okele. See *kele*, watery, and *kele*, to sail.

hō'oki. See *oki*, to stop.

hō'oki. See *'oki*, to cut.

ho'oki'eki'e. See *ki'eki'e*, height.

ho'okīnā. See *kīnā*, blemish.

ho'okino. See *kino*, body.

ho'okipa. See *kipa*.

ho'okipi. See *kipi*, rebellion.

ho'okō. See *kō*, to fulfill.

ho'okoe. See *koe*, to remain.

ho'okohu. See *kohu*, resemblance, and *-kohu*.

ho'oko'iko'i. See *ko'iko'i*, weight.

ho'okokoke. See *kokoke*, near.

ho'okolokolo. See *kolokolo*.

ho'okomo. See *komo*, to enter, and *komo*, to dress.

ho'okū. See *kū*, to stand, and *kū*, in a state of.

ho'okū'ē. See *kū'ē*, to oppose.

ho'oku'i. See *ku'i*, to pound.

ho'okūkū. See *kūkū*, to shake, and *-kūkū*.

ho'okuli. See *kuli*, deaf.

ho'okumu. See *kumu*, beginning.

ho'okū'ono'ono. See *kū'ono'ono*, well-off.

ho'okupa. See *kupa*, citizen.

ho'okupu. See *kupu*, sprout, and *-kupu*.

ho'oku'u. See *ku'u*, to release.

ho'olā. See *lā*, sun.

hō'ōla. See *ola*, life.

ho'ola'a. See *la'a*, 1.

ho'olaha. See *laha*, extended.

ho'olaka. To tame. See *laka*.

ho'olako. See *lako*.

ho'olalau. See *lalau*, mistake.

ho'olana. See *lana*, floating, and *-lana*.

ho'olapa. See *lapa*, ridge, and *lapa*, energetic.

ho'ōlā pāna'i. See *ola pāna'i*.

ho'olapu. See *lapu*, ghost.

ho'olau. See *lau*, leaf; *lau*, dragnet; and *lau*, much.

ho'olaulā. See *laulā*, broad.

ho'olaule'a. See *laule'a*.

ho'olauna. See *launa*, friendly.

ho'olawa. See *lawa*, 1.

ho'olawe. See *lawe*.

ho'olawehala. See *lawehala*, sin.

hō'ole. See *'ole*.

ho'olei. See *lei*, 2.

ho'olele. See *lele*, 1.

ho'olewa. See *lewa*, to float, and *-lewa*.

ho'olilo. See *lilo*, 1, 3.

ho'olimalima. See *limalima*.

ho'olohe. See *lohe*, to hear, obey.

ho'ololi. See *loli*, to change.

ho'olono. See *lono*, 1.

hō'olu. See *'olu*, cool.

ho'olua. See *lua*, 1, 3.

ho'oluhi. See *luhi*.

ho'oluli. See *luli*, to shake.

hō'olu'olu. See *'olu'olu*.

ho'olu'u. See *lu'u*, to dive.
ho'oma'ama'a. See *ma'ama'a*.
ho'oma'ema'e. See *ma'ema'e*.
ho'omaha. See *maha*, rest.
ho'omahana. See *mahana*, 1.
ho'omāhua. See *māhua*.
ho'omaika'i. See *maika'i*, good.
ho'omaka. See *maka*, 3.
ho'omāka'ika'i. See *māka'ika'i*,
to visit.
ho'omaka'u. See *maka'u*.
ho'omākaukau. See *mākaukau*.
ho'omake. See *make*, to die.
ho'omāke'aka. See -*māke'aka*.
ho'omālamalama. See *mālamalama*.
ho'omalimali. See *malimali*.
ho'omalolo. See *malolo*, to rest.
ho'omalu. See *malu*, shade.
ho'omāluhiluhi. See *māluhiluhi*.
ho'omana. See *mana*, power.
ho'omānalo. See *mānalo*, sweet.
ho'omanamana. See *manamana*.
ho'omana'o. See *mana'o*.
ho'omanawanui. See *manawanui*, patience.
ho'omaopopo. See *maopopo*.
ho'omau. See *mau*, 1, 2.
ho'omo'a. See *mo'a*, cooked.
ho'omoana. See *moana*, campground, and *moana*, broad.
ho'omoe. See *moe*, to sleep,
and *moe*, to marry.
ho'omū. See *mū*, 2, 3.
ho'onā. See *nā*, calmed.
ho'ona'auao. See *na'auao*.
ho'onanea. See *nanea*.
ho'onanenane. See *nanenane*.
ho'onani. See *nani*.
ho'ōne. See *one*, sand.
ho'one'e. See *ne'e*, to move
along.
hō'oni. See '*oni*, to move.
ho'onipo. See *nipo*, 1, 2.
hō'ono. See '*ono*, delicious.
ho'onui. See *nui*.
hō'o'opa. See '*o'opa*, lame.
ho'opā. See *pā*, to touch.
ho'opa'a. See *pa'a*.
ho'opa'apa'a. See *pa'apa'a*.

ho'opae. See *pae*, cluster, and
pae, to land.
ho'opahe'e. See *pahe'e*, slippery.
ho'opai. See *pai*.
ho'opa'i. See *pa'i*, to slap.
ho'opailua. See *pailua*, nausea.
ho'opakele. See *pakele*, to escape.
ho'opala. See *pala*, ripe, and
pala, dab.
ho'opale. See *pale*, 1.
ho'opāna'i. See *pāna'i*, revenge.
ho'opāpā. See *pāpā*, to touch.
ho'opau. See *pau*, finished.
ho'opaumanawa. See -*pauma-
nawa*.
ho'opē. See *pē*, crushed; *pē*,
perfumed; and *pē*, drenched.
hō'ope. See '*ope*, bundle.
ho'opiha. See *piha*, full.
ho'opi'i. See *pi'i*, 1, 2, and -*pi'i*.
ho'opili. See *pili*, to cling, *pili*,
to refer.
ho'oponopono. See *ponopono*,
1.
ho'opū'iwa. See *pū'iwa*, startled.
ho'opuka. See *puka*, 1, 2, 3.
ho'opulapula. See *pulapula*,
seedling.
ho'opulu. See *pulu*, wet, and
pulu, mulch.
ho'opuni. See *puni*, 1, 2, 3.
ho'oū'i. See *u'i*.
ho'oūka. See -*uka*.
ho'oūku. See *uku*, pay.
ho'oūli. See *uli*, 1, dark.
ho'oūlu. See *ulu*, 1, 2.
ho'oūna. See -*una*.
ho'owā. See *wā*, roar.
ho'owahāwahā. See *wahāwahā*.
ho'owalewale. See *walewale*.
ho'oweliweli. See *weli*.
ho'owili. See *wili*, to turn.
hope. 1. After, behind; last,
rear; afterwards. (This common word occurs without a
preceding *k*-demonstrative or
k-possessive; it frequently follows *ma*-. *Mahope*, afterwards, by-and-by. *I hope*, in
back, behind. PPN *sope*. 2.

Result, conclusion, end. 3. Deputy, assistant, acting officer. 4. Posterior, buttocks.

hopena. Result, conclusion, ending.

hope-ʻō. Wasp, yellow jacket. *Lit.*, spearing rear.

hope pelekikena (peresidena). Vice-president.

hope poʻo. Acting or deputy head, director.

hōpoe. 1. Fully developed. 2. (*Cap.*) A legendary woman in the Pele and Hiʻi-aka legend cycle.

hopohopo. Anxiety, uncertainty, doubt; in doubt, fearful. **hoʻohopohopo.** To produce anxiety.

hopu. To seize, grasp, arrest; taking, seizure. PEP (*f,s*) *opu.*

hopuna. 1. Grasping, taking; arrest. 2. Pronunciation.

hopunaʻōlelo. 1. Pronunciation. 2. Paragraph. 3. Syllable.

hou. 1. New, fresh, recent. PPN *foʻou.* 2. Again, more. *Hana hou,* to do again, encore. 3. To push, stab, inject. PPN *fohu.* 4. Perspiration, sweat; to perspire, sweat.

hōʻuluʻulu. See ʻuluʻulu, collection.

houpo. Diaphragm, chest.

houpo-ʻume-pau. Heart attack.

hū. 1. To rise or swell, as yeast or souring *poi;* to ferment, boil over; to surge or rise to the surface, as emotion; rising, swelling; overflow. **hoʻohū.** (a) To leaven, cause to rise. (b) Yeast, baking powder, leaven. 2. To roar, grunt, hum. PPN *fuu.*

hua. 1. Fruit, egg, ovum, seed; to bear fruit, seed; to bear a child; fruitful. **hoʻohua.** To bear fruit, reproduce, give birth; to swell high, as a wave. PPN *fua.* 2. Result, effect; credit, as for a university course. 3. Testicles. PNP

fua. 4. Word, letter. PEP *fua.*

huʻa. Foam, bubble, suds. PEP *fuka.*

huaʻai. Edible fruit or seed.

huaʻala. Nutmeg. *Lit.*, fragrant fruit.

huaale. Pill. *Lit.*, seed to swallow.

huaale hoʻomoe. Sleeping tablet.

hua ʻē. Child born out of wedlock, that is accepted by the husband or wife of the parent and treated as his own. *Lit.*, strange fruit.

hua hapa. Half note, as in music.

hua hapahā. Quarter note, as in music.

hua hāʻule. Fallen fruit or seed. *Fig.*, friendless, illegitimate child (modern); foetus lost through miscarriage.

huahekili. Hail. *Lit.*, thunder fruit.

huahelu. Figure, number (the character).

huahua. 1. Fruitful, productive; to bear many fruits; to lay many eggs. 2. Testicles.

huahuaʻi. Redup. of *huaʻi;* to boil up, as water in a spring; to gush forth.

huʻahuʻa-kai. Sea foam; crest of a wave breaking into foam.

huʻahuʻa kopa (sopa). Soapsuds.

huaʻi. To disclose, reveal, uncover, as an oven; to pour forth; to churn water, as the propeller of a ship.

hua iki. Small letter; small fruit.

hua kahi. An only child or offspring. PNP *fuatasi.*

hua kai. Scrambled eggs.

huakaʻi. Trip, voyage; procession, parade; to travel.

huakaʻi hele. Travels, a long trip; to keep traveling.

huakaʻi pō. Night procession or parade, especially the night procession of ghosts that is sometimes called *'oi'o*.

huakanu. Seed, as of mango; bulb.

huakē. Full and plump, as a healthy person.

hu'a kopa. Soap bubble.

hua kukui. *Kukui* (candlenut) nuts.

hu'alepo. To scatter dust; to hit an underhanded blow.

huali. Bright, polished clean, pure, white, gleaming; morally pure.

hua loa'a. Product, answer, as in arithmetic.

hu'a lole. Trimmings or borders of a garment; hem of a dress.

hū'alu. Loose skin over the eyeball.

hua mele. Notes in music; words of a song.

huamoa. Chicken egg.

hua mua. Offering to a Congregational church of the first earnings in a new job or undertaking; offerings in gratitude for a particular success, as a big fish catch. *Lit.*, first fruit.

hua nui. 1. Large fruit, egg. **2.** Capital letter.

hua 'oko'a. Whole note in music.

hua 'ole. Fruitless, unproductive, worthless.

hua'ōlelo. Word.

hua pākā. Scrambled eggs, omelet.

huapalaoa. Wheat. *Lit.*, flour (*Eng.*) seed.

hua palapala. Letter of the alphabet. *Lit.*, writing letter.

hua pāma. Date (the fruit).

hua pōpolo. *Pōpolo* berry.

huawaina. Grape, grapes. *Lit.*, wine (*Eng.*) fruit.

huawaina malo'o. Raisins. *Lit.*, dry grapes.

hue. Gourd, water calabash, any narrow-necked vessel for holding water. PEP *fue*.

hu'e. To remove, lift off, uncover; to open, as an oven; to wash out, as flood waters. PPN *fuke*.

huehue. Pimples, acne; to have pimples. PPN *fuafua*.

huelo. Tail, as of dog, cat, pig; train of a dress.

hū'ena. Very angry.

hue wai. Gourd water container, bottle.

hue wai pū'ali. Gourd water container with constriction around the middle.

hue wai pueo. Water gourd shaped like an hourglass. *Lit.*, owl water gourd.

hūhā. Chat, talk; to chat.

huhu. A wood-boring insect; worm-eaten, rotten. PEP $(f,s)u(f,s)u$.

huhū. Angry, offended; anger, wrath; to scold, become angry. **ho'ohuhū.** To provoke anger.

huhui. Cluster.

huhui waina. Cluster of grapes.

huhuki. Redup. of *huki;* to pull hard or frequently. **ho'ohuhuki.** To pull, cause to pull.

huhū wale. Short-tempered; angry without cause.

hui. 1. Club, association; firm, partnership, union; to form a society or organization; to meet. **ho'ohui.** To form a society. **2.** To join, unite, combine. **ho'ohui.** To join, as two rods; to add on, annex, append; to introduce one person to another; meeting of persons. PPN *fuhi*. **3.** A plus sign. **4.** Cluster, as of grapes or coconuts; bunch, as of bananas. **5.** Chorus of a song.

hūi. Haloo. *Modern.*

hu'i. Aching; ache. *Niho hu'i,* toothache. PPN *suki*.

hui hō'ai'ē kālā (dālā). Credit union. *Lit.*, society for loaning money.

hui ho'opa'a. Insurance company.

huihui. 1. Mixed, mingled,

joined; to pool together, as to buy cooperatively. 2. Cluster, collection, bunch. 3. Constellation.

hu'ihu'i. Cold, cool, chilly; numbing, tingling, as love. ho'ohu'ihu'i. To make cold, chill, as by refrigeration.

huihui a kōlea. To gather together like a flock of kōlea birds.

hui 'ia. Incorporated, united, joined.

huika, huita. Wheat. Eng.

hui kahi. United in one.

huikala. To absolve entirely, forgive all faults.

hui kālepa. Trading company, mercantile firm.

huikau. Mixed, confused; mix-up. ho'ohuikau. To mix, confuse.

Hui Ke'a 'Ula'ula. Red Cross.

hui kinai ahi. Fire department.

huila. Wheel. Eng.

huila kaulike. Disc wheel of a sewing machine.

huila nui. Large wheel; fly-wheel, as of a sewing machine.

huilawai. Water wheel, windmill.

hui malū. Any secret society or fraternity, as the Masons; Masonic; to meet secretly.

huina. 1. Sum, total. 2. Angle; corner, as of a house or street; crossroads, intersection.

huina-. Geometric figure. See huinahā, huinakolu, and others.

huina alanui. Crossroads, street corner.

huinahā. Quadrangle, quadrilateral.

huinahā kaulike. Square.

huina helu. 1. Sum of several numbers, total. 2. General arithmetic.

huinakolu. Triangle.

huina kūpono. Right angle.

huinalima. 1. Pentagon. 2. Joining of two hands, especially in hand wrestling (uma).

huini. 1. Needle-pointed, sharp-pointed. ho'ohuini. To carve or sharpen into a point. 2. Sharp, shrill sounds.

hui pū. To mix, unite, combine. 'Amelika-Hui-Pū-'Ia, United States of America.

hui puhi 'ohe. Band (musical).

huka. Hook, as on a door; to hook. Eng.

huki. 1. To pull, as on a rope; to draw, stretch, reach. ho'ohuki. To pull gently; headstrong, willful. PPN futi. 2. A fit of any kind, convulsion, stroke, epileptic fit; cramp, as in the leg; to have a fit or cramp.

hukihuki. 1. To pull or draw frequently, or by many persons; to pull by jerks, as in the tug-of-war game. 2. To disagree, quarrel; not cooperative, headstrong. 3. Tug-of-war game; to play the game.

hukilau. A seine; to fish with the seine. Lit., pull ropes (lau).

huki like. To pull together, cooperate.

huki wai. To draw water; one who draws water.

hula. 1. The hula, a hula dancer; to dance the hula. PEP fula. 2. Song or chant used for the hula; to sing or chant for a hula.

hulahula. Ballroom dancing with partners, American dancing, massed hula dancing; to dance thus.

hula 'ili'ili. Hula in which smooth water-worn stones are used as clappers or castanets; the pebble hula.

hula kōlea. A kneeling hula imitative of the kōlea, plover.

hula ku'i Moloka'i. An ancient fast dance of Moloka'i.

hulali. Shining, glittering,

glossy; to shine, reflect light.

hūlalilali. Redup. and intensification of *hulali.*

hula ʻuliʻuli. Hula with *ʻuliʻuli,* gourd rattles.

huli. 1. To turn; to curl over, as a breaker: *Fig.,* to change, as an opinion or manner of living. **hoʻohuli.** To turn, change, convert. PPN *fuli.* 2. To look for, search. **hoʻohuli.** To look for. 3. Section, as of a town or place. 4. Taro top. PPN *suli.*

huli ʻaoʻao. To lean over to one side, turn to the side.

huliau. 1. Turning point, time of change. 2. To think of the past, recall the past.

huli hele. To search here and there.

hulihia. Passive/imperative of *huli 1, 2;* overturned; a complete change, overthrow; turned upside down. PNP *fulisia.*

hulihuli. Redup. of *huli, 1, 2;* to search repeatedly or long.

huli kanaka. Profound studies, moral philosophy, science; to engage in such.

huli kua. To turn one's back, refuse to help, ignore.

hulili. Dazzling light, vibration; to dazzle, swell.

huli manaʻo. To seek an opinion; to change an opinion. **hoʻohuli manaʻo.** To induce change of opinion.

huli pau. To overturn completely; to search everywhere.

huli pū. To overturn, turn upside down, overthrow.

hulu. 1. Feather. PPN *fulu.* 2. Esteemed, choice; esteemed older relative, as of parents' or grandparents' generations. **hoʻohulu.** To esteem, prize. 3. Fur, wool, fleece, human body hair (contrasting with *lauoho,* head hair). PPN *fulu.*

huluʻānai. Scrubbing or painting brush, formerly made of a coconut husk.

hulu hipa. Sheep wool, fleece; woolen cloth.

huluhulu. 1. Body hair, hair of eyelashes, fleece, fur; hairy. PPN *fulufulu.* 2. Frayed, rough, not smooth. 3. Feathers. 4. Down or fuzz on plant stems. 5. Flannel. 6. Blanket.

hulu kuʻemaka. Eyebrow.

hulu manu. Bird feather.

hulumanu. Tick used for mattresses and pillow covers, so called because they were stuffed with bird feathers.

hulu-moa. The Hawaiian mistletoes (*Korthalsella* spp.), evergreen, cylindrical- or flat-stemmed shrubs with tiny, inconspicuous leaves and flowers.

hulu pena. Paintbrush.

hume. To bind about the loins, as a *malo;* to put on a *malo;* to wear a sanitary napkin. PEP (*f, s*)*ume.*

humehume. Redup. of *hume.*

humu. To sew, stitch; seam, stitch; to bind, as a book. PEP (*f, s*)*umu.*

humu hoʻi. Back stitching; to sew with back stitching.

humu (humuhumu) hoʻoholoholo. Running stitch, basting.

humuhumu. 1. Redup. of *humu;* to sew. 2. Triggerfish. PPN *sumu.*

humuhumu-nukunuku-a-puaʻa. Varieties of *humuhumu* (*Rhinecanthus aculeatus, R. rectangulus*). Lit., *humuhumu* with a snout like a pig.

humuhumu puke. Bookbinding.

humuhumu puke ʻili lole. Cloth bookbinding.

humuhumu puke ʻili pepa. Paper bookbinding.

humuhumu ulana. To darn, as socks.

humuhumu-umauma-lei. Triggerfish (*Sufflamen bursa*). *Lit.*, lei [on] chest *humuhumu*.

humukā. Cross-stitching; to do cross-stitching.

humu kaulahao. Chain stitch; to make chain stitches.

humulau. To embroider.

humu pe'a. Sail making; to sew sails.

humu puka pihi. Buttonhole stitch.

huna. 1. Minute particle; small, little. **2.** Hidden secret.

hūnā. To hide, conceal. **ho'ohūnā.** To hide. PNP *funa*.

hunahuna. Fragments.

hunahuna-'ōlelo. Particle, as Hawaiian *ua*, *i*, *e*.

huna-kai. 1. White-flowered beach morning-glory (*Ipomea stolonifera*). **2.** Sanderling (*Crocethia alba*), a winter migrant to Hawaii. *Lit.*, sea foam, so called from the bird's habit of following close behind receding waves.

huna kai. Sea spray, sea foam.

huna wai. Drop of water, spray, mist.

huna wailele. Spray from a waterfall.

hune. 1. Poor, destitute; a poor person. **2.** Fine, tiny.

hunehune. Redup. and intensification of *hune*, *2*; very fine, delicate.

hune kai. Sea spray, sea foam.

hune one. Fine-grained sand, sand particles.

hūnōna. Son- or daughter-in-law, followed by *kāne* or *wahine* for specific designation of sex. PEP *funoonga*.

-hūnōwai. Father- or mother-in-law, usually after *makua* and followed by *kāne* or *wahine* for specific designation of sex. PNP *fungawai*.

huoi. Suspicion. **ho'ohuoi.** To suspect.

hupa. Hoop. *Eng.*

hūpē. Nasal mucus. PPN *isuupe'e*. PEP *suupee*.

hūpēkole. Running nose; to sniffle.

hūpō. Ignorant, unintelligent; fool. *Lit.*, swelling darkness.

hūwā, hua. Envy, jealousy; envious, jealous; to stir up trouble due to envy.

I

i. 1. Particle and clitic preceding nouns and marking direct and indirect objects, with additional meanings; to, at, in, on, by, because of, due to, by means of. PPN (')*i*, *ki*. **2.** Particle and clitic preceding subordinate verbs and marking completed or past action and state or condition. **3.** If. **4.** While, when, no sooner than.

'ī. To say.

ia. He, she, it, this. PPN *ia*.

iā. 1. Yard (unit of measure). *Eng.* **2.** Yard (spar on a sailing vessel). *Eng.* **3.** Particle replacing *i*, *1*, before pronouns and names of people, and, optionally, before place names.

'ia. Particle marking passive/imperative.

i'a. 1. Fish or any marine animal, as eel, oyster, crab. PPN *ika*. **2.** Meat or any flesh food. **3.** (*Cap.*) Milky Way.

i (verb) **ai.** Particles indicating completed aspect or state or condition and accompanying subordinate verbs.

iāia. 1. Him, her; to him, to her; because of or due to him or her. **2.** While he or she, as soon as he or she.

'iako. 1. Outrigger boom. PPN

kiato. 2. Forty, as in counting tapas.

i'a maka. Raw fish.

i'a-makika. Mosquitofish (*Gambusia affinis*).

ia nei. This person, he, she (after *'o*, subject marker).

lānuali, lanuari. January. *Eng.*

Iao. Name of Jupiter appearing as the morning star.

lāpana. Japan. *Eng.*

ia'u. 1. Me, to me; because of or due to me. See *-a'u.* 2. While I, at the time that I, as soon as I.

i'e. Tapa beater. PPN *ike.*

'ie. Aerial root of the *'ie'ie* vine; the vine itself.

lēhowa, lehova. Jehovah. *Biblical.*

'ie'ie. An endemic, woody, branching climber (*Freycinetia arborea*). PPN *kie.*

Ielukalema, Ierusalema. Jerusalem. *Eng.*

'iēwe. 1. Afterbirth, placenta. Also *ēwe.* 2. Relatives of a common ancestry.

ihe. 1. Spear, javelin, dart. 2. Halfbeak fish. PPN *ise.*

i hea. See *hea*, where.

ihe laumeki, ihe laumaki. Barbed spear.

ihe 'ō. Dart; piercing spear.

ihe pahe'e. Short spear.

ihe pakelo. Lance.

ihi. To strip, peal. PPN *hisi.*

'ihi. 1. Sacred, dignified; treated with reverence or respect. **hō'ihi.** To treat thus. 2. Wood sorrels (*Oxalis*, all species). PPN *kisi.*

ihihī. To neigh.

'ihi lani. Heavenly splendor; reverence due a chief.

iho. 1. To go down; to go south or before the wind. PPN *hifo.* 2. Core, as of apple; pith. PPN *uso*; PEP *iso.* 3. Down, below (directional particle following words). *Hele iho*, to go down, descend. 4. Same particle and reference as

above but with reflexive meaning, often following words describing activities of the body, as eating, drinking, thinking. *'Ai iho*, to eat. 5. Same particle and reference as above with meaning "self." *E hana ana 'oia nona iho*, he will work for himself. 6. Same particle and reference as *iho, 3, 4, 5*, but used with words of time. *'Ānō iho nei*, just now, recently. *Mahope iho*, afterwards.

ihola. Directional and reflexive particle *iho*, plus clitic demonstrative *la.*

iho-lena. A favorite and common native variety of banana.

ihona. Descent, incline.

i hope. See *hope.*

ihu. 1. Nose, snout; toe of a shoe; a kiss. PPN *isu.* 2. Prow or bow of a canoe or ship.

ihu 'e'eke. To wrinkle up the nose, as to show scorn.

ihu 'eka. Dirty nose, a disparaging epithet.

ihu hānuna. To snore or speak with nasalized sounds.

ihuihu. Rising upward, as the prow of a canoe. *Fig.*, scornful.

ihu kāma'a. Toe of shoes.

ihu kū. Tilted nose, pug nose. *Fig.*, haughty.

ihu pī. To breathe with difficulty due to partial obstruction of the nostrils, as of one with a cold. See *pī, 2.*

ihu pi'i. Elevated nose. *Fig.*, scornful, haughty.

ihu wa'a. Bow of a canoe, bowsprit.

'i'i. Small, stunted, undersized; dwarf.

'i'ike. To see well; observant; to recognize and accost in a friendly way.

'i'imi. To seek again and again; one seeking everywhere, as for knowledge.

i (verb phrase) **inā.** Same as *inā* (phrase) *inā.*

'i'ini. To desire, crave; liking.

'i'iwi. Scarlet Hawaiian honey-creeper (*Vestiaria coccinea*) found on all the main islands; its feathers were used extensively in featherwork. Also called *'iwi.*

'i'iwi-haole. Cape gooseberry.

ikā. To drift upon; to turn aside from a straight course; flotsam and jetsam. **ho'oikā.** To put or throw ashore.

ikaika. Strong, powerful; strength, force, energy. **ho-'oikaika, hō'ikaika.** To make a great effort, encourage. *Ho-'oikaika kino,* body-building exercise.

ikaika lio. Horsepower.

Ikalia, Italia. Italy; Italian. *Eng.*

ikamu, itamu. Item. *Eng.*

'ike. To see, know, feel, greet, recognize, understand; to know sexually; knowledge; sense, as of hearing or sight; vision. **hō'ike.** (a) To show, make known, display, exhibit, reveal, explain; proof, guide, exhibition. *Ha'awina hō'ike,* examination. (b) Witness, as in court. (c) School commencement. (d) Congregational convention of various Sunday Schools with singing and recitation. PPN *kite.*

'ike hānau. Instinct. *Lit.,* birth knowledge.

'ike'ike. Rare redup. of *'ike.* **hō'ike'ike.** To display, exhibit, as in a museum or show. *Hale hō'ike'ike,* museum.

'ike kumu. Basic or fundamental knowledge.

'ike maka. Eyewitness; visible.

'ikena. View, seeing, knowing.

'ikeoma. Idiom; idiomatic. *Eng.*

'ike pāpālua. To see double; to have the gift of second sight and commune with the spirits.

'ike pono. To see clearly; certain knowledge.

iki. Small, little, slightly, a little. **ho'oiki.** To lessen. PPN *'iti.*

ikiiki. 1. Stifling heat and humidity; acute discomfort. **2.** (*Cap.*) Name of a month in the summer season.

'ikuwā. 1. Noisy, clamorous, loud-voiced; to make a din. **2.** (*Cap.*) Month near the end of the Hawaiian year, named for the roar of surf, thunder, and cloudbursts of this month.

ila. Dark birthmark. PPN *'ila.*

i laila. See *laila.*

i lalo. See *lalo.*

ilāmuku. Executive officer, marshal, sheriff. PPN *'ilaamuku.*

ili. 1. Stranded, aground, as a ship on the reef; to run over, as with a car. **ho'īli, ho'oili.** To land upon, load, as freight on a ship; to transfer, transmit. PPN *hili.* **2.** Inheritance; to inherit. **ho'īli, ho'oili.** To bequeath or leave in a will; to save. **3.** To fall upon, as sorrow, responsibility, blessings, curses.

'ili. 1. Skin, hide, scalp, bark. PPN *kili.* **2.** Leather. **3.** Surface, area. **4.** Binding, cover. **5.** Land section. **6.** Strap of any kind, as reins, fan belt, hose.

-'īli. (With *hō-*) **hō'īli.** To collect; to bunch together as fish in a net.

'iliahi. All Hawaiian kinds of sandalwood (*Santalum* spp.). PPN *asi.*

'ili 'āina. 1. Land area. **2.** An *'ili* land division.

'ili hau. Bark of the *hau* tree, as used for rope and for modern grass skirts.

ilihia. Stricken with awe. PPN *ilifia.*

ili hinuhinu. Patent leather. *Lit.,* shiny leather.

'ili holoholona. Leather; fur, as about the neck.

'ili honua. Surface of the earth.

'ilihune. Poor, destitute; poverty, poor person. *Lit.*, tiny skin.

'ili'ili. 1. Pebble, small stone, as used in dances or *kōnane*. *Hula 'ili'ili*, pebble dance. PPN *kilikili*. 2. To pile, overlap. *hō'ili'ili*. To gather, collect, save, store away.

'ilikai. 1. Surface of the sea. 2. Horizontal.

'ili kala. Skin of *kala*, a fish, sometimes stretched over a coconut shell to form the top of the small *pūniu*, knee drum.

'ili kani. 1. A skin that sounds, as used in drums. 2. Tough skin.

'ili kea. Fair skin, of Hawaiians.

'ili ke'ehi. Stirrup.

'iliki. 1. To strike suddenly, pour down, as rain; downpour. 2. A varnish, as made of candlenut (*kukui*) bark, ti root, or banana stump.

'Ilikini. Indian (of America). *Eng.* Also *'Inikini*.

'ilikole. 1. Poverty-stricken, very poor; pauper (stronger than *'ilihune*). *Lit.*, bare skin. *hō'ilikole*. To cause poverty. 2. Flesh of half-ripe coconut.

'ilikona. Wart. *Lit.*, hard skin.

'ili kou. Dark-skinned, as dark Hawaiians. *Lit.*, *kou*-wood skin.

'ili kūpono. A nearly independent *'ili* land division within an *ahupua'a*.

'ili lā'au. Tree bark.

'ili lele. Portion of an *'ili* land division separated from the main part of the *'ili* but considered a part of it. Also called *lele*.

'ili luna. Epidermis; outer bark.

'ilima. Small to large native shrubs (all species of *Sida*, especially *S. fallax*). The *'ilima* is the flower of O'ahu.

'ili mānoanoa. Callous; calloused skin.

ilina. 1. Grave, tomb, cemetery, mausoleum, plot in a cemetery. 2. Recipient. **ho'oilina**, **ho'ilina.** Heir, inheritance; successor.

'ilio. Dog. Probably PPN *kulii*. (*Tuamotu, kurio*.)

'ilio 'aukai. 1. Sea dog, experienced sailor. 2. Warship.

'ilio hae. Fierce or vicious dog; wolf, jackal.

'ilio hahai holoholona. Hunting dog.

'ilio hahai manu. Bird dog.

'ilio hanu kanaka. Bloodhound. *Lit.*, dog that smells man.

'ilio hipa. Sheep dog, shepherd dog.

'ilio hohono. Skunk, bad-smelling dog.

'ilio 'i'i. Small curly-haired native dog.

ili 'ōlelo. A tattletale, talebearer; to gossip.

'ili 'ōmaka. Foreskin.

'ilio māku'e. Native dog, brown dog.

'ilio-pulu. Bulldog. *Lit.*, bull (*Eng.*) dog.

'ili pa'a. An *'ili* land division complete in one section, as distinguished from an *'ili lele*.

'ili palapala. Parchment.

'ili pala uli. Dark-complexioned.

'ili pale o kāma'a. Sole of a shoe.

'ili pāpa'a. Sunburned or tanned skin.

'ili pipi. Leather, cowhide.

'ili po'o. Scalp.

'ilipuakea. White person.

'iliwai. 1. Surface, as of water; level. **hō'iliwai.** To grade or level, as a road. 2. Carpenter's or surveyor's level. 3. Water hose.

ilo. 1. Maggot, grub; to creep, as worms. PNP *'ilo*. 2. Young shoot; to germinate, sprout. **ho'oilo.** To cause germination.

-ilo. hoʻoilo, hoʻīlo. Rainy, winterlike months, winter.

iloilo. Redup. of *ilo*, 1, 2; wormy; sprouting.

-iloilo. hoʻoiloilo. To predict disaster.

i loko. See *loko*.

ʻīloli. Unpleasant sensations of pregnancy; emotional disturbances; intense yearning, longing. **hoʻīloli.** To feel the discomforts of pregnancy; to suffer emotional disturbance.

i luna. See *luna*.

ʻimi. To look, hunt, search. PPN *kumi*, PNP *kimi*.

ʻimi a loaʻa. Discoverer; to discover.

ʻimi hala. To find fault with, blame.

ʻimi hana. 1. To seek work. 2. To stir up trouble.

ʻimi ʻike. To seek knowledge; a seeker of knowledge.

ʻimi kālā. To seek money, to earn a livelihood; commercial.

ʻimi loa. To seek far; distant traveler. *Fig.,* one with great knowledge.

ʻimina. Looking, seeking; search.

ʻimi naʻauao. To seek knowledge or education; ambitious to learn; one seeking education or learning.

ʻimi ʻōlelo. To lie, slander, stir up trouble by gossip.

ʻimi pono. To seek or strive for righteousness; endeavor.

ʻimo. To wink, twinkle; winking, twinkling.

ʻimoʻimo. Redup. of *ʻimo.* *Hōkū ʻimoʻimo,* twinkling star.

imu. Underground oven; food cooked in an *imu.* Also *umu.*

i mua. See *mua.*

inā. If, would that.

ʻina. Young of the sea urchin (*wana*), *Echinothrix* spp., especially *E. diadema.* PNP *kina.*

ināhea. When (in questions in the past).

ʻinaʻi. Accompaniment to *poi,* usually meat, fish, or vegetable. PNP *ki(i)naki.*

inaina. Anger, hatred, malice; to hate; moved with hatred, angry. **hoʻoinaina.** To stir up anger, rouse hate.

inā (phrase) **inā.** If... would. *Inā he nui ke kālā, inā ua holomua ka hana,* if there were much money, the work would progress.

ʻinamona. Relish made of the cooked kernel of candlenut (*kukui*) mashed with salt.

ʻinana. To come to life or activity, as of a sick person; animated; stirring of life. **hōʻinana.** To animate, give life to.

ʻinea. Hardship, suffering, distress.

inehinei. Yesterday (often written *i nehinei*).

i neʻi. See *neʻi,* here.

ʻInia. India; East Indian. *Eng.*

ʻIniana. Indian, as Indian Ocean. *Eng.*

ʻiniha. Inch. *Eng.*

ʻiniʻiniki. To pinch or nip repeatedly; tingling, as with cold.

ʻinika. Ink. *Eng.*

ʻiniki. To pinch; sharp and piercing, as wind or pangs of love. PPN *kini.*

ʻInikini. Same as *ʻIlikini,* Indian. *Eng.*

ʻinikiniki (sometimes pronounced *ʻinisinisi* in songs). Same as *ʻiniʻiniki.*

ʻinikua. Insurance. *Eng.*

ʻinikua kaʻa. Automobile insurance.

ʻinikua ola. Life insurance.

ʻinikua pau ahi. Fire insurance.

ʻinikua ulia. Accident insurance.

ʻino. 1. Wicked, sinful; sin. **hōʻino, hoʻoʻino.** To insult, dishonor. PNP *kino.* 2. Spoiled, contaminated. 3. To injure, harm. **ho'o'ino.** To harm, damage. **4.** Storm; stormy. **5.** Very, very much, intensely. *Aloha 'ino,* too bad, what a shame.

inoa (in fast speech often preceded by *ke*). **1.** Name. PPN *hingoa.* **2.** Name chant.

inoa kapakapa. See *kapakapa,* 2.

inoa pō. Dream name.

'ino'ino. 1. Spoiled, contaminated; damaged. **hō'ino'ino.** To mar, disfigure, damage, speak evil of. **2.** Stormy; storm. **3.** Wicked, sinful; sin.

inu. To drink; a drink, drinking. **ho'īnu, ho'oinu.** To give to drink. PPN *inu.*

inu lama. To drink rum or other alcoholic drink; one who drinks.

inu li'ili'i. To drink but a little, sip.

inumia. Passive of *inu.* PPN *inumia.*

inu 'ona. To drink until intoxicated.

io. Paddle rib. PPN *io.*

i 'ō. See *'ō,* yonder.

'io. 1. Hawaiian hawk (*Buteo solitarius*), an endemic hawk found only on the island of Hawai'i. **2.** To twitter, chirp. PPN *kio.*

'i'o. 1. Flesh, meat, flesh and blood. PNP *kiko.* **2.** True, genuine, significant, real; really, truly; true worth.

'i'o hipa. Mutton, flesh of sheep.

'i'o holoholona. Meat.

'i'o huki. Muscle.

ioio. Rounded grooves in carving, as made in *kukui* nuts used in necklaces; depression made by stitches in quilting.

'io'io. Redup. of *'io;* cheeping, peeping.

'i'o'i'o. Clitoris. PEP *kikokiko.*

'iolana. To soar; soaring hawk.

'io lani. Royal hawk.

'Io-lani. Name of the Palace and of a school in Honolulu.

i'ole. So that not, in order not.

'iole. Hawaiian rat (*Rattus exulans*); introduced rat. PNP *kiole.*

'iole-lāpaki (rabati). Rabbit.

'iole li'ili'i. Little rat; mouse.

'iole-manakuke. Mongoose.

'iole-nui. Introduced large rat.

'iole-pua'a. Guinea pig.

i ona. To him, her; him, her. *Lit.,* to his, hers.

'i'o nīoi. Condiment of boiled pulp of chili peppers (*nīoi*), often mixed with relish such as *'inamona.*

'i'o niu. Flesh of coconut.

'i'o pale niho. Gums. *Lit.,* tooth-protecting flesh.

'i'o pipi i wili 'ia. Hamburger, ground round steak. *Lit.,* ground beef flesh.

'i'o pua'a uahi. Bacon. *Lit.,* smoked pork flesh.

i o'u. To me, me. *Lit.,* to my.

ipo. Sweetheart, lover. **ho'oipo.** To make love, court. PEP *ipo.*

ipoipo, ho'oipoipo. To make love.

ipu. 1. Bottle gourd (*Lagenaria siceraria*). See *pōhue. ipu.* **2.** Watermelon (*Citrullus vulgaris*). **3.** General name for vessel or container, as dish, mug, calabash, pot, cup, pipe. **4.** Drum consisting of a single gourd or made of two large gourds of unequal size joined together.

ipu-'ai-maka. Watermelon, melon. *Lit.,* melon to eat raw.

ipu 'aina. Scrap bowl, refuse container.

ipu-'ala. 1. Cantaloupe melon (*Cucumis melo* var. *cantalupensis*). **2.** Container for perfume or other fragrant matter. *Lit.,* fragrant gourd.

ipu 'au'au. Washbasin; container of water for a bath.

ipu hao. Iron pot; kettle or saucepan of any sort, whether glass, aluminum, or enamel. *Lit.*, iron container.

ipu-haole. Watermelon. *Lit.*, foreign gourd. See *ipu*, 2.

ipu heke 'ole. Gourd drum consisting of a single gourd without a top section.

ipu hōkiokio. Same as *hōkiokio*, gourd whistle.

ipu holoi. Washbasin.

ipu holoi lima. Finger bowl. *Lit.*, container wash hand.

ipu hula. Dance drum made of two gourds sewed together.

ipu i'a. Meat dish.

'īpuka. Door, entrance, exit, gate, opening in the wall for the admission of light or air.

ipu kai. A dish for meat or any dish deep enough to hold gravy (*kai*); gravy boat.

ipu kālua. Baked pumpkin or squash.

ipu kī. Teapot.

ipu kuha. Spittoon.

ipukukui. Lamp, candlestick. *Hale ipukukui*, lighthouse.

ipukukui hele pō. Lantern. *Lit.*, light for going at night.

ipu-kula. The cup of gold (*Solandra hartwegii*). *Lit.*, golden (*Eng.*) container.

ipu lepo. Earthenware pot, clay pot. *Lit.*, dirt container.

ipu mimi. Chamber pot, container for urine.

ipu pa'i. Gourd drum. *Lit.*, gourd to beat.

ipu paka (baka). Tobacco pipe.

ipu-pū. Same as *pū*, a general name for pumpkin and squashes.

ipu pueo. Gourd with hourglass shape.

ipu wai. Water container, water bottle.

ipu wai 'au'au. Washbasin.

'iu. Lofty, sacred, revered, consecrated.

'iu'iu. Intensification of *'iu*; majestic, very high; distant, far away.

i uka. See *uka*.

lukaio, ludaio. Jew; Jewish.

lulai. July. *Eng.*

lune. June. *Eng.*

lupika, lupita. The planet Jupiter. *Eng.*

iwa. Ninth, nine. PPN *hiwa*.

'iwa. 1. Frigate or man-of-war bird (*Fregata minor palmerstoni*). *Fig.*, thief. PEP *kiwa*. 2. A fern (*Asplenium horridum*). PEP *kiwa*.

i waena. See *waena*.

i waho. See *waho*.

'iwa'iwa. All maidenhair ferns (*Adiantum* spp.).

iwakālua. Twenty.

iwi. 1. Bone. PNP *iwi*. 2. Shell, as of coconut, candlenut (*kukui*), gourd, egg, shellfish.

'iwi. 1. Same as *'i'iwi*. PEP *kiwi*. 2. Eye-twitching. PPN *kiwi*.

iwi ā. Jawbone.

iwi 'ao'ao. 1. Rib, rib bone. 2. Assistant leader in a hula troupe.

iwi hilo. Thighbone.

iwi hoehoe. Shoulder blade.

iwi hope. Bone forming the posterior segment of the skull.

iwi hua. Hipbone; round bone fitting into a socket.

iwiiwi. High cheekbone; bony; skinny. PPN *iwiiwi*.

iwi kamumu. Cartilage.

iwi kanaka. Human bone or skeleton.

iwi kānana. Bone of the anterior part of the skull, forming the skeleton of the forehead.

iwikuamo'o. 1. Spine, backbone. 2. Near and trusted relative of a chief who attended to his personal needs and possessions and executed private orders; family.

iwi lā'ī. Stem and midrib of a ti leaf.

iwilei. 1. Collarbone. PNP *iwilei*. 2. Measure of length from the collarbone to the tip of the middle finger with the arm extended; yard (measure).

iwi loa. A tall bone. *Fig.*, a tall person.

iwi 'ō. Wishbone.

iwi po'i. Kneecap.

iwi po'o. Skull, head bone.

iwi pūhaka. Pelvic bone.

iwi pū niu. Coconut shell. *Fig.*, skull.

iwi umauma. Breastbone, sternum.

J

For loanwords from English beginning with *j-*, substitute *i-* or *k-*. For example: for June, July, see *Iune, Iulai;* for Japanese, jury, see *Kepanī, kiule.*

K

ka. 1. The one, the person in question (usually followed by *i* and a verb). 2. Definite article; *ka* is replaced by *ke* before words beginning with *a-, e-, o-,* and *k-,* and before some words beginning with the glottal stop and *p-. Ka* is usually translated "the," except that it is not translated before English mass nouns or status titles.

kā. 1. To hit, strike, hack, hurl, dash, especially with a quick hard stroke; to bail water, as from a canoe; to turn a rope for children to jump; to snare, as birds. ho'okā. To dash down, shatter, break, strike. PPN *taa.* 2. Canoe bailer. PPN *taa.* 3. Exclamation of mild disapproval or surprise. Oh! So! (If spoken alone it is frequently pronounced Chā! or Sah!) *'O 'oe kā.* So it's you! 4. Of, belonging to (*a*-class possessive). PNP *ta'a.*

kā-. 1. A prefix with meaning similar to that of the causative/simulative *ho'o-,* but used with only a few bases. Cf. *kāhinu, kāko'o, kāwili,* etc. PPN *taa-.* 2. Inclusiveness, in pronouns *kāua, kākou* and possessives *kā kāua,* *kō kāua, kā kākou, kō kākou.* PNP *taa-.*

ka'a. 1. To roll, turn, twist, revolve; rolling, twisting. *Ka'a pa'akai,* to roll in salt. ho'oka'a. To cause a rolling, turning. PPN *taka.* 2. Vehicle, carriage, automobile, car. 3. To pay; paid. ho'oka'a. To pay a debt. *Ho'oka'a hapa,* partial payment.

ka'aahi. Train; locomotive engine. *Lit.*, fire wagon.

ka'a hale. Trailer, house on wheels.

ka'a hehi wāwae. Bicycle, tricycle. *Lit.*, vehicle press feet.

ka'ahele. To make a tour, travel about; a tour.

ka'a holo hau. Sled. *Lit.*, vehicle running [on] snow.

ka'a huila kahi. Wheelbarrow. *Lit.*, single-wheel vehicle.

ka'a huila lua. Any two-wheeled vehicle, as cart or buggy.

ka'a huki. Handcart. *Lit.*, pull vehicle.

ka'ai. Sash, belt.

ka'akepa. Diagonal, cut at an angle; to avoid, shy away from.

ka'a kinai ahi. Fire engine. *Lit.*, vehicle extinguish fire.

ka'ā kolu. Three-stranded; threefold.

ka'akūmākena. Period of mourning, especially wailing in grief.

ka'akupapa'u. Hearse.

kā'ala'ala. Vigorous, sturdy, as of an infant or young animal.

ka'a lā'au. To wield a war club.

ka'a lau niu. Coconut-leaf thatching.

ka'a lawe ma'i. Ambulance.

ka'alele. To sway, reel; to fly or soar, as birds.

ka'alina. To bruise; to pelt, as rain. Cf. 'ālina.

ka'a lio. Horse-drawn vehicle, wagon, carriage.

kā'alo. To pass by, go by. Cf. mā'alo. ho'okā'alo. To pass to and fro, to cause to pass. PPN ta(a)kalo.

kā'alo'alo. Redup. of kā'alo.

ka'alolohi. Slowmoving, slow to anger.

ka'ā lua. Two-ply, two-stranded.

ka'a ma'i. Siege of sickness; a long or chronic illness.

ka'a malo'o. To wipe dry, as dishes with a cloth.

ka'amola. To turn around loosely, as a screw or peg that does not fit; loose, unsteady.

kā'ana. To divide, share, apportion. ho'okā'ana. To divide equally among, share.

ka'anini. To writhe, squirm, as a fidgety child or one in a tantrum. Cf. niniu, spin.

ka'ao. Legend, tale, usually fanciful; fiction. PEP t(a,e) kao.

ka'a 'ōhua. Vehicle carrying passengers for hire, as a bus or taxi.

ka'aoki. To finish or complete, as a canoe; to put on the last touches.

ka'apā. To toss from side to side, as a restless child in bed; in spasms.

ka'āpahu. To cut off squarely or crosswise.

ka'a paikikala. Bicycle. Lit., bicycle (Eng.) vehicle.

ka'a pauahi. Fire engine. Also ka'a wai.

ka'apuni. 1. To make a tour, go around, travel. 'Aha ka-'apuni, circuit court. 2. The hula step now called "around the island." 3. Revolution, revolving.

ka'au. Forty. PPN tekau.

ka'a uila. Streetcar, electric bus.

ka'a wai. 1. Vehicle carrying water. 2. Fire engine.

ka'awale. Separate, free, empty; to separate; free time; distance separating places or objects. Manawa ka'awale, spare or free time. ho'oka-'awale. To separate, distinguish; to set aside, to establish as a separate entity.

ka'a wale. To turn or roll freely, independently, or without control. PPN taka wale.

kā'awe. To tie anything tightly around the neck, to choke, strangle, hang.

ka'awili. To turn, twist, writhe as in pain; to knead, as bread.

kae. 1. Refuse, rubbish. PNP tae. 2. Treated with contempt, scorn. ho'okae. To despise, treat with contempt or scorn; destroy. Ho'okae 'ili, race prejudice.

ka'e. 1. Brink, border, edge; toothless gums; projecting brow of a hill. He ka'e wale nō, only gums and no teeth. Perhaps PPN take. 2. To sulk, fuss. 3. To smudge, dab. hōka'e, ho'oka'e. To daub, smudge, soil.

ka'e'e. Hard, stiff, not soft or pliable; dried up, withered as by heat.

kā'ei pāpale. Hatband.

kā'ekā. Entangled, confused, twisted.

kaekae. Smooth, polished, perfect; young, attractive, desirable, as of a woman; tasty, mellow, soft, as of sweet potatoes; to rub smooth, polish, finish.

kāʻekeʻeke. Bamboo pipes varying in length from one to several feet, usually with one end open; to play bamboo pipes.

kaʻele. Empty and hollow, as of a bowl, poi board, hull; inside bottom, as of a calabash or poi board. PPN takele.

Kāʻelo. Name of a wet month.

kaena. To boast, brag, praise; boastful, conceited.

kāʻeo. 1. Full, as a food calabash. Fig., full of knowledge. 2. Strong, zealous.

kaʻe paʻa. Selvage of cloth. Lit., solid edge.

kāʻeuʻeu. Helpful, cooperative; joyous, active; larger. Cf. ʻeu. hoʻokāʻeuʻeu, hōkāʻeuʻeu. To encourage and rouse to action.

kaha. 1. To scratch, mark, draw, cut, cut open or slice lengthwise, as fish or animals; to operate, as on the sick; to give a grade or mark to; to engrave; a line in mathematics; punctuation mark; stripe, as in the flag or on uniforms of enlisted men in the armed forces; a grade, as earned in school; long striped cloth. See kaha kiʻi. He aha koʻu kaha? What was my grade? PPN tafa. 2. Place (today usually followed by a qualifier, as kahakai, kahaone, kahawai; often used without ke, as hele i kahakai, go to the beach.) PPN tafa. 3. To swoop, as a kite; to go by, pass by; to turn and go on; to surf, body surf. PEP ta(f, s)a.

kahaapo. Circumference, par-

entheses, brackets. Lit., mark embrace.

kahaʻea. Cumulus clouds, often colored, thought to be a sign of rain.

kāhāhā. Interjection of surprise, wonder, displeasure; to wonder or be surprised; astonished. hoʻokāhāhā. Surprising; to cause astonishment.

kahahui. Plus sign in arithmetic. Lit., joining mark.

Kahaʻi. A culture hero. PNP Tafaki.

kahakaha. 1. Redup. of kaha, 1; to mark frequently, to draw lines; to scarify, engrave. Pepa kahakaha, scratch paper. PPN tafatafa. 2. Redup. of kaha, 3. hoʻokahakaha. To parade back and forth, to make a display; to show off; to drill; parade. PEP ta(f,s)ata(f,s)a.

kahakai. Beach, seashore. PEP tafatai.

kaha kiʻi. To draw or paint a picture or draw plans; artist.

kaha kiʻi hale. Architect; to draw building plans.

kahakuhi. Reference mark in writing or printing to direct attention, as asterisk, dagger, arrow.

kāhala. Amberjack or yellowtail (Seriola spp.).

kaha loa. To turn and then go straight for a long distance.

kahana. Cutting, drawing of a line; turning point.

kaha nalu. Body surfing. Cf. kaha, 3.

kahaone. Sandy beach.

kahawai. Stream, river, ravine whether wet or dry; valley.

kahe. 1. To flow, trickle, menstruate; in heat (of a bitch). Kahe ka hāʻae, to drool at the mouth. hoʻokahe. To water or irrigate, to drain. PPN tafe. 2. To cut or slit longitudinally, circumcise. PPN *tefe*.

kāhea. To call, cry out; to name; recital of the first lines of a stanza by the dancer as a cue to the chanter; to greet; to give a military command; a call, alarm.

kāhea pau ahi. Fire alarm.

kāheka. Pool, especially a rock basin where the sea washes in through an opening and salt forms.

kahe koko. Flow of blood; hemorrhage. **ho'okahe koko.** To shed blood; bloodshed.

kāhela. To lie spread out; to sweep back and forth, as billows.

kahe ule. To circumcise. *Lit.*, cut penis.

kāhewa. To miss, not succeed; foiled in an attempt.

kahi. 1. One, only one, alone, some (usually following the numeral classifiers '*a*- and '*e*-, or *ho'o*-); also, besides; someone else. *Na'u kahi*, give me some. **ho'okahi.** One, alone; oneness; together as a unit, to make one. *Noho ho-'okahi*, to live alone. PPN *tasi*. 2. To cut longitudinally, shave, comb. PNP *tafi*.

kāhi. Place (contraction of *ka wahi*; never used with *ke*); duty; where; in case of. *Kāhi 'ē*, elsewhere.

kāhi 'ē. See *kāhi*.

Kahiki. Any foreign country; Tahiti. *Holo i Kahiki*, sail to Tahiti or to any foreign country. PEP *Tafiti*.

kahiko. Old, ancient; old person. (Usually in the singular; cf. *kāhiko, 2.*) *Wā kahiko*, old times. **ho'okahiko.** To think, act, speak in the old way; to speak of old times; to cling to old customs; old-fashioned. PPN *tafito*.

kāhiko. 1. Finery; to wear finery. **ho'okāhiko.** To wear

fine clothes. 2. Plural of *kahiko*.

kahikolu. Trinity; three in one.

kāhili. 1. Feather standard, symbolic of royalty. 2. Kāhili ginger (*Hedychium gardnerianum*).

kahi moe. Place to sleep, bed, cot.

kāhinu. To rub with oil, grease, vaseline. Cf. *hinuhinu*.

kahi 'ō. High-backed comb with long prongs ('*ō*) such as worn by Spanish women.

kahi 'umi'umi. To shave the whiskers; barber.

kāholo. 1. Hasty, nimble, swift, quick; to move fast. **ho'okāholo.** To cause to hurry; to speed, hurry. 2. To sew with long stitches; basting. *Lopi kāholo*, basting thread. 3. The "vamp" hula step.

kāhonua. Globe of the earth.

kahu. 1. Honored attendant, guardian, keeper, administrator; pastor of a church; one who has a dog, cat, or any pet. *Kona kahu*, his attendant. *'O ka 'īlio kahu*, dog with a master. **ho'okahu.** To act as a *kahu*. 2. To tend or cook at an oven; to build an oven fire; one who tends an oven, a cook. **ho'okahu.** To make a fire for cooking in the oven. PPN *tafu*.

kahua. 1. Foundation, base, site, grounds, platform, as of a house; an open place, as for camping or for sports; playground, camp. *Fig.*, declaration of principles, doctrine. *Ka Monroe kahua kālai 'āina*, Monroe doctrine about land division. **ho'okahua.** To lay a foundation; to camp, as soldiers; to settle down, as homesteaders. PEP *ta(f,s)ua*. 2. Base of a quilt on which the pattern (*lau*) is appliquéd.

kahua hale. House foundation or site.

kahua hana. Subject, as of a discussion; foundation principles, as a political platform.

kahua hōʻikeʻike holoholona. Zoo.

kahua hōlua. Sledding course.

kahua hoʻolele leo. Radiobroadcasting station. *Lit.*, site for making voice fly.

kahua hoʻolulu mokulele. Airport.

kahua hoʻoūka. Battleground; place used for competitive sports or contests. *Lit.*, site for attack.

kahua kaua lewa. Air base.

kahua kinai ahi. Fire station. *Lit.*, place quench fire.

kahua leʻa, kahua leʻaleʻa. Playground.

kahu aliʻi. Royal guardian in the family of a high chief.

kahua paʻa. Terra firma, the solid earth. *Fig.*, security.

kahua pāʻani. Stadium; playground of any kind. *Lit.*, site for play.

kahu ʻekālekia (ekalesia). Pastor of a church.

kahu hānai. Foster parent (of adopted children).

kahu hipa. Shepherd; to tend sheep.

kahu hoʻoponopono. Administrator.

kāhūhū. Interjection of surprise or anger.

kahu kula. Schoolmaster, school supervisor.

kahu kula nui. School superintendent.

kahuli. To overthrow, overturn, upset. **hoʻokahuli.** To overthrow. PPN *tafuli.*

kāhuli. 1. To change. 2. Land shells (*Philonesia* spp.).

kāhulihuli. Unsteady, shaky; to sway; tossed about, as a ship. PPN *tafulifuli.*

kahuli pū. Turned completely over, upside down.

kahu maʻi. Nurse.

kahu mālama. Custodian, caretaker.

kahu mālama hale. Housekeeper. *Lit.*, guardian to care for house.

kahuna. Priest, minister, sorcerer, expert in any profession; to act as priest or expert. **hoʻokahuna.** To ordain or train as a *kahuna.* PPN *tufunga*, PEP *tafunga.*

kāhuna. Plural of *kahuna.*

kahuna ʻanāʻanā. Sorcerer who practices black magic.

kahuna aʻo. Teaching preacher, minister.

kahuna haʻiʻōlelo. Preacher, especially an itinerant preacher.

kahuna hoʻoūlu ʻai. Agricultural expert.

kahuna kālai. Carving expert; sculptor.

kahuna kālai waʻa. Canoe builder.

kahuna kilokilo. Priest or expert who observed the skies for omens.

kahuna lapaʻau. Medical doctor, medical practitioner. *Lit.*, curing expert.

kahuna pule. Preacher, pastor, priest. *Lit.*, prayer expert.

kahu pipi. Herdsman, keeper of cattle, rancher.

kahu puke (buke). Librarian.

kahu wai. One in charge of water rights and division.

kahu waiwai. Trustee, executor. *Lit.*, custodian of wealth or property.

kai. 1. Sea, sea water. *I kai,* toward the sea. *Makai,* on the seaside, toward the sea, in the direction of the sea. PPN *tahi.* 2. Gravy, dressing. 3. Interjection. My, how much! How very! *Kai ke kolohe!* Oh, how mischievous!

ka i, kai. Contraction of *ka mea i*, the one who did.

kai-. Person (in sibling terms). PEP *tai-*.

kaī, kaīī. Interjection of displeasure, annoyance, prolonged to indicate greater force.

ka'i. To lead, direct; to walk in a row; to walk deliberately, as in a procession, or as a child learning to walk. Cf. *alaka'i, huaka'i*. PPN *taki*.

kai a malō, kai a malo'o. An extreme low tide with reef exposed. *Lit.*, dry sea.

kaiāmū. To sit in silence, as at a meeting.

kai a Pele. Tidal wave. *Lit.*, sea of Pele.

kai apo. Rising or high tide. *Lit.*, encircling sea.

kai au. Sea where a moving current is visible. *Lit.*, current sea.

kaiāulu. Community, neighborhood, village.

kai ea. Rising tide; sea washing higher on land than usual. *Lit.*, rising sea.

kai 'e'e. Tidal wave. Also *kai hō'e'e*. *Lit.*, mounting sea.

kaiehu. To scatter or stir up, as dust or dirt; tossed, as spray.

kai emi. Ebbing sea. *Lit.*, decreasing sea.

kai he'e. Receding sea or wave.

ka'i hele. To walk, move, proceed; to walk holding on to something or with uncertainty, as a child learning to walk; to move, as in checkers.

kai hō'e'e. Var. of *kai 'e'e*.

kai hohonu. Deep sea; high tide.

kai ho'i. Ebbing sea. *Lit.*, returning sea.

kai holo. Running sea or current.

kai ho'olulu. Calm sea water.

ka'i huaka'i. Parade; to march in a parade.

kā'i'ī. Hard, rigid; stingy; to refuse to help.

kaikaina. Younger sibling or cousin of the same sex, as younger brother or male cousin of a male, or younger sister or female cousin of a female. PPN *tahina*.

kaikamahine. Girl, daughter, niece. PPN *tama'afafine*.

kaikamāhine. Plural of *kaikamahine*.

kaikea. White sea foam, especially as washed up on a beach.

ka'i ke'a. Station of the cross (Catholic); procession of the cross.

kai kō. Sea with a strong current.

kaiko'eke. Brother-in-law or male cousin-in-law of a male; sister-in-law or female cousin-in-law of a female. PPN *ta-'okete*.

kaikua'ana, kaiku'ana. Older sibling or cousin of the same sex; sibling or cousin of the same sex of the senior line, whether older or younger. PEP *tuakana*.

kaikuahine. Sister or female cousin of a male. PPN *tuafafine*.

kaikunāne. Brother or male cousin of a female. PPN *tunga'ane*.

kai lawai'a. Fishing grounds.

kāili. Runner on sweet potato vine; string of fish.

kā'ili. To snatch, grab, take by force; to gasp.

kai make. Low tide.

kai malo'o. Low tide, as when much of the reef is exposed. *Lit.*, dry sea.

kaimana, daimana. Diamond. *Eng.*

Kaimana-Hila. Diamond Head. *Lit.*, Diamond Hill (*Eng.*).

kai mimiki. Receding sea, especially immediately before a tidal wave. *Lit.*, shrinking sea.

kai moku. Turning of the tide. *Lit.*, cut sea.

kaina. 1. Same as *kaikaina*, most used as term of address. PPN *tahina*. 2. Kind. *Eng*.

kainō, kainoa. Why not; I thought (but it was not so). *Kainō ua hele 'oe*, I thought you had gone.

kai nui. High tide, big sea.

kaiolohia. Calm, tranquil sea. *Fig.*, peace of mind.

kaio'o. Strong sea; to be such.

kai piha. High sea, high tide, full sea.

kai pi'i. High or rising tide.

kai po'i. Breaking waves or surf.

kai pupule. Crazy, restless, wild sea.

kai ulu. Sea at full tide; mounting sea.

Kai-waena-honua. Mediterranean Sea. *Lit.*, sea middle earth.

kai wahine. Calm, gentle sea. *Lit.*, feminine sea.

kaka. To rinse.

kākā. 1. To strike, dash, beat, chop; to thrash or beat out as grain; to strike, as flint and steel. 2. To excrete; excreta (a euphemism, taught to children).

kaka'a. To roll, turn over; to revolve, as a wheel; rolling, turning, etc. **ho'okaka'a.** To cause to turn, roll, etc.; to turn somersaults or cartwheels.

kakahiaka. Morning. *Kakahiaka nui*, early morning.

kākai. Handle, as of a bucket, pot, basket; strings by which a netted (*kōkō*) calabash is hung.

kaka'i. To walk along with a group; to follow in line, as chickens after a hen; procession.

kaka'ikahi. Scarce, sparse, rare, few; seldom, rarely.

kā kākou. Our, ours (*a*-class possessive, plural, inclusive). PNP *taa taatou*.

kākā lā'au. Spear fencing; to fence.

kakale. Redup. of *kale*.

kakalina. Gasoline. *Eng*.

kākāmaka. Raw salted meat; to cut raw meat into large pieces and salt it. *Lit.*, chop raw.

Kākana, Satana. Satan. *Eng*.

kakani. Noisy; to make repeated noises; pealing, ringing. **ho'okakani.** To make noises.

kākā'ōlelo. Orator, person skilled in use of language; advisor; storyteller; to orate. *Lit.*, to fence [with] words.

kākau. 1. To write; to print on tapa; writing. *Mea kākau.* writer, author. 2. To tattoo; tattooing. PPN *tatau*.

kā kāua. Our, ours (*a*-class possessive, dual, inclusive). PNP *taa taaua*.

kākau ho'opa'a. To register.

kākau inoa. To sign a name, register; to sign, signature.

kākau kaha. To make lines, print, mark, tattoo.

kākau lima. Handwriting; written by hand.

kākau mo'olelo. Author; secretary or recorder.

kākau 'ōlelo. Secretary, clerk.

kākau 'ōlelo pōkole. Stenographer; shorthand.

kake. 1. Chants with mixed or garbled words, for and by chiefs. **ho'okake.** To speak *kake;* to speak unclearly. 2. To slip back and forth; to mix. **ho'okake, hōkake.** To disturb.

kakekimo. Catechism.

kākela. 1. To perform well. 2. Castle. *Eng*.

kākele. 1. To rub with oil; to mix or stew with sauce or gravy. 2. To slide; to go rambling at will and hence to do as one pleases.

kākī. Khaki. *Eng.*

kakiana. Sergeant. *Eng.*

kākiʻi. To strike at, aim at; to brandish threateningly, as a war club.

kākini. Dozen; stocking, stock. *Eng.*

kākiʻo. Mange, impetigo, itch, itching pustules of the skin.

Kakōlika, Katolika. Catholic. *Eng.*

kākoʻo. To uphold, support, assist, prop up; girdle. Cf. *koʻo*, support.

kākou. We (plural, inclusive). *Kō kākou*, our, ours. PPN *kitatolu*, PNP *kitaatou*, PEP *taatou*.

kākū. Barracuda (*Sphyraena barracuda*).

kākua. To bind or fasten on, as a sarong. PEP *taatua*.

kala. 1. To loosen, untie, free; to forgive, pardon, excuse; proclaim. *E kala mai iaʻu*, excuse me. **hoʻokala.** To release. PPN *tala*. 2. Screwdriver. 3. Several species of surgeonfish (genus *Naso*). 4. Rough, as sharkskin. **hoʻokala.** To sharpen, grind. 5. Gable, as of a house. 6. A tern. PPN *tala*. 7. Thorn. PPN *tala*.

kālā, dala. Dollar, silver, money. *Eng.*

kālaʻau. Stick dancing; to stick dance.

kālaʻe. Clear, calm. **hoʻokālaʻe.** To cause to clear.

kalahala. Atonement; to pardon, absolve from sin. *Lit.*, forgive sin.

kālai. To carve, cut, hew; to divide, as land. PNP *talai*, PEP *taalai*.

kālaiʻāina. Political; politics; political economy. *Lit.*, land carving. *Kuhina Kālaiʻāina*, Minister of Interior.

kalaima, karaima. Crime; criminal. *Eng. Hana kalaima*, criminal act.

kālaimoku. Counselor; prime minister; to hold such office. *Lit.*, manage island.

kālai pōhaku. Stone cutter; to carve or hew stone.

kalaīwa, kalaiwa. To drive, as a car; driver. *Eng. Kalaīwa kaʻa*, to drive a car; car driver.

kālai waʻa. Canoe carver; to build a canoe.

kālā keʻokeʻo. Silver money.

kalakoa. Calico; variegated in color, as croton leaves; printed cotton cloth (modern). *Eng.*

kā lākou. Their, theirs (*a*-class possessive, plural). PNP *taa laatou.*

kalakupua. Magic; magical, mysterious. **hoʻokalakupua.** Magician, enchanter; to do wondrous acts.

kalalī. To go quickly, briskly, without noticing anyone; to walk or talk in a brisk, haughty way; proud.

kalana. Division of land smaller than a *moku* or district; county.

kālana. 1. Stationery. 2. Same as *kānana, 1, 2.*

kālana kākau. Notebook, tablet.

kālani, galani. Gallon. *Eng.*

kālā pepa. Paper money.

kalapu. 1. Club, society; club in a deck of cards. *Eng.* 2. To strap, tie; a strap. *Eng.*

kā lāua. Their, theirs (*a*-class possessive, dual). PNP *taa laaua.*

kalaunu (karauna). Crown, corona. *Eng.* Cf. also *pua-kalaunu.*

kālawa. Curve, as in the road or along a beach. Also *hālawa.*

kālawe. To hold and carry, as a pail.

Kalawina. Calvinistic, Congregational. *Eng.*

kale. Watery, nearly liquid, as thin poi. *Waha kale*, to talk excessively. PEP *tale*.

kalekale. Same as *kakale;* to gossip. **ho'okalekale.** To make watery; to lie, deceive; soft, spongy.

kālele. Support, railing; to lean upon, as a support; to have faith in. **ho'okālele.** To cause to support; stress.

kalelē. Celery. *Eng.*

kālelei. To turn toward, listen to.

kālele leo. Stress mark; emphasis.

kālele mana'o. To stress, emphasize.

kāleo. Saying, expression.

kālepa. Trader, merchant; to trade, sell as merchandise. *Lit.*, strike flag, so called because a salesman hoisted a small flag to show that poi or another article was for sale. *Moku kālepa*, trading ship.

Kaleponi. California. *Eng.*

kālewa. To move from place to place; to float or move with the wind, as clouds; to peddle (formerly of goods carried suspended and swinging on a carrying pole); to lie off, as a ship.

kali. To wait, loiter, hesitate; slow. **ho'okali.** To cause to wait; lingering. PPN *tali.*

kālī. Spine; string, as used to thread things upon, as flowers for a lei, or candlenuts for a torch.

kalia. A native tree (*Elaeocarpus bifidus*). PNP *tali(a,e)*.

kalika. Silk. *Eng.*

kālika, galika. Garlic. *Eng.* See more common *'aka'akaipūpū*.

Kalīkamaka. Same as *Kalīkimaka.*

kāliki. Corset, girdle; tight

waist binder; suspenders; to tie as a corset.

Kalīkiano. Kristiano. Christian. *Eng.*

Kalīkimaka. Christmas. *Eng.*

kāliki waiū. Brassiere, corset cover. *Lit.*, breast corset.

kalima. Cream. *Eng.*

kalima hamo. Face cream.

kalima waiū. Cream.

kalo. Taro (*Colocasia esculenta*). PPN *talo.*

kāloa. 1. Oval wooden dish or platter. 2. (*Cap.*) Names of three nights of the month; see below.

Kāloa-kū-kahi. Twenty-fourth day of the Hawaiian month. *Lit., Kāloa* standing first.

Kāloa-kū-lua. Twenty-fifth day of the Hawaiian month. *Lit., Kāloa* standing second.

Kāloa-pau. Twenty-sixth day of the Hawaiian month. *Lit.,* last *Kāloa.*

kalokalo. Conversational prayer to the gods. PNP *talo.*

kālole. Straight, as hair.

kalo pa'a. Cooked unpounded taro.

kālua. 1. To bake in the ground oven; baked. 2. Double, two-stranded.

kālua pa'a. To bake whole, as a pig.

kaluhā. Papyrus (*Cyperus papyrus*), a large sedge.

kāluhe. To droop, bend, vibrate as a leaf in the wind; to act as the coquette.

kama. Child, person. *Kama 'ole*, childless, barren. **ho'okama.** To adopt a child or adult one loves, but for whom one might not have the exclusive care. PPN *tama.*

kāma'a. Shoe, sandal, slipper; ti-leaf or tapa sandal. Cf. *ma'a*, to bind. **ho'okāma'a.** To put on shoes, to furnish shoes.

kāma'a hakahaka. Openwork

shoes, sandals. *Lit.*, shoes with spaces.

kāma'a hao. Horseshoe. *Lit.*, iron shoe.

kāma'a 'ili. Leather shoes.

kama'āina. Native-born; host; native plant; acquainted, familiar. *Lit.*, land child. **ho-'okama'āina.** To become acquainted with.

kāma'a lō'ihi. Boot, boots, hip boots. *Lit.*, tall shoes.

kāma'a pale wawae. Slippers. *Lit.*, shoes protecting feet.

Kamāhana. The constellation Gemini. *Lit.*, the twins.

kamaha'o. Wonderful, astonishing, surprising, remarkable. **ho'okamaha'o.** To be or do something wonderful.

kama hele. Traveler.

kamahine. Girl. See *kaikamahine.*

kama'ilio. To talk, converse; conversational. *Kama'ilio 'ana,* conversation.

kama kahi. Only child, single child.

-kamakama. **ho'okamakama.** To prostitute; prostitution. *Lit.*, to cause children.

kāmakamaka. 1. Fresh, as of leaves or fresh fish; to lay green leaves on an oven. 2. Prayer asking forgiveness. **ho'okāmakamaka.** To ask forgiveness, to seek restoration of friendship.

kā mākoi. To fish with a pole.

kā mākou. Our, ours (*a*-class possessive, plural, exclusive). PNP *taa maatou.*

kamalani. Child of a chief; a petted child. **ho'okamalani.** To make a favorite of a person; to treat with indulgence; to be finicky.

kama lei. Beloved child.

kamali'i. Children (used only in the plural; sometimes used without the particle *nā*). *Lit.*, small child. **ho'okamali'i.** Childish. PPN *tamariki.*

kamali'i wāhine. Girls, a group of girls.

kamāli'i wahine. Princess (short for *kama ali'i wahine*, female, chiefly child).

kamanā. Carpenter. *Eng.*

kamanā kāpili moku. Shipwright. *Lit.*, carpenter joining ships.

kamani. 1. A large tree (*Calophyllum inophyllum*). PPN *tamanu.* 2. Smooth, polished, as *kamani* wood. **ho'okamani.** To act the hypocrite; to deal falsely.

kamani-haole. The false *kamani* or tropical almond (*Terminalia catappa*).

kāmano. Salmon. *Eng.*

kāmano kini. Canned salmon.

kāmano lomi. Salted salmon, cut and mashed with onions and tomatoes and a little water.

Kama-pua'a. Name of the pig god famous in legend.

kāmau. 1. To keep on, continue, persevere. 2. To drink, especially intoxicants; a toast, somewhat like "to your health." 3. Card game; trumps; to trump.

kā māua. Our, ours (*a*-class possessive, dual, exclusive). PNP *taa maaua.*

kamawae. Selective, difficult to please, finicky. *Lit.*, person [who] chooses.

kāmeha'i. 1. Unusual, surprising, astonishing. 2. Illegitimate child, since the identity of the father may be unknown.

kameki. Cement. *Eng.*

kāmelo. Camel. *Eng.*

Kāmoa. Samoa; Samoan (old name was *Ha'amoa*).

kāmoe. 1. To go straight ahead; to recline; flattened. 2. Recumbent weft of mat, so called because the strands lie horizontally (*moe*); overcasting stitches that lie neatly in the same direction.

kamu. Gum. *Eng.*

kana. Tens (usually compounded with numbers from three to nine to indicate 30 to 90). *Kanaīwa,* ninety.

kāna. 1. His, hers, its (*a*-class possessive). PNP *taana.* 2. Also **Sana.** (*Cap.*) Saint (used in proper names). *Kāna Lui,* Saint Louis.

kānaenae. Chanted supplicating prayer; chant of eulogy.

kanahā. Forty.

kanahiku. Seventy.

kanaīwa. Ninety.

kanaka. Human being, man, human, mankind, person, individual; subject, as of a chief; human; inhabited; Hawaiian. PPN *tangata.*

kānaka. Plural of *kanaka.* PNP *taangata.*

kanaka ʻē. Foreigner.

kanaka hana. Worker, servant.

Kanakaloka. Santa Claus. *Eng.*

kanaka makua. Adult, mature person.

kanakē. Candy. *Eng.*

kanakolu. Thirty.

kanalima. Fifty.

Kanaloa. Name of one of the great Hawaiian gods. PPN *Tangaloa.*

kānalua. Doubtful, to doubt, hesitate.

kānana. 1. Sieve, strainer; to strain; to sift, as flour. 2. Writing paper. Also *kālana.*

kānana palaoa. Flour sifter; to sift flour.

-kananeʻo. hoʻokananeʻo. To disregard, as instruction, warning, danger; careless of danger.

kanaōno. Sixty.

kānāwai. Law, code, rule, statute; legal; to obey a law. *ʻAha kau kānāwai,* legislature, law-making body. **hoʻokānāwai.** To impose a law.

kānāwai koa. Military law.

kānāwai maʻamau. Common law, customary law.

kānāwai mele. Musical notes.

kanawalu. Eighty.

kane. Tinea, a fungus skin disease. PPN *tane.*

kāne. 1. Male, husband, male sweetheart, man; brother-in-law of a woman; male, masculine; to be a husband or brother-in-law of a woman. *Pipi kāne,* bull. PPN *taʻane.* 2. (*Cap.*) Name of one of the four leading Hawaiian gods. PEP *Taane.* 3. (*Cap.*) Name of the twenty-seventh night of the lunar month.

Kaneka, Saneta. Saint; holy.

kāne make. Widowed; dead husband. *Wahine kāne make,* widow.

kāne makua. Elder brother or elder male cousin in the senior line of a woman's husband.

kāne male (mare). Married man, bridegroom, husband to whom a woman is legally married.

kāne manuahi. Common-law husband, lover.

kāne ʻole. Spinster, one without a husband.

kāne ʻōpio. Younger brother or younger cousin in the junior line of a woman's husband.

kāne wahine make. Widower. *Lit.,* man [with] dead wife.

kani. Sound of any kind; pitch in music; to sound, cry out, ring, peal, crow; to strike, of a clock; voiced. Cf. *leokani. Kani ka moa,* the rooster crows. **hoʻokani.** To play a musical instrument, to cause to sound; to ring up on the telephone. PPN *tangi.*

kaniʻāʻī. Adam's apple, larynx, trachea, neck, throat. *Lit.,* hard neck.

kanikau. Dirge, lamentation, chant of mourning; to chant, wail. *Lit.,* sound chant.

kanikē. Tolling of a bell, ding-dong; sound of clashing objects.

kanikela, kanikele. Consul. *Eng.*

kani koʻo. Aged person; aged, so old that one walks with a cane. *Lit.*, sounding cane.

Kani-lehua. Name of a mist-like rain famous at Hilo. *Lit.*, [rain that] *lehua* flowers drink.

kaniwāwae. Infantryman; infantry. *Lit.*, sound [of] feet.

kano. Large, hard stem, as on a banana bunch; tool handle; bones of the lower arm or lower leg; male erection; stiffening; hard. **hoʻokano.** To harden.

-kano. hoʻokano. Haughty, proud, conceited, disdainful of others.

kānoa. Bowl. PPN *taanoʻa*.

kanu. To plant, bury; planting, burial. *Meakanu*, crops, plants. PPN *tanu*.

kānuku. Funnel.

kao. 1. Dart, javelin; spike as on tail of a stingray; sky-rocket; to throw a spear, javelin, etc. PPN *tao*. 2. Goat.

kāohi. To hold back, restrain, try to hold back, control. PPN *taʻofi*, PNP *taaʻofi*.

kao hihiu. Wild goat.

kao keiki. Kid, young goat.

kao lele. Dart, javelin, fireworks.

kaʻolo. Jowl, sagging chin, double chin.

kā ʻolua. Your, yours (*a*-class possessive, dual). PNP *taa koulua*, PEP *taa kolua*.

kaomi. To press down, squeeze with downward pressure; to suppress, as a thought. PPN *taʻomi*.

kaomi waina. Wine press.

kaona. 1. Hidden meaning in Hawaiian poetry. 2. Town. *Eng.*

kā ʻoukou. Your, yours (*a*-class possessive, plural). PNP *taa koutou*.

kapa. 1. Tapa, as made from *wauke* or *mamaki* bark; formerly quilt or clothes of any kind, or bedclothes. PEP *tapa*. 2. To call, term, give a name to. *Kapa ʻia*, called, named. PPN *tapa*. 3. Edge, border, boundary; side, as of a road (often not preceded by *ke*). PPN *tapa*. 4. Labia. PEP *tapa*.

kapa ʻāpana. Quilt with appliquéd designs. Also called *kapa lau*. *Lit.*, piece tapa.

kāpae. To set aside, turn aside, lay aside, spare, stow away. **hoʻokāpae.** To push aside, parry.

kapakahi. One-sided, crooked, lopsided; biased; to show favoritism. *Lit.*, one side.

kapakapa. 1. Plural of *kapa, 3*; human crotch. 2. Redup. of *kapa, 2*; to invoke, summon. *Inoa kapakapa*, nickname, fictitious name, pet name, pen name.

Kāpaki, Sabati. Sabbath. *Eng.*

kapakū. Overwhelmed, destroyed.

kāpala. Printing, blot, daub; to smear, smudge.

Kapalakiko. San Francisco. *Eng.*

kapa lau. Quilt with appliquéd designs. Also called *kapa ʻāpana*.

kapalili. Palpitating, as in fear or joy; trembling; quivering, as a leaf in the wind.

kapalulu. Whirring, as of quail taking flight; roaring, as of an airplane.

kapa moe. Blanket, quilt, bedspread (general name); sleeping tapa.

kapa poho, kapa pohopoho. Patchwork quilt of varied color or design. *Lit.*, patch quilt.

kapa pulu. Padded quilt, comforter. *Lit.*, pad covering.

kāpehi. To throw at, pelt, strike.

kāpeku. To splash the feet in the water, as in scaring fish. *Fig.*, blustering, harsh.

kāpena. 1. Captain. *Eng.* **2.** Cabin. *Eng.*

kāpī. To sprinkle, as with salt; to salt; to scatter, as sand or salt.

kapikala. Capital, capitol (city, building). *Eng.*

kāpiki. Cabbage. *Eng.*

kāpiki-pua. Cauliflower. *Lit.*, flowering cabbage.

kāpili. To build, put together, put on (as glasses), fit together, mend, repair, unite; to shoe, as a horse. PEP *taapili.*

kāpili manu. To catch birds with lime.

kāpili moku. Shipbuilding, shipbuilder.

kapolena. Tarpaulin, canvas. *Eng.*

kapu. Taboo, prohibition; special privilege or exemption from ordinary taboo; sacredness; forbidden; sacred, holy, consecrated. **hoʻokapu.** to make taboo, prohibit, sanctify. PPN *tapu.*

kapuahi. Fireplace, stove, furnace; censer for sacrifice. PEP *tapuafi.*

kapuahi ea. Gas stove.

kapuahi hoʻomahana hale. House heater, furnace.

kapuahi uila. Electric stove.

kapuaʻi. Sole of the foot, footprint, track; foot measure; paw of an animal. PEP *tapuwae.*

kapuaʻihao lio. Horseshoe. *Lit.*, horse iron tread.

kapu ʻauʻau. Bathtub.

kapu holoi. Washtub.

kapukapu. Dignity, regal appearance; entitled to respect and reverence, difficult of access because of rank, dignity, and station. **hoʻokapukapu.**

To impose a taboo, especially on something not previously taboo; to praise, glorify. PNP *taputapu.*

kāpulu. Careless, slovenly, unclean, gross, untidy.

kapu moe, kapu a moe. Prostration taboo.

kapu noho. Taboo requiring everyone to sit in the presence of the chief, or when his food container, bath water, and other articles were carried by.

kapuō. Var. spelling of *kapuwō.*

kapu wai. Washtub; water tub.

kapuwaʻi. Var. spelling of *kapuaʻi.*

kapuwō. A cry proclaiming a taboo on the approach of a sacred personage or as part of a ceremony.

kau. 1. To place, put, hang, suspend; to set, rest; to enact, impose, or pass, as a law; to levy, as a tax; to ride, as on a horse or in a car; to board, mount; to rise up, appear, as the moon; to come to rest, as the setting sun; to come to pass; to hang up, as a telephone receiver. **hoʻokau.** To put on, place on, lay on, as responsibility; to happen, come to pass. *Hoʻokau hiamoe*, to fall asleep. PPN *tau.* **2.** Period of time; any season, especially summer, session of a legislature; term, semester. PPN *taʻu.* **3.** A sacred chant. PPN *tau.* **4.** Particle indicating plural, much less commonly used than *nā* and *mau* except in the compounds *kauhale, kaukolu, kauwahi.* **5.** Particle expressing superlative, preceded by *hoʻi* or *mai hoʻi. He nani mai hoʻi kau!* Oh, so beautiful!

kāu. Yours, yours (singular, *a*-class possessive). PNP *taau.*

kaʻu. My, mine (*a*-class possessive). PNP *taku.*

-ka'u. Hesitation, fear. See *ka-'uka'u, ka'unē, maka'u.*

kaua. War, battle; army; to make war. PNP *tau'a.*

kāua. We (dual, inclusive). PPN *kitaua,* PNP *kitaaua,* PEP *taaua.*

Kaua'i. Kaua'i. See *kaula'i.*

kaua kūloko. Civil war, internal war.

kaua lio. Cavalry; cavalry war. *Lit.,* horse war.

ka ua mea. See *mea,* cause.

kau anu. Winter, cold season.

kaua paio. Combat, debate.

kau'eli'eli. To dig up the past, to review the past.

kauhale. Group of houses comprising a Hawaiian home. *Lit.,* plural house.

kauhola. To open, unfold, as a tapa; to expand, as a flower in bloom.

kauhua. State of pregnancy. **ho'okauhua.** To cause pregnancy; pregnancy sickness.

kau hua. Fruit season.

kauhuhu. Ridgepole. PPN *ta-'ofufu.*

kauila, kauwila. A native tree in the buckthorn family (*Alphitonia ponderosa*).

kau'ipuka. To loiter about the door of a house as though desiring food gifts; one who does so. *Lit.,* placed [at the] door.

kauka. Doctor, physician; medical. *Eng.*

kauka ha'iha'i iwi. Chiropractor. *Lit.,* bone-breaking doctor.

kaukahi. 1. Standing alone, solitary; singleness of purpose. 2. Single canoe. Cf. *kaulua.*

kauka holoholona. Veterinarian. *Lit.,* animal doctor.

kauka ho'ohānau. Obstetrician.

kauka kaha. Surgeon. *Lit.,* cutting doctor.

kauka lapa'au. Medical doctor.

kauka lomilomi. Osteopath. *Lit.,* massage doctor.

ka'ukama. Cucumber, introduced. *Eng.*

kaukani, tausani. Thousand. *Eng.*

kauka niho. Dentist. *Lit.,* tooth doctor.

kaukau. Chant of lamentation, as addressing the dead directly; to advise, admonish, especially in a kindly or affectionate manner.

ka'uka'u. To slow down, hesitate; reluctance.

kaukauali'i. Class of chiefs of lesser rank than the high chief.

kau koho pāloka. Election season, election.

kaula. Rope, cord, string, line; arc of a circle in geometry; chain, as used by surveyors and engineers. PPN *taula.*

kāula. Prophet, seer. PPN *taula,* PEP *taaula.*

Ka'ula. Name of an islet off Ni'ihau.

kaula ahi. Wick.

kaula hao. Chain. *Lit.,* iron rope.

kaula ho'ohei. Rope for lassoing or ensnaring.

kaula hope. Line from mast to stern.

kaula huki. Drawstring, rope or cord to pull on.

kaula huki pe'a. Halyard.

kaula'i. To hang up, as to dry in the sun. PPN *tauraki.*

kaula ihu. Line from mast to bow (*ihu*).

kaula'i iwi. To talk too much of one's ancestry and to reveal the secrets of the ancestors. *Lit.,* expose bones.

kaula'i lā. To sun; to bleach in the sun; sun bath.

kaula 'ili. Leather rope, lassoing rope, lariat.

kaula kaula'i lole. Clothesline. *Lit.,* line to dry clothes.

kaula lei. Cord on which flowers are strung into a lei; streamer.

kaula lī. Lacing, as for shoes or corset.

kaula lī kāmaʻa. Shoelace.

kaula lio. Halter. *Lit.,* horse rope.

kaula moku. 1. Ship line of any kind. **2.** Broken rope, string.

kaulana. 1. Famous, celebrated, renowned; fame; to become famous. **hoʻokaulana.** To make famous. **2.** Resting place; restful, quiet. PPN *taulanga.*

kaula paʻa lima. Leash. *Lit.,* rope held hand.

kaula uaki. Watch chain.

kaula waha. Bridle, reins; to bridle. *Lit.,* mouth chain.

kāula wahine. Prophetess, priestess.

kau lei. To sell leis; to hang leis.

kaulele. 1. To take flight; soaring, on the wing. **2.** Stress; to accent in music. **3.** Extraordinary, over and above the ordinary.

kauleo. To urge, exhort, command. *Lit.,* to place the voice.

kaʻuli. To creep along with a hissing sound, as fire.

kaulike. Equality, justice; equal, impartial; to balance evenly, make alike; treat fairly and impartially; dispense justice. **hoʻokaulike.** To equalize.

kau lio. To ride horseback.

kaulua. 1. Double canoe, pair, yoke, two of a kind; to put together, to yoke or harness together; to double in quantity. Cf. *kaukahi.* PPN *taulua.* **2.** (*Cap.*) One of the many names for the star Sirius.

kaumaha. 1. Heavy; weight, heaviness; sad, depressed. **hoʻokaumaha.** To burden, load down, oppress, cause sadness

or grief. PPN *mamafa.* **2.** Offering. PPN *taumafa.*

kaumaha lua. Very heavily laden; bearing a heavy load; extremely sad.

kaumahana. Native mistletoes. Also called *hulu-moa.*

kau maʻi. Period or time of sickness.

kau mau. Regular session, as of legislature.

kāuna. Four. *ʻEkolu kāuna,* twelve.

kaunaʻoa. A native dodder (*Cuscuta sandwichiana*), parasitic on other plants. **2.** A gastropod mollusk with a wormlike shell; family Vermetidae.

kaʻunē. Slow, lagging, delaying.

kāunu. Love-making.

kauō. Var. spelling of *kauwō.*

kauoha. Order, command, decree; to order, command, commit into the hands of.

Kauoha Hou. New Testament.

Kauoha Kahiko. Old Testament.

kau ʻokoʻa. Placed apart; to separate.

kaupale. Boundary, barrier; to thrust aside, parry; to cover an earth oven, especially with rocks on its edge to keep earth out. *Lit.,* place ward off. **hoʻokaupale.** To cause a separation.

kaupalena. To limit, mark a border, set a deadline; limitation.

kau paona. Scales, weight; to weigh. *Lit.,* place pound (*Eng.*).

kaupeʻa. Crisscross, interwoven.

kaupoku. Ridgepole, highest point, roof. (Often used without *ke.*) *Fig.,* greatest.

kaʻupu. A bird, probably albatross. PEP *takupu.*

kauwā. Untouchable, outcast, pariah; a caste which lived apart and was drawn on for sacrificial victims; slave.

kauwahi. Some, a little, a few; something; some place.

kau wale. To put or place for no reason; to ride free of charge; to ride bareback.

kau wela. Summer, hot season.

kauwila. Var. spelling of *kauila*.

kauwō. 1. To drag, haul, draw along. *Pipi kauwō*, oxen. **hoʻokauwo.** To cause to be dragged. 2. Yolk or white of an egg. Cf. *kauwō keʻokeʻo, kauwō melemele.*

kauwō keʻokeʻo. White of an egg.

kauwō melemele. Yolk of egg.

kawa. Leaping place, as a precipice above a pool.

kā waʻa. Canoe bailer; to bail a canoe.

kawakawa. Bonito, little tunny (*Euthynnus yaito*). PEP *tawatawa.*

kāwele. 1. Kind of chant with clear, distinct pronunciation. 2. A hula step. 3. Towel, napkin, dishcloth; to wipe or dry with a cloth. (*Eng.*, towel.)

kāwele ʻauʻau. Bath towel.

kāwele holoi. Washcloth.

kāwele wai. To mop or wipe with wet cloth or water.

kāwelowelo. To flutter, whip, as a flag in the wind.

kawewe. To clatter, as dishes; to roar, as a sudden downpour; to snap or crackle.

kāwili. To mix ingredients; to ensnare birds, as with lime; entwined, interwoven. PPN *taawiliwili.*

kāwili lāʻau. To mix ingredients, drugs; pharmacist.

kāwili palaoa. Flour mill; to grind flour.

kāwiliwili humuhumu. Sewing machine worked by hand rather than by a foot treadle.

-kāwōwō. hoʻokāwōwō. To roar, as a wind or waterfall.

ke. 1. Var. of *ka, 2,* often translated "the." *Ke* replaces *ka* before all words beginning with *k-, a-, e-,* and *o-,* and before some words beginning with *p-* or the glottal stop. PPN (*h*)*e,* PNP *te.* 2. Contraction of *ka mea e,* the one who will, should, or is; the thing that is, will, should. 3. A particle meaning "when, if" in a statement. *Ke hele ʻoe, hele au,* if you go, I'll go. 4. A particle connecting certain forms, as *hiki* and *pono,* with following verbs. *Hiki iaʻu ke hele,* I can go. 5. See *ke . . . nei.*

kē. 1. Protest, complaint, criticism; critic, especially a hula critic; to criticize; to push, shove, struggle against, avoid, abstain from, refuse. *Kē ʻai,* to fast. **hoʻokē.** To crowd, elbow, push aside, oppress, shun. 2. To clang, as a bell or gong; to dingdong, strike, as a clock.

kea. White, clear; fair-complexioned person. PPN *tea.*

keʻa. 1. Cross, crucifix, any crossed piece; main house purlin. *Fig.,* to hinder, obstruct, intercept. **hoʻokeʻa.** To cross, block. 2. Bow, dart; to shoot with bow and arrow. Probably PPN *tika,* PEP *teka.*

keʻahakahaka. Abdomen. PPN *fatafata.*

keaka. 1. Theater; theatrical. *Eng. Hale keaka,* theater building. 2. Jack (in a deck of cards). *Eng.* 3. To chat, speak. *Eng.*

keakea. Semen. *Fig.,* child, seed.

Keʻa ʻUlaʻula. Red Cross.

keʻe. Crookedness; fault, flaw; full of faults. *Nānā keʻe,* to look at with disfavor. **hoʻokeʻe.** To make a turn, as in cutting paper or cloth; to run, as in walking; to form an angle. PPN *teke.*

keʻehana. Any footrest, footprint; ground or floor stamped on or trodden on.

ke'ehi. To stamp, step, tread; to strike against; to put foot into stirrup in mounting a horse; to "put the foot down" in ending a situation. PNP *takafi.*

ke'eke'e. 1. Redup. of *ke'e.* **ho-'oke'eke'e.** Redup. of *ho-'oke'e* (see *ke'e*); zigzag, angular. **2.** Same as *kekē,* surly, cranky.

ke'ena. Office, room; department, board, bureau.

ke'ena hana. Place to work, office, laboratory.

ke'ena kapu. Taboo room; tabernacle, sanctuary.

ke'ena koho pāloka. Voting booth.

kēhau. Dew, mist, dewdrop.

kēhau anu. Cold dew, frost.

kēia. This, this person, this thing; the latter. Also, *keia.* PEP *te(e)ia.*

keiki. Child, offspring, descendant, boy, son; calf, colt, kid; to have or obtain a child; to be or become a child. Cf. *keiki kāne.* PEP *t(a,e)iti.*

keiki ali'i. Prince, child of a chief.

keiki hele kula. Schoolchild.

keiki hipa. Lamb. *Lit.,* sheep (*Eng.*) offspring.

keiki kameha'i. Illegitimate child whose father is not definitely known. *Lit.,* wonder child.

keiki kāne. Boy, son.

keiki makua 'ole. Orphan. *Lit.,* child without parent.

keiki manuahi. Illegitimate child. *Lit.,* gratis child.

keiki po'o 'ole. Illegitimate child. *Lit.,* headless child.

kekahi. A, some, one, other, another; besides, too, also, including; moreover; someone, anyone. *Kekahi lā,* another day, some other day, a certain day. PEP *tetasi.*

kēkake. Donkey, jackass. *Eng.*

kekē. 1. Scolding, shrieking angrily; exposure of the teeth, as in derision, anger; surly, sharp-tongued. **ho'okekē, ha-'akekē.** To scold, expose the teeth, etc. **2.** Indecent exposure by a woman or girl; admonition to a female to sit properly.

keke'e. 1. Redup. of *ke'e* but more common; crooked, twisted. **ho'okeke'e.** To crook, bend, twist out of shape.

kekele, degere. Degree. *Eng.*

Kēkēmapa, Dekemaba. December. *Eng.*

kekē niho. Surly, cross, violently rude, snarling, often in the sense of making threats that may not be carried out.

kekē nuku. About the same as *kekē niho,* but with more verbalization and scolding.

keko. Monkey, ape.

kekona, sekona. Second (the time unit). *Eng.*

kela. Excelling, exceeding, projecting beyond, reaching high above; to excel. **ho'okela.** To outdo, surpass; to show off; to show preference.

ke (verb) lā. Particle denoting present tense at a distance from the speaker. Cf. *ke (verb) nei.* PEP *te (verb) laa.*

kēlā. That, that one, he, she, it, that person or thing; the former. PNP *teelaa.*

kēlā . . . kēia. That and that, all, every, everything, here and there; miscellaneous. *I kēlā me kēia lā,* daily.

kelakela. Redup. of *kela.* **ho-'okelakela.** To brag, show off; overbearing.

kela (tela) lole. Tailor, dressmaker. *Lit.,* clothes tailor (*Eng.*).

kelamoku. 1. Sailor. *Lit.,* ship sailor (*Eng.*). **2.** Denim, usually bell-bottomed sailor trousers.

kelawini. Gale. *Lit.,* wind gale (*Eng.*).

kele. 1. Watery, muddy, swampy, greasy. *Fig.,* impurity. *Wao kele,* forested uplands. **ho'okele.** Same as *ho'okelekele* (see *kelekele, 1*). 2. To sail; reached by sailing. *Awa kele,* harbor that may be reached by sailing. **ho'okele.** Steersman, helmsman; to sail or navigate, as the master of a ship; to steer; to drive as a car. PPN *tere.*

keleawe. Brass, copper, tin.

kelekalama, teregarama. Telegram. *Eng.*

kelekalapa, telegarapa. Telegraph. *Eng.*

kelekele. 1. Redup. of *kele, 1;* mud, mire, slush, fat; muddy, oily, rich, greasy. **ho'okelekele.** To make muddy; to soak material, as pandanus leaves in water to make pliable for plaiting; to fatten. 2. Redup. of *kele, 2.* **ho'okelekele.** Redup. of *ho'okele* (see *kele, 2*); to steer, navigate or sail frequently.

Kelemania. Germany; German. *Eng.*

kelepona, telepona. Telephone; to telephone. *Eng.*

kelikoli, teritori. Territory; territorial. *Eng.*

kemokalaka, demokarata. Democrat; democratic. *Eng.*

kemu. 1. To absorb, consume. 2. Game. *Eng.*

kena. 1. Quenched; satisfied, of thirst. 2. Weary, as from heavy toil; grieved and distressed.

kēnā. 1. To command, order, give orders, send on business. 2. That (near the person addressed). PNP *teenaa.*

ke (verb) **nei.** Particle denoting present tense near the speaker. Cf. *ke* (verb) *la.* PEP *te* (verb) *nei.*

keneka. Cent. *Eng.*

kenekoa. Senator. *Eng.*

kenelala, generala. General. *Eng.*

keni. Change (money), small change. *Eng. He keni no kāu?* Have you change?

kenikeni. Dime, ten cents, small change. (*Eng.,* ten.)

ke'o. 1. White, clear. **ho'oke'o.** To whiten, bleach. 2. Clitoris. PEP *teko.* 3. Proud. PEP *teko.*

ke'oke'o. 1. White, clear. *Kālā ke'oke'o,* silver money. PEP *tekoteko.* 2. White muslin (usually followed by *maoli, pia,* or *wai*). 3. Proud.

ke'oke'o maoli. Bleached muslin of good quality. *Lit.,* genuine whiteness.

ke'oke'o pia. Bleached muslin of inferior quality.

ke'oke'o wai. Bleached muslin.

keōnimana. Gentleman. *Eng.* **ho'okeōnimana.** Gentlemanly conduct; to act as a gentleman.

kepa. Notched; cut or trimmed obliquely; to turn to one side.

Kepakemapa. September. *Eng.*

Kepanī. Japanese. *Eng.*

Kepania, Sepania. Spain; Spanish. *Eng.*

kēpau. Lead, pitch, tar, resin; gum, as on ripe breadfruit.

kēpau kāpili palapala. Sealing wax. *Lit.,* gum-stick document.

kepela, sepela. 1. Spelling. *Eng. Puke a'o kepela,* spelling book. 2. Also **zebera.** Zebra. *Eng.*

keu. Remaining, excessive, additional, extra, more, too much (often accompanied by *a*). *Kanahā a keu,* forty and more. *He keu a ke kolohe!* Very, very mischievous! PPN *teu.*

kewe. 1. Convex, concave;

crescent-shaped, as the moon.
2. Boom, crane.

kī. 1. Ti, a woody plant (*Cordyline terminalis*) in the lily family. PPN *tii*. 2. To shoot or aim, as with a gun; 'to squirt water, as with a syringe; to spit, as an angry cat. PEP *tii*. 3. Bundle of 40 pandanus leaves, sorted for size and length and set aside for plaiting. 4. Key, latch; key, pitch, and clef in music; to lock, as a door; to wind or set, as a clock. *Eng.* 5. Trigger of a gun. 6. Tea. *Eng.*

kia. 1. Pillar, prop, post; mast of a ship; nail; rod used in snaring birds with gum; one who so snares birds. PEP *tia*. 2. Also **dia**. Deer. *Eng.*

-kia. Canoe. See *kialoa, kiapā*.

kia'āina. Governor; governorship. *Lit.*, prop of the land.

kī'aha. 1. Cup, pitcher, tumbler, mug. 2. (*Cap.*) The Big Dipper (modern).

kī'aha aniani. Glass (for drinking). *Lit.*, glass cup.

kī'aha inu waina. Wineglass.

kia hō'ailona. Signpost.

kia ho'omana'o. Monument, gravestone.

kia'i. Guard, watchman; to watch; to overlook, as a bluff. **ho'okia'i.** To post a watch. PEP *tiaki*.

kia'i kai. Coast guard. *Lit.*, sea guard.

kia'i kino. Bodyguard.

kia'i ola. Lifeguard.

kia'i pō. Night watchman, night watch.

kia kahi. Sloop; one-masted vessel.

kia kolu. Three-masted vessel.

kialoa. Long, light, and swift canoe used for display and racing.

kia lua. Brig, two-masted vessel, two-masted schooner.

kia manu. Bird catcher, bird catching by gumming.

ki'amo. Plug, stopper; sanitary napkin.

kianapauka. Dynamite. *Lit.*, giant powder (*Eng.*).

kiapā. Swift-sailing canoe.

kiapolō, diabolo. Devil; devilish. *Eng.*

kī'apu. Ti leaf folded into a cup and used for dipping water; the two hands rounded to form a cup for drinking water.

kiawe. Algaroba tree (*Prosopis* sp.).

ki'ei. To peer, peep, as through a door or crevice.

ki'eki'e. Height, tallness; high, lofty, exalted, majestic, superior. **ho'oki'eki'e.** To elevate, promote; overbearing in conduct; conceit. PNP *tike*.

kiele. Gardenia. PPN *tiale*.

kiha. Supernatural lizard.

kīhā. 1. Belch, burp; to belch or burp. 2. To rise and pitch, as a canoe in a heavy sea.

kīhae. To tear or strip, as leaves; to remove thorns from pandanus leaves; to shred, as ti leaves for dance skirts.

kīhāpai. Small land division, smaller than a *paukū*; cultivated patch, small farm; parish of a church; department of a business or office.

kihe. Sneeze; to sneeze. PEP *ti(f,s)e*.

kīhei. Shawl, cape; rectangular tapa cloak tied in a knot on one shoulder; bed covering; to wear a *kīhei*.

kīhei moe. Light bedspread.

kihi. Outside corner, edge, tip; apex of an angle; to turn aside. *Maka kihi,* looking out of the corners of the eyes. *Kihi alanui,* street corner. **ho'okihi.** To make a corner by overlapping, as in plaiting. PEP *ti(f,s)i*.

kihikihi. 1. Corners; angular, full of corners. 2. A small fish (*Zanclus canescens*), also called the Moorish idol. PPN *tifitifi*.

kihi po'ohiwi. Points or edges of the shoulders; shoulder; shoulder of a mountain.

kī hō'alu. Slack key.

ki'i. 1. Image, statue, picture, doll, petroglyph; plans, as for a house. PEP *tiki*. 2. To fetch, procure, send for, go after. **ho'oki'i.** To send; to have sent for. PEP *tiki*.

-ki'i. See **hāki'i, hīki'i, mūki'i, nāki'i, nīki'i,** all meaning to tie, bind. PEP *-tiki*.

ki'i akua. Idol, image.

ki'ihele. To gad about, wander; such a person.

ki'i ho'ākaaka. Illustration, picture. *Lit.,* clarifying picture.

ki'i ho'olele. Enlargement of a picture.

ki'i kālai 'ia. Carved image, graven image.

ki'i 'oni'oni. Moving picture, movie.

ki'i palapala. Printed picture, as in a newspaper.

ki'i pena. Painting. *Lit.,* painted picture (*Eng.*).

ki'i pōhaku. Stone statue; petroglyph.

kika. 1. Slippery, slimy, as with mud. 2. Also **tita.** Sister. *Eng.* 3. Also **sida.** Cider. *Eng.* 4. Also **tiga.** Tiger. *Eng.*

kīkā. 1. Guitar. *Eng.* 2. Cigar. *Eng.* 3. The cigar flower (*Cuphea ignea*).

kīkaha. To soar, glide, poise; to turn aside; to maneuver, as fighting cocks.

Kikako. Chicago. *Eng.*

kīkala. Hip, coccyx; posterior; stern, as of a canoe.

kīkānia. 1. Cockleburs (*Xanthium* spp.). 2. Zizania, tares.

kīkā Pukīkī. Mandolin. *Lit.,* Portuguese guitar (*Eng.*).

kīkē. To rap, knock; to break open, as with a hammer; to click glasses, as in drinking a toast.

-kīkē. Back and forth. See *'ōlelokīkē, walakīkē, pākīkē, kīkē'ōlelo.* **ho'okīkē.** Ready with a rude retort.

kīke'e. To bend, crook; zigzag. *Alanui kīke'e,* zigzag road.

kīke'eke'e. Redup. of *kīke'e. Alanui kīke'eke'e,* road with many turns.

kīkē'ōlelo. To argue, talk back.

kīkepa. Tapa or sarong worn by women, the upper edge passing under one arm and over the shoulder of the opposite arm.

kiki. 1. To sting, as a bee; to peck, leap at, as a hen. 2. Plug. PEP *titi.*

kikī. To flow swiftly; to spurt, as water from a hose; to do swiftly.

kīkī. Redup. of *kī, 2;* to shoot, as a gun. *Wai-kīkī* (name), spouting water. PEP *tiitii.*

kīkīao. Sudden gust of wind, squall.

kikili. Same as *hekili.*

kīkīpani. Conclusion, last, end.

kikī wai. To shoot water with a hose or water pistol, to hose.

kiko. Dot, point, speck of any kind; punctuation mark; punctuation; section of a story; dot in music indicating time added to a note, also to repeat; dotted; to dot, mark; to pick up food, as chickens; to injure fruit, as by a fruit fly; tattooed with dots on the forehead. PEP *tito.*

kiko ho'omaha. Punctuation mark, indicative of a pause, as comma, colon, semicolon, period. *Lit.,* dot for resting.

kikoi. 1. Rude, sarcastic. 2. To do in irregular, haphazard fashion, as skipping about while reading; irregular.

kiko kahi. Period mark in punctuation. *Lit.*, single dot.

kikokiko. 1. Dotted, spotted; to dot frequently; to peck repeatedly, as a feeding hen. **2.** To type.

kikokiko hua. To typewrite; typist. Cf. *mīkini kikokiko hua.*

kiko koma. Semicolon. *Lit.*, dot comma. *Eng.*

kiko moe. Hyphen. *Lit.*, supine mark.

kiko nīnau. Question mark.

kīko'o. Span; extent; to stretch, extend, as the hands, or as a bird its wings; to shoot, as from a bow; to pay out money, draw money from the bank. PEP *tiitoko.*

kiko'olā. 1. Sarcastic, rude, impertinent. **2.** Haphazard; here, there, and everywhere; entangled; of awkward shape, as a package.

kīko'o pāna'i. Bill of exchange. *Lit.*, exchange disbursement.

kīko'o panakō. Bank check.

kiko pū'iwa. Exclamation mark.

kikowaena. Center of a circle; central, telephone operator, headquarters; bull's eye.

kila. Also **sila. 1.** Seal, deed, patent; sealed; to fix a seal. *Eng.* **2.** Steel, chisel, knife blade. *Eng.*

kilakila. Majestic, tall, strong.

kili. Raindrops; fine rain; to rain gently. See *kili hau, kilihune, kili nahe.*

kili hau. Ice-cold shower; to rain thus.

kilihē. Drenched, as by sea spray.

kilihune. Fine, light rain; windblown spray.

kilika. 1. Silk. *Eng.* **2.** The black mulberry (*Morus nigra*).

kilika lau. Brocaded silk.

kilika nehe. Taffeta. *Lit.*, rustling silk.

Kilīkiano, Kiritiano. Var. of *Kalīkiano,* Christian.

kili nahe. Light, soft, gentle rain.

kili noe. Fine, misty rain, somewhat heavier mist than the *kili 'ohu.*

kili 'ohu. Fine rain and light mist.

Kilipaki, Gilibati. Gilbert Islands; Gilbertese. *Eng.*

kilo. Stargazer, reader of omens, seer, astrologer; to watch closely. PPN *tiro.*

kilohana. The outside, decorated sheet of tapa in the *ku'inakapa,* bed coverings; the four inner layers were white, contrasting with the decorated *kilohana.* Hence extended meanings: best, superior, excellent.

kilo he'e. One who fishes for octopus by looking through a glass-bottomed box; to fish thus.

kilohia. Passive/imperative of *kilo.* PPN *tirofia.*

kilo hōkū. Astrologer, astronomer; to observe and study the stars.

kiloi. To throw away.

kilo i'a. A man who observes fish movements from a high place and directs fishermen.

kilo lani. Soothsayer who predicts the future by observing the sky.

kilo makani. One who observes the winds for purposes of navigation.

kilo moana. Oceanography, oceanographer; to observe and study the open seas.

kilo nānā lima, kilokilo nānā lima. Palmistry, palmist.

kilu. A small gourd or coconut shell, usually cut lengthwise, used for storing small, choice objects, or to feed favorite children from. Used also as a quoit in the *kilu* sexual game; to play *kilu.*

kimo. 1. A game similar to

jacks. PEP *timo*. **2.** (*Cap.*) James. *Eng.*

Kina. China; Chinese. *Eng.*

kinā. Blemish, blotch, disfigurement or physical defect of any sort; disfigured, maimed, etc. **ho'okinā.** To cause defect, disaster, etc.

kinai. To quench, as fire; to put out, as a light. PNP *tinai*.

kinai ahi. Fireman, fire extinguisher; to put out fires.

kinamu. Gingham. *Eng. Pua kinamu*, flower appliquéd, as on quilt or cushion cover.

kīnana. Mother hen or bird and her brood. Perhaps PNP *tinana*.

kīna'u. Stain, blemish, defect, minor flaw.

kini. **1.** Multitude, many; forty thousand. PEP *tini*. **2.** King. *Eng.* **3.** Also **tini.** Tin, pail, can. *Eng. Kini 'ai*, pail for carrying poi or other food. *Lit.*, food [or poi] pail. **4.** Also **gini.** Gin. *Eng.*

kini akua. The thousands of spirits and gods, the multitudinous spirits.

kinikini. **1.** Redup. of *kini, 1;* numerous. **2.** Marble, game of marbles; to play marbles.

kini lau. Numerous, very many.

kini 'ōpala. Garbage or rubbish can.

kinipōpō. Ball, baseball; to play ball.

kinipōpō hīna'i. Basketball.

kinipōpō pa'i. Tennis. *Lit.*, ball to strike.

kinipōpō peku. Football. *Lit.*, kick ball.

kino. **1.** Body, person, individual, self; bodily, physical. **ho'okino.** To take shape; to develop, as a puny infant; to take form, as a spirit. PNP *tino*. **2.** Person in grammar; personal. *Kino mua, kino kahi*, first person.

kinohi. Beginning, origin, genesis.

kīnohi. Decorated, ornamented; decoration.

kīnohinohi. Redup. of *kīnohi;* printed, as calico.

kino kanaka. Human form.

kino lau. Many forms taken by a supernatural, as Pele.

Kino o ka Haku. Corpus Christi.

kino'ole. Frail and thin.

kino wailua. Spirit of the dead; dead person, corpse.

kio. **1.** To cheep. PEP *tio*. **2.** A mollusk. PPN *tio*.

ki'o. Pool, cistern; to settle, as dregs; to excrete. Cf. *ki'o lepo*. Probably PPN *tiko*.

ki'o ahi. Fiery pit, hell.

kī'o'e. Ladle, dipper, cup; scoop or spoon made of coconut shell; arm or wrist motion in paddling or dipping; to dip, ladle, scoop.

kioea, kiowea. **1.** An extinct species of the honeyeater family of birds. **2.** Bristle-thighed curlew (*Numenius tahitiensis*).

kiola. To throw away.

ki'o lepo. Swamp, mire; mud puddle.

Kio-pa'a. North Star. *Lit.*, fixed projection.

kī'ope. A bundle; to make a bundle.

ki'o wai. Pool of water, water hydrant, fountain.

kipa. To visit, call. **ho'okipa.** To entertain; hospitality. PPN *tipa*.

kīpā. Chinese gambling game chee-fah; to play this game.

kīpa'i. To shoo away, as by clapping (*pa'i*).

kipaku. To send away, drive away, expel, banish.

kīpalalē. Disorder, jumble; rapid flow, as of a swollen stream; unsystematic; to extend in a disorderly fashion.

kīpapa. Pavement, level terrace; to pave.

kipa wale. To pay a visit without being asked; to intrude.

kīpehi. To pelt, throw at.

kipi. 1. Rebellion, revolt; to resist lawful authority; to conspire against. **ho'okipi.** To foment or act in revolt. **2.** To dig. PPN *tipi*.

kipikua. Pickaxe.

kīpou. To drive down, as a stake into the ground; to lean, as a post.

kīpū. To hold back or brace, as a canoe on a wave with a paddle; to rein in, as a horse; to fold tightly about one, as a blanket.

kī pū. To shoot, fire a gun. Cf. *laikini kī pū.*

kīpuka. 1. Variation or change of form (*puka*, hole), as an opening in a forest; especially an "island," often vegetated, of older lava land completely surrounded by a more recent lava flow. **2.** Short shoulder cape; cloak, poncho.

kīpūkai. Seaside heliotrope (*Heliotropium curassavicum*).

kīpuka 'ili. Leather lasso.

kiu. 1. Spy; to spy, observe secretly. Cf. *māka'i kiu*, detective. **2.** Northwest wind. PEP *tiu*.

kiule, kiure. Jury. *Eng.*

kiwi. Horn of an animal; curved object such as a sickle; curved, bent.

kīwila. Civil, civic; civilian. *Eng. Hana kīwila*, civil service.

kīwini. Brazen, bold.

kō. 1. Sugar cane (*Saccharum officinarum*). Perhaps PPN *toro*. **2.** Dragged; long, as a vowel sound; to drag; pull, tug. **3.** To fulfill, come to pass; fulfilled. **ho'okō.** Executive; to fulfill; to carry out, as a contract. PPN *toho*. **4.** Of (o-class possessive). *Kō kākou*, our (plural, inclusive). PNP *too*. **5.** Your (of one person; singuar possessed ob-

ject; replacing both *kou* and *kāu*).

koa. 1. Brave, fearless; bravery. PPN *to'a*. **2.** Soldier; martial. *Kānāwai koa*, martial law. **3.** An endemic forest tree (*Acacia koa*), the largest and most valued of the native trees; its fine wood was used for canoes, surfboards, calabashes. PPN *toa*.

ko'a. 1. Coral, coral head. PNP *toka*. **2.** Fishing grounds. **3.** Shrine used in certain ceremonies, as to make fish multiply.

kō'ā. Arid, barren.

koa'e. The tropicbird or boatswain bird, particularly the white-tailed tropicbird (*Phaethon lepturus dorotheae*). PPN *tawake*, PEP *toake*.

koa-haole. A common roadside shrub or small tree (*Leucaena glauca*). *Lit.*, foreign *koa*.

koa hele wāwae. Infantry soldier. *Lit.*, soldier goes afoot.

kō'ai. To stir with a circular motion of the hand; to creep around, as a vine.

koai'e. A native tree (*Acacia koaia*).

koa kahiko. Veteran, old soldier.

kō a kai. Shore dweller.

ko'a kea. White coral.

koa kia'i. Military sentry, guarding soldier.

kō'ala. To broil (of meat, fowl, fish). Cf. *kunu, pūlehu.*

koali, kowali. 1. Morning-glory (*Ipomoea* spp.). **2.** Swing; to swing, twirl about. *Lele koali*, to jump rope, ride in a swing.

koana. Spacing, space, as between rows of stitching in a quilt.

ko'ana. Dregs, sediment; to settle, as dregs.

kō a uka. Upland dweller.

koe. 1. To remain; remaining, excessive; remainder; except; soon, about to; only thing remaining, not yet. *Koe aku ia,* except for this; this is not known or included; I don't know. **ho'okoe.** To save, reserve for later use. PPN *toe.* 2. To scratch, scrape; to strip pandanus leaves; garden rake.

ko'e. Worm. PPN *toke.*

koehonua. A large remainder, a balance.

ko'eke. Same as *kaiko'eke,* most used as a term of address.

ko'ele. Tapping sound. PEP *to(o)kele.*

kō'ele. Small land unit farmed by a tenant for the chief.

koena. Remainder, surplus, balance (in accounts), remains. Cf. *koe, 1.* PPN *toenga.*

kohā. Crack of a whip, report of a pistol; to resound thus.

kohana. Nude, naked; alone, by itself. *Kū kohana,* to stand naked.

kohe. 1. Mortise; crease, as in the center of the crown of a hat; corner in a pandanus mat. **ho'okohe.** To fold pandanus matting to form a corner. 2. Vagina.

kōhi. To gather, as fruit; to split, as breadfruit. PEP *to(f, s)i.*

koho. Guess, election, choice, selection; to choose, vote, elect. *Lā koho,* election day.

kohola. Reef flats, bare reef. *Kai kohola,* lagoon.

koholā. Whale. PPN *t(a,o)fora'a.*

koho mua. First choice, first guess; hypothesis.

koho pāloka. To cast a ballot, vote; voting.

koho pololei. Right choice; to vote a straight ticket.

koho wae moho. Primary election. *Lit.,* candidate-selection election.

kohu. Resemblance, appearance, likeness; suitable, in good taste, attractive, resembling, alike. **ho'okohu.**

To assume a likeness to; to presume to. PEP *to(f,s)u.*

-kohu. ho'okohu. To appoint, authorize.

kohu like. Similar. See *kohu.*

kohu 'ole. Not matching, ill-suited; poor taste.

kohu pono. Decent, upright.

koi. To urge, implore, require, claim; requirement. PEP *toi.*

ko'i. Axe, adze. PPN *toki.*

kō ia ala. His, hers.

ko'ihonua. Genealogical chant; to sing such chants.

koikoi. Redup. of *koi.*

ko'iko'i. Weight, responsibility; stress, accent; heavy, weighty, prominent, emphatic; harsh. **ho'oko'iko'i.** To stress or emphasize in speech; to burden, oppress.

ko'iko'ina. Stressing, accent.

koi pohō. To sue for damages.

kō kākou. Our, ours (*o*-class possessive, plural, inclusive). PNP *too taatou.*

kō kāua. Our, ours (*o*-class possessive, dual, inclusive). PNP *too taaua.*

koke. Quick, near; quickly, soon, immediately. Cf. *kokoke.*

kōkeāno. Silent, deserted.

kōkī. Extremity, tiptop, topmost; upper limit.

koki'o. Native hibiscus (*Hibiscus kokio*) with red flowers.

koki'o kea. Native hibiscus, *koki'o ke'oke'o.* A native hibiscus (*Hibiscus arnottianus*) with white flowers.

koki'o-'ula'ula. Native hibiscus (*Hibiscus kokio*) with red flowers.

koko. Blood; rainbow-hued. *Ho'okomo koko,* blood transfusion. PPN *toto.*

kōkō. Carrying net, usually made of sennit, as used for hanging calabashes. PEP *too-too.*

kokoke. Near, close; to draw near. Cf. *koke,* fast. **ho'oko-**

koke. To draw near, approach.

kokoko. Bloody. PPN *totototo*.

kokoleka. Chocolate. *Eng.*

kokolo. Redup. of *kolo,* to creep.

kokololio. Wind gust; to blow in gusts.

kōko'o. Partnership, partner, companion (nearly always followed by a number designating the number of associated persons, as *kōko'olua, kōko'okolu*). PPN *toka*.

kōko'okolu. Partnership of three, one of three associates.

kōko'olua. Companion, partner, union (always of two).

koko pi'i. High blood pressure. *Lit.,* mounting blood.

kōkō 'ula. Network of red color, as of a spreading rainbow.

kōkua. Help, assistant, helper; comforter; cooperation; to help, assist, support; to second a motion.

kōkua kauka. Doctor's aide, intern.

kōkua kumu. Assistant teacher, substitute teacher.

kokuli. Ear wax.

kola. Hard, rigid, sexually excited. PNP *tola*.

kō laila. Those of that place.

kō lākou. Their, theirs (*o*-class possessive, plural). PNP *too laatou*.

kolamu. Column. *Eng.*

kō lāua. Their, theirs (*o*-class possessive, dual). PNP *too laaua*.

kole. 1. Raw, as meat; inflamed; red, as a raw wound or as red earth. *Kole ka ihu,* nose inflamed with cold. Perhaps PPN *tole*. **2.** Surgeonfish (*Ctenochaetus strigosus*).

kōlea. 1. Pacific golden plover (*Pluvialis dominica fulvus*). *Fig.,* to repeat, boast. PEP *toolea*. **2.** Stepparent, as *makuahine kōlea, makua kāne kōlea*. **3.** (*Cap.*) Korea; Korean. *Eng.*

kolekole. Redup. of *kole*. *Pipi mo'a kolekole,* beef cooked rare.

kolekolea. To cry or chirp, said of the *kōlea* bird and of the *kāhuli* (land shell) in Hawaiian belief.

koli. To whittle, pare; to trim, as a lamp or the raveled edges of a dress. PPN *toli*.

kolī. Same as *pā'aila,* castor bean or castor oil plant.

kolo. 1. To creep, crawl; to move along, as a gentle breeze or shower; to walk bent over as in respect to a chief or as indicative of humility. **ho'okolo.** To cause to creep, crawl; to follow a trail, track. PPN *tolo*. **2.** To pull, tow, drag; to pull a seine. See *mokukolo*.

koloa. Hawaiian duck (*Anas wyvilliana*). PPN *toloa*.

kolo-hala. Ring-necked pheasant (*Phasianus colchicus torquatus*). *Lit.,* creep go on.

kolohe. Mischievous, naughty; unethical or unprincipled in any way; rascal, prankster, vandal; to act in this fashion (very common use). **ho'okolohe.** To do mischief, play pranks, etc.; to disturb, annoy; to do amusing things to create laughter.

koloka. Cloak, cape. *Eng.*

kolokolo. 1. Redup. of *kolo, 1;* to track down, investigate. **ho'okolokolo.** To try in court; trial. See *hale ho'okolokolo*. **2.** Any creeping vine.

kololani. To go away silently.

kolomoku. Tugboat; to tow a ship.

kolona. 1. Colon. *Eng.* **2.** Also **korona.** Crown, rosary. *Eng.* Cf. *lei kolona*.

kolonahe. Gentle, pleasant breeze. *Lit.,* gentle creeping.

kolopā. Crowbar. *Eng.*

kolu. Three. PPN *tolu*.

kolū. 1. Glue. *Eng.* **2.** Bluing,

used in washing clothes. *Eng.*
3. Screw. *Eng.*

Kolukahi Hemolele. Holy Trinity.

koma. Comma. *Eng.*

kō mākou. Our, ours (*o*-class possessive, plural, exclusive). PNP *too maatou.*

kō māua. Our, ours (*o*-class possessive, dual, exclusive). PNP *too maaua.*

kōmike, komite. Committee. *Eng.*

komikina, komisina. Commissioner; commission. *Eng.*

komo. 1. To enter, go into; to join, as a class or organization; entered, filled. **hoʻokomo.** To insert, put in, enter, deposit. PNP *tomo.* **2.** To dress, put on, wear. **hoʻokomo.** To dress another person. **3.** Ring, thimble.

komohana. West, western, so called because the sun "enters" (*komo*) the sea in the west. PEP *tomo(f, s)anga.*

komohana hema. Southwest, southwestern.

komohewa. To trespass, enter by mistake or illegally; to put on in a wrong way, as clothes wrong side out.

komo humuhumu. Thimble. *Lit.,* sewing ring.

komo lole. To dress, put on clothes.

komo wale. To enter without permission or ceremony; to trespass, intrude.

komunio. Communion. *Eng.*

kona. 1. Leeward sides of the Hawaiian Islands. PPN *tonga.* **2.** (*Cap.*) Name of a leeward wind; to blow, of this wind. **3.** His, her, hers, its (*o*-class possessive). PPN *tona.*

konā. Hard, unyielding, haughty. Cf. *mākonā.*

konakona. Strong, bulging with muscles; rough and uneven, as a surface; hard. Cf. *pūkonakona.*

kōnane. 1. Bright moonlight; to shine, as the moon; clear, bright. **2.** Ancient game resembling checkers; to play *kōnane.* **3.** Tapa-beater design.

konela. 1. Colonel. *Eng.* **2.** Tunnel (also called *konela puka*). *Eng.*

koni. To throb, tingle, beat; to flutter, as the heart; to tug, as a fish on a hook. *ʻEha koni,* throbbing ache; *fig.,* pangs of love. PNP *tongi.*

kono. 1. To invite, ask in, entice. *Palapala kono,* (written) invitation. **hoʻokono.** To invite. PEP *tono.* **2.** See *kono manu.*

konohiki. Headman of an *ahupuaʻa* land division under the chief; land or fishing rights under control of the *konohiki;* such rights are sometimes called *konohiki* rights. Perhaps PPN *tongafiti.*

kono manu. To entice a bird, as by imitating its call, and then to snare it; a bird catcher. Cf. *kono, 2.*

-konu. See *waenakonu,* center. PPN *tonu, tone.*

konuwaena. Same as *waenakonu.*

koʻo. Brace, support, prop; to uphold. Cf. *kākoʻo.* **hoʻokoʻo.** Prop with a pole. PPN *toko.*

koʻo-. Partner. See *koʻolua.* PPN *toko-.*

koʻokoʻo. Cane, staff, rod; support, means of livelihood; staff in music. **hoʻokoʻokoʻo.** To push, brace, resist, lean back and brace oneself. PPN *tokotoko.*

koʻokoʻolau. All kinds of beggar ticks (*Bidens* spp.); the leaves are used medicinally by Hawaiians, as a tonic in tea; sometimes used in preference to commercial tea.

koʻokoʻona. To reach far for; to rest one hand for support (*ko'oko'o*) and reach out with the other.

Ko'olau. Windward sides of the Hawaiian Islands. PPN *Tokelau.*

ko'olua. Var. of *kōko'olua.*

kō 'olua. Your, yours (*o*-class possessive, dual). PNP *too koulua,* PEP *too kolua.*

kō 'oukou. Your, yours (*o*-class possessive, plural). PNP *too koutou.*

kopa, sopa. Soap; to cover with soap. *Eng.*

kōpa'a. Sugar. *Lit.,* hard sugarcane.

kopalā. Shovel. *Eng.*

kope. 1. Rake, shovel; to rake, scratch. PEP *tope.* 2. Coffee, coffee beans. *Eng.* 3. Copy; to copy. *Eng.*

kope ahi. Fire shovel, rake for ashes.

kōpī. To sprinkle, as salt, sand; to salt, as fish or meat.

kopiana. Scorpion. *Eng.*

kou. 1. A tree (*Cordia subcordata*) widely distributed from East Africa to Polynesia; its soft, beautiful wood was used for cups, dishes, and calabashes. PPN *tou.* 2. (*Cap.*) Old name for Honolulu harbor and vicinity. 3. Your, yours (*o*-class possessive, singular). PNP *tou.*

-kou. Indicator of plurality in the plural pronouns and possessives only (*kākou, mākou, 'oukou, lākou*). PPN *-tolu,* PNP *-tou.*

ko'u. My, mine, of me (*o*-class possessive). PNP *toku.*

kōwā. Intervening space or time; channel, strait; separated, as by a passage or channel.

kowali. Var. spelling of *koali.*

kōwelo, koelo. To stream, flutter; to trail behind, as the train of a gown.

Kristiano. Var. spelling of *Kilīkiano.*

kū. 1. To stand, stop, halt, anchor; to rise, as dust; to hit; to park, as a car; to stay, remain; to reach, extend; upright, standing, parked. **ho-'okū.** To set up, make stand, establish, as a society; to brace a canoe with a paddle while sailing or coasting over waves in order to steer and steady the canoe; to carry on, as a family name. PPN *tu'u.* 2. Stand, pedestal. 3. In a state of; resembling, like; due to, because of (often followed by *i* or *a*). **ho'okū.** To produce a likeness. 4. To appear, show, reveal; to change into; beginning, appearance, arrival. 5. To run in schools, as fish. 6. Suitable, proper, O.K.; ready, prepared. Cf. *kūpono.* 7. (*Cap.*) Name for the third, fourth, fifth, and sixth days of the month. 8. (*Cap.*) Name of a major god. PEP *Tuu.*

kua. 1. Back; burden. PPN *tu'a.* 2. Yoke of a dress; back of a garment. 3. Poles used in quilt making. 4. Var. of *akua,* god. 5. To cut, chop, hew. PNP *tua.* 6. Tapa-beating anvil. PPN *tutua.*

kua-. Generations back, two (or sometimes today, one) more than the suffixed number; see *kuakahi, kualua, kuakolu, kuahā.* PNP *tua-.*

kū a. To turn into. *Kū a pōhaku,* to turn to stone. See *kū, 4.*

kua'āina. Country (as distinct from the city); person from the country, rustic. *Lit.,* back land. **ho'okua'āina.** To act like one from the country; countrified.

kua'ana. Term of address for older sibling or cousin of the same sex, or cousin of the same sex of the senior line of a family; also sometimes used to replace the much more common *kaikuaʻana* or *kaikuʻana*. PEP *tuakana*.

kuaehu. Silent, still, lonely.

kuahā. Six generations removed. Cf. *kua-*.

kua hao. Anvil, as used by blacksmiths.

kuahaua. Proclamation, declaration; to proclaim.

kuahine. 1. Term of address for a male's sister or female cousin, sometimes replacing the more common *kaikuahine*. PPN *tuafafine*. 2. (*Cap.*) Name of a rain in Mānoa Valley, Oʻahu. Often called *ua Tuahine*.

kuahiwi. Mountain, high hill. PPN *tuʻasiwi*.

kuahu. Altar.

kuāhua. Heap, pile; heaped, piled up; hunchback. *Lit.*, back heap (*āhua*).

kuai. To scour, scrape. PNP *tuai*.

kuaʻi. To remove internal organs of animals; to clean, as chickens. PEP *tuaki*.

kūʻai. To buy, barter. *Lit.*, to stand up food. *Kūʻai mai*, to buy. *Kūʻai aku*, to sell. *Kūʻai hele*, to go shopping.

kuaka. Quart. *Eng.*

kuakahi. 1. Once, singly; first; single. 2. Three generations removed, as great-grandparent (*kupuna kuakahi*) and great-grandchild (*moʻopuna kuakahi*). Sometimes today *kuakahi* denotes two generations removed.

kuakea. Faded, bleached; white and encrusted, as salt deposits left by evaporated sea water; to bleach white; foam. **hoʻokuakea.** To bleach or whiten.

kū ākea. To stand openly or in public; to take a public stand.

kuakini. Innumerable.

kuakolu. 1. Five generations removed; for some speakers, four generations removed. 2. Thrice, three times.

kua lāʻau. Hewer of wood; axman.

kualana. Lazy, indolent, bored.

kualapa. Ridge.

kualima. 1. Seven generations removed. Cf. *kua-*. 2. Five times; by fives.

kualono. Area near mountain tops.

kualua. 1. Four generations removed. 2. Twice, second.

kuamoʻo. Backbone, spine; road, path. Cf. *iwikuamoʻo*. PEP *tuamoko*.

kūamuamu. To revile, blaspheme, curse.

kua nalu. Surf just before it breaks; place where the surf breaks.

kuanoʻo. Thoughtful, meditative, comprehending.

kūʻaoʻao. Attendant or witness at a wedding. *Lit.*, standing [at the] side. *Kūʻaoʻao o ke kāne*, best man. *Kūʻaoʻao o ka wahine*, bridesmaid, maid of honor.

kuapā. 1. Dashing, slashing, as waves on a shore. 2. Wall of a fish pond.

kuapapa. 1. Heap, pile; to heap or pile up; heaped up. 2. Peace, quiet, tranquility.

kuapo. Belt; to put on a belt.

kuapoʻi. Weatherboard covering a canoe top fore and aft.

kuapoʻimaka. Eyelid.

kuapo ʻōpū. Belt.

kuapuʻu. Hunchback; hunchbacked; hump, as of a camel. PEP *tuapuku*.

kūʻauhau. Genealogy, pedigree; genealogist; to recite genealogy.

kuaʻula. Ribbed or grooved tapa cloth, as made with a grooved board.

kuauli. Verdant countryside. *Lit.*, green back.

kūʻaulima. Arm below the elbow.

kūʻauwāwae. Leg; shinbone.

kūʻau wili. Crank. *Lit.*, turning handle.

kuawa. Guava (*Psidium guajava*). *Eng.*

kūʻē. To oppose, resist; objection, opposite. *Lit.*, stand different. **hoʻokūʻē.** To cause opposition; to stir up resistance.

kuea. 1. Square. *Eng. Kamaki Kuea*, Thomas Square. **2.** To swear. *Eng. ʻŌlelo kuea*, oath.

kūʻēʻē. Redup. of *kūʻē*; disagreement, opposition; to quarrel, disagree. **hoʻokūʻēʻē.** To stir up opposition or disagreement.

kuehu. To shake, stir up, as dust; to toss up, as spray.

kueka. Sweater. *Eng.*

kuʻekuʻe. Elbow, wristbone, joint, knuckle. **hoʻokuʻekuʻe.** To elbow, push with the elbows. PEP *tuketuke.*

kuʻekuʻe lima. Elbow.

kuʻekuʻemaka. Eyebrow. **hoʻokuʻekuʻemaka.** To frown. PEP *tukemata.*

kuʻekuʻe pipi. Beef joint or knuckle; soupbone.

kuʻekuʻe wāwae. Ankle joint, heel.

kuʻemaka. Eyebrow. **hoʻokuʻemaka.** To frown. PEP *tukemata.*

kuene. Waiter, steward; to wait on table; to supervise. *Kuene wahine*, waitress.

kuewa. Vagabond, wanderer; wandering, homeless.

kuha. Saliva, spittle; to spit. PEP *tufa.*

kūhalahala. To find fault with, criticize.

kūhaʻo. Standing alone, independent.

kū hele. To get up and go. *Kū hele pēlā!* Get out!

kūhewa. Sudden attack, stroke, as of heart failure; sudden

wind gust; suddenly attacked by a stroke.

kuhi. 1. To point, gesture, as in speaking, directing an orchestra, or dancing the hula; gesture, pointing. PPN *tusi.* **2.** To suppose, infer.

kuhihewa. To suppose wrongly; to err in judgment; to mistake a person for someone else.

kuhikuhi. Redup. of *kuhi*, 1,2; to show, designate, teach, point out.

kuhikuhipuʻuone. Seer, soothsayer.

kuhina. Minister, premier, regent, ambassador; cabinet member. Probably PNP *tusinga.*

kuhina nui. Powerful officer in the days of the monarchy.

kuhina o nā ʻāina ʻē. Minister of foreign affairs.

kuhina waiwai. Minister of finances.

kui. 1. To string pierced objects, as flowers in a lei, or fish; to thread, as beads. PPN *tui.* **2.** Needle, pin, spike, nail, screw.

kuʻi. 1. To pound, punch; to beat out, as metals; to boom as thunder. **hoʻokuʻi.** To hit, pound. PPN *tuki.* **2.** To join, stitch, sew; joined; seam. **hoʻokuʻi.** (a) To join, connect; to spell; to dovetail; to add up, as numbers. (b) Zenith. **3.** Artificial. *Lauoho kuʻi*, wig. **4.** To disseminate news.

kuʻia. Passive/imperative of *kuʻi, 1*; to meet an obstacle, stumble; to waver or be unsettled mentally.

kui hao. Nail, iron, spike.

kuʻi hao. To pound and shape iron; to forge; blacksmith.

kui humuhumu. Needle.

kui iwi. Bone awl.

kuʻikahi. Treaty, covenant, agreement; united. *Kuʻikahi like*, agreement. **hoʻokuʻikahi.**

To unite, reconcile, make a peace treaty or armistice.

Ku'ikahi Pāna'i Like. Reciprocity Treaty.

kui kaiapa. Safety pin. *Lit.*, diaper pin.

kui kala. Screwdriver. Commonly called *kala*.

ku'i kālā (dala). Silversmith; to weld silver.

kūikawā. Temporary, for the time being, special, free and independent. *Lit.*, standing at the time.

kū'ike. 1. To know by sight; to understand or know in advance. 2. Cash. *Uku kū'ike*, cash payment.

kui kele. Large needle, as for darning or on a sewing machine. *Lit.*, steering instrument.

kuiki. Quilting; to quilt. *Eng.*

kuikui, Same as *kukui*, candlenut. Ni'ihau. PPN *tuitui.*

ku'iku'i. 1. Redup. of *ku'i, 1*; boxing; to box. PPN *tukituki.* 2. Redup. of *ku'i, 2*. 3. Redup. of *ku'i, 4*.

kui lā'au. Wooden peg.

kui lauoho. Hairpin.

kui lei. To string flowers, beads, seeds, shells into leis; a lei stringer.

kui lihilihi. Crochet hook.

kui lima, kuikui lima. To go arm in arm, to hold hands; arm in arm.

ku'i lima. Boxer, pugilist; to strike with the fist.

kuina. A stringing together, as of leis.

ku'ina. 1. Blow, punch; peal, as of thunder. PPN *tukinga.* 2. Joint, joining, seam. *Fig.*, center, key.

kui nao. Screw, large nail.

ku'inehe. Quiet and still, without rustling.

ku'ineki. Crowded, as a street.

kuini. Queen. *Eng.*

kui 'ōmou. Stickpin, common pin. *Lit.*, pin to attach.

ku'i 'opihi. To pry *'opihi* (limpets) loose, done formerly with stones.

ku'i-pa'a. Lockjaw. *Lit.*, tight molar.

kui pahu. Thumbtack. *Lit.*, pushing nail.

kuipapa. Method of making a hat lei by sewing leaves and flowers to a pandanus strip; to make such a lei. *Lit.*, string on a base.

ku'i pehi. To pummel, pound, abuse horribly. *Lit.*, pound pelt.

kui ulana. Knitting needle.

kuka. Coat. *Eng.*

kūkā. Same as *kūkākūkā*, 'Aha *kūkā*, council, conference.

kūka'a. 1. Roll, bolt of cloth; rolled pack, as of pandanus leaves ready for plaiting; to roll up, as a bundle of cloth or tapa. 2. Wholesale.

kuka'aila. Raincoat.

kūkae. Excreta. PPN *ta'e*, PEP *tuutae.*

kūkaehao. Rust; rusty. *Lit.*, iron excrement.

kūkaelio. Toadstool, mushroom. *Lit.*, horse dung.

kūkaeloli. Mildew; mildewed. *Lit.*, sea cucumber dung.

kūkae manu. Bird dung, guano.

kūkaenalo. 1. Mole on the body, believed to be deposits of flies during infancy. *Lit.*, fly dung. 2. Beeswax.

kūkae-pa'a. Constipation. *Lit.*, hard excreta.

kūkaepele. Sulphur, brimstone, match. *Lit.*, Pele's dung.

kūkae-pua'a. A small weedy, creeping grass (*Digitaria pruriens*).

kūkaeuli. Ink squirted by octopus to discolor water.

kūkaha. To stand sideways, as in making room for another to pass.

kūkahekahe. To while the time away in pleasant conversation; chatting. *Lit.,* stand flowing.

kū kahi. Standing alone, outstanding, unique, first.

kūka'i. To exchange, as greeting (*aloha*), conversation (*kama'ilio*), letters (*leka*). PNP *tu'utaki.*

kūka'i leka. To correspond back and forth; to exchange letters.

kūka'i 'ōlelo. To converse.

kūkā kama'ilio. Interview, conference. *Lit.,* confer chat.

kūkākūkā. Consultation, discussion; to consult, confer.

kūkala. To proclaim publicly, tell abroad, announce.

kūkālā, kudala. Auction; to sell at auction. *Lit.,* stand dollar (*Eng.*).

kukaua. Raincoat.

kukaweke. Raincoat. (Perhaps *Eng.,* coat and [sou']wester.)

kuke. 1. To nudge, push, jostle. **ho'okuke.** To shoe, banish. PEP *tute.* 2. Cook; to cook. *Eng.* 3. Customs duty. *Eng.* 4. Also **duke.** Duke. *Eng.*

kuke awa. Harbor duty or tax.

kuke kū. To push with elbows and shoulders, as forcing a way through a crowd.

kūkele. 1. Muddy, slippery; to slip, slide, as in mud. 2. To sail, as a boat.

kuki. See *mea'ono kuki,* cookie.

kūkini. 1. Runner, swift messenger, as employed by chiefs, with a premium on their speed. 2. Close together, in great numbers, as plants. 3. Cushion. *Eng.*

kūki'o. Small pool of water. *Lit.,* standing pool.

kuko. Lust. Probably PEP *tuto.*

kuku. 1. To beat, as tapa. PPN *tutu.* 2. Stick, as used to support a net. PEP *tutu.*

kukū. 1. Thorn, spine, burr; barbed, thorny; hurt by a

thorn. 2. Redup. of *kū, 1;* crowded.

kūkū. 1. (Usually pronounced *tūtū.*) Granny, grandma, grandpa; any relative of grandparent's generation. 2. To shake in jerks, bounce, trot, as on a horse. *Holo kūkū,* to trot. **ho'okūkū.** To cause to shake; uncomfortably full, as after overeating. 3. Gourd beat, as used for hula dancing.

-kūkū. ho'okūkū. 1. Contest, game, match; to hold a contest. **Ho'okūkū hīmeni,** song contest. 2. To fit, as a garment; a fitting.

kuku'e. Clubfoot; one with a twisted or deformed foot.

kukui. 1. Candlenut tree (*Aleurites moluccana*), the State tree. 2. Lamp, light, torch. *Fig.,* guide, leader.

kukui-haole. General name for any nut not native to Hawai'i.

kukui hele pō. Lantern. *Lit.,* light [for] going [at] night.

kuku'i 'ōlelo. Storyteller; to recite, narrate. *Lit.,* joining speech.

kukui pa'a lima. Flashlight. *Lit.,* light hold hand.

kukui uila. Electric light.

Kukui-wana'ao. Morning Star. *Lit.,* early morning light.

kukuli. Redup. of *kuli, 1;* kneecap; to kneel; to crouch or lie as an animal, with feet under the body. *Noho kukuli,* to sit on bended knees, with the feet stretched backwards, and with the front of the toes down. PEP *tuutuli.*

kūkulu. 1. Pillar, post; horizon. *Nā kūkulu 'ehā,* four cardinal points. 2. To build, as a house; to establish, set up; to put up, as a tent; to found, as a society; to establish, as a name or dynasty. **3.** To tie, tether; to park.

kukuluāe'o. 1. Stilts; to walk on stilts. **2.** Hawaiian stilt (the bird; *Himantopus himantopus*). Perhaps PNP *kuli.*

kukuna. Ray, as of the sun; radius of a circle; spoke of a wheel. *Kukuna X,* x-ray.

kukuna-o-ka-lā. Mangrove (*Bruguiera* spp.); calyx of a mangrove flower, as used in leis. *Lit.,* ray of the sun.

kula. 1. Plain, field, open country, pasture. **2.** Source; container. See *kula kakalina, kula wai, kula waiwai.* **3.** School; to teach school, go to school; to hold school or class sessions. *Eng.* **4.** Also **gula.** Gold; golden. *Eng.*

kula aupuni. Public school, government school.

kula hānai. Boarding school. *Lit.,* feeding school. Also called *kula noho pa'a.*

kula'i. To push over, knock down, overthrow. PPN *tul(a, e)ki.*

kulaīwi. Native land, native. *Ku'u home kulaīwi,* my own homeland.

kula kahuna pule. Theological seminary. *Lit.,* minister school.

kula kakalina. Gasoline drum.

kula kamali'i. Primary school, kindergarten. *Lit.,* children's school.

kula Kāpaki (Sabati). Sunday school.

kula ki'eki'e. High school.

kula koa. Military academy.

kula kumu. Teachers' training school, normal school.

kula manu. Gathering place of birds.

kulana. To tilt, rock, reel, sway.

kūlana. Station, rank, position, place, situation; outstanding, prominent. PNP *tuulanga.*

kūlanakauhale. Village, town,

city. *Lit.,* place [of] households.

kūlana nalu. Place where the waves swell up and the surfrider starts paddling and racing the wave, usually at the most distant line of breakers. Also called *kūlana he'enalu.*

kūlana pa'a. Standard, as weight or money.

kūlana pule. Prayer meeting or other religious service.

kulanui. University, college; formerly high school. *Lit.,* big school.

kulapepeiao. 1. Earring. *Lit.,* gold [for] ears. **2.** Fuchsia (*Fuchsia magellanica*).

kula pō. Night school.

kula uku. Private school. *Lit.,* paying school.

kula wai. Watering trough, water source.

kula waiwai. Source of income or livelihood.

kuleana. Right, title, property, responsibility, jurisdiction, authority, claim, ownership; reason, cause, justification; small piece of property; tenure. **ho'okuleana.** To entitle, give right to possess. See *palapala ho'okuleana.*

kūlepe. 1. Split open from head to tail, as fish prepared for drying and salting; to split thus. **2.** To flap, flutter; strong, of wind. **3.** Same as *'ūlepe.*

kūlewa. Moving slowly through space, as clouds.

kuli. 1. Knee. PPN *turi.* **2.** Deafness, deaf person; deaf; noisy. **ho'okuli.** Deaf; to feign deafness. PPN *tuli.*

kūlia. 1. Passive/imperative of *kū, 1;* to stand. **2.** To try, strive.

kūlike. Alike, identical; standing in similar fashion or in even rows. **ho'okūlike.** To conform, make alike.

kulikuli. Noise, din; noisy, deafening. Be quiet! Keep still! Shut up! PEP *tulituli.*

kūlina, kurina. Corn, maize (*Zea mays*). *Eng.*

kūlina-'ono. Sweet corn. *Lit.,* delicious corn.

kūlina-pohāpohā. Popcorn.

kulipe'e. To creep along, as a sick person; to walk as though weak-kneed.

kūlipo. Dark, deep, as a cave. *Fig.,* extremely, intense.

kūli'u. Deep, as a voice; penetrating, profound, as thoughts.

kūloko. Local, domestic. *Lit.,* state of being inside. *Kaua kūloko,* civil war.

kūloku. Falling, flowing, as rain or stream; flattened, as plants by rain.

kūlolo. Pudding made of baked or steamed grated taro and coconut cream.

kūlono. Sheer, precipitous.

kūlou. To bow the head, bend. Also *kūnou.* **ho'okūlou.** To bow down, humiliate; to subdue, as an enemy. PPN *tulou.*

kūlou po'o. To bow the head; to dive headfirst.

kulu. 1. To drip, leak, trickle; to flow, as tears; a drop; general name for distilled liquor. PPN *tulu.* 2. Timber used in houses, as sticks, posts.

kuluaumoe. Late at night.

kulukulu. Redup. of *kulu, 1;* to drip, leak, drop.

kuluma. Accustomed to; acquainted with; customary.

kūmā-. Prefix to numbers, as *'umi kūmākahi, 'umi kūmālua,* etc.

kūmaka. Seen by the eye, visible; to see for oneself.

kūmakahiki. Annual, yearly.

kūmakani. Windbreak; wind resisting.

kūmākena. To lament, bewail, mourn loudly for the dead.

kumamā-. Same as *kūmā-* (rarely used in conversation, Biblical).

kūmau. Customary, usual, regular. *Uku kūmau,* usual fees, taxes, dues.

kūmimi. Xanthid crab (*Lophozozymus intonsus*).

kūmoe. Bedstead. *Lit.,* standing bed.

kūmoena. 1. Longitudinal mat commencement. 2. Pile of mats; spread out as a mat.

kumu. 1. Bottom, base, foundation, basis, main stalk of a tree; basic, hereditary. PPN *tumu.* 2. Teacher, manual, primer. 3. Beginning, source, origin. **ho'okumu.** To make a beginning, establish, start. 4. Reason, cause. 5. An article bought, sold, or exchanged; price. Cf. *kumu kū'ai.*

kūmū. 1. Goatfish (*Parupeneus porphyreus*). 2. Good-looking, handsome, especially of a sweetheart. *Modern slang.*

kumu a'o. Teaching; teacher.

kumuhana. Topic, subject (as topic of discourse or as grammatical subject). *Lit.,* work source.

kumu hele. Crotch. *Lit.,* source of going.

kumu hipa. Flock of sheep.

kumu honua. Beginning of the world, origin of the earth.

kumu ho'olaha. Means of propagation, source of progeny.

kumuipukukui. Lamp, not including the chimney; candlestick. *Lit.,* base light bowl.

kumu kahi. Origin, beginning.

kumukānāwai. Constitution, law code. *Lit.,* source of laws.

kumu kū'ai. Price. *Kumu kū-'ai nui,* high-priced, expensive.

kumu kula. Schoolteacher.

kumulā'au. Tree.

kumulani. Base of the sky; horizon.

kumulipo. Origin, source of life; name of the Hawaiian creation chant.

kumumana'o. Topic, subject; text, as of a sermon.

kumu niu. Trunk of the coconut tree.

kumupa'a. 1. Principal, capital (contrasting with interest). **2.** Firm foundation, ancient times; firmly established.

kumu 'ūhā. Groin, joining of leg and torso. *Lit.*, source of thigh.

kumu wai. Source of a stream, spring.

kumu waiwai. Source of wealth; resources; capital.

kuna. 1. A freshwater eel. PPN *tuna*. **2.** Schooner. *Eng.*

kūna'e. To stand firmly against opposition; unyielding.

kūnāhihi. Weak, as from shock; dismayed, horrified.

kūnānā. 1. Puzzled, stumped, at wit's end. *Lit.*, stand look. **2.** Goat.

kunāne. Brother or male cousin of a female, usually used only as term of address or as an affectionate variation of *kaikunāne*. PPN *tunga-'ane*.

kūneki. Filled to overflowing; to flow away.

kuni. 1. To burn, blaze, kindle, scorch, brand; to etch, in leather. *Hao kuni*, branding iron. PPN *tungi*. **2.** Postmark, seal; to stamp. **3.** Type of black magic that results in the death of a sorcerer.

kuni ahi. Fire kindler; to kindle or light a fire.

kūnihi. Steep.

kūnou. Var. of *kūlou*.

kunu. 1. To broil on coals, as of meat, fish. PPN *tunu*. **2.** To cough. PEP *tungu*.

kunukunu. To grumble, complain.

kū'oko'a. Independence, liberty, freedom; independent. **ho-'okū'oko'a.** To establish independence.

kuolo. 1. To rub, scrub, polish. **2.** To tremble, as the voice; to shake, as with palsy; to vibrate, resonate, as a chanting voice. *Kai kuolo*, sea with an undertow. PEP *tuolo*.

kū'olo. Sagging, baggy, as of clothes; old, as of a person with sagging cheeks. PEP *tuukolo*.

kū'ono. 1. Nook, cranny, gulf, bay; inside corner. **ho'okū'ono.** To indent, form a bay. **2.** Deep, as a cave; profound.

kū'ono'ono. 1. Well-off, comfortably situated, wealthy. **ho'okū'ono'ono.** To prosper. **2.** Redup. of *kū'ono*, 2.

kupa. Citizen, native; well-acquainted. **ho'okupa.** To naturalize, make a citizen.

kūpa'a. Steadfast, firm, immovable; loyal, faithful; constant; loyalty, firmness. **ho-'okūpa'a.** To remain loyal, to strengthen, establish.

kupaianaha. Surprising, strange, wonderful, extraordinary, marvellous. Also *kupanaha*.

kūpale. Defense; to defend, ward off.

kupanaha. Same as *kupaianaha*.

kūpaoa. 1. Strong permeating fragrance, as of jasmine. **ho'okūpaoa.** To emit fragrance; fragrant. **2.** Night cestrum (*Cestrum nocturnum*) and the endemic Hawaiian *Railliardia*, both having very fragrant flowers.

kūpāpā. 1. To grope, feel, as when looking for flaws in a wooden bowl. **2.** Hand-to-hand fight, struggle; to fight thus.

kūpapakū. Bedrock; to stand

on bedrock; depths of the earth.

kupapa'u. Corpse, dead body. PEP *tupapaku.*

kūpau. Entirely finished.

kūpe'e. Bracelet, anklet; fetters, manacles, handcuffs; to put on or tie on bracelets, anklets, fetters.

kūpe'e niho 'īlio. Dog-tooth anklets.

kūpe'e pipi. To bind feet of cattle, especially with the lasso.

kūpehi. To pelt, throw at. Cf. *pehi,* to throw.

kūpele. To knead, as bread dough or very hard fresh poi.

kūpihipihi. Tiny, small, insignificant; to become insignificant.

kūpiki'ō. Agitated, raging, as wind or storm. *Fig.,* mentally disturbed.

kūpola. To roll, wrap up, as a package; to wither and curl up, as a banana leaf.

kūpono. Upright, perpendicular, honest, proper, right, just, fair; worth, merit. **ho'okūpono.** To behave uprightly, honestly; to conform to.

kūpono 'ole. Unsuitable, improper.

kūpou. To go down, walk downhill fast, stagger; to bend far forward, as one reeling drunk.

kūpouli. Befuddled, mentally clouded, stricken.

kūpoupou. Redup. of *kūpou.*

kupu. Sprout, growth; offspring; upstart, as one rising suddenly and conspicuously to high position; to sprout, increase. **ho'okupu.** To cause growth, sprouting; to sprout. PPN *tupu.*

-kupu. ho'okupu. Tribute, tax, ceremonial gift-giving to a chief as a sign of honor and respect; to pay such tribute; church offering.

kupua. Demigod, especially a supernatural being possessing several forms. PPN *tupu'a.*

kupu'eu. 1. Rascal, scamp. **2.** Hero, wondrous one.

kūpuku. Clustered, thick, rank.

kupukupu. 1. Redup. of *kupu.* **2.** General name for ferns on a single stem, such as *3.* **3.** Sword fern (*Nephrolepis exaltata*).

kupukupu-'ala. Rose geranium (*Pelargonium graveolens*). Also called *kupukupu-haole.*

kupulau. Spring season. *Lit.,* leaf sprouting.

kūpule. Days set aside for prayer; to set aside time for prayer.

kupuna. Grandparent, ancestor, relative of the grandparent's generation, grandaunt, granduncle. **ho'okupuna.** To take an unrelated person as a grandparent or grandaunt or granduncle because of affection; to act as a grandparent. PNP *tupunga,* PEP *tupuna.*

kūpuna. Plural of *kupuna.* PEP *tuupuna.*

kupuna kāne. Grandfather, granduncle, male ancestor.

kupuna wahine. Grandmother, grandaunt, female ancestor.

kūpuni. To stand around, surround.

kupupu'u. Redup. of *kūpu'u.*

kūpu'u. To take potluck.

ku'u. 1. To release; to free, give up; to pay out, as a line or cable; to lower, as a net; to settle, as earth. *Fig.,* at peace. **ho'oku'u.** To release, let go, send away; to expel, as from school; to discharge, as from work; to free, liberate. PPN *tuku.* **2.** My, mine (this form may replace either *ka'u* .or *ko'u*).

kū'ula. Any stone god used to

attract fish; open altar near the sea for worship of fish gods. *Lit.*, red *Kū*.

kū'ululū. To shiver and be numb with cold.

ku'upau. To do with all one's might or strength, to go the limit; to release all checks, restraints.

kū uwaki. To stand a watch; watchman, sentinel, guard.

ku'uwelu. To hang loose; to float in the wind; to fall, as ripened fruit; fringed; tassel.

kūwaho. Outside, outer, foreign.

kuwala, kuala. 1. Somersault; to fall backwards; to turn somersaults. **2.** Interest, usury.

kūwili. To move restlessly, embrace; to spin in a dance. *Lit.*, interwoven state.

kūwiliwili. Redup. of *kūwili*.

kūwō, kūō. To cry loudly, as with joy or pain; to howl, as a dog; to roar, as a lion.

L

lā. 1. Sun, sun heat; sunny. **ho-'olā.** To sun, put out in the sunlight. PPN *la'aa*, PEP *laa*. **2.** Day. *Kēia lā*, today. PEP *laa*. **3.** Fin. *Kua lā*, dorsal fin. **4.** Sail. PPN *laa*. **5.** There, then, that (after directionals and major words). *Ua kanaka lā*, that afore-mentioned person. PNP *laa*. **6.** Particle expressing doubt. *Pehea lā!* How, I don't know! PNP *la'a*. **7.** The letter "l."

lā-. 1. Short for *lau, 1*, with *k-* of the following word omitted: *lā'alo* for *lau kalo*, taro leaf. **2.** Third person, in the dual and plural pronouns only, *lāua* and *lākou*. PNP *kilaa-*, PEP *laa-*.

la'a. 1. Sacred, holy, consecrated, dedicated. **ho'ola'a.** To consecrate, dedicate, hallow. PEP *laka*. **2.** Time, season. Cf. *la'a make*. **3.** Also, together with, besides. *E la'a me kēia*, besides, this, like this.

lā 'aha'aina. Feast day.

la'a kea. Sacred light, sacred things of day, as sunshine, knowledge, happiness. *Lit.*, light sacredness.

la'alā'au. Small sticks, twigs,

shrubs, bush. *Pā la'alā'au*, hedge.

la'a make. Season when plants die or grow slowly. *Lit.*, dead season.

lā'au. 1. Tree, plant, wood, timber, forest, stick, club; blow of a club; wooden, woody. PPN *ra'akau*. **2.** Medicine; medical.

la'a ua. Rainy season.

lā'au-'aila. Castor-oil plant. *Lit.*, oil plant.

lā'au 'ala. Fragrant wood, especially sandalwood.

lā'au ana. Yardstick, ruler, surveying rod, measuring stick.

lā'au-ho'ohiamoe. Drug, narcotic, anesthetic, medicine to cause sleep, chloroform.

lā'au ho'oka'a. Rolling pin, any wooden roller.

lā'au kāhea. A type of faith healing of broken or crushed bones or sprains. *Lit.*, calling medicine.

lā'au Kalīkimaka. Christmas tree.

lā'au ke'a. Wooden cross or crucifix; bar to hold a gate shut, brace.

lā'au kia. Stick for snaring birds.

lā'au ku'i. Ladder, tree with

crosspieces used as a ladder.
Lit., joined wood.

la'a 'ula. Autumn. *Lit.*, red
time [of leaves].

lā'au lalo. Boom of a vessel.
Lit., down stick.

lā'au lapa'au. Medicine. *Lit.*,
curing medicine.

la'a ulu. Spring, time of growth.

lā'au māka'i. Policeman's club.

lā'au make. Poison.

lā'au 'ōhikihiki niho. Toothpick. *Lit.*, stick to pick teeth.

lā'au pa'i kinipōpō. Ball bat,
tennis racket, ping-pong paddle; any kind of paddle for
hitting a ball. *Lit.*, stick for
beating ball.

lā'au pālau. War club.

-la'a wa'a. ho'ola'a wa'a. Blessing of a canoe launching; to
dedicate a canoe.

lae. 1. Cape, point, promontory.
PEP *lae*. 2. Forehead, brow.
PPN *la'e*. 3. Wisdom; mental
or emotional qualities. Cf.
lae o'o, *lae pa'a*, *lae 'ula*.

la'e. Same as *la'ela'e*. **ho'ola'e.**
To clear up, brighten.

la'ela'e. Bright, shiny, clear,
serene, calm, pleasant. **ho-
'ola'ela'e.** Redup. of *ho'ola'e*.

lae la lae. Syllables repeated in
songs at ends of verses to
mark time and for gay effect.

laenihi. Various high-headed
labroid fishes of the genera
Hemipteronotus and *Iniistius*.

lae o'o. An expert. *Lit.*, mature
brow. Cf. *lae 'ula*.

lae pa'a. Hard-headed, obstinate, closed in mind and hostile to new ideas. *Lit.*, hard
brow.

lae 'ula. A well-trained, clever
person; expert. *Lit.*, red brow
[red being the sacred color].
Cf. *lae o'o*.

laha. Extended, spread out,
broad, published, circulated,
distributed, broadcast; increased, numerous. **ho'olaha.**
To spread abroad, publish,

broadcast, advertise. PPN
lafa.

lahalaha. Redup. of *laha*.

lā hana. Workday.

lā hānau. Birthday. *Hau'oli lā
hānau*, happy birthday.

laha 'ole. Rare, choice, unique.

lahi. Thin, frail; delicate. PEP
la(f,s)i.

lā hiki. Eastern sun, rising sun;
eastern. *Mai ka lā hiki a ka
lā kau*, from sunrise to sunset
[a whole day or whole life
span].

lahilahi. Redup. of *lahi*. *Kou
pāpālina lahilahi* (song), your
dainty cheeks.

laho. 1. Scrotum. PPN *laso*. 2.
Male, as *pipi laho*, bull.

Lā Ho'ālohaloha. Thanksgiving
Day. *Lit.*, day for expression
of affection.

lā ho'āno. Holy day, day of
worship.

laholio. Rubber, automobile
tire. *Lit.*, horse scrotum.

Lā Ho'omaika'i. Thanksgiving
Day. *Lit.*, day to bless.

lā ho'omana'o. Day of com-
memoration, anniversary day.

lāhui. Nation, race, tribe, people, nationality; species, as of
animal or fish; national, ra-
cial. **ho'olāhui.** To form a
nation, race, etc.

lāhui hui pū. United nation. *Nā
lāhui hui pū 'ia*, united nations.

lāhui kanaka. Nation, people,
tribe, multitude.

lai. A fish of the genus *Scom-
beroides*. PPN *lai*.

la'i. Calm, stillness, quiet, as of
sea, sky, wind; peace, con-
tentment; quiet, silent, peaceful. *Pō la'i, 'ihi'ihi e*, silent
night, holy. **ho'ola'i.** To
cause to be still; to quiet, as
a mob; calm, peaceful, quiet.

-la'i. A transitivizer occurring
in *kaula'i, kula'i*. PPN *-raki*.

lā'ī. Ti leaf (contraction of *lau
kī*).

lā'ie. Short for *lau 'ie*, *'ie* vine leaf.

laiki, raisi. Rice. *Eng.*

laikī. Litchi. *Eng.*

lā'iki. Tight, as a dress; painfully stuffed, as the stomach after overeating; narrow, as a gate opening (contraction of *lā'ā*, wide, and *iki*, small). *Lima lā'iki*, long, narrow sleeve.

laikini. License. *Eng.*

laikini ka'a. Auto or vehicle license.

laikini kī pū. Firearms license.

laila. There. (Follows particles with varying meanings: *A laila*, then. *I laila*, there, at that place. *Kō laila*, of that place, local. *Malaila*, there. *Mai laila*, from there, thence. *No laila*, therefore, for that reason, hence; belonging to that place. *O laila*, of that place.) PEP *leila*.

laina. 1. Line. *Eng.* 2. Cane trash (*Eng.*, rind), bagasse.

laina mokuahi. Steamship line.

laipela, raifela. Rifle. *Eng.*

laipila. Libel; to libel. *Eng.*

laka. 1. Tame, domesticated, gentle; attracted to, fond of; to tame, domesticate. **ho'olaka.** To tame; to treat with kindness. PPN *lata*. 2. (*Cap.*) Goddess of the hula. 3. (*Cap.*) A god of canoe makers. 4. (*Cap.*) Name of a legendary hero. Probably PNP *Lata*. 5. Lock; to lock. *Eng.*

lākana. 1. Lantana (*Lantana camara*). *Eng.* 2. (*Cap.*) Also **Ladana.** London. *Eng.*

Lā Kāpaki. Sabbath Day.

lā kau. Setting sun. See *lā hiki*.

Lā Kau Pua. Decoration Day. *Lit.*, day [to] place flowers.

laki. Luck; lucky. *Eng.* **ho'olaki.** To bring luck; lucky.

lākī. Ti leaf (short for *lau kī*).

lākike, latike. Lattice. *Eng.*

lakikū, latitu. Latitude. *Eng.*

Lākina, Latina. Latin. *Eng.*

lako. Supply, provisions; wealth; well-supplied, well-furnished, well-equipped; rich, prosperous. **ho'olako.** To supply, provide, furnish, enrich.

lākō. Sugarcane leaf (same as *lā'ō*, contraction of *lau kō*).

lako hale. Furniture and fixtures for a house. Same as *pono hale*.

lako kākau. Stationery supplies.

lako ke'ena. Office supplies.

lako kula. 1. School supplies. 2. Also **lako gula.** Jewelry, especially gold.

lākou. They, them (more than two). *Kā lākou*, their (*a*-class). *Kō lākou*, their (*o*-class). PNP *laatou*.

lala. 1. Diagonal, slanting, oblique; diagonal surfing or surf. **ho'olala.** To turn aside. PEP *lala*. 2. To warm, as over a fire; to bask in the sun; to cook over a fire. **ho-'olala.** To heat, as by holding over a fire; to warm. PPN *rara*.

lālā. 1. Branch, limb, bough; timber, as of outrigger boom or float; to branch out, form branches. **ho'olālā.** To cause to branch out, as by topping a tree; to branch out. Possibly PPN *ra'ara'a*; PNP *la-'ala'a*. 2. Member, as of a society. 3. Slip, as of a plant.

lālā kanu. A cutting (to plant).

lalana. 1. Spider. Also called *lanalana, nananana*. 2. Warming, as at a fire. Cf. *lala*, warm.

lālani. Row, rank, line; verse of poetry.

lalau. Mistake, blunder, going astray; to wander, err. **ho-'olalau.** To cause to wander, to lead astray; to dillydally, kill time.

lālau. To seize, take hold of, reach out for.

lalau hewa. To wander in error; to sin.

lale. To hasten, hurry, push on; to encourage, urge on. ho-'olale. To hasten, hurry; to urge.

lali. Greasy, as pork fat; slippery and shiny, glittering; sticky. ho'olali. To cause greasiness, glitter. Probably PEP lali.

lalo. 1. Down, downward, under, beneath; depths (frequently preceded by i or ma, sometimes joined as one word). I lalo, malalo, below, underneath. PPN lalo. 2. Leeward, southern.

lama. 1. Native Hawaiian trees of the genus Diospyros (ebony family). PNP lama. 2. Torch, light, lamp. Lama wood was used in building temples, and a piece of it was placed on altars of the goddess Laka because its name suggested enlightenment. PPN rama. 3. Also rama. Rum; any intoxicating drink. Eng.

lamalama. Torch fishing; to go torch fishing.

lama pa'ipa'i 'ia. Mixed alcoholic drink, cocktail, highball.

lana. 1. Floating, buoyant; to lie at anchor, as a fishing canoe; calm, still, as water. ho-'olana. To cause to float, to right a canoe. PNP langa. 2. Also rana. Frog.

-lana. ho'olana. Cheerful, hopeful; to cheer up.

-lana. Nominalyzing suffix corresponding to 'ana. PPN -langa.

lana hele. To drift, as a ship.

lānahu. Charcoal, coal. See nā-nahu.

lānai. Porch, veranda; temporary open-sided roofed structure near a house.

Lāna'i. Lāna'i Island.

lanakila. Victory; to triumph, win. PEP langatila.

lanalana. 1. Redup. of lana, 1.

ho'olanalana. Redup. of ho-'olana. 2. Lashings, as of ornamental sennit binding the float (ama) to outrigger booms ('iako). 3. Spider. Also lalana, nananana.

lani. 1. Sky, heaven; heavenly, spiritual. PPN langi. 2. Very high chief, majesty, high born, aristocratic.

lani pa'a. Firmament. Lit., solid heaven.

lanipō. Dense, dark, as of plants, rain; said of luxuriant growth.

lānui. Holiday, important or big day.

Lānui ō nā Limahana. Labor Day. Lit., holiday of the laborers.

lā'ō. 1. Same as lau kō, sugarcane leaf. 2. Ornated wrasse (Halichores ornatissimus).

lapa. 1. Ridge, steep side of a ravine; ridged. ho'olapa. to form a ridge; ridge. 2. Overactive, energetic, mischievous. ho'olapa. To rise up; to boil; to swell, as a blister; to excite, animate. PPN lapa. 3. Clot, as of blood.

lapa'au. Medical practice; to treat with medicine, heal, cure; medical, medicinal. Kauka lapa'au, medical doctor.

lāpaki. Rabbit. Eng.

lapalapa. 1. Redup. of lapa, 1; steep-ridged; many-ridged. 2. Redup. of lapa, 2; to bubble, boil; to cavort. 3. Clotted.

lapa uila. Lightning flash; to flash, as lightning.

lapawāwae. Shin. Lit., leg ridge.

lapu. Ghost, apparition; haunted; to haunt. ho'olapu. To pretend to be a ghost, as children on Hallowe'en.

Lāpule. Sunday. Lit., prayer day.

lapuwale. Vanity, worthlessness; of no value.

lau. 1. Leaf; to leaf out. Lau is

sometimes contracted to *lā*-, as *lā'ī*, *lā'ie*. **ho'olau**. To grow leaves. PPN *lau*. **2.** Dragnet, seine. **ho'olau**. To use a *lau*. PPN *rau*. **3.** To be much, many; very many, numerous; four hundred. **ho-'olau**. To make numerous; to assemble, as of numerous persons or animals. PPN *lau*. **4.** Tip, as of the tongue.

lāua. They, them (dual). PPN *kilaua*, PNP *kilaaua*, PEP *laaua*.

laua'e, lauwa'e. 1. A fern (*Microsorium scolopendria*); some varieties have a *maile*-like fragrance. **2.** Beloved, sweet, of a lover. **ho'olaua'e**. To cherish, as a beloved memory.

lauahi. To destroy, as by fire or lava flow.

lau 'ai. Salad. *Lit.,* edible leaves.

lau alelo. Tongue tip.

lau hala. Pandanus leaf, especially as used in plaiting.

lauhulu. Dry banana leaf.

lau'ī. Ti leaf. Also *lā'ī*, *lau kī*.

lau'īpala. Surgeonfish (*Zebrasoma flavescens*).

lau-kahi. Broad-leafed plantain (*Plantago major*), a cosmopolitan weed. *Lit.,* single leaf.

lau kanaka. Densely populated, having many people; many people. **ho'olau kanaka**. To have many people about one; to dispel loneliness with people.

lau kī. 1. Ti leaf. **2.** Tea leaf.

laukō. Dragnet.

laulā. Broad, wide; liberal; widely known; publicly. *Hele laulā*, to act with freedom or liberty.

laulau. Wrapping, wrapped package; individual servings of pork or beef, salted fish, and taro tops, wrapped in ti leaves or banana leaves, and baked in the ground oven, steamed or broiled; any cloth, net, or leaves used as a wrapper or carrier; to wrap or carry in such bundles. PPN *laulau*.

laule'a. Peace, happiness, friendship; happy, peaceful. **ho-'olaule'a**. Celebration, gathering for a celebration, large party; satisfaction; to hold a celebration; to preserve friendship and good will.

lau li'i. Small-leafed; qualifying term for some plants, as *maile*.

laulima. Cooperation; group of people working together; community food patch; to work together. **ho'olaulima**. To cause to cooperate.

lauloa. Long wave or surf, as extending the entire length of the beach.

lau loa. 1. A long leaf. **2.** Length; lengthwise.

lau mau'u. Blade of grass.

laumeki. 1. A kind of barbed spear. **2.** To recede, ebb, as the tide or flood waters. **3.** To wilt, as plants without water.

launa. Friendly, sociable; to associate with, meet with. Used idiomatically with *'a'ohe*, *'a'ole*, *'ole*: *'A'ohe launa ka maka'u*, terrible fear; there's no limit to the fear; *lit.,* no meeting the fear. **ho'olauna**. To introduce one person to another; to be friendly.

lau nahele. Plants, forest growth or leaves.

lau niu. Coconut leaf, frond.

lau'ō. 1. Sugarcane leaf (same as *lau kō*). **2.** Young white coconut leaves near the heart.

lauoho. Hair of the head. *Lit.,* head leaf.

lauoho o Pele. Pele's hair: fine, glassy filaments of lava.

lau pala. Fading leaf turning yellow, red, or brown. *Fig.,* person failing in health.

laupapa. 1. A broad flat area,

as of coral, lava, reef. PPN *laupapa*. 2. Board, lumber. *Pā laupapa*, wooden fence.

lawa. 1. Enough, sufficient, ample; to have enough. **hoʻolawa.** To supply, apportion sufficiently. PPN *lawa*. 2. Possessed of enough or ample knowledge, hence wise, capable. 3. As soon as. *I lawa no a pau ka hana, hoʻi kāua*, as soon as the work is finished, we'll leave. 4. To tie. PPN *lawa*.

lawaiʻa. Fisherman; fishing technique; to fish, to catch fish. PEP *lawaika*.

-lawalawa. hoʻolawalawa. Redup. of *hoʻolawa*, to supply.

lāwalu. Fish or meat bound in ti leaves and broiled on coals; to cook thus.

lawa puni. Enough for all, well-supplied.

lawe. To take, accept, carry, bring; portable; bearer. **hoʻolawe.** To cause to take, deduct, subtract. PPN *lawe*.

lawehala. Sin, sinner, delinquency; evil, sinful; to sin. *Keiki lawehala*, delinquent child. **hoʻolawehala.** Accusation; to accuse; to grow worse, of a sickness.

lawehana. Workman, laborer; industrious; to do labor. *Hoa lawehana*, fellow worker.

lawe hānai. To adopt, as a child.

lawe kāhili. Bearer of the feather standard of royalty (*kāhili*).

lawelawe. 1. To serve, work for, minister to, attend to, do; to treat, as the sick; to wait, as on tables; to handle. PPN *lawelawe*. 2. To pilfer, make off with. *Lima lawelawe*, pilfering hand.

lawelawe hana. Function, administration.

lawelawe lima. To pitch in and

lend a hand; to assault, beat, tackle.

lawe leka. Mail carrier, postman; to carry mail or letters.

lawe lima. To carry by hand. *Puke lawe lima*, handbook.

lawe ʻōhua. Passenger carrier; to carry passengers.

lawe ʻōlelo. Talebearer; gossip; to gossip, bear tales.

lawe wale. Extortion, seizure of property with the owner's knowledge; to take without right.

leʻa. 1. Joy, pleasure, happiness; pleasing, delightful, merry; delighted, pleased. *Hāʻawi manawaleʻa*, to give gladly; *lit.*, to give [with] happy heart. **hoʻoleʻa.** To cause pleasure, joy; to praise, please, delight. PEP *leka*. 2. Clearly, perfectly, thoroughly, successfully.

leʻaleʻa. 1. Redup. of *leʻa, 1*. **hoʻoleʻaleʻa.** Redup. of *hoʻoleʻa;* to amuse oneself, have fun. PEP *lekaleka*.

lehe. Lip. See *lehe luhe, lehe ʻoi*.

lehelehe. Lips; labia of vagina.

lehelehe nui. hoʻolehelehe nui. Sullen, sulky, pouting.

lehe luhe. Pouting lip.

lehe ʻoi. Sharp-lipped; sharp-tongued, of one who makes cutting remarks.

leho. 1. General name for cowrie shell, as *Cypraea tigris*. PPN *fole*, PEP *lefo*. 2. Callus, as on shoulders from carrying heavy loads. 3. Covetous. Cf. *maka leho*.

lehu. 1. Ashes; ash-colored, as a chicken. *Lā Hāpala Lehu*, Ash Wednesday. **hoʻolehu.** To reduce to ashes. PPN *refu*. 2. The number 400,000; numerous, very many. Cf. *lehulehu*.

lehua. 1. The flower of the ʻōhiʻa tree (*Metrosideros col-*

lina); also the tree itself, a favorite native tree; the *lehua* is the flower of the island of Hawai'i, famous in song and tale. *Fig.*, a warrior, a beloved friend or relative, a sweetheart, an expert. 2. (*Cap.*) Name of the small island beyond Ni'ihau.

-lehua. ho'olehua. Swift, strong.

lehulehu. Multitude, crowd, great number, the public; numerous.

lehu pele. Volcanic ash.

lei. 1. Lei, garland, wreath; necklace of flowers, leaves, shells, ivory, feathers, or paper; beads; any ornament worn around the head or about the neck; to wear a lei; crown. *Fig.*, a beloved child, wife, husband, sweetheart, younger sibling. **ho-'olei.** To put a lei on oneself or on someone else; to crown. PPN *lei*. 2. To leap, fling; toss. Usually used with *ho'o-*. **ho'olei.** To cast, throw, toss, pitch; to stretch. PEP *lei*.

lei 'ā'ī. Lei for the neck; necktie, scarf, neckerchief. *Fig.*, beloved person, especially mate or child. *Lit.*, neck lei.

lei ali'i. Royal lei, chief's lei, crown, diadem.

lei hala. Lei made principally or solely of pandanus keys.

lei hulu. Feather lei. *Fig.*, dearly beloved child or favorite person.

lei kolona (korona). Rosary, prayer beads. *Lit.*, crown (*Eng.*) lei.

lei kukui. Lei of candlenut (*kukui*) nuts.

leina. Spring, leap, bound; place to leap from. PEP *leinga*.

lei niho 'ilio. Dog-tooth necklace.

lei niho palaoa. Same as *lei palaoa*.

lei palaoa. Ivory pendant, originally probably whale's tooth suspended by two coils of braided human hair; necklace of beads of whale's teeth; today, any pendant shaped like the old whale-tooth pendant. *Lit.*, ivory lei.

lei po'o. Lei worn on the head (*po'o*).

lei pūpū. Shell lei.

leke. Also **lede.** Lady. *Eng.*

lēkō. Watercress.

lele. 1. To fly, jump, leap, hop, burst forth; to sail through the air, as a meteor; to get out of, as from a car; to land, disembark, as from a canoe; to move, as stars in the sky; a jump, leap, attack. **ho'olele.** To cause to fly; to fly, as a kite; to embark, as on a project. PPN *lele*. 2. Windblown, of the rain. 3. A detached part or plot of land belonging to one *'ili*, but located in another *'ili*.

lelea. A kind of prayer to send kava essence to the gods. PPN *lelea*.

lele 'ao'ao. To leap sideways; to shy, as a horse.

lele 'ē. To speak prematurely or before one is spoken to; to jump to conclusions.

lelehuna, lelehune. Fine windblown rain.

lele'ino. To spring or leap violently, as in an attack or fright; to rush violently. *Lit.*, to fly evil.

lele kawa. To leap feet first from a cliff into water without splashing, or (at Ka'ū) into soft earth. *Papa lele kawa*, diving board.

lele koa'e. Flight of tropicbirds; to fly like a tropicbird. *Fig.*, sheer, steep.

lele koali. To swing; to jump rope; swinging on a *koali* vine rope, an ancient sport.

lele koke. To leap suddenly, immediately. *Fig.*, short-tempered, excitable, quick to fight.

lele lā'au. Pole-vaulting; to pole-vault.

-lele leo. ho'olele leo. To broadcast; radiobroadcast.

-lele lupe. ho'olele lupe. To fly kites.

leleo. Redup. of *leo.* PNP *lele'o.*

lele'oi. Excessive, very great. *Lit.,* excessive leap.

lele pali. To leap or fall from a cliff; to practice the ancient sport of leaping from a precipice into water.

lelepau. To trust completely.

lele pi'o. To fly or jump in a curve; to fly as a comet through the sky.

lelepo'o. To dive headfirst.

lele ua. Windblown rain.

lelewa. 1. Redup. of *lewa,* 2. PEP *lelewa.* 2. Hangers-on about a chief; parasitic persons.

lele wale. To fly, jump, move of one's own accord or for no reason.

lelo. Tongue (short for *alelo, elelo*).

lemi. Lemon, lime. *Eng. Wai lemi,* lemonade, limeade.

lemu. Buttocks. PPN *lemu.*

lena. 1. Yellow, yellowish; jaundice; bile. PPN *renga.* 2. Variant name for the *'ōlena* or turmeric plant. PPN *renga.* 3. To stretch out, as to dry; to sight or aim; to bend, as a bow.

lenalena. Redup. of *lena,* 1. PPN *rengarenga.*

leo. Voice, tone, tune, sound, command, advice, syllable; to speak, make a sound. Cf. *leoleo, leo 'ole.* PPN *le'o.*

leo ho'onani. Song of praise, hymn.

leo kāne. Male voice, bass.

leo kani. Vowel. *Lit.,* voiced sound.

leokanipū. Consonant. *Lit.,* sound said together.

leokū pāhā. Quartet.

leokū pākahi. Solo. *Lit.,* single standing speech.

leokū pākolu, leokū pāpākolu. Trio. *Lit.,* triple standing speech.

leokū pālua. Duet. *Lit.,* double standing speech.

leoleo. To speak loudly, angrily; to wail, as for the dead.

leo mele. Song tune; notes on the scale.

leo nui. Loud voice; to speak loudly.

leo 'ole. Uncomplaining, agreeable; considerate of feelings of others; giving generously. *Lit.,* no voice.

leo pa'a. Deaf-mute, dumb person. *Lit.,* held voice.

leo wahine. Soprano, soprano voice, feminine voice.

lepa. Flag, tapa cloth on end of a stick, as used to mark a taboo area. Cf. *kālepa.* PEP *lepa.*

lepe. 1. Hem or fringe, as of a garment; any loose attachment, as of torn cloth or torn flesh. **ho'olepe.** To cut, tear; to stir, as water. 2. Rooster's comb; turkey wattles. PEP *lepe.*

lēpela, lepera. Leprosy, leper; leprous. *Eng.*

lepelepe. 1. Redup. of *lepe, 1;* fringed. 2. Wattles.

lepelepe-o-Hina. Monarch butterfly; Kamehameha butterfly.

lepo. Dirt, earth, ground, filth, excrement (euphemism); dirty, soiled. PPN *repo.*

lepolepo. Dirty, turbid; contaminated, as water.

lepo lo'i. Taro-patch mud.

lepopele. Match, sulphur (euphemism for *kūkaepele*). *Lit.,* volcanic dirt.

lepupalika, repubalika. Republic; Republican. *Eng.*

lewa. 1. Sky, atmosphere, upper heavens. PEP *lewa*. 2. To float, dangle, swing, hang; swinging, pendulous, unstable. *Hōkū lewa*, moving star, planet. **ho'olewa.** (a) To float, as a cloud; to lift up and carry, as on a stretcher. (b) To rotate the hips in dancing. PNP *lewa*.

-lewa. ho'olewa. Funeral.

lewa lani. Highest level of the heavens.

lewalewa. Redup. of *lewa*, 2.

lewa luna lilo. Highest atmosphere, outer space.

lī. 1. Chills; to have chills; to tremble with cold; shuddery feeling of horror. *Lī ka 'ili, lī ka 'i'o*, to have goose flesh. 2. Lace, as of shoes; to lace or tie. PNP *lii*.

lī-. A prefix to many kinds of seaweeds, short for *limu*.

lia. Same as *liha, 1*. PPN *liha*.

-lia. Suffix corresponding to *'ia* but inseparably bound to a base. PNP *-lia*.

li'a. Strong desire, yearning; to wish for ardently.

liha. Nit, louse egg. Also *lia*. PPN *lisa*. 2. Same as *liliha;* dreadful, fearful.

lihaliha. 1. Same as *liliha*. 2. Redup. of *liha, 1;* many nits.

līhau. Gentle cool rain that was considered lucky for fishermen; moist and fresh, as plants in the dew or rain; cool, fresh, as dew-laden air.

lihi. 1. Edge, rim, border, boundary. Also *nihi*. 2. Small quantity, particle, a little bit, slight. *'Ike lihi*, to glimpse. PPN *nifi*.

lihilihi. 1. Same as *lihi, 1, 2*. 2. Eyelashes, eyelid. 3. Lace.

lihilihi hana lima. Handmade lace; crocheting; any handmade trimming, as of knitting, tatting.

li'i. 1. Small, tiny. PPN *riki*. 2. Short for *ali'i*, chief, being especially common after *nā: nā li'i*, the chiefs.

li'ili'i. Here and there, piecemeal, a little at a time; small, little, in bits, diminutive, infantile. *Kū'ai li'ili'i*, retail buying or selling. **ho'oli'ili'i.** To decrease, lessen, make small. PPN *rikiriki*.

lī kāma'a. Shoelace; to lace shoes.

like. Alike, like, similar, resembling, equal. Cf. *'ālike, ālike; hālike*. *'Ālike ālike*, midway, equally. *Like pū*, just the same. PEP *lite*.

likelike. Redup. of *like*.

like 'ole. Various, all, different, not alike.

like pū. See *like*.

likiki. Ticket, receipt. *Eng*.

liko. 1. Leaf bud; newly opened leaf; to bud; to put forth leaves. *Fig.*, a child; youth. PPN *lito*. 2. Shining, glistening, as with dew, sparkling.

lilā. Spindly. PPN *lila*, PEP *liilaa*.

lili. Jealous; highly sensitive to criticism; jealousy; anger and mental anguish felt if one's loved ones are criticized. **ho'olili.** To provoke jealousy; jealous. PPN *lili*.

lilia. Any kind of lily. *Eng*.

liliha. Nauseated, nauseating, of rich or fatty foods only; very rich, of fatty, oily food; revolted; dreadful.

liliko'i. The purple water lemon or purple granadilla (*Passiflora edulis*), one of many passion flower or passion fruit vines). The yellow *liliko'i* which has better-tasting fruit, is grown commercially in Hawai'i and widely used for desserts and beverages.

lilinoe. Fine mist, rain.

lili'u Scorching, burning, smarting, as salt in a raw wound or pain in the eyes.

lilo. 1. To accrue, be lost, pass

into the possession of, be gone; to become, turn into; to overcome; taken. **hoʻolilo.** To transfer, change. PPN *lilo.* **2.** Busy, absorbed, engrossed, devoted, dedicated. **3.** Expense, expenditure. **hoʻoliʻo.** Expense; to spend; to lose; to buy or sell. **4.** Far, distant, out of sight, completely. *I luna lilo,* way up.

lilo loa. Completely engrossed, dedicated, absorbed; permanently lost or taken, entirely gone.

lima. 1. Arm, hand; sleeve; finger. PPN *lima.* **2.** Five; fifth. PPN *lima.*

lima ʻākau. Right hand; right-handed; dependable helper, right-hand man.

limahana. Labor, laborer, worker; busy.

lima hema. Left hand; left-handed.

lima ikaika. Strong hand or arm; power, strength; strong-arm.

lima iki. Small hand; little finger.

lima kākau. Handwriting; hand to write with.

lima kuhi. Index finger. *Lit.,* pointing finger.

lima kuhikuhi. Hands of a clock. *Lit.,* pointing hands.

limalima. 1. To handle, use the hands; to pilfer. **2.** To hire. **hoʻolimalima.** To rent, hire, employ, lease, charter; a lease, rental.

lima nui. Big hand, thumb.

limu. A general name for all kinds of plants living under water, both fresh and salt; also algae growing in any damp place, as on the ground, on rocks, and on other plants; also mosses, liverworts, lichens. PPN *limu.*

limu kala. Common long brown seaweeds (*Sargassum* spp.).

limu kele. Moss growing on trees in rain forests.

limu-kohu. A soft, succulent, small red seaweed (*Asparagopsis sanfordiana*), one of the best-known and best-liked of edible seaweeds. Also called *limu-koko.*

lina. 1. Soft; adhesive, sticky; glutinous, as taro of poor quality. Cf. *papālina.* **2.** Scar. Cf. *ʻālina.* **hoʻolina.** To scar. **3.** Ring (*Eng.*), hoop, race-track.

lino. 1. Bright, shiny, dazzling, brilliant. **2.** To weave, twist, braid, tie. PPN *lino.* **3.** Same as *linolino, 2.*

linolino. 1. Redup. of *lino, 1, 2.* **2.** Calm, unruffled. Cf. *malino.*

lio. Horse. *Holo lio,* to ride horseback.

liʻō. To act wild, as a frightened animal; to open the eyes wide in terror. **hoʻoliʻō.** To frighten, cause to shy, leap.

lio heihei. Racehorse.

lio lāʻau. Merry-go-round; horse on a merry-go-round; sawhorse; wooden horse, as used in quilting. *Holo lio lāʻau,* to ride on a merry-go-round.

lio lawe ukana. Packhorse. *Lit.,* horse carry gear.

liʻoliʻo. Bright, dazzling; dazzled. PEP *likoliko.*

liona. Lion. *Eng. Hui Liona,* Lions Club.

liona kai. Sea lion.

lio wahine. Mare.

līpahapaha. All kinds of sea lettuce (*Ulva* spp. and *Monostroma* spp.), edible but not well liked.

lipaki, libati. Liberty. *Eng.*

līpeʻe. Some native species of edible red seaweeds of the genus *Laurencia.* *Lit.,* hiding seaweed.

līpeʻepeʻe. Same as *līpeʻe.*

lipelala, liberala. Liberal. *Eng.*

lipi. Adze, chisel; any sharp

edge; sharp mountain ridge; sharp, tapering. PPN *lipi.*

lipilipi. Redup. of *lipi.* PPN *lipilipi.*

lipina, rubina. Var. of *lipine.*

lipine, ribine. Ribbon; tape, of a tape recorder. *Eng.*

lipine kikokiko. Typewriter ribbon.

lipo. Deep blue-black, as a cavern, the sea, or dense forest; dim, distant. *Kumulipo,* the origin in the deep, blue-black past [a Hawaiian creation poem].

lipoa. Two popular edible brown seaweeds (*Dictyopteris australis, D. plagioeranama*).

lipu'upu'u. An edible green seaweed.

liu. Bilge water, leakage; to leak. PPN *liu.*

li'u. 1. Slow, tardy, taking a long time; a long time. 2. Well-salted, salty; seasoned. *Fig.,* deep, profound, as of skill or knowledge.

li'ulā. Twilight; mirage.

liuliu. Prepared, ready; to make ready. **ho'oliuliu.** To prepare.

li'uli'u. Redup. of *li'u,* 1; to pass much time; to spend much time. **ho'oli'uli'u.** To cause a delay, prolong.

lō. Earwig. PPN *loo.*

loa. 1. Distance, length, height; distant, long, far, permanent. Cf. *loloa.* **ho'oloa.** To stretch, extend, prolong, lengthen. PPN *loa.* 2. Very, very much; too; most. *Maika'i loa,* very good. *Aloha nui loa,* very much *aloha.* PEP *loa.*

loa'a. To find, get, obtain, acquire, have, gain, receive; gain, earnings, profit, wealth, success; to have a child, beget a child; to be born; unequalled, incomparable. (This extremely common word takes an agent preceded by *i* or *iā.*) *Loa'a ka hale i ke*

ali'i, the chief has a house. PEP *loaka.*

loea. Skill, ingenuity, cleverness; expert, clever, skillful; skilled person.

loha. Drooping, wilting; hanging low, as a branch; beaten down, as by rain. *Fig.,* sullen, spiritless. PPN *lofa.*

lohe. To hear; to mind, obey; to feel, as the tug of a fishing line; obedient. **ho'olohe.** To obey.

lohelohe. 1. Redup. of *lohe;* to listen carefully, eavesdrop. 2. Dragonfly larva, cocoon.

lohe 'ōlelo. Hearsay, gossip.

lohe pepeiao. Hearsay; to hear of.

lohi. 1. Slow, tardy, late. *'Ōlelo lohi,* speak slowly. **ho'olohi.** To delay, make slow, detain; to go slowly. PEP *lo(f,s)i.* 2. Short for *'alohi,* sparkle.

loi. To look over critically.

lo'i. Irrigated terrace, especially for taro, but also for rice.

lō'ihi. Length, height; long, tall; distance. *Lō'ihi ke ala,* a long road. **ho'olō'ihi.** To lengthen, extend, prolong.

loina. Rule, custom; principle, as of a political party.

loio. 1. Thin, spindly. 2. Lawyer (*Eng.*), attorney; to act the lawyer; to judge. **ho'oloio.** To act the lawyer; to show off knowledge.

loio ho'okolokolo. Prosecutor.

loio kuhina. Attorney general.

lōkahi. Unity, agreement, accord; agreed, in unity. *Mana'o lōkahi,* unanimous. **ho'olōkahi.** To bring about unity; to make peace and unity.

loke. 1. Rose; rosy. *Eng.* 2. Also **roke.** Roast. *Eng. Pipi loke,* roast beef.

loke-lani, roselani. The common small red rose.

loke-lau. Green rose (*Rosa chinensis* var. *viridiflora*).

loko. 1. In, inside, within; interior, inside; internal organs, as tripe. **ho'oloko.** To insinuate, suggest, implant a thought, either good or bad. PPN *loto.* 2. Character, disposition, heart. Cf. *loko hāiki, loko 'ino, lokomaika'i.* 3. Pond, lake, pool. 4. Mainland of the United States. *I loko aku nei au,* I've been to the mainland. 5. In spite of. *I loko nō o ka waiwai, hana nō,* in spite of wealth, working anyway. 6. By means of.

loko hāiki. Hard-hearted; narrow-minded; tight-fisted.

loko 'ino. Merciless, evil, cruel; such a person.

loko kai. Lagoon.

lokomaika'i. Generosity, kindness, good will; benevolent.

loko pa'akai. Salt pond or lake.

loku. Downpour of rain; blowing of wind; to pour, of rain. *Fig.,* to feel deep emotion, pain, sorrow. **ho'oloku.** To pour, as rain; to disturb. PEP *lotu.*

lola. 1. Drooping, hanging downward; lazy, idle. 2. Roller, rolling pin; to roll. *Eng.*

lole. 1. Cloth, clothes, dress; to wear clothes. 2. To unfold, turn inside out, reverse. PEP *lole.*

lole holoi. Laundry; soiled clothes ready to be washed.

lole komo. Clothes. *Lit.,* clothes to put on.

lole moe pō. Nightgown. *Lit.,* night-sleeping clothes.

lole wāwae. Trousers, pants, panties, slacks. *Lit.,* leg clothes.

loli. 1. To turn, change, alter, turn over. **ho'ololi.** To change, take a new form; to amend, as laws. PEP *loli.* 2. Sea slug, bêche-de-mer, sea cucumber, trepang (*Holothuria* spp.). PPN *loli.*

loliloli. Redup. of *loli, 1;* changing, turning, changeable.

lolo. 1. Brains, bone marrow. PPN *lolo.* 2. Religious ceremony at which the brain of the sacrificed animal was eaten (such ceremonies occurred at a canoe launching, the start of a journey, completion of instruction); to have completed the *lolo* ceremony, hence expert, skilled. 3. A strikingly colored species of wrasse fish. PEP *lolo.*

lōlō. Paralyzed, numb; feebleminded.

loloa. Redup. of *loa, 1. Lima loloa,* long sleeve. PPN *loloa.*

lolohe. Redup. of *lohe;* to listen carefully, attentively. **ho'ololohe.** To listen carefully; to strain the ear to hear.

lolo iwi. Bone marrow.

loloka'a. Dizziness, with spinning head.

lolo po'o. Brain. *Lit.,* head brain.

lolo wa'a. Canoe-launching ceremony; to perform the ceremony.

loma. Idle.

lomi. To rub, press, crush, massage, rub out; to work in and out, as claws of a contented cat. PPN *lomi.*

lōmilo. To spin with fingers; to twist, as thread in making rope or cord. Cf. *milo,* to twist.

lomilomi. Redup. of *lomi;* masseur, masseuse. PPN *lomilomi.*

lonikū, lonitu. Longitude. *Eng.*

lono. 1. News, report, remembrance, rumor (sometimes formerly preceded by *ke*). **ho'olono.** To listen, hear, obey; obedient. PPN *rongo.* 2. (*Cap.*) One of the four major gods brought from Tahiti, the god of the *makahiki* harvest festivities and of agriculture. PEP *Longo.*

3. (*Cap.*) The twenty-eighth day of the lunar month. 4. (*Cap.*) Hawaiian name for Captain Cook.

lo'ohia. Possessed, overwhelmed, overcome; to befall, happen. PEP *loko(f,s)-ia.*

lōpā. Shiftless; poor tenant farmer. PEP *loopaa.*

lopi, ropi. Thread. (*Eng.,* rope.)

lopi ho'oholoholo. Basting thread.

lopi kāholo. Basting thread.

lou. Hook; to hook, to fasten with a hook. **ho'olou.** To hook; to put on a hook, as bait. 2. Fruit-plucking pole; to pluck with a *lou.* PPN *lohu.*

lo'u. To overhang, as a cliff; to bend over, as with grief or laughter; bent over, as a laden branch. PPN *loku.*

loulu. All species of native fan palms (*Pritchardia*).

lū. To scatter, throw, as ashes; to sow; to shed, as a chicken its feathers or a tree its leaves; to shake; to cast off, as grief; to squander. See *lūlū.* PEP *luu.*

lua. 1. Hole, pit, grave, den, cave, mine, crater. **ho'olua.** To bake in the oven. Cf. *kālua.* PPN *lua.* 2. Toilet, outhouse. 3. Two, second, secondary, twice; doubly, much, a great deal. **ho'olua.** To do twice, repeat, do over and over. PPN *rua.* 4. Equal likeness, duplicate, copy, match. Cf. *lua 'ole.* 5. Companion, mate. Cf. *kōko'o.*

-lua. 1. **ho'olua.** (*Cap.*) Name of a strong north wind. 2. Dual number, only in pronoun and possessive *'olua.* PPN *-rua.*

lu'a. Old and wrinkled; worn and shabby with use.

-lu'a. ho'olu'a. (a) To bear many children. (b) To lay an egg.

lua ahi. Pit of fire; hell.

lua 'eli pōhaku. Quarry. *Lit.,* pit [for] digging stones.

luahine, luwahine. Old woman, old lady; to be an old woman. **ho'oluahine.** To act or dress like an old lady. PEP *luafine.*

lua'i. Vomit; volcanic eruptions; to vomit, erupt. Cf. *lua'i koko.* **ho'olua'i.** Emetic; causing vomiting; to cause a vomiting. PPN *lua + 'aki.*

lua'i koko. Any kind of sickness with vomiting of blood; to vomit blood.

lua'i pele. Volcanic eruption, lava, sulphur, brimstone.

luakaha. Enjoyable, pleasant, as a place to which one is attached; to while away the time enjoyably.

luakini. Temple, church, cathedral, tabernacle; large *heiau* where ruling chiefs prayed and human sacrifices were offered.

lua kupapa'u. Tomb, grave. *Lit.,* corpse pit.

lua li'ili'i. Outhouse, toilet.

luana. To be at leisure; to enjoy pleasant surroundings and associates; to live in comfort and ease. **ho'oluana.** To be at leisure.

luana iki. To pause a moment; to enjoy oneself a little.

lua 'ole. Superior, incomparable, unequalled, second to none.

lua 'ōpala. Rubbish pit.

lua pele. Volcano, crater. *Lit.,* volcanic pit.

lua puhi. Blowhole, eel hole.

lū'au. 1. Young taro tops, especially as baked with coconut cream and chicken or octopus. PPN *luu,* PNP *lu(u)kau.* 2. Hawaiian feast.

luawai. Well, pool, pond, reservoir.

luea. Seasickness, nausea, dizziness.

luhe. To droop.

lūheʻe. Fishing for octopus with line and cowry lure; the octopus lure; to fish thus.

lū heleleʻi. To scatter, strew; to let hair hang loose and unbound.

luhi. Weary, tired, fatigued; wearisome, tiresome, tedious; burden; labor, work, pains. **hoʻoluhi.** To bother, disturb, trouble, overburden. PEP *lu(f,s)i.*

luhia. A species of shark. PPN *rufi.*

luhiluhi. Redup. of *luhi.* **hoʻoluhiluhi.** To make tired, disturbed. PEP *lu(f,s)ilu(f,s)i.*

luina. Sailor.

lukānela, lutanela. Lieutenant. *Eng.*

Lukia, Rusia. Russia; Russian. *Eng.*

Lūkini. Russian. *Eng.*

luku. Massacre, slaughter, destruction; to destroy, massacre, lay waste, exterminate. PEP *lutu.*

luku wale. Vandalism, useless slaughter or destruction; to destroy thus.

lula, rula. Ruler, tape measure; rules, manners, regulations. *Eng.*

lula kumu. Fundamental or basic rule.

luli. To shake, as the head in approval or disapproval; to roll, as a ship; to sway to and fro. **hoʻoluli.** To rock, as a child; to sway. PEP *luli.*

lulu. Calm, peace, shelter, lee, protection, shield; to lie at anchor. **hoʻolulu.** To lie quietly in calm water, as a ship in port; to be calm. PPN *ruru.*

lūlū. 1. Redup. of *lū;* to scatter, sow, as seeds; to shake, as an earthquake. PPN *lu(u)-luu.* 2. Donation, offering, as in church; raffle; to make an offering.

lūlū lima. To shake hands; handshake.

luma, lumaʻi. To douse, duck; to upset, tumble, as in the surf. PEP *lumaki.*

lumakika, rumatika. Rheumatism. *Eng.*

lumi, rumi. Room. *Eng.*

lumi ʻaina. Dining room.

lumi ʻauʻau. Bathroom. *Lit.,* washing room.

lumi hoʻokipa. Parlor, living room. *Lit.,* entertaining room.

lumi kuke. Kitchen. *Lit.,* cooking room.

lumi moe. Bedroom. *Lit.,* sleeping room.

lumi waiho pā. Pantry. *Lit.,* room [for] leaving plates.

luna. 1. High, upper, above, over, up; on, in, into. *Luna* follows particles expressing place, as *a, i, kō, ma-, mai, no, o. Kau i luna o ke kaʻa,* get into the car. PPN *lunga.* 2. Foreman, boss, overseer, supervisor. **hoʻoluna.** To appoint as foreman, officer, etc.

luna ʻauhau. Tax collector.

luna aupuni. Government official.

luna hana. Overseer, foreman, anyone in charge of work.

luna helu. Census taker. *Lit.,* counting supervisor.

luna helu kālā. Teller, as of a bank. *Lit.,* officer who counts money.

luna hoʻohana. Manager, administrative head, overseer. *Lit.,* supervisor to cause work to be done.

luna hoʻomalu. Chairman; speaker, as of the House of Representatives.

luna hoʻoponopono. Editor.

luna hoʻopuka. Publisher. *Lit.,* officer who makes appear.

lunaʻikehala. Conscience. *Lit.,* officer who knows wrong.

lunakahiko. Elder; elderly leader.

luna kānāwai. Judge, magistrate; Book of Judges in the Old Testament; judicial. *Lit.,* law officer.

luna kānāwai kiʻekiʻe. Chief justice.

luna kiaʻi. Supervisor.

luna kula. School superintendent, schoolmaster.

luna leka. Postmaster. *Lit.,* letter officer.

lunamakaʻāinana. Representative in the legislature. *Lit.,* people's officer.

luna mākaʻi. District sheriff, chief of police.

luna nui. Chief officer or foreman, especially head overseer of a sugar plantation.

lupe. 1. Kite. *Hoʻolele lupe,* to fly a kite. **2.** Same as *hīhīmanu,* stingray.

lupo. Wolf.

lūpō. Same as *pāpiopio.* Probably PPN *lupo.*

luʻu. To dive, plunge into water, immerse; to dip in, as a shrimp net. **hoʻoluʻu.** To dip, immerse, etc. PPN *ruku.*

luʻuluʻu. Bent or bowed down, as with weight, sorrow, or trouble; painful, sorrowful. **hoʻoluʻuluʻu.** To cause sorrow, grief; to oppress. PPN *rukuruku.*

M

ma. At, in, on, beside, through, by means of, because of, according to (*mā* usually before primary stress). *Makai,* at the sea, seaward. *Mauka,* inland.

ma-. Stative derivative former, as in *mahae.* PPN *ma-.*

mā. 1. Faded, clear. PPN *maʻa.* **2.** Particle following names of persons: and company, and others, and associates, and wife. *Ke aliʻi mā,* the chief and his retinue. *Mea mā,* they. PNP *maʻa.* **3.** Variant of *ma-.*

mā-. Exclusiveness, in pronouns (*mākou, māua*) and possessives. PPN *ma(a).*

maʻa. 1. Accustomed, used to, knowing thoroughly, experienced. Cf. *maʻamaʻa, maʻamau.* **hoʻomaʻa.** To practice, gain experience or skill, become accustomed (less used than *hoʻomaʻamaʻa*). **2.** To tie. Cf. *kāmaʻa.* **3.** Sling. PPN *maka.*

maʻalahi. Easy, simple.

maʻalea. Cunning, craft, trickery; crafty, deceitful, shrewd, skillful.

maʻalili. Cooled, of what has been hot, as food; abated, calmed, of anger, love, passion. **hoʻomaʻalili.** To cause to cool; soothe. PNP *makalili.*

māʻalo. To pass along, by, or alongside, as to overtake and pass a car; to pass through, as land. PPN *ma(a)kalo.*

māʻaloʻalo. Redup. of *māʻalo;* to pass to and fro, back and forth; to pass frequently.

maʻamaʻa. Redup. of *maʻa, 1;* accustomed, experienced, used. **hoʻomaʻamaʻa.** Same as *hoʻomaʻa;* to practice, become accustomed.

maʻamau. Usual, customary, regular, habitual, ordinary. *Uku maʻamau,* customary fee. **hoʻomaʻamau.** To become accustomed, familiar.

maʻaneʻi. See *ʻaneʻi.*

ma'awe. Fiber, thread, strand, as of a spider web; to tread, track, follow, as a trail; weak, sickly. ho'oma'awe. To make a tracing; footprint, track; to make small fibers or threads. PNP makawe.

mā'awe'awe. Redup. of ma-'awe; streaked, as with different colors.

mae. To fade, wilt, wither; partially dry, as clothes; to fade away; to waste away, as with illness. ho'omae. To cause to wilt, fade; to fade. PPN mae.

maea. Malodorous. PPN mae.

mā'e'ele. Numb, as a foot that has "gone to sleep"; numb with cold or deeply moved by love; shocked; stricken with fear, horror, grief. ho'omā-'e'ele. To cause numbness, shock, great love.

mā'ele. Same as mā'e'ele.

ma'ema'e. Clean, pure, attractive, chaste; cleanliness, purity. ho'oma'ema'e. To clean, cleanse.

māewa. Swaying, swinging, as something with an anchored base, as seaweed, hair, or leaves; fluttering; unstable. PEP ma(a)ewa.

ma'ewa. Reproachful, scornful, mocking, sneering; scorned, abused. ho'oma'ewa. To reproach, sneer at, mimic.

mā'ewa'ewa. Redup. of ma-'ewa.

maha. 1. Temple, side of the head. PNP mafa. 2. Rest, repose; freedom from pain; at ease. See mahamaha. ho-'omaha. Vacation; rest in music; to take a rest or vacation; to retire, stop work; to obtain relief.

mahae. To tear, split, separate. Mahae lua, to split in two. Also nahae. PPN masae.

mahaehae. Redup. of mahae; to tear to shreds.

mahalo. 1. Thanks, gratitude; to thank. Mahalo nui loa, thank you very much. 2. Admiration, praise; to admire, praise. Probably PPN masal(a,o).

mahamaha. Redup. of maha, 2; to rest, stop.

mahana. 1. Warmth; warm. Cf. hahana, pumehana. ho-'omahana. To warm, create warmth, heat. PPN mafana. 2. Rest. Cf. maha, 2. ho-'omahana. Vacation, rest.

māhana. Twins; double; having two branches or forks. PPN maasanga.

maha'oi. Bold, impertinent, nervy, brazen. Lit., sharp temple.

mahea. See hea, 3, where.

Māhea-lani. Sixteenth night of the lunar month; night of the full moon.

māhelahela. Clearly shown, as wood grain. Perhaps PPN mafela.

māhele. Portion, division, department; share, as of stocks; measure in music; land division of 1848; the Great Māhele; part, as of the body; to divide, apportion, cut into parts. ho'omāhele. To have a division made, etc. PPN sele.'

māhele lā'au. Portion of medicine, dose.

māhele manawa. Division of time, as of a fiscal period.

māhele 'ōlelo. Interpreter, translator; to translate, interpret.

mahi. 1. To cultivate, farm; a farm, plantation. Cf. mahi'ai, mahina, mahina'ai. Mahi kō, sugar plantation. 2. Strong, energetic, as a worker. Moa mahi, fighting cock. PPN mafi.

mahi'ai. Farmer; to farm, cultivate; agricultural.

māhie. Delightful, charming,

pleasant. **ho'omāhie.** Delightful, charming.

māhiehie. Redup. of *māhie.*

mahiki. 1. To jump, leap, hop, move up and down; to teeter, seesaw. **ho'omahiki.** To cause to leap, jump, etc. PNP *mafiti.* **2.** To pry; peel off, as a scab; to appear.

māhikihiki. Redup. of *mahiki,* .*1, 2.*

mahimahi. Dolphin (*Coryphaena hippurus*). PPN *masimasi.*

mahina. 1. Moon, month; moonlight. *Mahina meli,* honeymoon. PPN *maasina.* **2.** Farm, plantation, patch.

mahina'ai. Same as *mahi'ai;* farm, to farm.

māhinahina. Pale moonlight.

mahina hou. 1. New moon, new month. **2.** Church offering on the first Sunday of the month, in Congregational churches.

mahina piha. Full moon.

mahina poepoe. Full moon. *Lit.,* round moon.

mahiole. Feather helmet, helmet; to wear a helmet.

mahi pua. Flower garden or patch; horticulture.

mahi waina. Vineyard; one who raises grapes; to cultivate grapes.

māhoe. Twins.

māhola. To spread out, extend. PPN *mafola.*

māhole. To bruise, skin, scrape, as a flesh wound; to injure, as the feelings. Cf. *hole,* peeled. PEP *maafole.*

mahope. See *hope,* after.

māhu. Steam, vapor; to steam, exude vapor.

mahū. Weak, flat, as stale beer; insipid. PPN *mafu(u).*

māhū. Homosexual, of either sex; hermaphrodite. **ho'omāhū.** To behave like a homosexual or hermaphrodite. PEP *maa(f,s)uu.*

māhua. Increase, growth; to increase, thrive, multiply. **ho'omāhua.** To increase, expand, enlarge, multiply. PPN *masua.*

māhuahua. Redup. of *māhua;* to grow strong, as a ruler. PPN *masuasua.*

mahu'i. To guess, surmise.

mahuka. To run away, escape. **ho'omahuka.** To assist or help escape. PEP *ma(f,s)uta.*

mai. 1. Direction toward the speaker. Come, come here; say, give (used without particles). *Hele mai,* come. PPN *mai.* **2.** Also *mai . . . mai.* From. *Mai Hilo mai ka lei,* the lei is from Hilo. PPN *m(a,e)i.* **3.** Particle of negative command. Don't. **4.** Almost, nearly. PPN *mei.*

ma'i. 1. Patient, sick person; sickness, disease; sick, ill. PNP *maki.* **2.** Genitals. *Mele ma'i,* song in honor of genitals, as of a chief, as composed on his or her birth.

mai'a. All kinds of bananas. PEP *meika.*

mai'a Pākē. Chinese banana (*Musa nana*).

maiau. Neat and careful in work; skillful, expert; correct, careful, as in speech.

ma'i-Hepela (Hebera). Smallpox. *Lit.,* Hebrew disease.

maika. Ancient Hawaiian game suggesting bowling; the stone used in the game; shot-put. Also, *'ulu maika.*

maika'i. Good, well, fine, excellent; handsome; goodness; well-being; good health. **ho'omaika'i.** To thank, bless, congratulate; to praise; to improve. *Ho'omaika'i!* Congratulations! PPN *ma'itaki.*

ma'i keiki. Pregnancy sickness; child's disease.

Maikonekia, Maikonikia. Micronesia; Micronesian. *Eng.*

maila. The directional *mai* plus *lā*, there, then.

mailani. To extol, praise. **ho-'omailani.** To praise.

maile. A native twining shrub (*Alyxia olivaeformis*), with shiny fragrant leaves, a favorite for decoration and leis. PPN *maile.*

maile-lau-li'i. A kind of *maile* with narrow, pointed leaves. *Lit.,* small-leaved *maile.*

maile-lau-nui. A kind of *maile* with large leaves. *Lit.,* big-leaved *maile.*

ma'i lele. Contagious disease. *Lit.,* jumping disease.

maile pilau. Stink vine (*Paederia foetida*). *Lit.,* stinking *maile.*

mā'ili. Pebble, as used for making sinkers for squid fishing; pebbly, full of pebbles.

mai . . . mai. See *mai, 2.*

māino. Cruelty, misery, harm; cruel, miserable. **ho'omāino.** To treat cruelly, abuse, persecute; to cause misery and suffering. PPN *'ingo.*

mā'ino'ino. To deface, mar, spoil; defamed, defaced. **ho-'omā'ino'ino.** To defame, slander, deface.

ma'i ola. To cure sickness; curable disease.

ma'i-Pākē. Leprosy. *Lit.,* Chinese disease.

ma'i-pu'upu'u-li'ili'i. Smallpox. *Lit.,* disease with many little pimples.

ma'i-pu'uwai. Heart disease, heart attack.

māi'u'u. Toe or finger nail; hoof, claw. Perhaps PPN *kuku;* PNP *maikuku.*

maka. 1. Eye, eye of a needle, face, countenance; presence, sight, view. PPN *mata.* **2.** Beloved one, favorite person. Cf. *makamaka* (very common). **3.** Point, bud; nipple, teat; sharp edge or blade of an instrument; point of a fish-

hook; land point; beginning, source. **ho'omaka.** To begin, start; to appear, of a child's first tooth; to put forth buds; to come to a head, as a boil. PPN *mata.* **4.** Mesh of a net; mesh in plaiting; stitch, in sewing. PPN *mata.* **5.** Raw, as fish; uncooked; green, unripe, as fruit; fresh as distinct from salted provisions. PPN *mata.*

māka. Mark, target; to mark. *Eng.*

maka 'āhewa. Walleyed; cross-eyed. *Lit.,* eyes that err.

maka'āinana. Commoner, populace, people in general; citizen. Cf. *lunamaka'āinana. Lit.,* people that attend the land. PNP *matakainanga.*

maka'ala. Alert, vigilant, watchful, wide-awake.

makaaniani. Eyeglasses, spectacles. *Lit.,* crystal eye.

maka'ē. To look at with disfavor; to look askance.

maka'ele'ele. Chilled, frozen.

mākaha. Fierce, savage, ferocious.

mākahakaha. Clearing, as rain. **ho'omākahakaha.** To show signs of clearing.

makahehi. Admiration, desire for, wonder, amazement; attractive; to admire.

makahekili. Hailstone. *Lit.,* thunder eye. PPN *maka + fatitili.*

maka hiamoe. Sleepy eyes; sleepy, drowsy.

makahiapo. First-born child, oldest child. *Lit.,* first-born person. PEP *mata(f,s)iapo.*

makahiki. 1. Year; annual, yearly (sometimes written M.H.). PEP *matafiti.* **2.** Ancient festival beginning about the middle of October and lasting about four months, with sports and religious festivities and taboo on war.

makahiki hou. New Year. *Hau-*

ʻoli Makahiki Hou, Happy New Year.

makahiki lele ʻoi. Leap year. *Lit.,* year jump ahead.

maka hilahila. Bashful eyes; bashful, timidly averting one's gaze.

maka hou. Beginning, new start. **hoʻomaka hou.** To begin again.

makai. See *kai,* ocean.

mākaʻi. Policeman, guard; to police, inspect, spy. Cf. *luna mākaʻi.* **hoʻomākaʻi.** To act as a policeman; to appoint or invest as a policeman.

maka ihe. Spear point.

mākaʻi hoʻomalu pō. Patrolling night police. *Lit.,* police making night peaceful.

maka ihu. Bowsprit of a canoe; sharp point at the bow. *Lit.,* bow point.

mākaʻikaʻi. To visit, see the sights; to stroll, take a walk. *Mākaʻikaʻi hele,* to stroll here and there. **hoʻomākaʻikaʻi.** To take others on a visit; to show the sights; to escort. PEP *maatakitaki.*

mākaʻikiu. Detective. *Lit.,* spying police.

mākaʻi koa. Military police. *Lit.,* soldier police.

mākaʻi nui. Sheriff.

mākaʻi pō. Night watchman, night police.

makaīwa. Mother-of-pearl eyes, as in an image, especially of the god Lono. *Lit.,* mysterious eye.

mākaʻi wahine. Police matron.

maka kiʻekiʻe. Proud look; haughty air.

maka kilo. Observant, watchful eyes; to watch with great attention.

makākiu. Spy, detective, spying eye; watchful, spying; to spy. **hoʻomakākiu.** To spy, watch, reconnoiter.

maka koa. Bold, unafraid,

fierce. *Lit.,* brave eye. PNP *mata toʻa.*

maka koʻa. Landmark for a fishing ground. *Lit.,* fishing-ground point.

maka kui. Needle or nail point; stitch.

makala. To loosen, undo, untie, open a little, set at liberty; to remit, as a debt; to open, as a flower. PPN *matala.*

mākala. 1. Myrtle. *Eng.* 2. Marshal. *Eng.* 3. (*Cap.*) Marshall (Islands). *Eng.*

makalapua. Handsome, beautiful; to blossom forth.

makalē. Mackerel, canned sardines. *Eng.*

maka leʻa. Twinkle-eyed, happy-eyed, mischievous.

maka leho. Covetous; lustful. *Lit.,* cowrie eyes.

makaliʻi. 1. Tiny, very small, fine, wee; small-meshed. PPN *mataliki.* 2. (*Cap.*) Pleiades; Castor and Pollux. PPN *Mataliki.* (If Tongan Mataliki is a Samoan loan, the reconstruction would be PNP instead of PPN.) 3. (*Cap.*) Name of a Hawaiian month; the six summer months collectively.

makalika. Marguerite, daisy. *Eng.*

maka loa. Very green, as a fruit; barely cooked, very raw.

maka lokomaikaʻi. Bountiful eye; one who looks kindly, charitably, and with good will. *Lit.,* good-hearted face.

maka luhi. Tired eyes, tired people, especially those who have been working hard on a community project.

makamae. Precious, of great value, highly prized, darling.

makamaka. Intimate friend with whom one is on terms of receiving and giving freely; host. Cf. *maka,* beloved. **hoʻomakamaka.** To befriend, be a friend to, make a friend, cause to be friends.

maka mua. First, beginning, commencement, first time; first child of a family. *Lit.*, first end.

makana. Gift, present; reward; prize; to give a gift. Cf. *maka, 2.*

makana aloha. Gift of friendship or love; free-will offering.

makana hele. Parting gift. *Lit.*, going gift.

makani. Wind, breeze; gas in the stomach; to blow. Cf. *ani.* PPN *matangi.*

maka 'oi. Piercing, penetrating, sharp eyes.

maka piapia. Eyes sticky with viscous matter; watery eyes.

makapō. Blindness, blind person; blind. *Lit.*, night eye. **ho'omakapō.** To cause blindness, to feign blindness, to blindfold. PEP *matapoo.*

makapōuli. Dizziness; dizzy, faint. *Lit.*, black-night eyes.

makau. Fishhook. PPN *maata'u*, PEP *matau.*

maka'u. Fear; frightened, afraid. **ho'omaka'u.** To frighten, scare, terrify; to pretend fear; to fear. PNP *mataku.*

maka'uhia. Passive/imperative of *maka'u.* PNP *matakufia.*

mākaukau. Able, competent, capable, efficient, skilled; prepared, ready; competence, efficiency, preparation; to know how, to know well. Cf. *'ākau*, right. **ho'omākaukau.** To prepare, make ready. PEP *maatautau.*

maka 'ula'ula. Pinkeye; inflamed eye. *Lit.*, red eye.

maka uli. Black eye, as from a bruise.

maka 'upena. Net mesh.

maka'u wale. Coward, cowardice; afraid for no reason, easily frightened.

maka wai. Watery-eyed; eyes welling with tears; tender-eyed.

makawalu. Numerous, many, much. *Lit.*, eight eyes.

makawela. Glowing, burning; full of hate.

make. 1. To die; defeated, killed, unfortunate; to faint; death, peril, destruction; to kill (when used transitively, the subject is preceded by *i* or *iā*); deathly, deadly. **ho-'omake.** To kill; to let die; to let diminish, grow faint. PPN *mate.* 2. Desire, want; to want. Cf. *make 'ai.* PEP *mate.*

make 'ai. Hungry. *Lit.*, want food. PEP *mate kai.*

-māke'aka. ho'omāke'aka. Witty, comic, funny; to cause laughter, exercise wit.

make'e. Covetous, greedy, desirous to have; to have affection for.

makehewa. Bad bargain, vain undertaking; in vain, useless, without profit. Cf. *makepono.*

mākeke. Market. *Eng.*

mākeke nui. Large market, supermarket.

make loa. To die (in contrast to *make*, which may mean "defeated, faint").

makemake. Desire, want, wish; to want, like, wish (often replaced colloquially by *ma-make*).

makemakika. Mathematics. *Eng.*

makepono. Bargain, profitable, reasonable in price. Cf. *makehewa.*

make wai. Thirst; thirsty. PEP *mate wai.*

make wale. To die of itself, to die without cause.

mākia. 1. Aim, motto, purpose; to aim or strive for. 2. Pin, nail, bolt; to nail, bolt, crucify, pin; to establish, as a kingdom; to drive stakes, as in surveying.

makika. Mosquito. *Eng.*

mākō. Rough, rocky; large. Perhaps PPN *mato.*

mākole. Inflamed eye; red-eyed; red-hot; red or yellow, as dying leaves. **ho'omākole.** To cause redness or soreness of the eyes.

mākolu. Thick, heavy, deep, as clouds; thick-coated, as dust; laden, as a high chief with taboo. PPN *matolu.*

mākonā. Hard, mean, hardhearted. **ho'omākonā.** To act mean, hard, etc.

mākou. We, us (plural, exclusive). PPN *kimatolu*, PNP *kimaatou*, PEP *maatou.*

makua. Parent, any relative of the parents' generation, as uncle, aunt, cousin; Father (God, in Christian prayers); Catholic father; main stalk of a plant; adult; full-grown, mature, older, senior. **ho'omakua.** To grow into maturity; to mature; to act the part of a parent; to adopt, as a child; to call or treat as a parent. PPN *matu'a.*

mākua. Plural of *makua.* PPN *maatu'a.*

makua ali'i, makuali'i. Progenitor, patriarch, head of a tribe.

makuahine. Mother, aunt, female cousin or relative of parents' generation. *Lit.*, female parent. *'Ōlelo makuahine*, mother tongue.

mākuahine. Plural of *makuahine.*

makuahine kōlea. Stepmother. *Lit.*, plover mother.

makuahine papakema. Godmother.

makuahūnōwai, makuahunoai. Parent-in-law; uncle- or aunt-in-law; cousin of parent-in-law (sex may be designated by addition of *kāne*, male, or *wahine*, female).

makua kāne. Father, uncle,

male cousin of parents' generation.

mākua kāne. Plural of *makua kāne.*

makua kāne kōlea. Stepfather.

makua kāne papakema. Godfather.

mākuʻe. 1. Dark brown, any dark color. PEP *matuke.* **2.** Frown, scowl; to frown, scowl.

makule. Aged, old, of people. Cf. *'elemakule*, old man.

mala. 1. Aching, as after unaccustomed exercise; stiff and sore; bruised. **ho'omala.** To cause such an aching. PPN *mala.* **2.** Sour, as fermented sweet potato. PPN *mara.*

māla. Garden, plantation, cultivated field, as *māla 'ai.* PPN *ma'ala.*

māla 'ai. Taro patch, food garden or plantation.

māla'e. Clear, calm; clear of weeds, as a field; serene, as a cloudless sky. **ho'omāla'e.** To clear, explain clearly; to calm, cheer, dispel gloom; to clear away, as brush or weeds.

malahia. Passive/imperative of *mala*, 1. PNP *maalasia.*

malaila. See *laila.*

malakeke. Molasses. *Eng.*

Malaki. March (the month). *Eng.*

malalo. See *lalo.*

malama. Light; month. Cf. *lama*, torch. PPN *maarama*, *malama.*

mālama. To take care of, care for, preserve; to keep or observe, as a taboo; to conduct, as a service; to serve, honor, as God; care, preservation, support; fidelity, loyalty; custodian, caretaker. Cf. *mālama hale*, *mālama moku.*

mālama hale. Custodian of a house, janitor, housekeeper.

mālamalama. Redup. of *malama*; light of knowledge,

clarity of thinking or explanation; shining, clear. **ho-ʻomālamalama.** To cause light, brighten, illuminate, enlighten, inform.

mālama moku. Mate of a ship.

mālama waihona puke. Librarian.

māla pua. Flower garden.

male. Phlegm, mucus from lungs or throat. PPN *male.*

malia. Perhaps, maybe (usually followed by *o* or *paha*).

mālie. Calm, quiet, still, gentle; calmly, slowly, quietly. *Noho mālie,* keep still, sit still. **hoʻomālie.** To calm, quiet, hush, soothe. PPN *maalie.*

malihini. Stranger, newcomer, guest; one unfamiliar with a place or custom; new, unusual, rare, or of foreign origin; for the first time. **hoʻomalihini.** To be or act as a stranger, guest. PEP *man(i, u)fili.*

māliko. To bud, as leaves.

malimali. To flatter, soothe, persuade with soft words, cajole. **hoʻomalimali.** To flatter; to mollify with soft words or a gift; to soothe, quiet. PEP *malimali.*

malino. Calm, quiet, as the sea. *Malino ke kai,* the sea is calm. PPN *malino.*

maliʻo. Dawn light, twilight, especially as it pierces the shadows of night. PNP *maliko.*

maliu. To heed, give attention, listen, look upon with favor, turn toward. **hoʻomaliu.** To cause to heed, heed. PPN *maliu.*

malo. Male's loincloth; chant in praise of chief's loincloth. PNP *malo.*

mālō. Taut, firm, straight. *Kino mālō,* straight body. **hoʻomālō.** To make straight, firm, as a cord; to tighten. PPN *maaloo.*

maloka, hoʻomaloka. Skeptical, unbelieving.

maloko. Inside. See *loko.*

malolo. To rest, pause, adjourn. **hoʻomalolo.** To cease work for a time, recess; adjourn temporarily. PPN *malolo.*

mālolo. General term for Hawaiian flying fishes. PPN *maalolo.*

maloʻo. Dry, dried up, evaporated; drought, dryness. **hoʻomaloʻo.** To dry out; to season, as lumber; tracing, as of genealogy.

malu. Shade, shelter, protection, peace; shaded, peaceful; reserved; taboo; the stillness and awe of taboo. **hoʻomalu.** To bring under the care and protection of, to protect; to keep quiet, still; to restrict; to make peace between warring parties; to preside, as at a meeting; probation. Cf. *hale hoʻomalu, luna hoʻomalu.* PPN *malu.*

malū. Secretly, clandestinely, illegally. *Lawe malū,* to take secretly. PPN *maluu.*

maluhia. Peace, quiet; serenity; safety; peaceful, restful. **hoʻomaluhia.** To cause or give peace, protect; to arbitrate between warring parties.

māluhiluhi. Tired, weary; tiresome, wearisome, fatiguing. **hoʻomāluhiluhi.** To cause fatigue, exhaust, tire; tiresome, exhausting.

malule. Limp, weak, flexible; soft and fragile, as some eggshells. **hoʻomalule.** To make lax, limp, weak; to relax, weaken; to change from a caterpillar into a butterfly.

maluna. See *luna.*

mama. To chew, masticate (but not swallow; cf. *nau*). PPN *mama.*

māmā. 1. Fast, nimble, speedy

of movement. **2.** Light, of weight. *Fig.*, eased, of pain, ache, or distress. *Eamāmā*, oxygen. **hoʻomāmā.** To lighten, as a load; to ease pain; to cheer. PPN *maʻamaʻa.* **3.** Mama, mother. *Eng.*

mamae. Redup. of *mae;* sickly, listless; weakening or withering effect of pain; wan or pale, as after illness. PNP *mamae.*

mamake. 1. Redup. of *make, 1;* to die, of several; to wilt, of plants. PPN *mamate.* **2.** Colloquial for *makemake,* to want, like.

māmaki. A small native tree (*Pipturus albidus*) whose bark yielded a coarse tapa.

māmala. 1. Fragment, splinter, piece. PPN *mala.* **2.** (*Cap.*) Bay outside Honolulu Harbor, from about Pearl Harbor to Kewalo Basin.

māmala hoa. Var. of *māmala hoe.*

māmala hoe. Name of Kamehameha I's famous law of the splintered paddle (*lit.,* paddle fragment) which guaranteed the safety of the highways to all—as women, children, sick, and aged.

mamalaʻōlelo. Sentence, clause, phrase. *Lit.,* speech fragment.

māmalu. 1. Redup. of *malu;* protection, shade; shaded. **hoʻomāmalu.** To protect; to make shady; to cast gloom. **2.** Umbrella, parasol.

mamane. A native leguminous tree (*Sophora chrysophylla*).

māmao. Far, distant; high in rank. **hoʻomamao.** To keep away; to keep one's distance; to go far. PPN *mamaʻo.*

mamo. 1. A mostly black Hawaiian honeycreeper (*Drepanis pacifica*); its few yellow feathers above and below the tail were used in choicest featherwork. **2.** Descendant,

posterity. **3.** Var. of *maomao.* PPN *mamo.*

mamua. See *mua.*

mamuli. See *muli.*

mana. 1. Supernatural or divine power, mana, miraculous power; a powerful nation, authority; to give mana to; to have mana, power; possessed of mana, power. *Mana makua,* parental authority. **hoʻomana.** (a) To place in authority, empower. (b) To worship; religion, sect. *Hoʻomana Kepanī,* Buddhist; Buddhism. PPN *mana.* **2.** Branch, limb; crosspiece, as of the cross; a line projecting from another line; stream branch; road branch; variant, version, as of a tale; to branch out, spread out. PPN *manga.*

māna. A chewed mass, as of kava for drinking, coconut or *kukui* nut for medicine. *Māna ʻai,* food chewed by adult for child; any mouthful of food. PPN *maʻanga.*

mānā. Arid; desert.

mānai. Needle for stringing leis; to string leis.

manakā. Boresome, tiresome, dull, monotonous; bored, uninterested. **hoʻomanakā.** Same as *manakā;* to cause boredom.

manakō. Mango (*Mangifera indica*).

manakō-kāne. Chutney mango.

manakuke. Mongoose. *Eng.*

mānalo. Sweet, potable, of water that may be drunk but is not deliciously cool (*huʻihuʻi*). **hoʻomānalo.** To remove bitterness or saltiness, as of overly salty salmon. PNP *maangalo.*

mana lua. Two branches, fork, as in a road.

manamana. 1. Redup. of *mana, 1.* **hoʻomanamana.** To impart mana, as to idols or ob-

jects; superstitious. **2.** Redup.
of *mana, 2;* appendages,
branches, rays, forks; to
branch out. PPN *mangaman-
ga.* **3.** Finger.

manamana kuhi. Index finger;
hand of a watch or clock.

manamana lima. Finger.

manamana lima nui. Thumb.
Lit., big finger.

manamana nui. Big branch; big
toe, thumb.

manamana wāwae. Toe.

mana'o. Thought, idea, opinion,
theory, meaning, mind; desire; to think, consider. **ho-
'omana'o.** To remember, recall, commemorate. PPN *ma-
nako.*

mana'oha'i. Something to say,
thought to express.

mana'o ho'ohālikelike. Comparison.

mana'o ho'onalonalo. Hidden
meaning.

mana'o 'ino. Evil thought or
idea; hatred.

mana'o'i'o. Faith, confidence;
to have faith, confidence; to
believe. *Kumu mana'o'i'o,*
creed.

mana'olana. Hope, confidence;
to hope. *Lit.,* floating thought.

mana'o maoli. Literal meaning;
a real or true opinion.

māna'ona'o. Horrible, dreadful, horrifying, gruesome;
shocked, horrified; heartsick.
ho'omāna'ona'o. To cause a
sensation of horror, grief.

mana'o nui. Important matter
or idea, meaning.

mana'opa'a. Conviction, deter-
mination; convinced.

mana'o ulu wale. Whim, fancy,
impulse.

manauea, manauwea. A kind
of small red seaweed (*Graci-
laria coronopifolia*), today
often called *ogo* (Japanese,
dialectal).

manawa. **1.** Time, turn, season;
chronology. Cf. *ha'i manawa.*

2. Anterior fontanel in the
heads of infants; top of the
head of adults at position of
the fontanel. PPN *manawa.*

manawahua. Discomfort of the
stomach, with gas and often
diarrhea; to grieve. *Lit.,* swollen stomach.

mana wai. Stream branch.

manawa 'ino. Evil disposition,
hard feelings; time of storm.

manawakolu. Eternal.

manawa kūpono. Opportune
time, appropriate time, opportunity.

manawale'a. A generous heart;
charity; to give freely; gratis,
free.

manawanui. Patience, stead-
fastness; fortitude; to have
patience; patient, steadfast;
courageous and persevering.
Lit., large disposition. **ho-
'omanawanui.** Same as *manawanui* (very common); to try
one's patience. PEP *manawanui.*

mānele. Sedan chair, palanquin,
litter, stretcher; to carry on
a stretcher, bier, sedan chair.

manene. Shuddery sensation of
fear, as on looking over a
precipice or if confronted by
sudden danger; sensation of
disgust or repugnance; to
shudder, quake.

mane'o. Itch; itchy; smarting,
as the throat; prickly; sexually titillated; ticklish; tick-
ling. **ho'omane'o.** To cause
to itch; to tickle. PNP *man-
geo.*

mānewanewa. Grief, sorrow,
mourning; exaggerated ex-
pression of grief. **ho'omāne-
wanewa.** To display violent
grief.

mania. **1.** Shuddering sensation
as on looking down from a
great height, or on hearing a
saw filed; dizziness; dizzy; to
shudder. PPN *mania.* **2.** Inactive, drowsy, sleepy. **ho-**

'omania. To cause sleepiness, drowsiness.

mānienie. Bermuda grass (*Cynodon dactylon*).

manini. **1.** Small striped surgeonfish (*Acanthurus sandvicensis*), very common on Hawaiian reefs. PPN *manini*. **2.** Stingy. *Modern slang.*

manino. Var. of *malino*, calm. PPN *malino*, PNP *manino*.

manioka. Cassava or manioc (*Manihot esculenta*). *Eng.*

mano. Many, numerous; four thousand; thick. Cf. *kini*, *lau*. ho'omano. To increase; to do repeatedly or persistently. PPN *mano*.

manō. Shark, general name. PPN *mangoo*.

mānoa. Thick, solid, vast; depth, thickness. ho'omānoa. To thicken.

manō-kihikihi. Hammerhead shark (*Sphyrna lewini*). Lit., angular shark.

manomano. Redup. of *mano*; great; greatness; four thousand times four thousand.

manu. **1.** Bird; any winged creature; wing of a kite. PPN *manu*. **2.** Canoe end-piece part. PNP *manu*.

manuahi, manuwahi. Gratis, free of charge; adulterous. *Keiki manuahi*, illegitimate child.

manu-'ai-mīkana, manu-'ai-papaia. Linnet, house finch, or papaya bird (*Carpodacus mexicanus frontalis*). Lit., papaya-eating bird.

manu-aloha. Lovebird, parakeet; parrot.

manu-kapalulu. Quail. *Lit.*, whirr bird.

manukū. Dove, pigeon. *Lit.*, coo bird. (*Eng.*)

manu-mele. Songbird, especially canary.

manu-'ula'ula. Cardinal, redbird. *Lit.*, red bird.

manuwā, manua. Man-of-war; warship. *Eng.*

mao. Cleared, as rain; alleviated, as grief; to clear up, as rain; to pass, as sadness. PPN *mao*.

ma o. Because of, due to, by means of, through. Cf. *ma*, *at*.

ma'o. **1.** Green. Cf. *'ōma'oma'o*. **2.** Native cotton (*Gossypium tomentosum*). **3.** Same as *'ōma'o*, Hawaiian thrush. PEP *mako*.

ma'ō. See *'ō*, there.

mā'oi. Same as *maha'oi*, bold. ho'omā'oi. To act bold, impertinent.

maoli. Native, indigenous, genuine, true, real; very, really, truly. *Maika'i maoli*, very good indeed. PPN *ma(a)'oli*.

maomao. A damselfish (*Abudeduf abdominalis*).

ma'oma'o. Green, greenness. ho'oma'oma'o. To paint green, make green.

mā'ona (usually pronounced but not written *mā'ana*). Satisfied after eating, full, satisfying; to have eaten, to eat one's fill. ho'omā'ona. To eat all one wants, to feed all that is wanted. PPN *maakona*.

maopopo. To understand, recognize; clear; plainly, clearly. ho'omaopopo. To understand; to make plain or clear, tell clearly; to pay attention in order to understand.

māpala. Marble (*Eng.*), granite.

māpela, mabela. Var. of *māpala*.

māpu. Fragrance, especially windblown fragrance; wafted; dipping, swooping. Perhaps PPN *mapu*.

māpuana. Same as *māpu*. PPN *maapuna*.

māpuna. Bubbling spring.

mau. **1.** Always; steady; constant; to continue; continuation. **ho'omau.** To continue, keep on, persist, renew. PNP *mau.* 2. Stopped, as menstruation; snagged, caught, as a fish or hook; grounded, as a canoe; stuck, stalled, as a car. **ho'omau.** To make fast, as an anchor in sand; to cause to be grounded, stopped. PPN *ma'u.* 3. Particle marking plural used principally after the *k*-class possessives and demonstratives, numerals, and *he.* PEP *mau.*

ma'ū. Damp, wet, moist, cool, refreshing. **ho'oma'ū.** To dampen, moisten, irrigate, soak; to shade, cool.

māua. We (dual, exclusive). Probably PPN *kimarua;* PNP *kimaaua,* PEP *maaua.*

Maui. Name of one of the Hawaiian islands. Cf. *Māui,* the demigod.

Māui. Name of the famous demigod and trickster who snared the sun and discovered fire. PPN *Maaui.*

mauka. See *uka,* inland.

ma'ukele. Rain forest.

ma'ule. Faint, fainthearted, dispirited. **ho'oma'ule.** To cause fainting; to faint; to feign fainting.

mauli. Life, heart, seat of life; ghost, spirit. PPN *ma'uri.*

mauli'awa. Hiccough; dying gasp; to hiccough, gasp in dying.

ma'uma'u. Same as *'āma'uma'u,* ferns.

mauna. Mountain, mountainous region; mountainous. PPN *ma'unga.*

mauna-loa. Vines (*Dioclea violacea,* a sea bean, and *Canavalia cathartica*). Both, and especially the latter, have flowers used in intricate and beautiful leis.

Mauna Loa. Names of mountains on Hawai'i and Moloka'i and of a Moloka'i village. *Lit.,* long mountain.

maunu. Bait; objects used in sorcery, as hair, spittle, nail parings, excreta, clothing, food leavings. PPN *maaunu.*

māunu. To moult; to change skin, as of snakes. PPN *maunu.*

mau'u. General name for grasses, sedges, rushes, herbs. PPN *m(a, o)huku.*

mau'u-Kepanī. Velvet grass (*Zoysia tenuifolia*). *Lit.,* Japanese grass.

mau'u-malo'o. Hay, straw, any dry grass.

māwae. 1. Cleft, fissure, crack, as in rocks; to crack, split. 2. To separate, sort, select; to cleanse, as from defilement. Cf. *wae,* to select. PPN *maawae.*

mawaena. See *waena.*

mawaho. See *waho.*

me. 1. With. *A me,* and. PEP *me.* 2. Like, as. *Like me 'oe,* like you. Cf. *mehe.* PEP *me.*

mea. 1. Thing, person. Cf. *mea 'ole.* PPN *me'a* 2. Possessor of. Cf. *mea 'āina, mea hale.* 3. One who does (in compounds; see *mea hula, mea kia'i, mea oli*). 4. What-d'you-call-it, so-and-so (said when one is at a loss for a word or name); such and such. *'O mea mā,* so-and-so and the others. 5. Cause, reason; means of; because. *No ka mea,* because. 6. Reddish brown, yellowish white. PPN *mea.*

mea'ai. Food.

mea'ai māmā. Light refreshment.

mea'ai momona. Dessert.

mea 'āina. Landowner.

mea 'ē. Extraordinary, unusual, strange, wonderful; unusual person; stranger, alien.

mea hale. House owner; something belonging to a house.

meahou. News; new. *He aha ka meahou?* What's new?

mea hula. Hula dancer.

mea iki. Trifle, inconsequential thing. *He mea iki,* it's a trifle, you're welcome [sometimes said in reply to "thank you"].

meainu. Beverage, drink.

mea kākau. Writer, author.

meakanu. A plant.

mea kia'i. Guard, preserver, protection.

mea koho. Voter.

mea nui. Beloved person or thing; important person; thing of importance.

mea 'ole. Inconsequential, trifling, insignificant; null and void; a mere nothing.

mea oli. Chanter of *oli;* one with an *oli* chant in his honor; *oli* chanter.

mea'ono. Cake of any kind, pastry, cooky. *Lit.,* delicious thing.

mea'ono-kuki. Cooky.

mea'ono-pua'a. Chinese pork cake.

mea ulu. Vegetable, growing plant.

me'e. Hero.

mehameha. Loneliness, solitariness, hushed silence; lonely, solitary; silent, as during the hush of taboo. **ho'omehameha.** To cause silence, loneliness; to hush.

mehe. Like, as though. PEP *mese.*

meheu. Track, footprint, tracing; trodden, beaten, as a path; walked on. **ho'omeheu.** To make a track.

Mei. May. *Eng.*

meia. Mayor. *Eng.*

me ia. With him, her.

meka, mesa. Mass. *Pule meka,* mass.

mekala. 1. Also **medala.** Medal. *Eng.* 2. Also **metala.** Metal (*Eng.*); tag, as a dog license.

makenika. Mechanic. *Eng.*

mekia. 1. Major (the military title). *Eng.* 2. Also **Mesia.** (*Cap.*) Messiah. *Biblical.*

Mekiko. Mexico; Mexican. *Eng.*

Melanikia. Melanesia; Melanesian. *Eng.*

mele. 1. Song, chant of any kind, poem; to sing, chant (preceded by both *ke* and *ka*). **ho'omele.** To cause to sing or chant. 2. Yellow. 3. Merry. *Eng. Mele Kalīkimaka,* Merry Christmas. 4. (*Cap.*) Mary. *Eng.*

mele aupuni. National anthem.

mele haipule. Hymn, religious song.

mele ho'ohiamoe keiki. Lullaby. *Lit.,* song to put children to sleep.

mele ho'oipoipo. Love song. *Lit.,* wooing song.

mele ho'onānā keiki. Lullaby, song to soothe children.

mele inoa. Name chant, i.e., chant composed in honor of a person, as a chief. Also called *inoa.*

mele kāhea. Chant for admittance to an old-time hula school. *Lit.,* calling song.

Mele Kalīkimaka. Merry Christmas. *Eng.*

mele kanikau. Dirge, mourning song.

melekule. Pot marigold (*Calendula officinalis*).

mele ma'i. See *ma'i, 2.*

melemele. 1. Yellow. **ho'omelemele.** To color or paint yellow. 2. (*Cap.*) Name of a star. PEP *Mele.*

meli. Bee, honey. *Nalo-meli,* bee. *Wai meli,* honey.

melia. All species and varieties of *Plumeria;* plumeria, frangipani.

mene. 1. Dullness, bluntness; dull, blunt, as a knife. **ho'omene.** To make dull; dull. 2. To move back, step back, shrink. PPN *mene.*

Menehune. Legendary race of small people who worked at

night building fishponds, roads, temples; if the work was not finished in one night, it remained unfinished. PEP *M(a, e)n(a, e)fune*.

me'o. To nag and tease, usually indirectly; to drool at the mouth while watching, as food being prepared; to linger about with greedy eyes.

me'ome'o. Redup. of *me'o*.

mī. 1. Urine; to urinate (less used than *mimi*). **2.** Seventh note in musical scale, ti. **3.** Mister. *Eng. Mī Laiana*, Mr. Lyons.

-mia. Suffix corresponding to *'ia*, but closely bound to a base. See *inumia*. PPN *-mia*.

mihi. Repentance; to repent, apologize, be sorry, regret; to confess, as to a priest. PNP *misi*.

mika. Mister. *Eng.*

mikana. Papaya (*Carica papaya*).

mikanele. Missionary. *Eng.* Also *mikinele, mikionali*. **ho'omikanele.** To act as a missionary; to be a goody-goody.

miki. 1. Quick, active, nimble, prompt, alert, fast and efficient in work; speed, alertness. **2.** To suck in, dip in; to shrink, as clothes or as salt beef in boiling; to spring together, as sides of a steel trap; to draw in, as an octopus; to recede, as an undertow; evaporated, as water by boiling. PPN *miti*.

miki'ala. Alert, prompt; early on hand.

miki'ao. Claw, nail, as of finger or toe. PEP *mitikao*.

mikilana, misilana. Chinese rice flower (*Aglaia odorata*), a shrub with dark, shiny leaves and fragrant flowers. (*Chinese, mei-sui-lan*.)

mikimiki. Redup. of *miki, 1, 2*.

mikinele. Same as *mikanele*, missionary.

mīkini. Machine (*Eng.*), motor.

mīkini helu. Adding machine, comptometer.

mīkini holoi. Washing machine.

mīkini humuhumu. Sewing machine.

mīkini kikokiko hua. Typewriter.

mīkini 'oki mau'u. Lawn mower. *Lit.*, grass-cutting machine.

mīkini pa'i nūpepa. Printing press. *Lit.*, machine to print newspapers.

mikinolia. Magnolia.

mikioi. Dainty and neat in craftsmanship, or in doing anything; excellently made, as result of workmanship. **ho'omikioi.** To do neatly and skillfully.

mikiona, misiona. Mission. *Eng.*

mikionali, misionari. Missionary. *Eng.* Also, *mikanele, mikinele*.

miko. 1. Seasoned with salt; salted. **ho'omiko.** To season with salt. **2.** To kink, snarl, become ensnared; kink.

mile. Mile. *Eng.*

mili. To handle, feel of, fondle, caress, as a beloved child; fondled, beloved. PPN *mili*.

mili 'apa. Slow, dilatory.

mililani. To praise, exalt; to give thanks; to treat as a favorite.

milimili. Redup. of *mili*; toy, plaything; favorite, beloved.

miliona. Million. *Eng.*

milo. 1. A shade tree (*Thespesia populnea*) growing usually near the beach; its beautiful wood was made into calabashes. PPN *milo*. **2.** Curl; to curl, twist, as sennit strands; to whirl, as water; abortion. PPN *milo*.

milu. 1. Soft, rotten. **2.** (*Cap.*)

Underworld, ruler of underworld.

mimi. Urine; to urinate. **ho-'omimi.** To cause urination; to help to urinate, as a child. PPN *mimi.*

mina. Same as *minamina,* 1, 2, 3. PEP *mina.*

minamina. 1. To regret, be sorry; to grieve for something that is lost; regret, sorrow. 2. To prize greatly, value greatly, especially something in danger of being lost; value, worth. 3. Saving, economical, miserly; covetous of things that one values; economy, thrift.

mino. Dimple, depression, dent; dimpled, wrinkled.

mino'aka. Smile; to smile. *Lit.,* laughing dimple. **ho'omino-'aka.** To cause to smile; to smile a little.

minuke, minute. Minute. *Eng.*

mio. 1. To disappear swiftly; to move swiftly, as a stream of water; to make off with quickly; to steal; to depart quickly. 2. Narrow, pointed, tapering.

miona. 1. Swift disappearance or movement. 2. Crease in the buttocks.

miula. Mule, ass. *Eng.*

miulana. Orange or white champak or mulang (*Michelia champaca* and *M. alba*), tall trees from the Himalayas related to the magnolia; they bear very fragrant orange or yellow flowers. The white-flowered species is the Chinese *pak-lan,* also called *pakalana* by Hawaiians.

mō. Short for *moku,* 1, 2. *Mōkapu* (place name), taboo district.

mō-. 1. Short for *mo'o,* succession. Cf. *mo'olelo,* story. 2. Short for *mo'o,* 1, 2, 3, 4. *Mō-'ili'ili* (place name), pebble lizard.

moa. Chicken. PPN *moa.*

mo'a. Cooked; burned, as by sun; cooking. **ho'omo'a.** To cook.

Moa'e. Trade wind. See *a'e,* 2.

mōakaaka, moakaka. Clear, plain, intelligible; clarity. Cf. *akaaka.* **ho'omōakaaka.** Explanation, definition; to explain clearly, clarify, define.

moa kāne. Rooster, cock. *Lit.,* male chicken.

moamoa. To act the part of a cock; to care for, attend to; to supply with food, as a child or ward. **ho'omoamoa.** To accompany, as a cock with hens; to care for, protect, cherish. 2. Same as *pahu,* 5, boxfishes. PPN *moa.*

moana. 1. Ocean, open sea. PPN *moana.* 2. Campground, consultation place for chiefs. **ho'omoana.** To camp. 3. Broad, wide, extended, expansive, spread out. **ho'omoana.** To spread down, as mats.

moani. Light or gentle breeze, usually associated with fragrance; wafted fragrance; to blow perfume.

moano. Two species of goatfish (*Parupeneus multifasciatus* and *P. bifasciatus*).

moa wahine. Hen. *Lit.,* female chicken.

moe. 1. To sleep, lie down; to lie in wait, ambush; to prostrate oneself, as before a chief; to lay down, as cards; to sit on eggs. **ho'omoe.** To put to sleep, to lay down, to set, as a hen or fish net; to "drop" a matter; to defer, postpone, to table, as a motion. PPN *mohe.* 2. To marry, mate with, sleep with; marriage. **ho'omoe.** To arrange a match. 3. Bed, sleeping place. 4. Dream.

moe 'ino. Nightmare; bad

dream; to toss, turn while sleeping.

moe ipo. To have an affair; to sleep with a lover; to commit adultery.

moekolohe. Adultery; to commit adultery, fornicate; adulterous. *Lit.*, mischievous mating. **ho'omoekolohe.** To lead into adultery.

moelepo. Earth sleeper; to sleep in the earth. *Fig.*, the dead; dirty, shiftless individual.

moemoe. Ambush, to lie in ambush; to lurk. **ho'omoemoe.** To cause to lie down; to hush or put to sleep; to arrange a match.

moena. Mat. Cf. *moe*, to lie down. PPN *moenga*.

moena weleweka. Soft carpet of any kind. *Lit.*, velvet (*Eng.*) mat.

moe paipai. Cradle. *Lit.*, rocking bed.

moe'uhane. Dream; to dream. *Lit.*, soul sleep.

mōhā. Fully developed, as a flower; of fine physique, as a person.

mōhai. Sacrifice, offering; to offer a sacrifice. Cf. *hai*.

mōhai aloha. Free-will offering; love offering.

mōhai ho'omalu. Peace offering.

mōhala. Unfolded, as flower petals; blossoming, opening up; blooming, as a youth just past adolescence; shining forth, as a light; appearing clear, as a thought; evolved, developed. **ho'omōhala.** To open, unfold, spread, recover; development, etc.

mōhalu. 1. Loose, slack; at ease, unrestrained, at liberty; comfortable. *Hale mōhalu*, house of relaxation. **ho'omōhalu.** To slacken, relax; to cause relaxation, ease. 2. To

open, unfold, as flowers. Also *mōhala*.

moho. 1. Candidate, as in politics; representative selected to participate in a race, or wrestling or betting contest. 2. Hawaiian rail (*Pennula sandwichensis*), an extinct flightless bird. PPN *moso*. 3. To unfold, of leaves. PEP *mo-(f,s)o*.

moi. Threadfin fish (*Polydactylus sexfilis*). PEP *moi*.

mō'ī. King, sovereign, ruler, queen.

mō'ī wahine. Queen.

mōkākī. Scattered, littered; disorder.

mokihana. A native tree (*Pelea anisata*), found only on Kaua'i, its small, leathery, anise-scented fruits are strung in leis.

mōkio. 1. To pucker or contract, as the lips for whistling, or the nostrils after diving. 2. Also **motio.** Motion. *Eng.*

moko. Same as *mokomoko*. PPN *moto*.

mokomoko. Rough, hand-to-hand fighting of any kind, whether boxing (*ku'i*) or free-for-all wrestling; a fighter, boxer; to box, fight.

moku. 1. To cut, sever, amputate, break in two, as a rope; to break loose, as a stream after heavy rains, or as a bound person. *Moku ka pawa*, ·dawn breaks. **ho-'omoku.** To cut and divide; a cutting, division, separation. PPN *motu*. 2. District, island, section; forest, grove; severed portion, fragment, cut. Cf. *mokupuni, momoku*. **ho'omoku.** To place an individual in charge of a *moku*, district. PPN *motu*. 3. Ship.

mokuahi. Steamship. *Lit.*, fire ship.

moku'āina. State, as of the

United States; district, island.

mokuhia. Passive/imperative of *moku*, 1. PPN *motusia*.

moku kaua. Battleship, warship.

moku kia kahi. One-masted ship, sloop.

moku kia kolu. Three-masted ship, bark.

moku kia lua. Two-masted ship, as a schooner; brig.

mokukolo. Tugboat.

moku lawe ʻōhua. Passenger ship.

moku lawe ukana. Freighter.

mokulele. Airplane.

mokumāhu. Steamship.

mokuna. Division, boundary, as of land; severed portion, cut piece, part; chapter, section, as of a book.

moku ʻō koholā. Whaling ship. *Lit.*, ship for piercing whales.

moku pāpapa. Low reef island.

moku peʻa. Sailing vessel.

mokupuni. Island.

mole. 1. Tap root, main root; bottom, as of a pit or of a glass; ancestral root; foundation, source, cause. PEP *mole*. 2. Smooth, round, bald. **hoʻomole.** To smooth.

mōlehu. Twilight, dusk; tipsy. Cf. *lehu*, ashes.

molemole. Redup. of *mole*, 2. **hoʻomolemole.** To smooth. PPN *molemole*.

Molemona, Moremona. Mormon. *Eng.*

mōlia. To set apart for the gods; to sacrifice or offer to the gods; to bless; to curse. PPN *mori*.

Molokaʻi. Name of a Hawaiian island.

molowā. Lazy.

momi. Pearl.

momoe. Redup. and plural of *moe*, 1, 2. PNP *momoe*.

momoku. Redup. of *moku*, 1; broken fragments, severed pieces; breaking forth, as of water from a dam.

momona. 1. Fat; fertile, rich, as soil; fruitful. **hoʻomomona.** To fatten, fertilize. *Hoʻomomona lepo*, fertilizer; to fertilize the soil. PPN *mo(o)mona*. 2. Sweet. **hoʻomomona.** To sweeten; candy.

moni. To swallow, gulp down, absorb. *Moni ka hāʻae*, to water at the mouth; *lit.*, swallow the saliva. PEP *moni*.

moʻo. 1. Lizard, reptile of any kind, dragon, serpent; water supernatural (extremely common in legends). PPN *moko*. 2. Succession, series, especially a genealogical line. Cf. *moʻo aliʻi, moʻoʻōlelo*. **hoʻomoʻo.** To follow a course, continue a procedure. 3. Story, tradition (less common than *moʻolelo*). 4. Narrow strip of land, smaller than an *ʻili*. Also called *moʻo ʻāina*.

moʻo aliʻi. Genealogy of chiefs, history of chiefs; chiefly line of succession.

moʻo kūʻauhau. Genealogical succession.

moʻolelo. Story, tale, history, tradition, legend, journal, record, article; minutes, as of a meeting (from *moʻo ʻōlelo*, succession of talk).

moʻolelo ʻahaʻōlelo lāhui. Congressional record. *Lit.*, national legislative journal.

moʻolelo hakuwale. Fiction; an invented story.

moʻolelo pōkole. Short story, anecdote.

moʻo lio. Sea horse. *Lit.*, horse reptile.

moʻoʻōlelo. Same as *moʻolelo*.

moʻopuna. Grandchild; grandniece or grandnephew; relatives two generations later, whether blood or adopted; descendant; posterity. *Kāna moʻopuna*, his grandchild. **hoʻomoʻopuna.** To claim a *moʻopuna* relationship; to address and treat as a *mo-*

'opuna, as from affection. PPN *mokopuna*.

mo'opuna kāne. Grandson.

mo'opuna wahine. Granddaughter.

mouo. Buoy; float, as on a fishing net; board or anything to float on; to lie at anchor.

mū. 1. General name for destructive insects that eat wood, cloth, or plants; cane borer; caterpillar in the cocoon stage. PPN *muu.* **2.** Silent; to shut the lips and make no sound. **ho'omū.** To sit in silence; to refuse to answer; speechless. **3.** Gathered together, of crowds of people. Cf. *mumulu.* **ho'omū.** Same as above; multitude; to cause a gathering. **4.** (*Cap.*) Legendary people, Kaua'i. **5.** A fish (*Monotaxis grandoculis*). PPN *muu.*

mua. Before; front; first, foremost; previously, beforehand; oldest, older brother or sister; senior branch of a family; leader, senior partner, senior; more than. *I mua! Mamua!* Forward! **ho'omua.** To push forward, to do something first; to claim to be senior. PPN *mu'a.*

mūhe'e. 1. Cuttlefish, squid. PPN *nguu feke*, PEP *mu(u)-feke.* **2.** Mother-of-pearl lure.

mui. Assembled, gathered together; an assembly. PNP *mui.*

mūkā. Sound of lips popped open; clicking sound, as in urging a horse to speed up; smack, as in eating.

mūkī. Sucking noise made by pursing the lips and expelling or drawing in the air, as in kissing; to suck into the mouth, as when lighting a

pipe; to sip, as birds sip honey.

mūki'i. To tie; tether. Also **nāki'i, hīki'i.**

muku. Cut short, shortened, amputated; at an end, ceased; anything cut off short. PPN *mutu.*

mukumuku. Fish species. PPN *mutumutu.*

muli. After, behind, afterward; last, following behind; younger; youngest; stern of a canoe. *Mamuli o kona akamai,* because of his cleverness. PPN *muri.*

muli hope. Youngest child; very last.

muliwai. River, river mouth; pool near mouth of a stream, as behind a sand bar, enlarged by ocean water left there by high tide; estuary. PPN *muriwai.*

mumuhu. Buzzing, humming sound, as of flies; to swarm. PPN *musu.*

mumuku. Redup. of *muku;* amputated, maimed; premature, as a baby.

mumule. Speechless, silent, taciturn, mute, sullen, sulky.

mumulu. To swarm, as flies, bees, mosquitoes.

mu'o. Leaf bud; to bud, of a leaf; younger branch of a family. PPN *muka.*

mu'umu'u. 1. Cut off, shortened, amputated, maimed; person with arms or legs missing, amputee. *Hula mu'umu'u,* a sitting dance. PNP *muku.* **2.** A woman's underslip or chemise; a long, loose gown, so called because formerly the yoke was omitted (cf. *mu'umu'u, 1*), and sometimes the sleeves were short. Cf. *holokū.*

N

na. By, for, belonging to (*a*-class). PEP *na(a)*.

-na. 1. Nominalizer. PPN *-nga*. 2. Passive/imperative suffix. PPN-*na*. 3. Third person singular possessive. PPN *-na*.

nā. 1. Calmed, quieted; settled, as a claim. **ho'onā.** To relieve pain, soothe, quiet; to settle a claim. PPN *na'a*. 2. To moan, groan, wail. PPN *ngaa*. 3. Plural definite article preceding nouns. PNP *na(a)*. 4. Demonstrative particle indicating the addressee. PPN *na(a)*.

na'ana'au. Small intestine.

na'au. Intestines, bowels; mind, heart; of the heart or mind. PPN *ngaakau*.

na'auao. Learned, intelligent; learning, science. Cf. *'imi na'auao*. *Lit.*, daylight mind. **ho'ona'auao.** To educate, instruct; educational.

na'au ho'oki'eki'e. Conceited, proud; proud heart.

na'au 'ino. Malicious; evil heart.

na'aukake. Sausage, wiener. *Lit.*, sausage (*Eng.*) intestines.

na'aumoa. Appendix. *Lit.*, chicken intestines.

na'aupō. Ignorant, unenlightened; ignorance. *Lit.*, night mind. Cf. *na'auao*. **ho'ona'aupō.** To cause or feign ignorance; ignorant.

na'au pono. Upright, just; right-minded.

nae. Shortness of breath; to puff. PNP *nae*.

na'e. But, yet, furthermore, still.

naha. 1. Bent, curved, bow-legged. 2. A chief whose parents were uncle and niece or aunt and nephew.

nahā. Cracked, broken, as a dish; smashed to bits, as masonry; to act as a purgative; to split. *Lā'au nahā*, purgative. **ho'onahā.** To smash, crack, split; to take a purgative.

nahae. Torn, rent; tear; to tear. See *mahae*.

naheka, nahesa. Snake.

nahele. Forest, grove, wilderness; trees, shrubs, vegetation, weeds. PEP *ngahele*.

nāhelehele. Redup. of *nahele*; weeds.

nahenahe. Soft, sweet, as music or a gentle voice; soft, as fine cloth; soft-spoken. PPN *ngasengase*.

nāhi. 1. Some, few, the little (contraction of *nā*, the, and *wahi*, little). PPN *ngaafi*. 2. The fires (contraction of *nā ahi*).

naho. Hollow; deep-set, as eyes of a starving person; eye sockets.

nāholo. To flee, of several; to run away; gone away. **ho'onāholo.** To cause to run, to chase. PPN *ngaasolo*.

nāholoholo. Redup. of *nāholo*.

nahu. To bite; to sting, as beating rain; pain, as of stomach ache or of childbirth. **ho'onahu.** To bite, cause a stomach ache.

nahunahu. Redup. of *nahu*; to suffer pangs of childbirth.

na'i. 1. To conquer, take by force; conqueror. PEP *ngaki*. 2. To strive to obtain, endeavor to examine or understand.

nai'a. Porpoise.

naio. 1. Pinworm, as in the rectum; larvae, as of mosquitos. PEP *ngaio*. 2. The bastard sandalwood (*Myoporum sandwicense*), a native tree. PEP *ngaio*.

naka. 1. To quiver, shake, as jello or as with cold or fear; shaky, unsteady, shivering. **2.** To crack open, as earth from the heat. **3.** A sea creature. PEP *ngata.*

nakeke. Rattling, as of a window; rustling, as of paper. **hoʻonakeke.** To make a rattling or rustling noise. PPN *ngatete.*

nakele. Soft, boggy, slippery; yielding, sinking in.

naki. Same as *nākiʻi.* PEP *nati.*

nākiʻi. To tie. Cf. *nīkiʻi.*

nākiʻikiʻi. Redup. of *nākiʻi.*

-nakoa. hoʻonakoa. Brave, daring.

nākolo. Rumbling, roaring, as of surf or thunder; reverberating.

nākolokolo. Redup. of *nākolo.*

naku. To root, wallow, as a hog; to tread, trample, push, as through mud or grass; to struggle; to roil, as water. PPN *natu.*

nākuʻi. To rumble, roar, thrum; rumbling; beating, as of the heart.

nakulu. Dripping, as water; patter, clatter, echo; rumbling, as the stomach; grumbling; to spread or circulate, as rumor.

nali. To nibble, gnaw. PPN *ngali.*

nalinali. Redup. of *nali.*

nalo. 1. Lost, vanished, concealed, forgotten; to pass away, disappear. **hoʻonalo.** To cause to be lost. PPN *ngalo.* **2.** The common housefly and other similar two-winged flies. PPN *lango.*

nalohia. Passive/imperative of *nalo, 1.* PEP *ngalo(f,s)ia.*

nalo-hope-ʻeha. Hornet and other Hymenoptera. *Lit.,* fly with stinging posterior.

nalo-meli. Honeybee. *Lit.,* honey fly.

nalo-meli mōʻī wahine. Queen bee.

nalonalo. Redup. of *nalo, 1.* **hoʻonalonalo.** Hidden; to cause to disappear. Cf. *ʻōlelo hoʻonalonalo, manaʻo hoʻonalonalo.*

nalowale. Lost, gone, forgotten, vanished; disappeared.

nalu. 1. Wave, surf; full of waves; to form waves. **hoʻonalu.** To form waves. PPN *ngalu.* **2.** To ponder. PPN *nanunga.* **3.** Meconium. PEP *nanu.*

nalulu. Dull headache; dull pain in the abdomen. **hoʻonalulu.** To cause a pain in head or stomach. PNP *ngaalulu.*

namu. 1. Unintelligible muttering, gibberish; any foreign language, especially English; to speak gibberish or a foreign language. *Namu haole,* English. **hoʻonamu.** To pretend to speak in a foreign language, to mutter, speak gibberish. PNP *namu.* **2.** To nibble; to chew with closed mouth.

namunamu. Redup. of *namu, 1, 2;* to grumble, complain.

namu-paʻi-ʻai, namu-paʻi-kalo. Pidgin English. *Lit.,* hard-poi gibberish, hard-taro gibberish.

nana. For him, her, it; by him, her, it (*a*-class). PEP *nana.*

nāna. Same as *nana.*

nanā. Snarling; to strut, as one looking for a fight. **hoʻonanā.** Aggressive, looking for a fight, threatening.

nānā. To look at, observe, see; to care for, pay attention to, take care of. **hoʻonānā.** To cause to look, show.

nānahu. Var. of *lānahu.* **hoʻonānahu.** To turn into charcoal, as burnt wood. PEP *ngaalahu.* Proto Hawaiian-Marquesan, *ngaanahu.*

nānaina. General appearance, view.

nānā-lā. Sunflower. *Lit.*, sun-gazer.

nānā maka. To look at without helping; indifference to one in trouble.

nananana. 1. Spider. 2. Var. of *lanalana, 1, 2.*

nānā 'ole. Disregard, heedless disregard; to pay no attention to.

nānā pono. To watch carefully, pay particular attention to, note carefully.

nane. Riddle, puzzle; parable, allegory; to riddle, speak in parables. **ho'onane.** To make riddles, speak in parables.

nanea. Of absorbing interest; fascinating, enjoyable; repose, leisure; relaxed; engaged, busy with. **ho'onanea.** To pass the time in ease, peace, and pleasure. PNP *nanea.*

naneha'i. Problem, riddle to be solved. *Lit.*, telling riddle.

nane huna. Hidden riddle, conundrum.

nanenane. Redup. of *nane.* **ho-'onanenane.** Same as *ho-'onane;* puzzling, riddling; figurative.

nani. Beauty, glory, splendor; beautiful, pretty, splendid. **ho'onani.** To beautify, adorn, decorate; to glorify, honor, exalt; decorative, glorifying.

nani-ahiahi. The four o'clock (*Mirabilis jalapa*). *Lit.*, evening beauty.

nani-ali'i. Allamandas with large yellow flowers (*Allamanda cathartica* and some varieties). *Lit.*, chiefly beauty.

nani-mau-loa. An everlasting or strawflower (*Helichrysum bracteatum*); also called *pua-pepa.*

nanue. Var. of *nenue.* PNP *na-nue.*

nao. 1. Ripple; ridge, as of twilled cloth or a tapa beater;

groove; thread of a screw; grooved. *Kui nao,* screw; *lit.*, nail with thread. PEP *ngao.* 2. To thrust the hands into an opening, as in fishing; to probe. PEP *nao.*

na'o. Spittle, phlegm, mucus; slimy. PPN *ngako.*

naonao. 1. Ants. Also called *nonanona.* 2. Redup. of *nao, 1, 2.*

na'ona'o. Redup. of *na'o.*

naonao-lele. Termite. *Lit.*, flying ant.

nao wili. A bit for a drill. *Lit.*, twisting thread.

napa. 1. Uneven, bent, crooked, out of shape; warped. 2. Flexible, springy, elastic. 3. Delay. **ho'onapa.** To cause delay.

napanapa. Redup. of *napa, 1, 2;* to writhe and twist, as an eel.

nape. Bending and swaying, as coconut fronds; surging, as the sea; to rise and fall, as the chest in breathing; yielding, springy.

napenape. Redup. of *nape;* fluttering, flickering.

napo'o. Cavity, hollow, depression; armpit; to sink, go down, set (of the sun), to enter or sink out of sight.

nāpo'opo'o. Redup. of *napo'o.*

nau. To chew, munch, masticate, gnash the teeth; grinder, as of a sugar mill. *Nau kamu,* to chew gum. PPN *ngau.*

nāu. Yours, belonging to you, for you, by you (singular, *a*-class). PEP *na(a)u.*

na'u. Mine, belonging to me, for me, by me (singular, *a*-class). PEP *naku.*

naue, nauwe. To move, shake, tremble; to quake, as the earth; to vibrate; to march; loose and insecure, as a tooth. **ho'onaue.** To cause to shake, revolve, sway, rock, etc. PPN *ngaue.*

nāueue, nauwuewe. Redup. of *naue.*

nauki. Impatient, irritable, cross. **hoʻonauki.** Causing irritation; aggravating, annoying.

nāuki. Intensive of *nauki;* vexation, anger.

nāukiuki. Redup. of *nauki.* **hoʻonāukiuki.** Redup. of *hoʻonauki.*

nāulu. Sudden shower; showery; to shower.

naupaka. Native species of mountain or seashore shrubs (*Scaevola*); the small, whitish flowers look like half flowers. PEP *naupaka.*

naupaka-kahakai. The beach *naupaka.*

naupaka-kuahiwi. All mountain species of *naupaka.*

nāwali. Weak, feeble, infirm, limp; weakness. **hoʻonāwali.** To cause weakness; to enfeeble; to feign weakness. See *wali.* PPN *ngaawari.*

nāwaliwali. Redup. of *nāwali,* weak.

neʻe. Moving along little by little or by fits and starts; to step, hitch along; to push along, as work; to squirm. **hoʻoneʻe.** To cause to move, hitch along, push ahead. PNP *neke.*

neʻehope. To retreat, move backward; to back up, as a car. **hoʻoneʻehope.** To back up, as a car. *Hoʻoneʻehope i ke kaʻa,* back up the car.

neʻemua. To advance, go forward, progress. **hoʻoneʻemua.** To cause progress.

neʻeneʻe. 1. Redup. of *neʻe;* to edge along. PNP *nekeneke.* **2.** Surgeonfish (*Acanthurus olivaceus*).

nehe. 1. To rustle, as leaves or the sea; rumbling; groping with the hands, as in searching. **2.** Taffeta, so called because it rustles (*nehe*).

nehinei. Yesterday (usually preceded by particle *i*).

nehu. A small fish (*Stolephorus purpureus*) similar to the herring; the most important tuna-bait fish in Hawaii.

nei. 1. To rumble, as an earthquake; sighing, as of the wind. **2.** This here. Cf. *ke* (verb) *nei. Hawaiʻi nei,* this Hawaiʻi. PPN *eni,* PNP *nei.* **3.** Last. *I ka pō nei,* last night.

neʻi. Here, this place (often preceded by *i, ma, o*). Cf. *ʻaneʻi, ʻoneʻi.*

neia. This. Same as *kēia.*

nele. Lacking, destitute, deprived of, needy, wanting, without. **hoʻonele.** To deprive, make destitute; to deny, impeach. PEP *ngele.*

nema. Criticizing; critical; to criticize, find fault, censure.

nemanema. Redup. of *nema.*

nemo. Smooth, smoothly polished; rounded smooth, bare. **hoʻonemo.** To polish, smooth.

nemonemo. Redup. of *nemo.*

nene. Same as *manene.* PPN *nene.*

nēnē. 1. To chirp, as a cricket; to croak, as a mudhen; crying, as in distress; rumor, gossip; to be attracted to; to cherish. **hoʻonēnē.** Same as above. **2.** Hawaiian goose (*Branta sandvicensis*).

nenue. Rudder fish (*Kyphosus cinerascens* and *Sectator ocyurus*); also *nanue.* PEP *nanue.*

neo. Empty, bare, desolated; nothing, naught; getting nowhere. **hoʻoneo.** To lay waste, make destitute; desolation.

newa. 1. War club; policeman's club. **2.** To reel, stagger; dizziness, vertigo; dizzy. **3.** (*Cap.*) A constellation, probably the Southern Cross.

newanewa. Redup. of *newa,* 2.

newe. Plump; filled out, full, as a pregnant woman.

newenewe. Redup. of *newe.*

nia. Smooth, round, bald; calm, as a smooth sea. **hoʻonia.** To make smooth and even, as in carving. PEP *nia.*

nīao. Mewing, purring.

nīʻau. 1. Coconut-leaf midrib; rib of an umbrella. PEP *niikau.* 2. Ramrod.

nīʻau kāhili. Broom made of coconut-leaf midribs tied together at one end.

nīʻau kani. A true Jew's harp. *Lit.*, sounding coconut midrib.

nīʻaupiʻo. Offspring of the marriage of a brother and sister, or half-brother and half-sister. *Lit.*, bent coconut midrib, i.e., of the same stalk.

nīʻau pūlumi. Broom straw. *Lit.*, broom (*Eng.*) coconut-leaf midrib.

nīele. To ask questions; inquisitive; to quiz, pump. As an exclamation of annoyance: you are too inquisitive! **hoʻonīele.** Questioning, especially by leading up indirectly rather than directly; curious.

nieniele. Redup. of *nīele;* to investigate.

nihi. 1. Edge, brink, rim, border; sideways, on edge, standing on edge. Also *lihi.* PEP *nifi.* 2. Stealthily, quietly; creeping silently and softly, as on tiptoe; circumspect; with discrimination.

nihinihi. Redup. of *nihi,* 1, 2; fastidious.

niho. Tooth; toothed; nipper, as of an insect; claw, as of a crab; tusk; stones set interlocking, as in a wall; biting, of the teeth. **hoʻoniho.** To lay stones interlocking; to set stones, as in a fence. PPN *nifo.*

nihoa. 1. Passive/imperative of *niho;* toothed, notched, jag-ged; firmly imbedded and interlocked, as stones in a fence. 2. (*Cap.*) Name of an island between Kauaʻi and Midway.

niho ʻelepani. Elephant tusk, ivory.

niho hoʻokomo. False tooth.

niho huʻi. Toothache; having a toothache.

nihoniho. Set with teeth, as a saw; toothed, notched; scalloped, as lace; scalloped, as potatoes. **hoʻonihoniho.** To make into a toothed, scalloped, notched design; to make teeth.

niho ʻoki. Shark's-tooth knife, used formerly for wood carving and cutting hair. *Lit.*, cutting tooth.

niho palaoa. Whale tooth, whale-tooth pendant, a symbol of royalty.

niho puaʻa. Pig tusk, especially that worn as an ornament.

niki. Same as *nīkiʻi.*

nīkiʻi. To tie, as a rope or knot. Also *hīkiʻi, hīkiʻikiʻi, mūkiʻi, nākiʻi, nākiʻikiʻi, niki, nikiniki.*

nikiniki. Redup. of *niki.*

ninaninau. Redup. of *nīnau.*

nīnau. Question; to ask a question; interrogation; interrogating. Cf. *noi,* to ask for something. **hoʻonīnau.** To ask a question; to have questions asked.

nīnau hōʻike. Interrogation, usually oral; quiz, examination; catechism. *Lit.*, revealing questions.

nini. 1. Ointment, balm; to apply ointment; to pour, spill. 2. Fence, line of stones; pavement. Cf. *pā-nini.*

ninini. To pour. PPN *lilingi.*

niniu. Redup. of *niu, 2;* to spin; worried, sad; dizzy; dizziness; blurred, indistinct. **hoʻoniniu.** To cause dizziness; to spin, as a top.

ni'o. Highest point; to reach the summit.

nioi. Any kind of red pepper.

nioi-pepa. Chili pepper.

nioi-pūha'uha'u. Bell pepper or sweet pepper.

nipo. 1. To yearn for; to be in love with; to love, long for. **ho'onipo.** To make love, court. 2. Drowsy, languid, sleepy. **ho'onipo.** To cause sleepiness.

niponipo. Redup. of *nipo*, 1, 2.

niu. 1. The coconut. *Wai niu*, coconut water. *Wai o ka niu*, coconut cream. PPN *niu*. 2. Spinning, whirling. Cf. *niniu*.

niuhi. A large, gray, man-eating shark. PPN *neiufi*, PNP *naiufi*, PEP *niufi*.

niu kahiki. Date palm. *Lit.*, foreign coconut.

niu malo'o. Copra, dry coconut meat.

no. Of, for, because of; resulting from, concerning, about, from (*o*-class). *No laila lākou?* They are from there? PEP *no(o)*.

nō. Intensifying particle. *Maika'i nō*, quite good, very good. *'O au noho'i*, really me.

noa. Freed of taboo, released from restrictions; to adjourn, as a meeting. **ho'onoa.** To cause to cease, of a taboo; to free from taboo. PPN *noa*.

noe. Mist, rain spray; to form a mist. *Ua noe*, misty rain. **ho'onoe.** To form mist, vapor, fog. PEP *noe*.

no'eau. Clever, skillful, wise. *'Ōlelo no'eau*, wise or entertaining proverb, saying.

nohea. Handsome, lovely, of fine appearance.

no hea. From where, whence.

noho. 1. Seat, chair, stool, bench, saddle; to sit. 2. To live, dwell; to be in session; to stay; to marry. **ho'onoho.** To take up residence; to install, establish, locate, rule;

to set, as type. PPN *nofo*. 3. To be, act as (followed by a complement). See *noho ali'i*. 4. Conduct, bearing, condition, way of life.

noho ali'i. Throne; reign, chieftainship; to reign, to act as chief.

noho aloha. Dwelling at peace, friendly relationship.

noho aupuni. To rule; a reign.

noho hale. House dweller.

noho huila. Wheel chair.

noho'i. See *nō*.

noho 'ie. Wicker chair.

noho kai. Dweller on the seashore; to live by the sea.

noho kālele. Armchair.

noho kāne. To marry, of a woman; to live with a man.

noho lio. Saddle.

noho loa. To remain long, permanently, for life.

noho-mālie. The yellow oleander or be-still tree (*Thevetia peruviana*). *Lit.*, be still.

nohona. Dwelling, residence, seat, mode of life, relationship. PEP *nofonga*.

nohonoho. Redup. of *noho*. **ho'onohonoho.** Redup. of *ho'onoho;* to arrange, classify.

noho paipai. Rocking chair.

noho papa. Arranged in order, as feathers in a hatband, shingles on a roof. **ho'onoho papa.** To arrange, put in order.

noho pono. Sitting properly, behaving well.

noho uka. Upland dweller; to live inland.

noho wahine. To marry, of a man; to live with a woman.

noho wale. To do nothing; to stay without working or payment.

nohu. Two fish species (*Scorpaenopsis cacopsis* and *S. gibbosa*), which resemble the tropical Pacific stonefish, but lack its poisonous spines. PPN *nofu.*

noi. To ask for something, make a request, make a motion; petition. Cf. *nīnau,* to ask a question. Cf. *noinoi, nonoi.* PPN *noʻi.*

noʻiau. Var. of *noʻeau.*

noiʻi. To seek information or knowledge in great detail.

noinoi. Redup. of *noi.*

noio. The white-capped noddy or Hawaiian tern (*Anous tenuirostris*). PPN *noio.*

nōkali, notari. Notary. *Eng.*

no ka mea. Because, whereas (in legal documents). *Lit.,* because of the thing. PEP *no te mea.*

noke. To persist, continue, persevere.

no ke aha? Why? See *aha.* PEP *no te aha.*

nokenoke. Redup. of *noke.*

no laila. See *laila.*

nolu. Soft, yielding. PEP *ngolu.*

nona. His, hers, its; for him, her, it. PEP *nona.*

nonanona. 1. Ant (same as more common *naonao*). 2. Gnat.

noni. Indian mulberry (*Morinda citrifolia*), a small tree or shrub, formerly useful to Hawaiians as a source of dyes, food, and medicines. PPN *non(o, u).*

nono. 1. Red, redness; rosy-cheeked; red-faced, as from sunburn; sunburned, bronzed. 2. Full of holes, perforated, moth-eaten; oozing, as water in the sand; seepage.

nonoi. Redup. of *noi.* PEP *nonoi.*

noʻonoʻo. Thought, reflection, meditation, thinking; to think, reflect; to consider, as a case at law; thoughtful. *Noʻonoʻo hāiki,* narrow-minded; a narrow mind. **hoʻonoʻonoʻo.** To cause to think, reflect; reminiscent.

nou. 1. To throw, pelt, pitch, hurl; buffeting, throwing; pitcher. **hoʻonou.** To throw, pelt; to put forth physical effort. PPN *nou.* 2. For you, yours, in your honor (singular, *o*-class). PEP *nou.*

noʻu. For me, mine, in my honor (*o*-class). PEP *noku.*

Nowemapa. November. *Eng.*

nū. 1. To cough; to roar, as wind; grunting, as of pigs; cooing, as of doves; patter, as of rain; groaning, deep sighing, moaning; worried, grief-stricken. **hoʻonū.** To moan, groan, sigh, roar, etc. PPN *nguu.* 2. The letter *"n."* *Eng.* 3. News. *Eng.* See *nūhou.*

nuha. Sulky, sullen; to sulk; balk. Cf. *nunuha.* **hoʻonuha.** To cause to sulk; to sulk.

nuhe. Same as *ʻenuhe.* PPN *nufe.*

nūhou. News, recent or late news. *Nūhou kūloko,* local news.

nui. Big, large, great, important; many, much; size, number, magnitude, quantity, the greater part; enough. Cf. *hapa nui, mea nui. Leo nui,* loud voice. *ʻAno nui,* important. *Aloha nui loa,* very much aloha. Before a noun, *nui* may mean "group," as *nui manō,* group of sharks, or *nui manu,* flock of birds. **hoʻonui.** To enlarge, increase, multiply, magnify. *Hoʻonui leo,* loudspeaker. PNP *nui.*

nui kino. Whole body.

Nuiōka. New York. *Eng.*

Nukilani. New Zealand. *Eng.*

nuku. 1. Beak, snout, tip, end; spout, the lip of a pitcher; mouth or entrance, as of a harbor, river, or mountain pass. *Nuku awa,* entrance to a harbor. PPN *ngutu.* 2. Scolding, raving, ranting, grumbling.

nukunuku. 1. Redup. of *nuku, 1, 2;* to scold. **2.** Short, broken off short, blunt.

nuku-pu'u. 1. A species of Hawaiian honeycreeper (*Hemignathus lucidus*), now very rare. *Lit.*, hunched beak. **2.** Protruding lips; to pout the lips.

nuku wai. Stream mouth.

numela, numera. Numeral. *Eng.*

numi. To subside gradually, as tears, laughter, emotions.

PEP *numi.*

numonia. Pneumonia. *Eng.*

nūnū. 1. Moaning, groaning, cooing, grunting. **2.** Trumpetfish (*Aulostomus chinensis*).

nunuha. Redup. of *nuha;* sulky, moody.

nunui. Plural of *nui.* PEP *nunui.*

nūpepa. Newspaper. *Eng.*

nūpepa-puka-lā. Daily newspaper.

nu'u. Height, high place; elevation; stratum. PPN *nuku.*

O

o. 1. Of (*o*-class). PPN (')*o.* **2.** Or, lest, if. **3.** Pre-verbal imperative marker.

ō. 1. To answer, reply yes, agree; yes (in reply). PNP (')*oo.* **2.** To remain, endure, survive, continue, go on, exist; continuing. See *'oia, 1; 'oia mau nō.*

ō-. Stative prefix. PEP *koo.*

'o. Particle marking the subject, especially common before names of people, the interrogative *wai,* and the pronoun *ia. 'O au nō,* it's I. PPN *ko.*

'ō. 1. Any piercing instrument, fork, pin, sharp-pointed stick, fishing spear; to pierce, prick, stab. **ho'ō.** To cause to enter, put in, thrust in, insert. PNP *koo.* **2.** There, yonder (very common, often following *ma-, i, mai, a;* written as one word with *ma-* and always stressed, *ma'ō*). *Noho ma'ō,* sit over there. PPN *koo.* **3.** The letter "o" *Eng.*

o'a. 1. House rafter. PPN *hoka.* **2.** Fish gill.

O'ahu. Name of one of the Hawaiian Islands.

'oama, 'owama. Young of the *weke,* a fish. PEP *koama.*

'o au. See *wau,* I.

'oe. You (singular). PPN *koe.*

oha. To greet; affection. PPN *'ofa.*

'ōhai. Monkeypod or rain tree (*Samanea saman*). PEP *koofai.*

'ōhai-'ula. Royal poinciana or flame tree (*Delonix regia*).

'ohana. 1. Family, relative, kin group; related. **2.** To gather for family prayers (short for *pule 'ohana*).

'ohe. All kinds of bamboo; reed; flute; pipe, tube; bamboo tube for preserving fish. *Puhi 'ohe,* to play a wind instrument; player of a wind instrument. PPN *kofe.*

'ōhelo. A small native shrub (*Vaccinium reticulatum*) in the cranberry family, bearing small, red or yellow edible berries; formerly sacred to the goddess Pele.

'ōhelohelo. Pink, rosy, of the color or *'ōhelo* berries. **ho-'ōhelohelo.** To color pink.

'ohe puluka. Flute. *Lit.*, flute (*Eng.*) bamboo.

'ohe-wai. Water pipe; bamboo water container.

ohi. Young animal, usually female; maiden just entering womanhood; youth; youthful growth. *Ohi moa,* young chicken, pullet. PEP *osi.*

'ohi. To gather; collect, as wages or taxes; to select. PEP *ko(f,s)i.*

'ohi'a. 1. Several species of trees belonging to two genera (*Metrosideros* and *Eugenia*): see *'ōhi'a-'ai, 'ōhi'a-lehua.* PPN *kafika.* 2. Tomato. See *'ōhi'a-lomi.*

'ōhi'a-'ai. Mountain apple (*Eugenia malaccensis*). *Lit.,* edible *'ōhi'a.*

'ōhi'a-lehua. The tree *Metrosideros collina;* see *lehua.*

'ōhi'a-loke. Rose apple (*Eugenia jambos*). *Lit.,* rose (*Eng.*) *'ōhi'a.*

'ōhi'a-lomi. The common table tomato, sometimes used for *lomi* salmon.

'ōhiki. 1. To probe, pry, pick out; to prod, as the earth with a digging stick; to shell, as peas; to pick, as the teeth or nose; to clean out, as the ears. 2. Sand crab, probably *Ocypode ceratophthalma.*

'ōhiki niho. Toothpick.

'ohina. Gathering, collecting; selection. Cf. *'ohi.*

'ōhinu. Shiny, greasy; piece of roasted meat; roast; grease.

ohiohi. To grow vigorously, flourish, of plants.

oho. 1. Hair of the head; leaves of plants; to leaf out, sprout. Cf. *lauoho.* 2. To call out, cry; outcry; to leap up, as startled birds. **ho'oho.** To exclaim, shout, halloo. PPN *ofo.*

ohohia. Enthusiasm; enthusiastic, delighted, pleased; enthusiastic acclaim.

ohoku'i. Wig, switch. *Lit.,* added hair.

'ohu. Mist, fog, vapor. **hō'ohu.** To form mist; misty, etc. PEP *kofu.*

ōhua. Retainers, dependents, servants; passengers, as on a vessel.

'ōhule. 1. Bald; bald person. **ho'ōhule.** To cause baldness; to shear the hair completely. 2. Defeated without getting a single score. **ho'ōhule.** To defeat.

'ōhulu. To feather out; to grow, especially of vines growing from discarded or broken bits of sweet potato.

'ōhuluhula. Hairy (of body hair), shaggy.

'ōhumu. To grumble, complain, find fault, conspire, plot. PEP *kohumu.*

'ōhumuhumu. Redup. of *'ōhumu;* to relate one's woes, as to a sympathetic friend. PEP *koohumuhumu.*

oi. To move; to turn sideways, as contemptuously; to slouch along; to pull away, as in anger. PNP *o'i.*

'oi. 1. Sharp; sharpness. **hō'oi.** To sharpen. PPN *kohi.* 2. Best, superior; exceeding, to exceed, excel; extra, above. *A 'oi, emi mai,* more or less. *Maui nō ka 'oi,* Maui is the best. **hō'oi.** To excel; best.

'o'i. To limp. PEP *koki.*

'oia. 1. Same as *ō, 2;* to keep doing, persevere. Cf. *'oia mau nō.* 2. Truth; true. **hō'oia.** To confirm, audit, verify. *Luna hō'oia,* auditor. 3. He, she, it (as subject); this, namely this, namely, thus; that's it, that's right, go ahead. *'Oia nō!* Yes, that's so; that's right! *'Oia paha,* maybe so.

'oia ana nō. It's the same result; regardless.

'oia ho'i hā. All right, then; so that's it after all.

'oiai. 1. While, meanwhile. 2. Although.

'oiā'i'o. True; truth; truly, certainly; faithfulness. **hō'oiā-'i'o.** To verify, prove; to acknowledge, as a title; deed, proof.

'oia mau nō. Same as ever, continuing the same, just the same (often said in answer to *Pehea 'oe?* How are you?) See *ō, 2; 'oia, 1.*

'oia paha. See *'oia, 3.*

'oihana. Occupation, trade, profession, job, industry, business; department, office; Biblical book of Acts; professional. *Noho 'oihana,* office holder, job holder; to stay in an office or job.

'oihana ho'ona'auao. Department of instruction, educational system.

'oihana kahuna. Priesthood, office and duties of a priest; book of Leviticus in the Old Testament.

'oihana kinai ahi. Fire department; job of putting out fires. *Lit.,* fire-extinguishing job or department.

'oihana leka. Postal department. *Lit.,* letter department.

'oihana wai. Water works, department of water.

'ō'ili. 1. To appear, come into view; appearance. *'Ō'ili ka maka,* to come up, as seeds, bulbs; to sprout. 2. Filefishes. PEP *kookili.*

-'oio. hō'oio. To show off; to assume an air of superiority, as a child who cuts capers; conceited.

'oilo. Young eel. PEP *ko(o)ilo.*

'ō'io. Bonefish, ladyfish. (*Albula vulpes*).

'oi'oi. Redup. of *'oi, 2;* superior person.

o'io'ina. Resting place for travelers, such as a shady tree, rock. PNP *okioki.*

'ōiwi. Native, native son. **ho-'ōiwi.** To pass oneself off as a native son; like a native son.

oka. Dregs, crumbs. PPN *'ota.*

'ōka'a. To revolve, spin; to roll, as a mat; a top; a roll.

'Okakopa, Okatopa. October. *Eng.*

'ōkala. 1. Gooseflesh, creepy sensation; to bristle. stand up, as hair. 2. Rough, coarse, as cloth.

'okana. 1. District or subdistrict, usually comprising several *ahupua'a;* portion, as of food (probably a contraction of *'oki 'ana,* cutting). 2. Organ. *Eng.*

ōkea. White sand or gravel (contraction of *one,* sand, and *kea,* white).

oki. To stop, finish, end. *Cf. uoki.* **ho'ōki.** To put an end to, finish, stop; end. PPN *'oti.*

'oki. To cut, sever, hew, separate, divorce, fell; to cut, as cards; to operate, amputate; a cut, division, operation, amputation. **hō'oki.** To pretend to cut short, to cause to cut, to cut; to divorce. PPN *koti.*

'okika. Orchid. *Eng.*

'okika-honohono. An orchid (*Dendrobium superbum*).

'oki male (mare). Divorce; to divorce. *Lit.,* cut marriage.

'oki mau'u. To mow the grass. *Mīkini 'oki mau'u,* lawn mower.

'okina. 1. Cutting off; ending, severance, separation. PPN *kotinga.* 2. Glottal stop.

'oki'oki. Redup. of *'oki;* to cut into pieces. PPN *kotikoti.*

'oki poepoe. Circumcision; to circumcise (Biblical; the old Hawaiian term was *kahe*). *Lit.,* round cut.

'oko'a. Different, another; whole; entirety; a whole note in music; entirely, wholly, completely; independently.

Cf. *holo'oko'a.* **hō'oko'a.** To make different, to set apart, separate, discriminate.

'ō koholā. Whaling; to whale. *Lit.,* pierce whale. Cf. *moku 'ō koholā.*

'ōkole. Anus, buttocks. PEP *kookole.*

'ōkolehao. Liquor distilled from ti root in a still of the same name; later, a gin as made from rice or pineapple juice. *Lit.,* iron bottom.

'ōkole-'oi'oi. Marigolds. *Lit.,* jutting buttocks. Cf. *melekule.*

'ōkomo. To insert; to calk, as a ship; to inlay.

'okomopila. Automobile. *Eng.*

'ōku'eku'e. Knuckles. See *ku'eku'e.*

ola. Life, health, well-being, living, salvation; alive, spared; healed; to live; to spare, heal, grant life. *Mālama ola,* financial support, means of livelihood. **ho'ōla.** To save, heal, cure, spare; salvation; healer; savior. PPN *ola.*

ola hou. To revive, resuscitate; resurrected; resurrection. **ho-'ōla hou.** To restore to life, revive.

ōla'i. Earthquake.

olakino. State of health. *Mea olakino,* things necessary for life, as food.

'ōlali. 1. To glide smoothly along, as a ship on the sea or as a fish slipping through one's hand. 2. Bright, shiny, glistening; brightness.

ola loa. Long life; completely cured or recovered.

'ōlani. To toast over a fire, broil, warm in sunlight.

'olapa. 1. To flash, as lightning; to blaze suddenly, flare up; to rumble uneasily, as a queasy stomach. 2. Dancer, as contrasted with the chanter or *ho'opa'a* (memorizer); now, any dance ac-

companied by chanting and drumming on a gourd drum.

ola pāna'i. Redeemed, ransomed, saved; to redeem. **ho-'ōla pāna'i.** To redeem, ransom; redeemer.

'ole. 1. Not, without, lacking; to deny; zero, nothingness. Cf. *'a'ole, mea 'ole, 'ole loa. Maika'i 'ole,* not good; bad. **hō'ole.** To deny, refuse, contradict; refusal, denial, negative. PEP *kole.* 2. (*Cap.*) Seventh, eighth, ninth, and tenth nights of the moon.

'olē. Helmet shell (*Cassis cornuta*).

'ōlelo. Language, speech, word; to speak, say, tell; oral, verbatim, verbal. PEP *koolelo.*

'ole loa. Not at all, not in the least, none whatsoever; of no value, worthless.

'ōlelo 'ē. Foreign language, incomprehensible lingo.

'ōlelo-ha'i-mua. Foreword, preface. *Lit.,* word told first.

'ōlelo hō'ike. Affidavit, testimony.

'ōleloho'oholo. Verdict (as of a jury), judgment, decision; resolution; conclusion.

'ōlelo ho'onalonalo. Figurative language; obscure speech with puns and poetical references; to speak thus.

'ōlelo huna. Secret language, speech with hidden meaning.

'ōlelokauoha. Decree, order, commandment; to order, decree.

'ōlelokīkē. Dialogue, repartee; to engage in dialogue. Cf. *kīkē'ōlelo.*

'ōlelo kūkā. Consultation, discussion; to discuss, consult.

'ōlelo maika'i. Good word, gospel.

'ōlelo makuahine. Mother tongue.

'ōlelo nane. Riddle, parable, allegory.

'ōlelo no'eau. Proverb, wise saying, traditional saying.

'ōlelo pa'i 'ai. Pidgin English. *Lit.*, hard-taro speech.

'ōlelo paipai. Word of encouragement, exhortation, commandment.

'ōlelo uwea 'ole. Wireless message.

'ōlena. Turmeric (*Curcuma domestica*), a kind of ginger; used medicinally and as a source of dyes. See *lena, 2*.

'ōlenalena. Yellow. See *lenalena*.

'ōlepe. 1. To turn, as on hinges; to shut and open, as Venetian blinds. **ho'ōlepe.** To cause to turn, shut. PEP *koolepe.* **2.** Any kind of bivalve, as a mussel or oyster.

'ōlepolepo. Somewhat dirty, sullied; to sully.

-'Olepope. Hō'olepope. Protestant. *Lit.*, Pope denier.

'ole wale! Not at all! Of no interest, value, use.

oli. Chant that was not danced to. *Mea oli*, chanter. PNP *oli*.

'oli. Joy, happiness, pleasure; happy, joyful. Cf. *hau'oli*. **ho-'oli.** To give joy, make happy. PNP *koli*.

'oliana. All kinds of oleander grown in Hawai'i (*Nerium* spp.) *Eng.*

'ōliko. To bud. See *liko*.

'ō lima. Arm vaccination. *Lit.*, arm piercing.

'ōlino. Bright, brilliant, dazzling; brightness. See *lino*.

'ōlinolino. Redup. of *'ōlino*.

olioli. Redup. of *oli*; chanter.

'oli'oli. Redup. of *'oli*. PNP *kolikoli*.

'oliwa, oliva. Olive tree (*Olea europaea*).

olo. 1. To rub back and forth, grate, saw; a saw. PPN *olo*. **2.** To resound, sound long. PPN *olo*. **3.** Long surfboard. **4.** Hill. PPN *kolo*.

'olo. Double chin, sagging skin,

jowls, calf of leg; scrotum; to roll with fat; to sag, hang down.

'oloa. Fine white tapa. PPN *koloa*.

olohaka. Empty, sunken, hollow, as eyes or cheeks; emptiness, deficiency.

'olohani. To strike, quit work; mutiny, riot (said to be from *Eng.* "all hands"). **hō'olohani.** To cause or foment a strike or mutiny.

ōlohe. Bare, naked, barren; hairless, as a dog; bald; destitute, needy.

ō'ohelohe. Redup. of *'ōlohe*.

oloka'a. To roll along, as a wheel; to remove; to transfer, as a debt.

ō'o kani. To sound.

olokē. Clamorous, incoherent, excited in speech or sound.

'oloke'a. Cross, gibbet, gallows, scaffolding; crisscross. **hō-'oloke'a.** To crisscross; to cross.

'olokele. Bog, swamp.

'ololī. Narrow.

olomea. A native shrub or small tree (*Perrottetia sandwicensis*).

olomio. Tapering, narrowing; to start to form a crust, as on a wound; to go quickly, vanish.

olonā. A native shrub (*Touchardia latifolia*); the very strong, durable fiber from the bark was used for fish nets and carrying nets, and as a base for feather capes, etc.

'olo'olo. 1. Redup. of *'olo*; to hang too low, as a petticoat; to hang loose and long. *Waiū 'olo'olo*, sagging breasts. **2.** To overflow, flood, as streams.

'olo'olo wāwae. Calf of the leg.

'olopū. Inflated, billowed out, as a sail in the wind; puffed out, as cheeks of a person eating; blistered, as hands from hard work. **hōʻolopū.** To dilate, inflate, blister. PEP *kolopu(u).*

ʻolu. Cool, refreshing; soft, flexible, elastic; pleasant, comfortable; polite, kind, courteous; coolness; comfort; courtesy, kindness. Cf. *ʻolu-ʻolu.* **hōʻolu.** To make soft, limber, pleasant, cool, comfortable; to comfort, please.

ʻolua. You two. PPN *kimourua,* PNP *koulua,* PEP *kolua.*

ʻoluʻolu. Redup. of *ʻolu. E ʻolu-ʻolu ʻoe e ʻhele mai,* please come here. **hōʻoluʻolu.** Redup. of **hōʻolu;** to retire to rest, to seek rest; parade rest, at ease (military commands).

ʻoma. Oven, baking pan; to roast; roasted.

ʻomaʻi. Sickly, weak, ailing, not well. See *maʻi.*

ʻomaʻimaʻi. Redup. of *ʻomaʻi.*

ʻomaka. Budding; beginning; source, as of a stream; to leaf out or bud; to nip off. See *maka, 3.*

ʻōmaka wai. Stream source.

ʻōmali. Weak, infirm, puny, shriveling.

ʻōmalu. Cloudy, overcast, shady. **hoʻōmalu.** To cast a heavy shade; overcast. See *malu.*

ʻōmaʻo. 1. Green, as plants. 2. Hawaiian thrush (*Phaeornis obscurus*). Also called *maʻo.* PEP *komako.*

ʻōmaʻomaʻo. Redup. of *ʻōmaʻo;* an emerald. **hōʻomaʻomaʻo.** To make green, paint green.

ʻōmea. Reddish; murky.

ʻōmilo. To twist, turn, drill, curl; to taper, as a baby's fingers by rolling the tips between thumb and index finger; to spin, as thread; to produce abortion, destroy. See *milo, 2.*

ʻomilu. Same as *ulua.*

omo. To suck; suckling; to evaporate, as water; suction tube, rubber nipple. *Keiki*

omo waiū, suckling child. Perhaps PPN *komo.*

ʻomo. Lid, cover, plug, cork, as of a calabash; lamp chimney. PEP *komo.*

ʻomo ipukukui. Lamp chimney.

omo koko. Bloodsucker, leech; to suck blood.

ʻōmole. Bottle.

ʻomoʻomo. Loaf; any long, oval body. **hōʻomoʻomo.** To mold, shape.

ʻomoʻomo palaoa. Loaf of bread.

omo waiū. Nipple for a milk bottle; to suck a nipple.

ʻōmuku. · Stump, projection, pommel of a saddle; to project; to cut off short. See *muku.*

ʻōmuʻo. Bud, budding; to have buds; to nip off, as a leaf bud; to be cut off, stopped. See *muʻo.*

ona. 1. Mite, louse 2. Infatuated, attracted. Cf. *onaona.* 3. His, hers, its (zero-class, *o*-class). PNP *ona.*

ʻona. 1. Drunk, dizzy and unsteady; intoxicating; intoxication. *Wai ʻona,* intoxicating liquor. **hōʻona.** Intoxicating. PPN *kona.* 2. Owner. *Eng.* Cf. *ʻona miliona.*

ʻona lama. Drunk on rum or any alcoholic liquor; drunkenness; alcoholic.

ʻona mau. Constantly drunk, alcoholic.

ʻona miliona. Millionaire. *Lit.,* owner [of a] million. *Eng.*

onaona. Softly fragrant; soft fragrance or perfume; gentle and sweet as the eyes or disposition; inviting, attractive. **hoʻōnaona.** To impart fragrance; attractive, sweet.

one. Sand; sandy; silt; poetic name for land (cf. *one hā-nau*). **hoʻōne.** Pumice; to rub and polish with sand. PPN *ʻone.*

one hānau. Birthplace.

'one'i. Here; local. *Kō 'one'i keiki*, the local people.

'oneki. Deck. *Eng.*

oneone. Sandy, gritty, grainy. PPN *'one'one*.

oni. To appear, reach out to, jut out.

'oni. To move, stir, shift; to take to court, as land matters; movement, motion, moving. *'Oni a puhi*, to squirm like an eel. hō'oni. To bestir, cause to move, shake, disturb. PNP *koni*.

'ōniho. Toothed, sharp-edged, tooth-edged. See *niho*.

'ōnini. A slight breeze, puff of wind; to gasp for breath.

'oni'oni. Redup. of *'oni*. See *ki'i 'oni'oni*. PEP *konikoni*.

'onipa'a. Fixed, immovable, steadfast, firm. *Lit.*, fixed movement. hō'onipa'a. To fix, establish firmly.

ono. 1. Long, slender mackerel- or tuna-like fish (*Acanthocybium solandri*); a fine food fish. PEP *ono*. 2. Six; sixth. PPN *ono*.

'ono. Delicious, tasty, savory; to relish, crave; deliciousness, savor. Cf. *mea'ono*. hō'ono. To tempt the appetite; to make tasty. PEP *kono*.

'ōnohi. Eyeball; center; setting, as of a ring. PEP *ko(o)no-(f,s)i*.

'ono'ono. Redup. of *'ono*. hō-'ono'ono. To make tasty, create a desire. *Hō'ono'ono 'ai*, appetizer, condiment, dressing, relish. PEP *konokono*.

'onou. To shove, push, force into, thrust on; to persuade.

'onou po'o. To shove or push into something headlong, regardless of consequences. *Lit.*, shove head.

'ono wai. Thirsty; to crave water.

o'o. Matured, ripe, as fruit; of mature age; to mature, as fruit; an adult human; to ripen.

'o'ō. To crow. PPN *kokoo*.

'ō'ō. 1. Redup. of *'ō, 1*; to pierce, poke, put in, insert. hō'ō'ō. To insert, put in, pierce, cause to pierce. PNP *koo*. 2. Digging stick, digging implement, spade. PEP *koo*. 3. Several endemic species of black honeyeaters (genus *Moho*), much prized by early Hawaiians for their few yellow feathers which were used in making feather capes and helmets. A separate species occurred on each of the four islands: Kaua'i, O'ahu, Moloka'i, and Hawai'i; all are now extinct except the very rare Kaua'i species. PPN *koo*.

'ō'ō hao. Iron tool for digging, plow.

'ō'ō ihe. To hurl spears; sport of spear throwing.

'ō'ō kila. Steel spade.

'o'ole'a. Hard, stiff, strong; hardness, strength. hō'o-'ole'a. To harden, stiffen, resist.

'o'oma. Concave; concavity, spout, gouge, flare of a bonnet; oval-shaped chisel; large sharp nose. hō'o'oma. To shape concavely; to turn down the rim of a hat on both sides of the face so that the front is like the flare of a bonnet.

'o'opa. Lame, crippled; a cripple, lame person; to limp, be lame. hō'o'opa. To cause lameness, to feign lameness. PEP *kokopa*.

'ō'ō pālahalaha. Trowel. *Lit.*, flat digging instrument.

'ō'ō palau. A plow; to plow. *Lit.*, plow (*Eng.*) digging implement.

'ō'ōpē. Spade. *Lit.*, spade (Eng.) digging implement.

'o'opu. General name for fishes

included in the families Eleotridae and Gobiidae (*gobies*); some live in salt water near the shore, others in fresh water, and still others prefer brackish water. PEP *kokopu*.

'o'opu-hue. Puffers, balloonfishes, globefishes (*Arothron hispidus* and other species).

'ōpā. 1. To press, squeeze, as in massaging or in working dough. **hō'ōpā.** To cause to squeeze. 2. To ache, as from sitting in a cramped position. **hō'ōpā.** To cause such aching.

'ōpae. General name for shrimps and prawns. PNP *pae*.

'ōpae-kai. Any sea shrimp, including bandana prawn (*Stenopus hispidus*).

'ōpae-kākala. Spiked prawn (*Saron marmoratus*).

'ōpae-kala-'ole. Species of fresh-water shrimp. Also called *'ōpae-kuahiwi*, mountain shrimp, and *'ōpae-kolo*, crawling shrimp. *Lit.*, spineless shrimp.

'ōpae-kolo. See *'ōpae-kala-'ole*.

'ōpae-kuahiwi. See *'ōpae-kala-'ole*.

'ōpakapaka. Blue snapper (*Pristipomoides microlepis*). an important market fish.

'ōpala. Trash, rubbish, refuse, litter, garbage. **hō'ōpala.** To litter, make rubbish. See *pala*.

'ōpalapala. Redup. of *'ōpala*; bits of trash and rubbish.

'ope. Bundle; to tie in a bundle. **hō'ope.** To tie a bundle. PNP *kope*.

'ope'a. To twist, bind, or cross the hands, as behind the back; to throw over the shoulder, as a shawl; to overturn, overthrow; to evict, as a tenant. **ho'ōpe'a.** Treach-erous, to cause to twist, cross, etc. See *pe'a, 1*.

'ōpe'a kua. To cross the hands behind the back, a gesture considered rude because it was thought to bring bad luck to a fisherman ōr one beginning a venture.

'ōpe'ape'a. 1. General name for starfish. 2. Bat. 3. Window shutters, Venetian blinds.

'ōpelu. Mackerel scad (*Decapterus pinnulatus*), an excellent food fish, also used as bait for tuna and marlin. PEP *koopelu*.

'ope'ope. Redup. of *'ope;* bundles, baggage; to fold up, as clothes; pillow.

'opi. Fold, crease; to fold, crease. PNP *kopi*.

'opihi. 1. Limpet (*Cellona* spp.). 2. Salted and dried abalone from the mainland.

'ōpikipiki. Anxiety, mental disturbance; agitated, as the sea.

'ōpili. Cramped or numbed, as by cold or sitting long in one position; aching; clamped together, as leaves of a sensitive plant when touched; a cramp. **ho'ōpili.** To cause a cramp, numbness, etc. See *pili*.

'ōpio. Youth, juvenile; young. *Kale 'ōpio*, Charles, junior. **ho'ōpio.** To make young, freshen, refresh; to act young. PEP *ko(o)pio*.

'ōpiopio. Young, immature, juvenile; unripe; youth, young person. **ho'ōpiopio.** Redup. of *ho'ōpio*.

'opiuma. 1. Opium. 2. Manila tamarind (*Pithecellobium dulce*).

'ōpū. Belly, stomach, abdomen, tripe, giblet, gizzard, bladder. PPN *koopuu*.

'ōpua. Puffy clouds, as banked up near the horizon. PEP *k(aa, oo)pua*.

'**ōpū ahonui.** Patient; patience; a patient person. *Lit.*, disposition of great breath.

'**opu-hue.** Balloonfish (*Arothron hispidus*). Also called *kēkē*.

'**ōpule.** A common labrid fish or wrasse (*Anampses cuvieri, A. godeffroyi*).

'**ōpū makani.** Bellows. *Lit.*, wind belly.

'**ōpū mimi.** Bladder. *Lit.*, urine belly.

'**ōpū nui.** Corpulent, large-bellied; corpulency; big belly.

'**ōpū pipi.** Beef tripe.

'**ōpū pua'a.** Pig intestine; tripe.

'**opu'u.** 1. A bud, the budding breasts of a girl; to bud; a child. 2. A whale-tooth pendant, not tongue-shaped like the *lei palaoa*.

'**opu'u mai'a.** The root bud and buds of a banana plant, and the sheaths enclosing them.

'**ōpu'upu'u.** 1. Lumpy, bumpy, hilly, rough, as cloth or a road. 2. Knuckle, as on the hand.

ou. Your, yours (singular, zero-class, *o*-class). PNP *ou.*

o'u. Mine, my, of me (zero-class, *o*-class). PNP *oku.*

'**ou.** To protrude, project, puncture. PEP *kou.*

'**oukou.** You (plural). *Kō 'oukou,* your (*o*-class). *Kā 'oukou,* your (*a*-class). PNP *koutou.*

'**ōuli.** Sign, omen, portent; nature, symptom, character.

'**owā, oa.** 1. Split, cracked, burst; to split, crack. **hō-'owā.** To cause to split, crack. 2. To retch, gag.

'**owai.** See *wai,* who.

'**ōwali.** Weak, sickly, puny. Cf. *wali, nāwali.*

'**o wau, 'o au.** See *au,* I, and '*o.*

'**owē, 'oē.** Murmuring, rustling, soughing, whining, as of surf, leaves, water, wind, a bullet; to sound thus; sound of tearing, as of cloth; buzzing of insects.

'**ōwela.** Hottish, feverish; burned and blistered, as by sun; heat. See *wela.*

'**ōwili.** Roll, bolt, as of cloth or paper; skein, coil; to roll up, twist; to fold, as the arms. See *wili.*

'**ōwiliwili.** Redup. of '*ōwili.* See *wiliwili.*

P

pā. 1. Fence, wall, pen, corral, sty, (house) lot, enclosure, yard; to build a fence or enclosure. PPN *paa.* 2. Dish, plate, pan (preceded by *ke*). 3. Mother-of-pearl shell; pearl-shell lure. PPN *paa.* 4. To touch, get, contact, reach, hit, experience, blow (of wind), shine (as moon or sun), drink, hear. **ho'opā.** To touch. PPN *paa.* 5. Barren, as a female. PPN *pa'a.*

pa-. In the nature of, having the quality of. Also, *pā-.* PPN *pa-.*

pā-. At a time, at once, number of times (prefix to numerals).

pa'a. Firm, solid, fixed, fast, stuck, secure, closed, busy, steady, steadfast, permanent, finished, completed; learned, memorized, stubborn, determined, solid or fast (of colors), strong, vigorous, learned; to hold, keep, retain, bear; a solid, as in

geometry. **ho'opa'a.** To make
fast, firm, tight, solid; to
bind; to learn, memorize,
complete, keep, detain, withhold; to subscribe, as to a
newspaper; to order, reserve,
register, insure, bolt; drum-
mer and hula chanter; in-
surance. *Ho'opa'a manawa,*
to make an appointment. *Ho-
'opa'a mo'olelo,* record a
story, keep minutes. *Leka
i ho'opa'a 'ia,* registered letter. *Ho'opa'a hao,* to weld.
Ho'opa'a kuleana, copyright;
to copyright.

pa'a 'āina. Landholder; to hold
land.

pa'ahana. Busy, industrious,
hard-working; laborer, worker.

pa'ahao. Prisoner, convict. *Lit.,*
iron-held. **ho'opa'ahao.** To
jail, imprison.

pā'aila. Castor oil plant (*Ricinus communis*).

pa'a'ili. A solid (usually with
number of sides given), as
pa'a'ili hā, four-sided solid.

pa'a kāhili. Bearer of the
feather standard; to carry a
kāhili.

pa'akai. Salt.

pa'a kāma'a. Pair of shoes.

pa'akea. Limestone, coral beds.

pa'akikī. Hard, compact, difficult, stubborn, obstinate.

pa'alima. Pentagon.

pa'a lole. Suit of clothes.

pa'alula. Formal, according to
rules.

pa'a male. Married couple.

pa'a mau. Regular, customary,
usual.

pa'a mo'olelo. Versed in lore,
legends, history, tradition;
one so versed.

pa'ana'au. Memorized, remem-
bered. **ho'opa'ana'au.** To
memorize.

pā'ani. Play, sport, game,
amusement, joke; to play,
sport. *Pā'ani kinipōpō,* to

play ball; ball player. *Pā-
'ani pepa,* to play cards. *Mea
pā'ani,* plaything, toy.

pa'apa'a. Dispute, argument,
quarrel. **ho'opa'apa'a.** To
argue, dispute; argument.

pa'apani. Playful.

pa'apū. Covered with, solid
with, as people, fog, clouds.

pa'a uma. Hand wrestling.

**-pa'a waiwai. ho'opa'a wai-
wai.** To insure property.

pae. 1. Cluster, row, bank.
ho'opae. To build up an em-
bankment, row. PPN *pae.* **2.**
To land, as a surfrider;
washed or drifted ashore.
Probably PPN *pae.*

pae 'āina. Group of islands,
archipelago.

pā'ele. Negro; dark, black; to
blacken.

pae moku. Group of islands,
archipelago.

paepae. Pavement, support,
house platform; to support,
hold.

pae pu'u. Row or cluster of
hills.

pa'ewa. Crooked, misshapen,
uneven, odd, imperfect,
wrong, incorrect; error, mistake.

paha. 1. Maybe, perhaps (very
common, making speech less
blunt; often preceded by
pēlā or *'a'ole,* and never occurring after a pause). *A
. . . paha,* or. *'Elua a 'ekolu
paha,* two or three. PEP
pa(f,s)a. **2.** Chant, especially an improvised chant; to
chant thus. PEP *pa(f,s)a.*

pā hale. House lot, yard, or
fence.

pā halihali. Tray (preceded by
ke).

pāha'oha'o. Mysterious, puzzling.

pahē. Soft-spoken, soft-man-
nered; soft. See *waipahē.*

pāheahea. To call, especially
to invite someone to eat.

pahe'e. Slippery, smooth, soft, satiny; to slide, slip, skid. **ho'opahe'e.** To cause to slip. PPN *paseke.*

pahe'e 'ulu. To bowl; bowling.

pahele. Snare, noose, trap; to ensnare, trap; deceit, treachery. **ho'opahele.** To ensnare, deceive.

pāhemahema. About the same as *hemahema;* awkward, unskilled.

pāhenehene. To ridicule, laugh at, make fun of.

pahi. Knife.

pahi kaua. Sword.

pahi keke'e. Sickle.

pahi koli. Carving knife.

pahi 'ō. Dagger.

pahi olo. Saw; to saw.

pahi pelu. Jackknife, penknife.

pahi 'umi'umi. Razor. *Lit.,* beard knife.

pāhoa. Dagger.

pāhoehoe. Smooth, unbroken type of lava, contrasting with *'a'ā.*

pā holoi. Wash basin.

pāhono. To mend, patch, repair.

pā ho'okani. Phonograph record.

pahu. 1. Box, drum, chest, barrel, ship binnacle, collection box, ark, coffin. PPN *pasu.* 2. Stick, stake, staff, post. 3. To push, shove, thrust. PPN *pasu.* 4. To cut off short. 5. Boxfishes, cowfishes (esp. *Ostracion meleagris*). Also, *moamoa.*

pahū. To explode, burst, blast, thud. **ho'opahū.** To set off, as firecrackers or dynamite. PPN *pasuu.*

pahu aniani. Glass box, especially a glass-bottomed box for fishing; glass case.

pahu hao. Safe.

pahu hau. Icebox, refrigerator.

pahu hope. Final goal or stake.

pahu hula. Hula drum.

pahu kui. Hypodermic injec-tion; to be injected. *Lit.,* needle piercing.

pahu kupapa'u. Coffin. *Lit.,* corpse box.

pā hula. Hula troupe.

pahulu. 1. Nightmare. **ho'opahulu.** To have a nightmare; to haunt, bring bad luck; unlucky. 2. Exhausted, worn out, of soil.

pahu manamana. Crossroads, intersection.

pahu meli. Beehive.

pahu 'ōlelo. Phonograph.

pahu pā. Cupboard, meat safe.

pahupahu. Billiards, pool; to play such.

pahūpahū. Redup. of *pahū.*

pahu pa'i. Small sharkskin hula drum.

pahu pa'i ki'i. Camera, kodak. *Lit.,* box for printing pictures.

pahu pānānā. Binnacle.

pahu 'ume. Drawer; bureau.

pahu wai. Water barrel, tank.

pai. 1. To urge, encourage, rouse, excite. **ho'opai.** To encourage. PEP *pai.* 2. To raise, lift up. 3. To laud, praise, exalt. 4. To pamper, spoil, make a pet of.

pa'i. 1. To slap, clap, print; printing (preceded by *ke*). **ho'opa'i.** To slap, hit, punish, revenge; punishment, revenge, fine, penalty. *'Ōlelo ho'opa'i,* sentence. PPN *paki.* 2. To tie; a draw, equal.

paia. Wall, side of a house; clearing of trees; walled in. *Paia 'ala i ka hala,* forest bower fragrant with pandanus.

pa'i 'ai. Hard, pounded, undiluted taro. See *'ōlelo pa'i 'ai.*

pa'i 'ana. Printing, edition.

pai'ea. An edible crab, perhaps a species of the genus *Grapsus.* PPN *pa'ikea.*

pa'i hakahaka. Printing; form, questionnaire.

pa'i hewa. Misprint, typographical error; to make such.

pa'ihi. Clear, bright, neat, tidy. PEP *pakisi*.

pai hua. Custard pie, egg pie, fruit pie.

paikau. To march, drill, parade, practice firearms.

paiki. Bag, suitcase, pocketbook, purse. *Eng.*

pa'i ki'i. To take pictures, photographs; photographer. *Lit.*, snap picture.

paikikala. Bicycle. *Eng.*

paila. 1. Pile, healp. *Eng.* 2. Also **baila.** To boil. *Eng.*

pā ilina. Cemetery, graveyard.

pailua. Nausea; abominable. **ho'opailua.** To cause nausea; nauseating, disgusting, loathsome.

pa'imalau. Portuguese man-of-war (*Physalia*).

paina. Pine, all kinds of conifers, ironwood. *Eng.*

pa'ina. To crackle, snap, click, tick, pop. PEP *pakinga*.

pā'ina. Dinner, small party with dinner.

pā'ina male. Wedding feast or reception.

paio. To quarrel, argue, debate, fight; argument, battle, struggle. See *hoa paio*.

paipai. Redup. of *pai*, *1*, *2*, *3*. See *noho paipai*.

pa'ipa'i. 1. Redup. of *pa'i*, *1*; to applaud, clap; applause. 2. To mix, as ingredients. See *lama pa'ipa'i 'ia*.

pa'ipa'i lima. To clap, applaud; applause.

Paipala, Baibala. Bible; Biblical. *Eng.*

pa'i palapala. Printing press; to print.

paipu. Pipe, faucet. *Eng. Paipu lawe 'ino*, sewage system.

pā ipu. Calabash, wooden dish or bowl.

pa'i umauma. Chest-slapping hula.

paka. 1. To criticize. 2. Raindrops. PNP *pata*. 3. Also **bata.** Butter. *Eng.* 4. Tobacco. *Eng.*

pāka. 1. Park. *Eng.* 2. To park, as a car. *Eng.*

pākaha. To cheat, fleece, rob, raid.

pāka lāhui. National park.

pakalaki. Bad luck, unlucky. *Eng.*

pakalana. Chinese violet (*Telosma cordata*). See *miulana*.

paka ua. Raindrops.

pākaukau. Table, counter.

pākaukau 'aina. Dining table.

pākaukau 'opi'opi. Folding table.

Pākē. China; Chinese.

pākela. Excess; excessive, surpassing; to exceed, surpass, excel.

pākela 'ai. To eat to excess; gluttonous; glutton.

pakele. To escape, get away. **ho'opakele.** To rescue.

pakelo. To slip, thrust.

pakeneka. Percent, percentage. *Eng.*

pakī. To splash, spatter, squirt. PEP *patii*.

paki'i. Various flatfishes (*Bothus pantherinus*, etc.). PEP *paatiki*.

pakika. Slippery, smooth.

pākīkē. Rude, sarcastic, saucy, impudent.

Pākīpika. Pacific. *Eng.*

Pakoa. Catholic term for Easter, Passover.

pākōlī. Musical scale.

paku. To drive away. PEP *patu*.

pākū. Curtain, screen, partition, veil. PEP *paatuu*.

pāku'i. To splice, add on, annex.

pāku'iku'i. Surgeonfish (*Acanthurus achilles*).

pala. 1. Ripe, mellow, rotten. **ho'opala.** To ripen. PPN *pala*. 2. Daub, smear, smudge, blot, dab of excreta. **ho'opala.** To daub, besmear.

PPN *pala*. **3.** A fern (*Marattia douglasii*). PEP *pala*.

pala'ā. Lace fern (*Sphenomeris chusana*).

pālaha. Spread out, extended, flattened, wide, broad. *See laha.*

palahī. Diarrhea.

palahū. 1. Rotten. **2.** Same as *pelehū*, turkey.

palai. A native fern (*Microlepia setosa*).

pala'ie. Game of loop and ball (played with a flexible stick made of braided coconut fiber with a loop at one end and a tapa ball on a string attached below the loop; the object was to catch the ball in the loop).

palaka. 1. Indifferent, inactive, uninterested. **2.** Sturdy blue-and-white checked cloth, used originally for work clothing. *Eng.*, block.

palaki. Brush; to brush. *Eng.*

palaki lauoho. Hairbrush.

palaki niho. Toothbrush.

palalā. A rumbling sound. PPN *palalaa.*

pālama. Sacred taboo enclosure.

palamimo. To pilfer.

palani. A surgeonfish (*Acanthurus dussumieri*). PPN *palangi*. **2.** (*Cap.*) Also, **Farani.** France, Frenchman; French; Frank. *Eng.* **3.** Also, **barani.** Brandy. *Eng.*

palaoa. 1. Whale, ivory. See *lei palaoa*. PEP *pala(a)oa*. **2.** Flour, bread, wheat. *Eng.*

palaoa li'ili'i. Roll, biscuit.

palaoa maka. Flour.

palaoa palai. Pancake.

palaoa pāpa'a. Toast. *Lit.*, crisp bread.

palapala. Document of any kind, bill, deed, warrant, certificate, tract, writ, manuscript; formerly, the Scriptures or book learning in general.

palapala 'ae. Permit, license.

palapala 'aelike. Written contract, as for labor; treaty.

palapala 'ai'ē. Note (to pay money), bond. *Lit.*, debt document.

palapala 'āina. Map.

palapala hānau. Birth certificate.

Palapala Hemolele. Holy Scriptures.

palapala ho'ālohaloha. Written condolence.

palapala ho'āmana. Power of attorney.

palapala ho'āpono. Passport, document granting permission.

palapala hō'ike. Affidavit, report.

palapala hō'ike no ke ola. Bill of health.

palapala hō'ike pilikino. Identification papers.

palapala ho'ohanohano. Honorary diploma or document.

palapala ho'ohiki 'ia. Affidavit.

palapala hō'oia. Certificate.

palapala hō'oiā'i'o. Voucher.

palapala hō'oia kulanui. College diploma.

palapala ho'oilina. Last will or testament.

palapala ho'oka'a. Receipt, as for paying a bill.

palapala ho'okō. Award, verdict, written decision, warrant.

palapala ho'okohu. Certificate of appointment, power of attorney.

palapala ho'okuleana. Patent, copyright.

palapala ho'olauna. Letter of introduction.

palapala ho'olimalima. Lease.

palapala ho'omaika'i. Letter of commendation, graduation diploma, certificate of merit.

palapala ho'opa'a. Bond, insurance policy.

palapala hopu. Warrant of arrest.

palapala ʻinikua. Insurance policy.

palapala kākoʻo. Letter of recommendation or support.

palapala kauoha. Last will and testament.

palapala kikoʻo. Check, draft, warrant.

palapala kila (sila). Deed, patent.

palapala kono. Invitation.

palapala kūʻai. Deed or bill of sale.

palapala kuhikuhi kino. Certificate of identification, as a passport.

palapala male. Marriage license or certificate.

palapala noi. Written petition.

palapala puka. Graduation diploma.

palapala waiho ʻoihana. Letter of resignation.

palau. 1. Betrothal; engaged to marry. hoʻopalau. To become engaged. 2. Plow; to plow. *Eng.*

pālau. 1. To tell tall tales, exaggerate. PPN *pa(a)lau.* 2. War club.

palaualelo. Lazy, idle, especially of a verbose person; such a person.

pale. 1. To ward off, thrust aside, parry; to ignore a command or law, make void, break; protection, defense, guard. hoʻopale. To fend or ward off. See *ʻili pale o kāmaʻa.* PPN *pale.* 2. Canto of a song, division of a hula song. 3. To deliver, as a child.

pale ahi. Fire protection; fireproof.

pā lehu. Ash tray (preceded by *ke*).

pale huila. Fender, as of a car.

paleʻili. Undershirt.

pale kaʻa. Car bumper.

pale kai. Breakwater.

palekaiko, paredaiso. Paradise. *Eng.*

pale kaua. Shield, war defense.

paleki. Brake. *Eng.*

palekikena, paresidena. Var. of *pelekikena,* president.

palekoki. Petticoat, skirt. *Eng.*

palemaʻi. Underdrawers.

pale makani. Windshield.

palemo. To sink, drown, vanish. PPN *m(a,e)lemo,* PEP *palemo.*

palena. Boundary, limit, border, juncture, separation. See *kaupalena.*

palena ʻāina. Land boundary.

palena ʻole. Boundless, without limit.

pale pākaukau. Table cloth.

pale-piwa. All species of *Eucalyptus* trees. *Lit.,* ward off fever (so called because the leaves were used as medicine for fever and in steam baths).

pale uhi. Veil, covering.

pale uluna. Pillowcase.

pale waiū. Brassiere.

pale wāwae. House slippers, sandals.

pali. Cliff, precipice, steep hill. *Fig.,* haughty, disdainful, difficult. PEP *pali.*

pali kuʻi. Notched cliff.

palila. A rare Hawaiian honeycreeper (*Psittirostra bailleui*), endemic to the island of Hawaiʻi.

Pali-uli. A legendary land of plenty and joy, said to be on Hawaiʻi. *Lit.,* green cliff.

pāloa. Seine. PEP *paaloa.*

pāloka, balota. Ballot, vote. *Eng.* See *koho pāloka.*

pālolo. Clay, sticky mud, mortar.

palu. Relish made of head or stomach of fish, with *kukui* relish, garlic, chili peppers; bait. PPN *palu.*

palū. Flu, influenza. *Eng.*

pālua. Two by two, double, twofold, twice.

palula. Cooked sweet-potato leaves.

pālule. Shirt.

pālulu. Screen, shield, protection. PEP *paalulu*.

pālulu kukui. Lamp shade.

pālulu makani. Windbreak.

pāluna, baluna. Balloon. *Eng.*

palupalu. Weak, soft, limber, flexible, tender.

pāma. Palm. *Eng.*

pā-makani. 1. A native hibiscus (*Hibiscus arnottianus*), same as *kokiʻo-keʻokeʻo*. 2. A native violet (*Viola tracheliifolia*).

pana. 1. To shoot, as marbles, arrows, a bow; bow and arrows; to snap, as with fingers. 2. Heart beat, pulse, beat in music; to beat time, pulsate, throb. *Nānā i ka pana*, to take the pulse. PEP *pana*. 3. Celebrated, noted, or legendary place.

pānaʻi. 1. Revenge, reciprocity, reward; to revenge, pay back, reward, reciprocate, replace, substitute. **hoʻopānaʻi.** To seek revenge, reward, etc. 2. To splice, graft, lengthen.

panakō, banako. Bank. *Eng.*

panalāʻau. Colony, dependency, province; colonist.

pānānā. Compass; pilot.

pana pua. To shoot with bow and arrow; archer, archery.

panau. To move restlessly. PEP *panau*.

pane. 1. Answer, reply; to answer. 2. Hind part of the head; top, summit (preceded by *ke*). PEP *pane*.

paneʻe. 1. To move along, push along a little. *Paneʻe i mua*, to progress. 2. Delayed, postponed; delay, postponement; to do in installments. **hoʻopaneʻe.** To postpone, delay, put off, procrastinate. See *uku hoʻopaneʻe*.

panepane. To retort, talk back.

pani. To close, shut, substitute, replace; closure, stopper, lid, cover, gate, door, substitute. PEP *pani*.

pani hakahaka. To substitute, fill a vacancy, replace; substitute, replacement, successor, proxy.

paniinoa. Pronoun. *Lit.*, name substitute.

pani kai. Levee, dike, protection against the sea.

panina. End, closing, conclusion, finish.

pā-nini. Prickly pear (*Opuntia megacantha*), the common wild cactus of Hawaiʻi; the fruits are edible. *Lit.*, fence wall.

pā-nini-o-Kapunahou. Night-blooming cereus (*Hylocereus undatus*). *Lit.*, Kapunahou cactus (for the famous hedge at Punahou School).

paniolo. Cowboy, Spaniard, Spain; Spanish. Spanish, *español*.

pani ʻōmole. Bottle stopper, cork.

pani puka. Door, gate; beggar sitting near a doorway.

pani-pūpū. Cat's eye, operculum or valve that closes a shell.

pani wai. Dam, sluice, levee, dike.

pano. Dark, as clouds; black. PEP *pango*.

pānoʻo. Same as *pāoʻo*. PEP *panoko*.

pao. 1. To scoop out, dub out, chisel out, peck, bore. 2. Cave, pit, cavern.

paoa. Strongly odoriferous; a strong odor.

paoka, paoda. Powder. *Eng.*

paona. Pound, balance, scales, weight. *Eng.* See *kau paona*.

paona kaulike. Balance, scales.

pāoʻo. Name for several species of blennies (the fish family Blenniidae). PEP *pa(a)oko*.

pāoʻo-kauila. Blenny (*Runula evaensis*).

papa. Flat surface, stratum, layer, level, foundation, reef, board, lumber, story of a building; class, rank, order; flat, level, wooden. PPN *papa*.

pāpā. 1. To forbid, prohibit. 2. To touch. hoʻopāpā. To touch repeatedly; contest in wit or strength; repartee. PPN *paapaa*.

papaʻa. Redup. of *paʻa;* tight, secure.

pāpaʻa. Cooked crisp, overdone, burned, parched; scab. PEP *paʻa*.

papa ʻaiana. Ironing board.

pāpaʻa lā. Sunburned, tanned, parched.

pāpaʻa palaoa. Slice of bread.

papa heʻe nalu. Surfboard. *Lit.,* board [for] sliding waves.

papahele. Floor.

papa helu. Table, list, enumeration, statistics.

papa hīmeni. Choir.

papa hōʻike. Program, timetable.

papa hoʻolaha. Billboard.

papa hoʻonaʻauao. Board of education.

papa hulei. Seesaw, teeter.

pāpaʻi. 1. General name for crabs. PEP *paapaka*. 2. Temporary hut or shelter.

papa inoa. List or catalog of names.

papakema, bapatema. Baptism. *Eng.*

papa kuhikuhi. Table of contents, index, program, timetable.

papa kuhikuhi manawa. Schedule, as of ship arrivals.

papa kuʻi ʻai. Poi-pounding board.

pāpala. All species of a native genus (*Charpentiera*) of shrubs and small trees.

papa lāʻau. Board, plank, large platter.

pā pālahalaha. Platter (preceded by *ke*).

pā palai. Frying pan (preceded by *ke*).

papale. Redup. of *pale*, to ward off.

pāpale. Hat; to put on or wear a hat. PPN *pale*.

pāpale aliʻi. Crown.

pāpale kapu. Cap.

papa lele kawa. Springboard for diving.

pāpale ʻoʻoma. Bonnet, sunbonnet.

pāpālina, papālina. Cheek, cheeks, PEP *pa(a)paalinga*.

papa luna kiaʻi. Board of supervisors.

papani. Redup. of *pani*, to close; interception.

papa niho. Row of teeth, set of teeth, jaw.

papa noho. Bench.

papa ola. Board of health.

pāpāʻōlelo. To converse, talk.

papa o nā kahu kula o ke kulanui. Board of regents of the university.

pāpapa. 1. Low, flat. 2. Beans, peas, lentils.

papa paʻi. Printing press.

papa palapala. Writing desk, board, flat surface for writing.

papa puʻukani. Choir, choral group.

papau. Deeply engaged, absorbed, engrossed; united; all together.

papaʻu. Shallow, shoal. PNP *papaku*.

papekema, bapetema. Same as papakema.

Papekike, Bapetite. Baptist. *Eng.*

papekiko, bapetiso. To baptize; baptismal; (*cap.*) Baptist.

papio. Same as pāpiopio, a fish. PEP *papio*.

pāpiopio. Young stage of growth of *ulua*, a fish.

pāpū. 1. Fort, fortress. 2. Clear, unobstructed. PEP *paapuu.*

pāpū lewa. Flying fortress, battleship.

pau. Finished, ended, completed, over, all done, final; entirely, completely, very much; all, to have all, to be completely possessed, consumed, destroyed. *Pau Pele, pau manō,* consumed by Pele, consumed by a shark (an oath meaning "May I be destroyed if I have not spoken truth"). *Pau iā kākou,* we've finished. **ho'opau.** To put an end to, finish, stop, cancel, revoke, repeal, abolish, consume, discharge. See *ho'opaumanawa.* PNP *pau.*

pa'u. 1. Soot, smudge. **ho-'opa'u.** To soil, smudge. 2. Drudgery, slavery, tedious work.

pa'ū. Moist, damp, moldy.

pā'ū. Woman's skirt or sarong, especially as worn by female horseback riders.

paua. A clam. PPN *pa'aua.*

pau ahi. Destruction by fire, burned; to put out a fire. See *'inikua pau ahi, kāhea pau ahi.*

pauaho. Out of breath, panting, discouraged, despairing, weary, exhausted. **ho'opauaho.** To cause shortness of breath or weariness.

pau apau. Everyone, all the people.

pauka, pauda. Powder. *Eng.*

paukū. Section, link, piece, stanza, verse, article (as of law), paragraph; to section off, cut in sections, slice.

paukū manawa. Portion of time, era.

paukū 'oloka'a. Cylinder.

paula. Powder. *Eng.*

paulele. Faith, confidence, trust; to have faith, confidence.

pauloa. All, everything; to have all.

pāuma. 1. Large curved needle. 2. Bent, curved. 3. Breastbone.

pā uma. Standing wrist wrestling.

-paumanawa. ho'opaumanawa. To waste time; not worth doing, waste of effort or time.

pā'ume'ume. 1. Tug-of-war game; to play this. 2. Contentious, quarreling, fighting.

pā'ū-o-Hi'iaka. A native beach vine (*Jacquemontia sandwicensis*) in the morning-glory family.

pau pilikia. Finished trouble. **ho'opau pilikia.** To attend the calls of nature. *Wahi ho'opau pilikia,* toilet, outhouse.

pau pono. Completely finished.

pau pū. All together, including all; completely demolished.

pawa. Darkness just before dawn.

pā wa'a. Canoe enclosure.

pāwehe. Generic name for colored geometric motifs, as on *makaloa* mats made on Ni-'ihau, bowls and gourds; to make such.

pe, pē-. Thus, so, like. See *pehea, pēia, pēlā, penei.* PPN *pehee.*

pē. 1. Crushed, flattened, humble, low. **ho'opē.** To crush. PPN *pe'e.* 2. Perfumed, fragrant. **ho'opē.** To perfume, anoint. 3. Drenched, soaked. **ho'opē.** To drench, soak. PEP *pe'e.*

pea. 1. Also **fea.** Fair; to be fair. *Eng.* 2. Pear, avocado. *Eng.* 3. Also **bea.** Bear. *Eng.*

pe'a. 1. Cross; to cross, turn and go. PEP *peka.* 2. Kite. 3. Bat. PPN *peka.* 4. Sail, as of a canoe. 5. See *hale pe'a.*

pe'ahi. Fan; to fan, brush, signal. PEP *peka(f,s)i.*

pe'ahi uila. Electric fan.

pe'a nui. Mainsail.

pe'ape'ahi. Redup. of *pe'ahi.*

pe'e. To hide; hiding.

pe'elua. Caterpillar.

pe'epe'e. Redup. of *pe'e.*

pehea. How? What? How about it? *Pehea 'oe?* How are you? *Pehea lā!* I don't know how. PPN *peheefea.*

pehi. To throw, throw at. PNP *pesi.*

pehu. Swollen; to swell; dropsy.

pēia. Thus, like this, this way; to say.

pekapeka. To tattle, tell tales; stool pigeon.

peke. Dwarf, brownie.

peki. 1. Pace, to move along step by step, trudge. *Eng.* 2. To back up. *Eng.* 3. Spade. *Eng.*

peku. Kick; to kick.

pekunia. Petunia.

pela. Fertilizer, decayed flesh. PPN *pela.*

pēlā. In that way, like that, thus, so, that way; to say. *Pēlā paha,* maybe so. PNP *peelaa.*

pela moe. Mattress.

pelapela. Filthy, dirty, nasty, obscene. PPN *pelapela.*

pele. 1. Lava flow, volcano, eruption. 2. (*Cap.*) The volcano goddess.

pelehū. Turkey. *Lit.,* swollen swelling.

Pelekane. Britain, British, England, English, Englishman. *Eng.*

Pelekania, Beretania. Britain, British. *Eng.*

peleki. Brake; to apply brakes. *Eng.*

pelekikena, peresidena. President; presidential. *Eng.*

pelekunu. Musty, rank, or moldy odor.

pelena, berena. Crackers, bread.

pelu. To fold, turn over, turn under; hem, tuck; to take a hem or tuck. PPN *pelu.*

pena. Paint; to paint. *Eng.*

penei. This way, like this, thus, as follows; to be thus. Probably PPN *peheeni;* PNP *pe(e)nei.*

peni. Pen, pencil. *Eng.*

penikala. Pencil (sometimes preceded by *ke*).

penu. To sop up, as gravy; to dunk, dab. PPN *penu.*

pepa. 1. Paper, card, playing cards; to play cards. *Eng.* 2. Pepper. *Eng.*

pepa hahau. Playing cards.

pepa hale. Wallpaper.

pepa hāleu. Toilet paper.

pepa kalakala. Sandpaper.

pepa kīko'o. Check, for paying money.

pepa lahilahi. Tissue paper, thin paper.

pepa mānoanoa. Cardboard.

pepa po'oleka. Postcard.

pepe. Flat, low, squatty.

pēpē. Redup. of *pē,* 1. *Na'au pēpē,* modest spirit.

pepe'e. Twisted, crooked, deformed.

pepehi. To beat, strike, pound, kill. PNP *pepesi.*

pepehi kanaka. Murder, murderer, manslaughter; to commit murder.

pepeiao. 1. Ear. 2. Chinese cake stuffed with meat.

pepeiao-akua. Tree fungus, bracket fungus, Jew's-ear (*Auricularia polytricha*).

pepeiao-'eha. Earache.

pepeiaohao. Horn of an animal.

pepeiao kuli. A deaf ear, deafness, disobedience, refusal to listen to advice.

Pepeluali. February. *Eng.*

peu. To thrust or push up, uproot, prod.

pewa. Tail of fish, shrimp, lobster. Perhaps PPN *pewa.*

pī. 1. Stingy (sometimes preceded by *ke*). 2. To sputter, snort. 3. To sprinkle. PPN *pii.* 4. Peas, beans. *Eng.* 5. The letter "p." *Eng.*

pia. 1. Polynesian arrowroot (*Tacca leontopetaloides*). PNP *pia.* 2. Starch. 3. Also bia. Beer. *Eng.*

pi'a. A kind of yam (*Dioscorea pentaphylla*).

pi'alu. Wrinkled.

pī'āpā. Alphabet.

piapia. Encrusted white matter in the eyes, as after sleeping or from sore eyes, "sand" in the eyes. PNP *piapia.*

pi'ena. Fiery-tempered.

piha. Full, complete, filled, full-blooded; completion, capacity, fullness; pregnant. **ho-'opiha.** To fill, complete, stuff, eat one's fill; to load, as a gun.

piha-'ekelo. Mynah bird (*Acridotheres tristis*).

piha makahiki. Yearly anniversary; to have such. *Lā piha makahiki,* birthday.

pihapiha. Full, complete, filled. **ho'opihapiha.** To fill, complete, file (as cards); questionnaire, form to be filled in.

-pihapiha 'ōlelo. ho'opihapiha 'ōlelo. To stir up dislike, gossip.

piha pono. Completely full, complete. *Piha pono ka mana'o,* completely clear and intelligible idea.

pihe. Din of voices, crying, shouting; to mourn, shout. PEP *pi(f,s)e.*

pihi. 1. Scab, scar. 2. Button, badge; to button (preceded by *ke*). PEP *pi(f,s)i.* 3. Blunt, dull.

pihi pūlima. Cuff button.

pihoihoi. Disturbed, excited, worried. **ho'opihoihoi.** To cause anxiety, worry; to worry, excite, astonish.

pihole. To fidget, paw, squirm.

piholo. To sink, founder, drown, be swamped.

pīhopa, bihopa. Bishop; Episcopalian. *Eng.*

pi'i. 1. To go inland (whether uphill or not); to go up, climb, ascend, mount, rise. **ho'opi'i.** To cause to rise. PPN *piki.* 2. To experience, as heat, cold, emotion. *Pi'i ke anu,* to get chills. *Pi'i ka wela,* to get a fever; to feel the heat of anger. **ho'opi'i.** To stir up ill feelings.

-pi'i. ho'opi'i. To sue, bring suit, accuse in court; lawsuit, court case.

pi'ikoi. To claim honors not rightfully due, seek preferment, aspire to the best.

pi'ina. Climb, ascent, rise.

pi'ipi'i. 1. Redup. of *pi'i, 1, 2;* bubbling forth, overflowing; to arouse anger, jealousy. 2. Curly, curled, wavy.

pi'ipi'i 'ōlelo. Words of anger, emotion, controversy.

pī kai. To sprinkle with sea water or salted water, as to remove taboo.

pīkake. 1. Arabian jasmine (*Jasminum sambac*), a shrub with fragrant, small white flowers used for leis. 2. Peafowl (*Pavo cristata*).

pīkake-hōkū. Star jasmine (*Jasminum multiflorum*).

pika wai. Water pitcher.

piki. 1. Shrunk, shortened, irregular. *Lei piki,* lei made of feathers of uneven length. PEP *piti.* 2. Peach. *Eng.*

Pīkī. Fiji, Fijian. *Eng.*

pikipiki'ō. Rough, stormy, choppy, agitated.

piko. 1. Navel, navel string, umbilical cord, genitals. *Pehea kō piko?* How is your navel? (a facetious greeting avoided by many because of the double meaning). PPN *pito.* 2. Summit of a hill or mountain, crown of the head, ear tip, end of a rope.

pīkoi. 1. Core, as of breadfruit

or pandanus. **2.** Tripping club.

piku, fiku. Fig (*Ficus carica*).

pila. 1. Any musical instrument, formerly the fiddle. *Ho'okani pila*, to play music. **2.** Also **bila.** Bill; to make out a bill. *Eng.*

pila 'ai'ē. Voucher.

pila kīko'o. Check, draft, bill.

pila kīko'o hale leka. Money order.

pila koi. Requisition.

pīlali. Gum, as from the bark of the *kukui* tree; resin, wax; sticky, gummy.

pilapuhipuhi. Harmonica, mouth organ.

pilau. Rot, stench, rottenness; to stink; putrid, spoiled, rotten, decomposed. *PPN pilau.*

pila'ume'ume. Accordion.

pila waiwai. Account, reckoning.

pili. 1. To cling, stick, adhere, touch, join, associate with, be with; clinging, sticking; close relationship. *E pili kāua*, let's be together. See *hoa pili.* **ho-'opili.** To bring together, stick. *PPN pili.* **2.** A grass (*Heteropogon contortus*), formerly used for house thatch; thatch. See *hale pili.* **3.** To refer, concern, relate, apply. **ho'opili.** To refer. **4.** Wager, bet; to bet.

pilialoha. Close friendship, beloved companionship; to have such.

pilikia. Trouble of any kind, tragedy, nuisance, bother, distress, accident, inconvenience. **ho'opilikia.** To cause trouble, bother.

pili-ko'a. Hawkfishes (*Paracirrhites forsteri, P. arcatus, Cirrhitops pinnulatus*). *Lit.,* coral-clinging.

pili koko. Blood relationship or relative.

pilimua. Article (the part of speech): *ka, ke, nā, he.*

pilina. Association, relationship, union; joining.

-pilipili 'ōlelo. ho'opilipili 'ōlelo. Word play, punning; to illustrate with parable, story, or anecdote.

Pilipino, Filipino. Philippines, Filipino. *Eng.*

pili pono. Well-suited, well-matched, close-fitting; to refer exactly or concisely.

pili pū. To unite, join, cling to.

piliwaiwai. Gambling, betting, gambler; to bet, gamble.

piliwi. To believe. *Eng.*

pilo. Swampy, foul odor; halitosis; polluted. *PNP pilo.*

pīna'i. Again and again, repeatedly; to come or do repeatedly; close together, crowded.

pinana. To climb; a climb.

pinao. Dragonfly.

pine. Pin, peg, bolt, picket; to pin. *Eng.*

pineki. Peanut. *Eng.*

pinepine. Frequent, often, frequently. *PNP pine.*

pinika. Vinegar. *Eng.*

pio. 1. Captive, prisoner; conquered, captured; game of tag. **ho'opio.** To conquer, make prisoner, capture. **2.** Extinguished or out, as a fire or light. **bo'opio.** To put out, extinguish. *PEP pio.* **3.** To peep, chirp.

pi'o. Arch, arc; bent, arched, curved; to arch, as the rainbow. *PPN piko.*

pi'oe. General name for barnacles.

pi'oloke. Alarmed, startled, confused, agitated.

pipi. 1. Pearl oyster (*Pinctada radiata*). *PPN pipi.* **2.** Also **bipi.** Beef, cattle. *Eng.*

pipī. Redup. of *pī, 2*; squinting; twinkling.

pīpī. Redup. of *pī, 1, 3*; to urinate (*Eng.*) *Pīpī holo ka'ao,* sprinkled, the tale runs on (phrase used at the end of tales). PPN *piipii.*

pipi'i. 1. Expensive, high-priced. **2.** Bubbling, overflowing. *Wai pipi'i,* bubbling water, charged water.

pipika. To draw away, shrink away, crinkle up, avoid.

pipi kāne. Bull.

pipi kaula. Beef salted and dried, then broiled before being eaten. *Lit.,* rope beef.

pipi keiki. Calf.

pipiki. Shrunk, crinkled, tight, cramped.

pipine. Promiscuous; promiscuous person.

pīpine. Miserly, stingy.

pipi palai. Beefsteak.

pipipi. General name for small mollusks, including *Nerita picea* and *N. neglecta.*

pipipi-kōlea. Periwinkle (*Littorina pintado, L. scabra*).

pipi po'a. Steer. *Lit.,* castrated beef.

pipi pulu. Bull.

pipi wahine. Cow.

pipi waiū. Milk cow.

piula. 1. Mule, donkey. **2.** Tired, exhausted. *Slang.* **3.** Pewter, tin, corrugated iron. See *wai piula.*

pīwa 1. Also **fiwa.** Fever. *Eng.* **2.** Also **biwa.** Beaver. *Eng.*

pīwa-ho'onāwaliwali. Typhoid fever.

pīwa-lenalena. Yellow fever.

pīwa-'ula'ula. Scarlet fever.

pō. Night, darkness; realm of the gods; dark, benighted. *Ua pō,* it's late ' not necessarily night). *Ua hana māua a pō ka lā,* we worked until night (until day darkened). *Ka pō nei,* last night. PPN *poo.*

po'a. 1. Castrated; eunuch. PPN *poka.* **2.** Sudden sound; to make such. **3.** To dig under, undermine.

pō'ae'ae. Armpit.

pō'aha. Circle, as of flowers; trailing plant.

Pō'ahā. Thursday. *Lit.,* fourth day.

pō'aha mālamalama. Halo. *Lit.,* light circle.

poahi. 1. Dim, obscure. **2.** To revolve, spin, rotate.

pō'ai. Circle, circuit, hoop, girdle, group (as of friends); to make a circuit, go around, encircle. PPN *pookai.*

pō'ai hapalua. Semicircle, half circle.

pō'ai-waena-honua. Equator.

Pō'akahi. Monday. *Lit.,* first day.

Pō'akolu. Wednesday. *Lit.,* third day.

Pō'akolu Kau Lehu. Ash Wednesday.

Pō'alima. Friday. *Lit.,* fifth day.

Pō'alima Hemolele, Pō'alima Maika'i. Good Friday.

pō'alo. To gouge out, scoop out, pluck, extract; to shell, as beans.

Pō'alua. Tuesday. *Lit.,* second day.

Pō'aōno. Saturday. *Lit.,* sixth day. *Ho'omana Pō'aōno,* Seventh Day Adventist religion.

poe. Round, rounded. **ho'opoe.** To round, shape. *Pipi ho'opoe,* meat ball.

po'e. People, persons, group of people, number of. *Ka po'e wāhine,* the women. *Po'e hale,* group of houses.

poehi, powehi. Dim, obscure.

poeko, poweko. Fluent, clever in speaking.

pō'ele. Black, dark, dark night; ignorant.

pō'ele'ele. Redup. of *pō'ele.*

poepoe. Round, rounded; compact, compressed; full, as the moon; globe, sphere.

poepoe honua. Globe of the earth.

pohā. 1. To burst, crack, break forth. **2.** Cape gooseberry, ground cherry (*Physalis peruviana*).

pōhae. Torn, fragile.

pōhāhā ahi. Fireball.

pōhāhā wai. Bubble.

pōhai. Circle, group; gathering.

pōhaku. Rock, stone, mineral, tablet; rocky, stony. See haku, 3. PEP poofatu.

pōhaku hānau. Stones at Kūkani-loko, O'ahu, and Holoholokū, Kaua'i, against which chiefesses rested as they gave birth.

pōhaku ke'oke'o. Marble.

pōhaku kihi. Cornerstone.

pōhaku ku'i 'ai, pōhaku ku'i poi. Poi pounder.

pōhaku lepo. Brick, adobe.

pōhaku maika'i. Precious stone.

pōhaku 'ōma'oma'o. Emerald.

pōhaku pa'a. General name for hard rocks, such as those used for adzes.

pōhaku pele. Lava rock.

pohala. 1. To revive after fainting, recover consciousness; to recover from sickness; relieved of worry; relief, rest. 2. To open, as petals.

pohāpohā. 1. Redup. of pohā, 1. 2. A kind of passion flower called running pop or love-in-a-mist (Passiflora foetida).

pohe haole. Nasturtium.

pōheo. Knob or knoblike object; penis head.

pōheoheo. Knob or knoblike object.

pohihihi. Obscure, entangled, intricate, confusing, difficult.

pōhina. 1. Gray, misty, foggy, hazy. 2. To topple, fall prone.

poho. 1. Hollow or palm of the hand; depression, hollow; container, receptacle. 2. Mortar; to knead. 3. Patch, as in clothes or in a calabash. 4. To belly out, puff out. 5. Chalk.

pohō. 1. Loss, damage, out of luck. See koi pohō. ho-'opohō. To cause a loss, sell at a loss. 2. Bog, swamp, mire, slough.

poho ahi. Matchbox.

poholalo. Underhanded, deceitful, dishonest; to burrow, filch, deal dishonestly.

pohole. Bruised, skinned, scraped, peeled.

poho lima. Palm or hollow of the hand, handful.

poholo. To sink, slip into, vanish; to miscarry.

poholua. To billow out, as sails.

poho meakanu. Flower pot.

poho pa'akai. Salt shaker, salt container.

poho pauka. Powder container, compact, vanity case.

pohopoho. Redup. of poho, 1–4; patched. Kapa pohopoho, crazy quilt or patchwork quilt.

poho wāwae. Hollow of the foot.

pohu. Calm, quiet, calmed, soothed; to calm down.

pōhue. 1. General name for gourd plant; potsherd. Also called ipu. PEP poohue. 2. A climbing legume (Canavalia sericea).

pōhuehue. Beach morning-glory (Ipomoea pes-caprae).

pōhuku. Swollen, protruding, heaped.

pōhuli. Sucker, sprout; to sprout, as bananas.

poi. Poi, the Hawaiian staff of life, made from cooked taro corms, or rarely breadfruit, pounded until smooth and thinned with water. PPN po'oi.

po'i. 1. Cover, lid; to cover (preceded by ke). PEP poki. 2. Top or crest of a breaking wave; to break, of waves. 3. To pounce, catch between cupped hands, snatch.

poi mai'a. Mashed ripe bananas and water.

po'imalau. Portuguese man-of-war (Physalia).

poina. To forget, forgotten. Mai poina 'oe ia'u, don't forget me.

pō'ino. Misfortune, ill luck, distress, misery, damage, injury; unfortunate. **ho'opō'ino.** To harm, injure, devastate; to cause distress, damage. *Ho-'opō'ino malū,* to harm secretly; sabotage.

po'ipū. To cover completely, as with clouds or waves; to attack, overwhelm; attack.

po'i wai holoi. Washbasin, finger bowl.

pōkā. Bullet, cannonball.

pōka'a. Ball, coil, roll, spool; to wind, roll, coil, revolve.

pōkā lū. Buckshot, grapeshot.

pōka'o. Barren, dry, tasteless, naked, destitute, boring.

pōkā pahū. Bomb, bombardment; to bomb.

pōkā pū. Bullet.

poke. To slice, cut crosswise; section, slice, piece.

pōkē. Bouquet; to make a bouquet. *Eng.*

pōkeokeo. 1. Turkey gobble, turkey. 2. Plump, prosperous.

pōki'i. Younger brother or sister or closely related younger cousin. PEP *pootiki.*

pōki'i kaina. Younger sibling of one's own sex.

pokipoki. 1. Box crab (*Calappa* sp.). 2. Sowbug, pill bug. PEP *potipoti.*

poko. Short for *pōkole.* PPN *poto.*

pōkole. Short; shortage. **ho-'opōkole.** To shorten, abbreviate.

Pokoliko. Puerto Rico. *Eng.*

pola. 1. Flap, as of a loincloth; tail of a kite. 2. Also **bola.** Bowl, cup (preceded by *ke*). *Eng.*

polapola. 1. Recovered from sickness; well after sickness; sprouting, as a bud. **ho'opo-lapola.** To cure; to fill out, as after sickness. 2. (*Cap.*) Tahiti, Borabora; Tahitian.

Polenekia. Polynesia; Polynesian. *Eng.*

poli. Bosom, breast, depression, heart, arms. *Ma ka poli iho nei,* in the arms. Perhaps PEP *poli.*

polinahe. Soft and gentle, as a breeze.

poli wāwae. Hollow of the foot, instep.

polohiwa. Dark, glistening black, as clouds.

poloka. Frog, toad. *Eng.*

poloke. Broken, broke (without funds). *Eng.*

pololei. 1. Straight, correct, right, accurate, all right. **ho'opololei.** To straighten, correct. 2. A land shell (*Lamellaxis*).

pōloli. Hunger; hungry.

pololoi. Var. of *pololei, 1.*

pololū. Long spear.

polopeka. Professor; professorial; to be a professor. *Eng.*

polū. Blue. *Eng.*

poluea. Nausea, dizziness, seasickness, hangover; seasick.

pōmaika'i. Good fortune, blessedness, blessing, prosperity; prosperous, fortunate, lucky; benefits and improvements to property. **ho'opomaika'i.** To cause good fortune; to bless, say grace.

pona. 1. Socket, eyeball; joint of sugarcane stalk or bamboo. PPN *pona.* 2. Also **bona.** Bond. *Eng.*

pōna'ana'a. Confused, bewildered.

pōnalo. Plant louse, gnat, small fly such as *Drosophila;* blight; shriveled; swarming.

pō nei. Last night.

poni. 1. To anoint, consecrate, oil, crown, ordain, inaugurate, daub; ointment. **ho-'oponi.** To anoint, crown, ordain, consecrate, inaugurate. 2. Purple.

poni mō'ī. Coronation; to crown a king or queen.

ponimō'ī. Carnation (*Dianthus caryophyllus*).

ponimōʻī-liʻiliʻi. Sweet william (*Dianthus barbatus*).

poniponi. Redup. of *poni, 2.*

pōniu. Dizzy, giddy; dizziness; to rotate, whirl, spin.

pōniuniu. Redup. of *pōniu.*

pono. 1. Goodness, morality, moral qualities, correct or proper procedure, excellence, well-being, prosperity, welfare, duty; moral, fitting, proper, right, just, fair, successful; should, ought, must, necessary. *Ka pono kahiko,* the old morality. *Pono i ke kānāwai,* legal. *Pono ʻole ka manaʻo,* disturbed, worried. *Me ka pono,* respectfully. *E pono iā ʻoe ke hele,* you should go. **hoʻopono.** To correct, behave correctly. PEP *pono.* **2.** completely, properly, carefully, much. *Pau pono,* completely finished. *Nānā pono,* look carefully. **3.** Property, gear, possessions, necessities.

pono hale. Furniture, household goods.

pono hana. Tools.

ponoʻī. Self, own; directly, exactly. *ʻO wau ponoʻī,* I, myself. *Hawaiʻi ponoʻī,* Hawaiʻi's own [people].

pono kīwila. Civil rights.

ponokope. Copyright; to copyright.

ponopono. 1. Neat, in order, arranged. **hoʻoponopono.** To correct, revise, edit, put to right; mental cleansing, as by family discussion. *Luna hoʻoponopono,* editor, administrator. See *hale hoʻoponopono.* **2.** Redup. of *pono, 1*; well off, wealthy.

pono ʻuhane. Spiritual welfare.

poʻo. 1. Head, summit, director; end, as of rope, pole, cane (preceded by *ke*). PEP *upoko.* **2.** Depression, cavity; to dip, scoop, dub, erode. PPN *poko.*

poʻohiwi. Shoulder, wing of bird or kite.

poʻo kanaka. Human head, skull. See *heiau poʻo kanaka.*

poʻokela. Foremost, best, superior, champion; to excel.

poʻolā. Stevedore.

poʻoleka. Postage stamp.

poʻolua. Child sired by other than the husband, but accepted by both husband and sire.

poʻomanaʻo. Topic, theme, headline.

poʻoʻōlelo. Title, text.

poʻo-paʻa. Hawkfish (*Cirrhites pinnulatus*). Lit., hard head.

poʻopoʻo. Redup. of *poʻo, 2*; sunken; nook, cranny.

Pope. Pope, papist, Catholic. *Eng. Hōʻole Pope,* Protestant.

pōpilikia. Trouble, distress, misfortune. **hoʻopōpilikia.** To cause distress, trouble.

popo. Rot. PPN *popo.*

pōpō. 1. Ball, cluster, bunch. PPN *poʻopoʻo.* **2.** Short for *ʻapōpō,* tomorrow.

pōpōahi. Fireball.

pōpō-hau. Hydrangea.

popohe. Round, shapely, neat.

pōpoki. Cat.

pōpolo. 1. Black nightshade (*Solanum nigrum* or *S. nodiflorum*), herbaceous plant important in Hawaiian medicine; bears clusters of small, black, edible berries. PPN *polo.* **2.** Negro. Slang. **3.** An endemic lobelia (*Cyanea solanacea*).

pōpolohua. Purplish blue; dark, as a bruise.

popopo. Rot, decay; rotten, decayed.

pou. 1. Post. PPN *pou.* **2.** Ridge, as of nose.

pou kihi. Corner post.

pouli. 1. Dark, darkness, ignorance. **hoʻopouli.** To darken, mislead. PPN *po(o)ʻuli.* **2.** Eclipse.

pōuliuli. Redup. of *pouli, 1.*

poupou. Short and stocky, stout.

pōwā. Robber; to rob, plunder.

powehi. Var. spelling of *poehi*.

poweko. Var. spelling of *poeko*.

pū. 1. Large triton conch shell or triton's trumpet (*Charonia tritonis*); wind instrument, as horn, trumpet, cornet. PNP *puu*. 2. Gun, pistol. 3. General name for pumpkin or squash. 4. Tree with cluster of several stalks, as banana, pandanus, or kava; clump, as of sugarcane. PPN *pu'u*. 5. Together, entirely. *Like pū*, just the same. *'O wau pū*, me too. 6. Sluggish, inactive, quiet, bored.

pua. 1. Flower, blossom. PPN *pua*. 2. To appear, come forth, emerge; to smoke, blow, speak, shine. 3. Child, descendant, young fish, fry. 4. Arrow, dart.

pū'ā. 1. Flock, herd; to flock. 2. Sheaf, bundle; to tie in bundles.

pua'a. 1. Pig, hog, swine, pork. PPN *puaka*. 2. Bank of fog or clouds.

pū'ā'ā. Scattered, dispersed; to flee.

pua'a hame. Ham.

pua ahi, puahi. To glow like fire.

pua ahiahi. Same as *nani-ahiahi*, four-o'clock flower.

pua ali'i. Descendant of a chief.

pua aloalo. See *aloalo*.

puaaneane, pūaneane. Extreme old age.

pua'a wahine. Sow.

pua-hilahila. Sensitive plant (*Mimosa pudica*).

pua hipa. Lamb.

pū'ā hipa. Flock of sheep.

pua-hōkū-hihi. Waxflower or wax plant (*Hoya carnosa*).

pua'i. To flow out, as water; to bubble, gurgle, boil, vomit; to utter, as speech. PNP *puaki*.

pū'ā'ī. Adam's apple.

pua-kala. 1. Beach poppy or prickly poppy (*Argemone glauca*); the yellowish juice, which contains a narcotic, was used by Hawaiians to relieve pain. 2. Spear thistle (*Cirsium vulgare*).

pua-kalaunu. Crown flower (*Calotropis gigantea*); large shrub of the milkweed family, bearing small white crown-shaped flowers often used in leis.

puakea. Pale; a tint between white and pink, as sunset clouds. See *'ilipuakea*.

pua-kenikeni. A shrub or small tree (*Fagraea berteriana*), bearing fragrant yellow flowers used in leis.

pua-kīkā. Cigar flower (*Cuphea ignea*).

pua kō. Stem and tassel of sugarcane.

pua-lele. Sow thistle (*Sonchus oleraceus*).

pualena. 1. Yellow. 2. Lazy.

pū'ali. 1. Warrior. 2. To gird tightly about the waist; notch, tight belt.

Pū'ali Ho'ōla. Salvation Army.

pū'ali inu wai. Temperance league. *Lit.*, water-drinking host.

pū'ali kaua ka'i wāwae. Infantry. *Lit.*, war army going afoot.

pū'ali koa. Armed forces.

pū'aloalo. Same as *pua aloalo*, hibiscus flower.

pualu, puwalu. A species of surgeonfish.

pū'alu. Loose, slack, crumpled.

pua makahiki. Annual flower.

puana. 1. Beginning of a song; to begin a song; summary refrain of a song; theme of a song. *Ha'ina 'ia mai ana ka puana*, tell the summary refrain. 2. Pronunciation.

pua-nānā-lā. Common sunflower.

pūanuanu. Cold, chilly, damp.

pū'ao. 1. Mesh. 2. Womb.

pua'ohi. To chatter, gush, ramble verbally.

pua-pepa. Same as *nani-mauloa*. *Lit.*, paper flower.

pua-pihi. All kinds of zinnias, especially *Zinnia elegans*.

pua-pilipili. Spanish clover (*Desmodium uncinatum*).

pū'ā pipi. Herd of cattle.

puapua. 1. Tail feathers, streamer. 2. Redup. of *pua, 2.*

pua pua'a. Piglet.

puapua'i. Redup. of *pua'i*.

pue. To huddle, sit crouched.

pu'e. 1. Hill, as of sweet potatoes; dune; to hill up. PPN *puke*. 2. To attack.

pu'e'eke. To shrink away from, wrinkle up; to shorten, contract.

puehu. Scattered, dispersed, routed, gone. PEP *pu(u)efu*.

pūehuehu. Redup. of *puehu*; tousled.

pueo. Hawaiian short-eared owl (*Asio flammeus sandwichensis*).

pu'eone. Sand dune or sandbar.

pu'e wale. To force, attack, rape.

pūhā. 1. Abscess, burst sore, ulcer; to break, burst. 2. Hollow, as in a tree. 3. To belch, clear the throat. PEP *pu(u)-ha(a)*. 4. To breathe air, as a turtle. PEP *pu(u)(f,s)a(a)*.

pūhaka. Loins.

pū hala. Pandanus tree. PEP *puu fala*.

pūhā lā'au. Hollow in a tree.

puhalu. Soft, flabby, loose, sagging, deflated; to loosen, stretch, sag. *Fig.*, relaxed, unenthusiastic.

pūhau. Cool spring.

pūheheo. Round and swirling, as a full skirt.

puhemo. 1. Loose, set free, released. 2. Weak, listless.

puhi. 1. To burn, set on fire, bake; to smoke, as tobacco. 2. To blow, puff; blowhole. PPN *pusi*. 3. Eel. PNP *pusi*.

puhi kō. To burn cane trash or a cane field.

puhi 'ohe. To play a wind instrument; player of a wind instrument; flute. See *hui puhi 'ohe*.

puhi-'ōni'o. Moray eel (*Gymnothorax meleagris*). *Lit.*, spotted eel.

puhi paka. To smoke tobacco; one who smokes; smoking.

puhi-paka. Moray eel (*Gymnothorax flavimarginatus*). *Lit.*, fierce eel.

pūhi'u. To break wind audibly; to be rude.

puhi-ūhā. Moray eel (*Conger marginatus*).

pūholo. To steam, as of pig; to take a sweat bath.

pū ho'okani. Conch trumpet, wind instrument.

pūhuluhulu. Hairy, shaggy, downy, hirsute.

puia. Sweet-smelling; diffused, as fragrance; permeated with fragrance. ho'opuia. To perfume.

pū'ili. 1. Bamboo rattles, as used for dancing. 2. To clasp, hold firmly in the hand, embrace.

pu'ipu'i. Plump, stout, stocky.

pū'iwa. Startled, surprised, astonished, frightened; fright, surprise. ho'opū'iwa. To startle, astonish, etc.

pū'iwa'iwa. Redup. of *pū'iwa*.

puka. 1. Hole (perforation; cf. *lua*, pit); door, gate, opening. ho'opuka. To make a hole or opening. PEP *puta*. 2. To pass through, appear, issue, come into sight; to rise, as the sun. *Puka lā*, daily issue, as of a newspaper. ho'opuka. To issue, as a permit; to acquit, as a defendant in court. 3. To graduate. ho'opuka. To graduate. 4. To say, utter.

ho‘opuka. To proclaim, say, pronounce. *Ho‘opuka ‘ana*, pronunciation. **5.** To gain, win, profit, draw interest; winnings, gain, profit. ho‘opuka. To invest, make a profit.

Puka ‘ana. Exodus (in the Bible), exit.

pukaaniani, pukaniani. Window.

puka hale. Door of a house, window.

pukana lā. Sunrise.

pū kani. Trumpet.

puka pihi. Buttonhole.

pūkaua. General, war leader, champion.

pū kaua. Artillery.

puka uahi. Smokestack, chimney.

puke, buke. Book. *Eng.*

puke heluhelu. Reader.

puke ho‘omana‘o. Memorandum, memoirs, diary, journal.

puke kuhikuhi. Manual, book of instructions.

puke pakeke. Pocketbook.

puke wehewehe ‘ōlelo. Dictionary. *Lit.*, book explaining words.

pūkiawe. A native shrub (*Styphelia tameiameiae*).

pūkiawe lei. Black-eyed susan (*Abrus precatorius*).

pūki‘i. To tie.

Pukikī. Portuguese. *Palaoa Pukikī*, Portuguese sweetbread. *Eng.*

pūkipa. Bookkeeper. *Eng.*

pū kō. Clump of sugarcane.

pūko‘a. Coral head. PEP *puutoka.*

pūkolu. Trio, triplet.

pūkonakona. Strong, husky, tough. Cf. *konakona.*

puku. To gather together, pucker; shrunken. PPN *putu.*

pūku‘i. **1.** To collect, assemble; council, assembly. PPN *pu(u)tuki.* **2.** To sit doubled up; to nestle together, hug. **3.** Hub.

pūku‘iku‘i. Redup. of *pūku‘i*, 2.

pū kuni ahi. Cannon. *Lit.*, gun burning fire.

pukupuku. Redup. of *puku;* wrinkles, frowns; to wrinkle, frown. PPN *putuputu.*

pula. Particle, as dust; particle in the eye, mote; to have something in the eye. PEP *pula.*

pula lānahu. Cinder.

pūlale. To hurry, rush.

pūlama. **1.** Torch. **2.** To care for, cherish, save.

pulapula. Seedlings, sprouts, cuttings; descendant, offspring. ho‘opulapula. To start seedlings or cuttings; to multiply, rehabilitate; rehabilitation. *Ho‘opulapula lāhui*, rehabilitation of the nation. *‘Āina ho‘opulapula*, homesteading land. PPN *pulapula.*

pule. **1.** Prayer, church, grace, blessing; to pray. *Pule a ka Haku*, Lord's prayer. See *kahuna pule, Lāpule.* PPN *pule.* **2.** Week. *Kēia pule a‘e*, next week. *Kēlā pule aku nei*, last week.

pule ho‘ola‘a. Dedicatory prayer.

pule ho‘omaika‘i. Prayer of thanks, benediction, grace; to say grace, offer a prayer of thanks.

pule ho‘opōmaika‘i. Blessing; to ask a blessing.

pūlehu. To broil.

pūlehulehu. Dusk, twilight. PEP *puulefu.*

pulelehua. **1.** Butterfly, moth, the Kamehameha butterfly (*Vanessa tameamea*). ho‘opulelehua. To act the butterfly, talk much but say little; frivolous. **2.** Wind-blown, as spray.

pulelo. To float, wave, as a flag (sometimes in sense of triumph).

pule ‘ohana. Family prayer; to hold such.

pulepule. 1. Crazy. See *pupule.* **2.** Spotted, speckled. PPN *pulepule.*

pūlewa. 1. To float back and forth; unstable, changeable, unsteady. **2.** Weak, feeble. **3.** Same as *hālili*, sundial shell.

pūliki. 1. To embrace, hug, gird on, grip tightly. **2.** Vest.

pūlima. 1. Wrist, cuff; to clasp hands. See *pihi pūlima.* **2.** Handwriting, signature.

pulo, buro. Bureau, agency. *Eng.*

pulo ʻeʻe moku. Bureau of immigration.

pulo hoʻokō. Executive board.

pūloʻu. Head covering; to cover the head.

pūloʻuloʻu. Redup. of *pūloʻu.* **2.** A tapa-covered ball on a stick carried before a chief as insignia of taboo. **3.** Steam bath.

pulu. 1. Wet, moist, soaked. **hoʻopulu.** To wet, soak, moisten. PEP *pulu.* **2.** Soft, glossy, yellowish wool on the base of tree-fern leaf stalks, formerly used to stuff mattresses and pillows. **3.** Mulch, any greenery or underbrush used as mulch, coconut fiber, cushion, fine linen, tinder, kindling (preceded by *ke*). See *kapa pulu.* **hoʻopulu.** To mulch, fertilize with compost. PPN *pulu.* **4.** Also **bulu.** Bull. *Eng. Keoni Pulu*, John Bull. **5.** Fool; to fool. *Eng.*

pūlumi, burumi. Broom; to sweep. *Eng.*

pūlumi hale. To sweep a house; janitor.

pūluna. One's child's parents-in-law or aunts and uncles by marriage (often followed by *kāne*, male, or *wahine*, female).

pulu niu. Coconut husk or fiber.

pulu pē. Thoroughly drenched, soaked; drunk.

pulupulu. Redup. of *pulu, 1, 2, 3.* **2.** Cotton.

pulupulu ahi. Fire kindling; to kindle fire; hot-tempered.

pulupulu-haole. The cotton plant.

pū maiʻa. Banana stalk.

pumehana. Warm, warm-hearted; warmth, affection. *Me ke aloha pumehana*, with warm affection. **hoʻopumehana.** To warm, heat.

puna. 1. Spring (of water). PPN *puna.* **2.** Coral, lime, plaster. PPN *punga.* **3.** Section between joints or nodes, as of bamboo or sugarcane. **4.** Spoon. *Eng.*

punahele. A favorite; to treat as a favorite.

punalua. Formerly, spouses sharing a spouse.

pūnana. Nest, hive; to nest. PPN *punanga.*

pūnana meli. Beehive.

pūnanana. 1. Same as *nananana*, a spider. **2.** Spider's web.

pūnāwai. Water spring.

punawelewele. Cobweb, spider web, spinning spider.

pūneʻe. Movable couch. See *hikieʻe.*

puni. 1. Surrounded, controlled, overcome; to gain control of. **hoʻopuni.** To surround, get control of. PNP *puni.* **2.** To be fond of, love, covet; favorite thing, delight, love. **hoʻopuni.** To be charmed by, desire greatly. **3.** Deceived. **hoʻopuni.** To deceive. **4.** Completed.

puni ʻai. Fond of eating; glutton.

punihei. Ensnared, entangled; gullible; captivating, entrancing. *Moʻolelo punihei*, fascinating tale. **hoʻopunihei.** To fascinate, charm, ensnare, decoy, trap.

puni hele. Fond of going about from place to place.

puni kālā. Avaricious, mercenary.

puni koko. Bloodthirsty.

puni le'ale'a. Pleasure-loving, fond of fun.

punipuni. Redup. of *puni*, 3. **ho'opunipuni.** To lie; lie, liar.

pūniu. 1. Polished coconut shell or bowl. 2. Small knee drum. 3. Human skull. 4. Fontanel of an infant. 5. To spin, as a top.

puni waiwai. Avaricious.

puni wale. Gullible, easily deceived.

pūnohu. To rise, as smoke or mist; to billow or spread.

pūnono. Gorgeously red, everbeautiful, flushed.

pūnua. Young bird, fledgling. PNP *punua*.

pūnuku. Muzzle, halter; to muzzle.

pū'o'a. Tower, steeple, pyramid, peak.

pū'ohe'ohe. Job's-tears (*Coix lachryma-jobi*).

puoho. Startled; to cry out in fright.

pū 'olē'olē. Conch horn.

pū'olo. Bundle, bag, container; to tie in a bundle.

pūpanapana. Pistol.

pū po'ohiwi. Musket.

pupū. To stall, move slowly; stuck, blocked.

pūpū. 1. General name for sea and land shells; beads. PPN *puupuu*. 2. Relish, snack, hors d'oeuvre; formerly, fish, chicken or banana served with kava. 3. Bunch, bundle, as of grass; bouquet.

pūpū-'alā. Cone shell (*Conus* sp.).

pūpū-'awa. A sea shell (*Drupa ricinus, Thais aperta*).

pupue. Redup. of *pue*.

pupu'e. Redup. of *pu'e, 2;* to attack, force.

pupuhi. Redup. of *puhi, 1, 2;* to spit.

pū puhi. Trumpet, horn, conch shell trumpet.

pupuka. Ugly, unsightly.

pupule. Crazy, insane. **ho'opupule.** To drive insane.

pūpū-loloa. Auger shell (*Terebra* sp.).

pūpū-momi. Small mother-of-pearl shell.

pupuni. Redup. of *puni, 1–4.*

pūpū-Ni'ihau. A shell (Columbellidae) found on Ni'ihau and Kaua'i.

pūpū-'ōkole-'oi'oi. Trochidae shell.

pupupu. 1. Numerous, crowded, congested. 2. Doubleflowering.

pūpū-puhi. Sundial shell (*Solarium perspectivum*); also called *hālili*.

pupu'u. To double up.

pūpū weuweu. Clump of greenery.

pu'u. 1. Any kind of protuberance from a pimple (*pu'u,* 2) to a hill; hill, peak, mound, bulge, heap, quantity, mass, clot, knob; heaped. PPN *puku*. 2. Any of various round parts or protuberances of the body, as pimple, wart, mole, callus, lump, Adam's apple, throat, larynx, tonsils, fist, knuckle, gizzard.

pu'u 'ako. Throat inflammation.

pu'u'eha. Sore throat.

pu'uhonua. Place of refuge, asylum, place of peace and safety.

pu'u kālā. Sum of money.

pu'ukani. Sweet-voiced, sweettoned; singer.

pu'ukaua. Fort, fortification.

pū'uki'uki. Crowded, packed tightly, difficult.

pu'u koko. Blood clot, heart, foetus.

pu'ukole. *Mons pubis.*

pu'ukū. Treasurer.

pu'ulele. Rupture, hernia.

pū'ulu. Group, crowd, army,

party; to form a group; to crowd, assemble.

pūʻulu kaua. Army, fighting band, division.

puʻumimi. Bladder.

puʻumoni, puʻumoniʻai. Throat.

puʻunaue, puʻunauwe. To divide, share; division.

puʻunaue loa. Long division.

puʻunaue pōkole. Short division.

puʻu-ōlaʻi. A fish, one of the sharpbacked puffers (*Canthigaster amboinensis*).

puʻuone. 1. Divination. 2. Pond near the shore.

puʻu one. Sand dune or heap.

puʻupā. Obstacle, struck object.

puʻupaʻa. 1. Virgin, virginity. 2. Kidneys.

puʻupau. Sore throat, throat cancer.

puʻu pele. Volcanic mound, hill.

puʻu pepa. Deck or hand of cards; pile of paper.

puʻupuʻu. 1. Redup. of *puʻu, 1;* lumpy, heaped, swollen. PPN *pukupuku.* 2. Redup. of *puʻu, 2;* knuckles, joints; pimply, full of blotches; scurvy.

puʻupuʻu liʻiliʻi. Smallpox.

puʻupuʻu lima. Clenched fist, knuckles, blow of the fist.

puʻupuʻu maneʻo. Itching skin irritation or eruption.

puʻupuʻu wāwae. Ankle, ankle bones.

puʻuwai. Heart.

puʻu welu. Heap of rags.

puwalu, pualu. 1. All together, in unison, united, cooperative. 2. Var. spelling of *pualu,* surgeonfish.

puwō, puō. To roar, wail, howl.

R

All loan words from English sometimes spelled with initial *r-* are entered under *l-*. For example: *raisi,* see *laiki,* rice; *ropi,* see *lopi,* rope; *rumi,* see *lumi,* room.

S

All loan words from English sometimes spelled with initial *s-* are entered under *k-*. For example: *Sabati,* see *Kāpaki,* Sabbath; *sopa,* see *kopa,* soap.

T

All loan words from English sometimes spelled with initial *t-* are entered under *k-*. For example: *tausani,* see *kaukani,* thousand; *tiga,* see *kika,* tiger.

U

u-. Prefix to some words to denote plural, as *uhaele, ulawaiʻa, unonoho.*

-u. Second person singular possessive. PPN *-u.*

ū. Breast, teat, udder. Cf. *waiū.*

PPN *huhu*. 2. Moist; to drip, drizzle; impregnated, as with salt. Cf. *ma'ū*.

-**'u.** First person singular possessive. PPN *-ku*.

'ū. 1. To grunt, groan, moan, sigh, mourn, grieve; sorrow; an exclamation of delight or assent. *Noho 'ū*, grief; grief-stricken. **ho'o'ū, hō'ū.** To grunt and strain, as with physical exertion; to mourn. PNP *kuu*. 2. The letter "u."

ua. 1. Rain; to rain; rainy. *Ua loa*, long period of rain. **ho-'oua.** To cause rain. PPN *'uha*. 2. Afore-mentioned, the one talked of (a demonstrative preceding a noun, which is usually followed by *nei*, here, or *lā*, there.) 3. A very common particle preceding verbs and denoting completed action. PPN *kua*.

uahi, uwahi. Smoke; smoked; dustlike; spray, wisps. *Pipi uahi*, smoked beef. **ho'ouahi.** To smoke, emit smoke, cure by smoking. PPN *'ahu*, PEP *auafi*.

uakea. 1. Mist (famous at Hāna, Maui). *Lit.*, white rain. 2. White as mist, mist-white, white as breaking surf or snow.

uaki, uati. Var. spellings of *uwaki*, watch.

'uala, 'uwala. Sweet potato (*Ipomoea batatas*). PEP *kumala*. (Cognates elsewhere in Polynesia may be borrowings from PEP: Green, 1973.)

'uala-kahiki. White or Irish potato (*Solanum tuberosum*). *Lit.*, foreign sweet potato.

'uala pilau. Turnip. *Lit.*, smelly potato.

ualo. Var. spelling of *uwalo*.

'uao, 'uwao. To intercede, arbitrate, reconcile; conciliator, peacemaker.

uapo. Var. spelling of *uwapo*.

'ua'u, 'uwa'u. Dark-rumped petrel (*Pterodroma phaeopygia sandwichensis*), a sea bird.

uaua. Tough, glutinous, willful. PPN *uaua*.

ue, uwe. 1. To jerk, pull, twist, sway. Cf. *naue*. PEP *ue*. 2. A hula step.

uē. Var. spelling of *uwē*.

uea. Var. spelling of *uwea*, wire.

'uehe. Var. spelling of *'uwehe*.

ueka. Var. spelling of *uweka*.

ueko. Var. spelling of *uweko*.

uene, uwene. To move back and forth.

uepa. Var. spelling of *uwepa*.

ueue, uweuwe. Redup. of *ue, 1*; to wriggle, squirm.

'uha. Wasteful, extravagant; waste, extravagance.

'ūhā. Thigh, lap; shoulder, hindquarters, as of a horse or pig. *'Ūhā moa*, drumstick of chicken. PEP *kuufaa*.

uhaele. Plural of *haele*, to go, come.

'ūhā hame. Leg of ham.

'ūhā hipa. Leg of mutton.

'ūhā hope. Hindquarters, as of pig, beef.

uhai. Same as *hahai*.

uha'i. Same as *uhaki*, to break.

'uhane. Soul, spirit, ghost.

'Uhane Hemolele. Holy Ghost.

uhau. Var. of *hahau*.

'uhene. To play a merry tune, converse quietly and romantically; exclamation of exultation, as in songs.

'uhe'uhene. Redup. of *'uhene*; tra-la-la.

uhi. 1. Covering, cover, veil, lid; solid tattooing; to cover, engulf, overwhelm; to don, as a feather cloak. PPN *ufi*. 2. Large bluish-brown birthmark. 3. Yam (*Dioscorea alata*). PPN *'ufi*. 4. Mother-of-pearl bivalve, mother-of-pearl shank. PPN *'ufi*.

uhikino. Body covering, garment, shield.

uhi moe. Bedspread.

uhina. Covering; throw or cast net.

'ūhini. Long-horn grasshopper; cricket; locust.

'ūhini-lele. Beetle, cricket. *Lit.*, flying grasshopper.

uhi pākaukau. Tablecloth.

uhi pūku'i. Hubcap.

uhiuhi. 1. Redup. of *uhi*, 1. PPN *ufi'ufi*. **2.** An endemic Hawaiian forest tree (*Mezo̱neuron kauaiense*) of the legume family, with pink to red flowers.

uhu. The parrotfishes, of which *Scarus perspicillatus* is among the most abundant and largest. PPN *ufu*.

ui. To ask, question, appeal, turn to for help or advice, query; question, catechism. PEP *ui*.

ūi. Halloo.

u'i. Youthful, handsome, pretty, beautiful; youth; youthful vigor and beauty; youthful hero. **ho'oū'i.** To beautify.

'uiki, 'uwiki. 1. To glimmer, especially of a light through a hole, crack, or narrow opening; to twinkle faintly. **hō-'uiki.** To open a crack or sliver; to cause to gleam. **2.** Piping, as used for dress trimming. **3.** Var. spelling of *'uwiki*, wick.

uila, uwila. Lightning, electricity; electric. *Kapuahi uila*, electric stove. **ho'ouila, hō-'uila.** To flash, as lightning. PPN *'uhila*.

'u'ina. 1. Sharp report, as crack of a pistol; to crack, snap, crackle, creak (as joints); to make a splashing sound. **2.** Glottal stop.

'u'inakolo. Rustle, roar; to rustle (*'u'ina* and *nākolo*).

uka. Inland, upland, toward the mountain; shore, uplands; shoreward (from at sea) (often preceded by the particles *i, ma-,* or *o* and often written *mauka*). *Kō uka*, those belonging to the uplands; mountain folk. PPN *'uta*.

-uka. ho'oūka. To load, as cargo or freight; to put on, as gear on a horse. Cf. *ukana*. PPN *uta*.

ukali. To follow, come after, succeed; follower, attendant. *Lede ukali*, lady in waiting. **ho'oūkali.** To cause, pretend, or try to follow, accompany, attend.

Ukali-ali'i. The planet Mercury. *Lit.*, following the chief (i.e., the sun).

ukana. Baggage, luggage, freight, cargo, supplies. **ho'oūkana.** To bundle up, pack up, load, as freight. PEP *utanga*.

'ūke'e. Twisted, crooked, as the mouth. **hō'ūke'e.** To screw or twist the mouth to one side, as in disapproval or dislike.

'ūkēkē. A variety of musical bow having two or three strings which were strummed.

'ūkele. Muddy; oily.

'uki-haole. All cultivated forms of gladiolus.

ukiuki. Anger, resentment; angry, annoyed, offended, vexed, irritated. **ho'oukiuki.** To provoke, offend, displease.

uku. 1. Pay, wages, fee, fine, tax; to pay, remunerate, compensate, repay. **ho'oūku.** To make someone pay; to levy a tax, fine, assess, charge. Probably PPN *utu*. **2.** Deep-sea snapper (*Aprion* spp.). PPN *utu*.

'uku. 1. Louse, flea. PPN *kutu*. **2.** Small, tiny (less used than *'u'uku*).

uku hana. Wages, salary, pay for work; to pay wages.

uku hapa. Installment payment; to pay in part.

ukuhi. To pour out, dip, as water; to wean, as a child.

ukuhina. A pouring out, dipping, weaning.

uku hoʻopaʻi. A fine.

uku hoʻopaneʻe. Interest, usury. *Lit.*, delayed payment.

uku kaʻa. Carfare.

ʻuku-kapa. Body louse. *Lit.*, tapa louse.

uku komo. Entrance fee.

uku kūʻike. Cash payment.

uku kula. School tuition.

uku leka, uku leta. Postage.

ʻukulele. Ukulele. *Lit.*, leaping flea.

ʻuku-lele. Flea.

uku makana. Tip, gift payment.

uku male (mare). Dowry; marriage fee, as to the minister. *Lit.*, marriage payment.

uku manawa. Installment payment; to make installment payments.

uku moku. Steamship fare.

ukupau. Piece labor, pay by the job rather than according to time; used in pidgin for any work that everyone should pitch in gladly to finish. *Lit.*, finished pay.

uku pohō. Damages; to pay damages.

ʻuku-poʻo. Head louse.

ula. Hawaiian or spiny lobsters (*Panulirus japonicus* and *P. pencillatus*). PPN *ʻura*.

ʻula. 1. Red, scarlet; brown, as skin of Hawaiians; to appear red. *Piʻi ka ʻula*, to blush. *hōʻula*. To redden. PPN *kula*. **2.** Sacred; sacredness; regal.

ula ahi. Fire flames.

ʻula aliʻi. Chiefly blood.

ulae. Lizardfish (*Saurida gracilis*).

ʻulāliʻi. Measles; red spots of measles.

ulana. To plait, weave, knit, braid; plaiting, weaving. PPN *langa*.

ula-pāpapa. Spiny lobster (*Scyllarides squammosus*).

ʻulaʻula. 1. Redup. of *ʻula*, 1. *hōʻulaʻula*. Same as *hōʻula*.

PPN *kulakula*. **2.** One of the red snappers (*Etelis marshi*, family Lutjanidae). **3.** The cardinal, Kentucky cardinal (*Richmondena cardinalis*).

ulawaiʻa. To fish (of many persons or often).

ule. Penis. PPN *ule*.

ule kahe. Circumcised penis. *Kahe ule*, to circumcise.

ulele. 1. To leap at, get into action, do quickly. **2.** To set, as type.

ʻulepe. Harelip. Also, *kūlepe*.

uleʻulu. Male breadfruit flower. *Lit.*, breadfruit penis.

uli. 1. Any dark color, including the deep blue of the sea, the ordinary green of vegetation, and the dark of black clouds; the black-and-blue of a bruise. *Kai uli*, the deep sea. *hoʻouli*. To darken, to make blue, green, etc; to make the skin black and blue. PPN *ʻuli*. **2.** To steer; steersman. PPN *ʻuli*. **3.** Shellfish species. PPN *huli*.

ulia. Accident; sudden; to come upon suddenly. *Ulia kaʻa*, auto accident. PPN *ulia*.

ʻūlili. Wandering tattler (*Heteroscelus incanum*); the cry of the bird; to cry thus. **hoʻūlili.** To act like the tattler bird. PEP *ku(u)lili*.

ʻulīʻulī. A gourd rattle containing seeds and fitted with colored feathers at the top, used in certain hulas; to rattle. **hōʻulīʻulī.** To shake the *ʻulīʻulī*; to rattle.

ʻūlōlohi. Same as *lohi*, slow.

ulu. 1. To grow, increase, spread; grove, growth, collection; an increase or rising of the wind. **hoʻoulu.** To grow, cause to increase, as the surf. PPN *ʻulu*. **2.** Possessed by a spirit; inspired by a spirit, god, ideal, person; stirred; to enter in and inspire. **hoʻoūlu, hoʻoulu.** To

stir up, inspire, excite. PPN
huru.

'ulu. 1. Breadfruit (*Artocarpus
communis*). PPN *kulu.* 2.
Round, smooth stone as used
in *'ulu maika* game; bowling ball; bell clapper.

ulua. Various species of jack
crevally, important game and
food fishes. PPN *'ulua.*

uluhe. All Hawaiian species
of false staghorn fern (the
four species are of the genera *Dicranopteris, Hicriop-
teris, Sticherus*).

uluhia. Passive/imperative of
ulu, 1, 2. PNP *ulufia.*

uluhua. Vexed, annoyed, discouraged, displeased, har-
assed. ho'oūluhua. To annoy,
weary, vex.

ulu kanu. Garden patch.

ulu kukui. Candlenut grove.

ulu lā'au. Forest, grove of
trees.

ulumāhiehie. Festive, attrac-
tively adorned and arrayed;
pleasing.   ho'oūlumāhiehie.
To adorn, decorate attrac-
tively.

'ulu maika. Same as *maika;* the
stone used in the game; to
play the *'ulu maika* game;
bowling.

ulu manu. Flock of birds.

ulu moku. Fleet, collection of
ships.

uluna. 1. Pillow, cushion; formerly made of pandanus
leaves; to use as a pillow.
PPN *'ulunga.* 2. Upper part
of the arm.

ulunahele. Wilderness, place of
wild growth.

ulu niu. Coconut grove.

ulu pua. Flower garden, growth
of flowers.

'ulu'ulu. Collection, gathering,
assembly. hō'ulu'ulu. To collect, assemble; addition, to
add; collection.

uluwehi. Lush and beautiful
verdure; festively adorned.

ho'oūluwehi.   To   bedeck
with plants.

uluwehiwehi. Redup. of *uluwehi.*

uma. Hand wrestling; to push,
grip; to pry, as a lever.

umauma. Chest, breast.

'ume. 1. To draw, pull, attract;
attractive, alluring; attraction.
PEP *kume.* 2. Same as *kala,*
a fish. Perhaps PPN *'ume.*

'umeke. Bowl, calabash, circular vessel, as of wood or
gourd. PPN *kumete.*

'umeke 'ai. *Poi* bowl. *Fig.,*
source of vegetable food, of
the uplands.

'umeke lā'au. Wooden bowl.

'umena. An attraction, pulling.
See *'ume,* 1.

'umi. 1. To strangle, choke, suf-
focate, throttle; to repress,
as desire. PPN *kumi.* 2. Ten;
tenth. PNP *kumi.*

'ūmi'i.   Clamp,   clip,   clasp,
buckle, vise; to pinch, clip,
clasp, clamp, squeeze; sharp
body pain or cramp, as in the
side. *Makaaniani 'ūmi'i,* spectacles held on the nose with
clips; pince-nez.

'ūmi'i 'iole. Rattrap, mousetrap.

'ūmi'i lauoho. Hair clasp.

'ūmi'i pepa. Paper clip, clamp,
staple.

'umi kūmā-. An element compounded with numbers from
one to nine to indicate 11 to
19, as *'umi kūmāhā,* fourteen.

'umi kumamā-. Same as *'umi
kūmā-.* Numbers one to nine
are suffixed to this also. *Biblical.*

'umina. Strangling, choking,
etc. See *'umi,* 1.

'umi'umi. 1. Whiskers, beard,
mustache; tendril; barbel or
feelers on lower jaw of a fish.
PPN *kumikumi.* 2. Redup.
of *'umi,* 1.

'umoki. Cork, stopper, bung;

to cork, stop up; wad of a gun.

umu. Oven, furnace. More commonly called *imu.* **ho-'oūmu.** To make an *umu.* PPN *'umu.*

-una. ho'oūna. To send, transmit, send on an errand, to put to work.

unahi. Scales of a fish; scaly; to scale. PPN *'unafi.*

una'oa. Same as *kauna'oa,* a mollusk. PPN *'ungako(a,o).*

unauna. Hermit crabs in general. PPN *'unga.*

unele. Honk of a goose; to honk.

'ūniki. Graduation exercises, as for *hula, lua* fighting, and other ancient arts.

uniona. Union, labor union. *Eng.*

unonoho. Plural and frequentive of *noho.*

uno'o. Scorched, partly consumed by fire, inflamed. Probably PNP *unoko.*

unu. Small stone, pebble, stone chip.

'unu. To shorten, hoist, jerk upwards; to pull or draw together, as the hair.

unuhi. To take out, withdraw, as money from a bank; to take off, as a ring; to translate, interpret. *Mea unuhi,* translator, interpreter. **ho-'ounuhi.** To have something translated, withdrawn, etc. PPN *unusi.*

unuhia. Passive/imperative of *unuhi.*

unuhina. Translation.

unuhi pili. Close, literal translation.

unuunu. To singe, pluck, as the feathers of a chicken before dressing it.

'uo, 'uwo. A group of feathers tied together in a small bunch, to be made into a feather lei or cloak; to tie thus; to string on a needle; to

splice, as strands of a rope. PEP *kuo.*

uoki, uwoki. Stop it! Quit! Don't touch!

'ūpā. Any instrument that opens and shuts, as shears, scissors, tongs, bellows, carpenter's compass; to beat, as the heart; to open and shut, as the mouth champing food.

'upa'i. To flap, as wings, or clothes in the wind; to bend in the wind, as a branch.

'ūpā mau'u. Grass shears.

'ūpā miki'ao. Fingernail scissors.

'ūpā nui. Shears.

'upāpalu. Cardinalfish (*Apogon menesemus*).

'ūpā 'ūmi'i. Pliers.

'upa'upā. Redup. of *'ūpā;* to rub clothes up and down on a washboard.

ūpē. Crushed; humble, bashful. **ho'oūpē.** To crush, belittle.

'ūpē. Mucus. *Fig.,* tears, grief.

'upena. Fishing net, net, web. PPN *kupenga.*

'upena kiloi, 'upena kiola. Throwing net.

'upena lauoho. Hairnet.

'upena nananana. Spider web. Also, *punawelewele.*

'ūpepe. Flat-nosed.

'ūpiki. Trap, snare, clamp; to snap or clamp together, as a trap, the jaws, or a bivalve; to shut, as a flower.

'ūpiki 'iole. Rattrap, mousetrap.

'ūpiki lima. Handcuff.

'ūpo'i maka. Eyelid.

'upu. Recurring thought, desire, attachment, hope; to desire, long for, covet. PPN *kupu.*

'u'u. To strip, as leaves or *maile* bark; to draw in, as a line on a ship; to hoist, as a sail; to pour suddenly, as rain. PPN *kuku.*

'ū'ū. 1. Redup. of *'ū, 1;* to stutter, stammer. **2.** Squirrelfish or menpachi (*Myripristis* *argyromus*). Perhaps PEP *kuukuu.*

'u'uku. Tiny, small; few. **ho-'o'u'uku.** To make small, reduce.

'uwā. To shout, cry out, sound loud.

uwahi. Var. spelling of *uahi.*

uwaki, uaki, waki, uati. Watch, clock; a watch, as on shipboard. *Eng.*

uwaki ho'āla. Alarm clock.

uwaki pūlima. Wrist watch.

'uwala. Var. spelling of *'uala.*

uwalo, ualo. To call out, as for help; to resound. Cf. *walo.*

uwapo, uapo. Wharf, pier, bridge. *Eng.*

'uwa'u. See *'ua'u.*

uwē. To cry, weep, lament, mourn; a cry, lamentation. *Uwē wale,* to cry for no reason; cry-baby. **ho'ouwē.** To cause weeping, to make someone cry.

uwea, uea. Wire. *Eng.*

uwea hakahaka. Wire screen. *Lit.,* space wire.

uwea kelepona. Telephone wire.

uwea maka 'upena. Chicken wire. *Lit.,* net-mesh wire.

uwea moana. Undersea cable.

uwea 'ole. Wireless.

'uwehe, 'uehe. 1. To open, uncover, reveal; to pry open, as a bivalve. Cf. *wehe.* **2.** Hula step.

uweka, ueka. Dirty, bleary, as the eyes. Cf. *weka.*

uweko, ueko. Bad-smelling, musty.

uwepa, uepa. 1. Wafer. *Eng.* **2.** Whip.

uwēuwē. Redup. of *uwē.*

'uwī, 'uī. 1. To squeak, squeal; to gnash, as teeth. Cf. *wī.* **2.** To twist, squeeze, wring; to express, as juice from fruit; to milk, as a cow.

'uwiki. 1. Var. spelling of *'uiki,* to glimmer. **2.** Also **'uiki.** Wick. *Eng.*

uwila. Var. spelling of *uila.*

'uwo. Var. spelling of *'uo.*

uwoki. Var. spelling of *uoki.*

W

wā. 1. Period of time, epoch, era, time, season, age. *Ia wā,* then, at that time. PPN *waa.* **2.** Tense, in grammar. *Wā i hala,* past tense. **3.** To make a noise, roar, din; noisy. Cf. *wawā.* **ho'owā.** To make a sound, roar; to cause gossip, talk. PPN *waa.* **4.** Space, interval, as between objects; channel. Cf. *kōwā.* PPN *waa.* **5.** Fret of an ukulele, guitar, or similar instrument.

wa'a. Canoe. **ho'owa'a.** To make or shape a canoe. PPN *waka.*

wa'a kaukahi. Single canoe. *Lit.,* single-placed canoe.

wa'a kaulua. Double canoe. *Lit.,* double-placed canoe.

wā ānō. Present tense.

wa'apā. Skiff, rowboat; ferryboat. *Lit.,* board canoe.

wae. To choose, select, sort, separate; to draft, as soldiers; to preen, as of a chicken; finicky. **ho'owae.** To choose, pretend to choose; finicky. PPN *wahe.*

waele. To weed. PEP *waele.*

waena. 1. Middle, between, center (often preceded by *i,* *ma-,* or *mai*); mean, average. PEP *waenga.* **2.** Cultivated field, garden, vegetable plot.

waenakonu. Center, middle.

waha. 1. Mouth; opening; oral; to talk too much. **ho'owaha.** To talk excessively, insult; to make an opening. PEP *fafa.* **2.** To carry on the back, as a child. PPN *fafa.*

wahahe'e. To lie; lying, deceitful; a lie, liar. *Lit.*, slippery mouth.

waha nui. A big mouth; to talk too much, tattle; tattler.

waha 'ōlelo. Spokesman; speaking mouth.

wahapa'a. To goad, tease; argumentative. *Lit.*, hard mouth.

wahāwahā. ho'owahāwahā. To treat with contempt, despise, abhor, ridicule.

wahi. 1. Place. (*Ka wahi* contracts to *kāhi*.) PPN *fa'asi*. 2. Some, a little, a few, a bit of. 3. To say (usually followed by the possessive *a*, and not preceded by either verb or noun particles. *Wahi a wai?* Who said so?

wahī. Wrapper, envelope, covering; to wrap, cover, bundle up; to dress, as a wound. PEP *fafi(i)*.

wāhi. To cleave, split, burst through, break through. PPN *fa'asi*.

wahie. Fuel, firewood; to serve as firewood. PPN *fafie*.

wahī leka. Envelope.

wahi moe. Bed, place to sleep.

wahine. Woman, lady, wife; sister-in-law, female cousin-in-law of a man; queen in a deck of cards; womanliness, female, femininity; feminine; Mrs.; to become a woman, as an adolescent. **ho-'owahine.** To behave like a woman, to imitate the ways of a woman; to grow into womanhood; to become a wife; to take a wife; feminine. PPN *fafine*.

wāhine. Plural of *wahine. Nā wāhine,* the women. PPN *fafine*, PNP *faafine.*

wahine kāne make. Widow. *Lit.*, woman with dead husband.

wahine kāne 'ole. Spinster, woman without a husband, single woman.

wahine male (mare). Married woman, bride.

wahi noho. Dwelling place.

waho. Outside, beyond, out, outer, outward (frequently preceded by *i, ma-,* or *mai*). *Mawaho aku 'olua!* Go out, you two! PPN *fafo.*

wai. 1. Water, liquid of any kind other than sea water, juice, sap, honey; any liquid discharged from the body, as blood, semen; color, dye; to flow like water; fluid. Cf. *hanawai.* PPN *wai.* 2. (*Cap.*) Place names beginning with *Wai-*, river, stream. 3. Who, whom, whose, what (in questions only and referring to persons). *'Owai?* Who? *'Owai kou inoa?* What is your name? PPN *hai.*

wai 'ale'ale. Rippling water, artesian water.

wai anuhea. Tepid water, neither hot nor cold.

wai au. Swirling water of a current.

wai 'au'au. Bath water; bathing place or pool.

wai hau. Ice water.

waiho. To leave, lay down, place before, present, deposit; to cease, stop, resign, abandon; a leaving, depository, etc. **ho'owaiho.** To leave, abandon, ignore. See *waiwai.* PEP *waifo.*

wai ho'āno. Holy water.

waiho loa. To abandon completely, give up.

waihona. Depository, place for putting things in safekeeping; funds, treasury; fiscal.

waihona kālā (dala). Treasury, money depository. *Lit.*, dollar depository.

waihona meli. Honeycomb.

waihona panakō. Bank account, depository.

waihona puke (buke). Library.

waihona waiwai. Treasury, depository for goods, property.

waiho‘olu‘u. Dye, water for coloring; color.

waiho wale. To leave without reason; to leave about carelessly.

wai inu. Drinking water, potable water.

waikahe. Stream; to flow, overflow, as a stream. *Lit.*, flowing water. PPN *waitafe*.

wai kī. Water in which tea has been brewed.

wailele. Waterfall, cataract. *Lit.*, leaping water.

wai lemi. Lemon juice, lemonade, limeade.

waimaka. Tears. *Lit.*, eye water. PEP *waimata*.

wai meli. Honey. *Lit.*, bee liquor.

wai momona. Soda water, sweet water.

waina. Wine. *Eng.*

waina malo‘o. Raisins. *Lit.*, dry grapes.

wai niu. Coconut water.

waioleka. Fragrant cultivated violets. *Eng.*

waiolina. Violin. *Eng.*

wai ‘ona. Intoxicating liquor.

waipa‘a. Ice. *Lit.*, hard, solid water.

wai pa‘akai. Salty water, brine.

waipahē. Gentlemanly, courteous. See *pahē*.

waipahū. Gunpowder. *Lit.*, explosive liquid.

wai piu!a. Water from a faucet.

wai puhia. Wind-blown water, especially of a waterfall; name of the "upside-down" waterfall in Nu‘u-anu Valley.

waipu‘ilani. Waterspout.

wai puna. Spring water.

waiū. Milk; wet nurse; breast. *Lit.*, breast liquid. PEP *waiuu*.

waiū kini. Canned milk.

wai ‘ula. Red liquid, blood, menstrual flow, rain run-off red with soil.

waiūpa‘a. Cheese. *Lit.*, solidified milk.

waiūpaka, waiu bata. Butter.

waiwai. Goods, property; value, worth; estate; rich, costly; financial. Ho‘oponopono *waiwai*, administrator of property or of an estate. **ho‘owaiwai.** To enrich, bring prosperity. See *waiho*.

waiwai ho‘oilina. Inherited property.

waiwai ho‘opa‘a. Security.

waiwai kālepa. Merchandise.

waiwai kaua. War goods, spoils.

wā kamali‘i. Childhood. Also called *wā li‘ili‘i*.

waki. Var. spelling of *uwaki*, watch.

Wakinekona, Wasinetona. Washington. *Eng.*

wala‘au. To talk, speak; formerly, to talk loudly, shout. **ho‘owala‘au.** To cause talk, start talk or conversation. PNP *walakau*.

walakīkē. To toss, hurl back and forth, as spears in battle.

walania. Anguish, burning pain, woe, torment. **ho‘owalania.** To cause pain, wound.

wale. 1. Slime, mucus, phlegm; sticky sap, as from cuts in tree ferns and *mamaki* wood. PNP *wale*. **2.** A common particle that follows modified words and has many meanings, as: only; just; very; alone; without pay, cause, reason; easily; gratuitous, free, casual. See *hele wale*, *hikiwale*. PPN *wale*.

walea. 1. Same as *nanea*. PEP *walea*. **2.** Accustomed; so familiar that one does a thing without effort, as a dance. Ua hana a *walea*, done until automatic.

wale nō. Only; just; all. ‘Elua *wale nō*, only two.

walewale. Redup. of *wale, 1*. **ho‘owalewale.** To tempt, decoy, lead astray; tempter; temptation. PPN *walewale*.

wali. Smooth, thin, as *poi;* fine, mashed, soft; supple, limber, as a dancer's body. **ho'owali.** To make soft, smooth; to mix, as *poi* or dough. See *nāwali.* PEP *wali.*

wā li'ili'i. See *wā kamali'i.*

waliwali. Redup. of *wali;* gentle, easygoing.

walo. Same as *uwalo,* to call, resound. PPN *walo.*

walohia. Passive/imperative of *walo;* pathos, touching.

walu. 1. To claw, scratch, rub, grate, rasp. PPN *waru.* 2. Eight, eighth. PPN *walu.*

wana. 1. Sea urchin with long, pointed dangerous spines, especially the species *Echinothrix diadema.* PPN *wana.* 2. Sharp-pointed, as sea urchin spines. 3. A long spike or ray of light, as at dawn; to appear, as a ray of light. Cf. *wana'ao.*

wana'ao. Dawn; to dawn.

wānana. Prophecy; to prophesy, predict. PEP *waananga.*

wanawana. Redup. of *wana,* 2; spiny, thorny, as cactus. PEP *wanawana.*

wanila. Vanilla. *Eng.*

wao. General term for inland region, usually not precipitous and often uninhabited. PPN *wao.*

wao kele. Rain belt.

wao nahele. Inland forest region.

wā 'ōpio. Youth (time of).

wau, au. I (often preceded by '*a*). PPN *au.*

wa'u. To grate, scrape, claw, wear away by friction; grater. PPN *waku.*

wā ua. Rainy season.

wauke. Paper mulberry (*Broussonetia papyrifera*), a small tree or shrub the bark of which was used to make tapa. PEP *aute.*

wa'u niu. Coconut grater; to grate coconut.

wā 'u'uku. Childhood. *Lit.,* small time.

wawā. Redup. of *wā, 3;* tumultuous; sound of distant voices, roar; rumored. **ho-'owawā.** To cause a loud shouting. PPN *wawaa.*

wāwae. Leg, foot, PPN *wa'e.*

wāwae huki. Cramps in the foot or leg.

wāwae-'iole. 1. Club moss (*Lyccpodium cernum*) a creeping, evergreen, mosslike plant used in Hawai'i for Christmas wreaths, etc. 2. Same as *'a'ala-'ula,* a seaweed.

wāwahi. Redup. of *wāhi;* to tear down, break into, demolish.

wāwahi hale. Burglary, housebreaking; to break and enter.

wāwahi panakō. To break the bank, as in *chee-fah* or other games.

wawe. Quickly; fast. See *hiki-wawe.* PPN *wawe.*

we. The letter "w".

wehe. To open, untie, loosen; to take off, as clothes; to tip, as a hat. **ho'owehe.** To cause to open, undo, etc. PEP *wese.*

wehena. Opening, unfastening, taking off; solution, as of a problem.

wehewehe. To explain. *Wehewehe 'ana,* explanation, definition.

wehi. Decoration, adornment; to decorate. **ho'owehi.** To beautify, decorate, adorn.

wehiwehi. Redup. of *wehi.* Cf. *uluwehiwehi.*

weka. 1. Ink discharged by squid or octopus. 2. Also **weta.** Weight. *Eng.*

weke. 1. Crack, narrow opening: to open a crack, as a door; to loosen, free. PPN *wete.* 2. Certain species of goatfishes, much prized since early times as food fishes. PPN *wete*.

weke-ʻaʻā. Goatfish (*Mulloidichthys somoensis*). *Lit.*, staring goatfish.

wekekē. Whiskey. *Eng.*

wēkiu. Tip, top, topmost, summit; of the highest rank or station.

wela. Hot, burned; heat, temperature. **hoʻowela.** To heat, burn, arouse passion. PPN *wela*.

wēlau. Tip, top, extremity, end.

Wēlau-ʻākau. North Pole.

Wēlau-hema. South Pole.

wele. 1. Suspended, hanging; fine, thin, as thread. 2. To weed. PNP *wele*.

weleweka. Velvet. *Eng.*

weli. 1. Fear, terror; fearful, afraid. *Kau ka weli*, full of fear. **hoʻoweli.** To frighten, terrify, arouse fear. PEP *weliweli*. 2. Sea cucumber. PPN *weli*.

welina. A greeting of affection, similar to *aloha*.

weliweli. Redup. of *weli*, 1; respectful, as of the word of a chief. **hoʻoweliweli.** Redup. of *hoʻoweli*.

welo. To flutter, float or stream, as in the wind.

welu. Rag, ragged fragment; ragged, frayed. PEP *welu*.

weluwelu. Redup. of *welu*; shredded to bits.

wena. Glow, as of sunrise or fire. *Wena ʻula*, red glow.

weuweu. Herbage, grass; bushy or fuzzy, as a beard.

wewe. Same as *ʻiēwe*, navel string.

wī. 1. Famine; to suffer a famine. 2. To squeal, tinkle; the sound of wind, of gnashing teeth; any high shrill sound. 3. The *wī* tree or Otaheite apple (*Spondias dulcis*), which bears edible apple-flavored fruits. PPN *wii*. 4. The tamarind (*Tamarindus in-*

dica) tree; also *wī-ʻawaʻawa*.

wiki, wikiwiki. To hurry, hasten; quick. *Hele wiki*, quick time; quick step. **hoʻowiki.** To hurry, hasten. PEP *witiwiti*.

wiko, vito. Veto; to veto. *Eng.*

wili. 1. To wind, twist, writhe, crank, grind, mix; to dial, as a telephone; to roll up, as a mat; coil, lock, as of hair. **hoʻowili.** To wind, coil, drill; to mill about, as a school of fish. PPN *wili*. 2. Mill, drill; bit.

wilia. Passive imperative of *wili*, 1.

wilikī. Engineer, turnkey; engineering. *Lit.*, turn key.

wili kō. Sugar mill, sugar grinder; to grind sugarcane.

wili kope. Coffee mill, coffee grinder.

wili makani. Windmill.

wili oho. Coil or strand of hair, as in a *lei palaoa* necklace.

wilipuaʻa. Corkscrew, hand drill, gimlet, screw auger. *Lit.*, pig twist.

wiliwili. 1. Redup. of *wili*, 1. **hoʻowiliwili.** Redup. of *hoʻowili*. PPN *wiliwili*. 2. A native Hawaiian leguminous tree (*Erythrina sandwicensis*).

wiliwili-haole. Tigers claw or coral tree (*Erythrina variegata* var. *orientalis*), resembling the *wiliwili*, but having thorned branches and bearing long clusters of scarlet blossoms.

wīneka, vinega. Vinegar. *Eng.*

wini. Sharp, as a point. **hoʻowiʻi.** To sharpen, make a point.

wiola, viola. Viol. *Eng.*

wīwī. Thin, slender. Perhaps PPN *iwiiwi*.

wiwo. 1. Fearful, bashful, modest, afraid, timid. Perhaps

PEP *wiwo*. **2.** Obedient; to mind, obey.

wiwo 'ole. Fearless, brave, bold.

wiwowiwo. Redup. of *wiwo*, *1*, *2*.

wōwō. To bellow, roar.

Z

Loan words from English sometimes spelled with initial z- are entered under *k*-. For example: *zebela*, see *kepela*, zebra; *zizania*, see *kīkānia*.

English-Hawaiian

A

a. 1. *The letter,* 'Ā. 2. *Article.* He, kekahi, ho'okahi.

aa. 'A'ā.

abalone. 'Opihi malihini.

abandon. Ha'alele, waiho, ho-'oku'u.

abbreviate. Ho'opōkole.

abbreviation. Hua hō'ailona, ho'opōkole 'ana.

ability. Hiki, mākaukau.

able. Hiki, mākaukau.

abnormal. 'Ano 'ē.

aboard. Maluna.

abolish. Ho'opau.

abominable. Ho'opailua, 'ino loa.

abomination. Mea 'ino, mea haumia.

aboriginal. Maoli, kupa maoli. *Hawaiian aboriginal,* Hawai'i maoli.

abortion. 'Ōmilo, milo, milo-milo.

about. 1. *Concerning.* E pili ana nō, nō, i. 2. *See* **almost.**

above. Maluna, i luna.

abroad. Ma ka 'āina 'ē (*in foreign lands*).

absence. Hele 'ole mai.

absent. Ma kahi 'ē, ma kahi 'oko'a, 'a'ole i hiki mai.

abundant. Nui, nui 'ino, mānoa.

accent. 1. *Speech.* Hōpuna. 2. *Stress.* Kaulele, kālele leo. 3. *Diacritical mark.* Kaha, kiko.

accept. 'Āpono, ho'āpono, 'ae, lawe.

accident. Ulia, pilikia.

accompany. Hele pū, ukali, 'alo, hahai.

accumulate. Ho'āhu, hō'ili'ili, ho'ākoakoa.

accurate. Pololei, pono.

accuse. Ho'āhewa, ho'olawe-hala.

accustomed. Ma'a, ma'ama'a.

ache. 'Eha, hu'i.

acquainted. Kama'āina.

acquire. Loa'a, lawe.

acre. 'Eka.

across. Ma kēlā 'ao'ao.

act. 1. *To do.* Hana. *To act as,* noho. 2. *Theatrical.* Māhele (*of a play*). *To act in a play,* hana keaka. 3. *Law.* Kānāwai. 4. *To pretend.* Ho'omeamea, ho'omea.

action. Hana.

active. 'Eleu, miki.

activity. Hana, 'oihana.

actor. Mea hana keaka, kanaka hana keaka.

actress. Wahine hana keaka.

actual. Maoli, 'oiā'i'o.

Adam's apple. Pu'u, pū'ā'ī, kani'ā'ī.

add. Hō'ulu'ulu, ho'ohui, pā-ku'i, ku'i lua, ho'onui; ho-'oku'i (*as numbers*).

addition. Hō'ulu'ulu.

address. 1. *Speech.* Ha'i'ōlelo. 2. *Residence.* Wahi noho.

adjacent. Kokoke, pili.

adjourn. Ho'omalolo.

adjust. Ho'oponopono.

administer. Ho'oponopono, ho-'ohana, ho'oholo.

administrator. Luna ho'opono-pono, kahu, kahu ho'opono-pono.

admire. Mahalo.

admit. 1. *Allow to enter.* Ho-'okomo, 'ae. 2. *Acknowledge.* 'Ae.

adopt. 1. *As a child.* Hānai, lawe hānai. 2. *To approve.* 'Āpono.

adore. Ho'onani, ho'omana.

adorn. Ho'ohiwahiwa, ho'onani, ho'okāhiko, ho'owehi, ho-'oūlumāhiehie.

adult. Makua, kanaka makua, o'o.

advance. Holomua, hele i mua.

advertise. Ho'olaha.

advice. 'Ōlelo a'o. *To give advice,* ha'i a'o.

adze. Ko'i, lipi.

affection. Aloha, aloha pume-hana.

aforementioned. Ua . . . nei, ua . . . lā.

aforesaid. I 'ōlelo 'ia.

afraid. Maka'u, weli, weliweli, wiwo.

after. Hope, mahope, muli, mamuli, pau.

afternoon. 'Auinalā.

afterward. Hope, mahope, mahope iho.

again. Hou. *To do again,* hana hou.

against. Kū'ē.

age. 1. *Period.* Au, manawa, wā. **2.** *Age of a person.* Kulana makahiki, heluna makahiki. *What is your age?* 'Ehia ou makahiki? He aha kou heluna makahiki?

agile. 'Eleu.

agitated. Pīhoihoi, pi'oloke.

ago. Mamua aku nei, wā i hala.

agree. 'Ae, 'aelike, lōkahi.

agreement. 'Aelike, palapala 'aelike, lōkahi.

agriculture. 'Oihana mahi'ai.

ah! 'Ā! Kāhāhā! *To oh and ah,* āhē, kāhāhā.

aha! Āhā!

ahead. I mua, mamua aku.

aid. Kōkua, kāko'o.

ailing. 'Ōma'ima'i, ma'ima'i, nāwali.

air. Ea, eaea, lewa.

air mail. Ho'oūna ma ka mokulele.

airplane. Mokulele, mokuea.

airport. Kahua ho'olulu mokulele.

air raid. Pākaha mai ka lewa.

alas! Aloha 'ino! Auwē!

alcoholic. 'Ona lama, 'ona mau.

alert. Maka'ala, miki'ala, 'eleu.

alga. Limu.

algaroba. Kiawe.

alike. Like, like pū, kohu like. *Just alike,* like loa, like 'ālike, kū like loa. *To make alike,* ho'ohālikelike, kaulike.

alive. Ola.

all. Apau, pauloa, pau.

all right. Hiki, hiki nō, pololei, maika'i. *All right, then,* 'oia ho'i hā. *It's all right,* 'oia a'e lā nō.

almost. Kokoke, 'ane'ane.

aloha. Aloha.

alone. Ho'okahi wale nō, wale, ho'okahi.

alphabet. Pī'āpā.

already. 'E, pau.

also. Ho'i, kekahi, kahi, eia kekahi. *I also,* 'o au pū.

altar. Ahu, lele, kuahu, ni'o, unu.

although. 'Oiai.

altogether. 'Oko'a, holo'oko'a. *All of us together,* kākou pū.

always. Mau, nā manawa apau loa, pau 'ole.

amen. 'Āmene.

America. 'Amelika.

among. Mawaena, i waena.

amuse. Ho'ole'ale'a, ho'okolohe, ho'ohoihoi.

amusement. Ho'ole'ale'a, le-'ale'a, pā'ani.

ancestor. Kupuna.

anchor. Helēuma.

ancient. Kahiko.

and. A (*usually preceding verbs*); a me (*usually preceding nouns*); eia ho'i.

angel. 'Ānela.

anger. Huhū, inaina, ukiuki, uluhua. *Very great anger,* huhū wela loa, huhū loa. *Anger without cause,* huhū wale. *To become angry,* pi'i ka huhū.

animal. Holoholona.

anniversary. Piha makahiki, lā ho'omana'o.

announce. Hō'ike, kūkala.

annoy. Ho'onaukiuki, ho'okolohe, ho'oūluhua.

annual. Makahiki, kūmakahiki, ma ka makahiki. *Annual report,* hō'ike makahiki. *Annual salary,* uku ma ka makahiki.

anoint. Poni.

another. Kekahi, ha'i, 'oko'a, 'ē a'e. *Another day,* kekahi lā.

answer. Pane; ha'ina (*as to a riddle*); hua loa'a, ha'i loa'a (*as to a problem*).

ant. Naonao.

anthem. Mele, hīmeni. *National anthem,* mele aupuni.

anthropology. Huli kanaka.

anxiety. Hopohopo, pīhoihoi.

any. Kekahi.

anybody. *See* anyone.

anyhow. *See* however.

anyone. Kekahi, kekahi mea, 'o ka mea nō e.

anything. Ka mea e loa'a ana.

anywhere. Aia no i kāhi e hele ai; ma nā wahi like 'ole.

apart. Ka'awale. *To stand apart,* kū ka'awale. *Placed apart,* kau 'oko'a.

apartment. Ke'ena noho. *Apartment building,* hale papa'i.

apiece. Pākahi.

apologize. Mihi, mimihi, mimimihi.

apostle. Luna'ōlelo.

appear. Puka, kau, hiki, maka, kū, 'ō'ili; pua'i (*as color*); wana (*as a ray of light*).

appetite. 'Ono ka 'ai.

applause. Pa'ipa'i lima, pa'ipa'i.

apple. 'Āpala, poma.

apply. 1. *Adhere.* Pili, ho'opili. 2. *Petition.* Noi.

appoint. Ho'onoho, ho'okohu, ho'okoho.

appointment. 1. *Engagement.* Ho'opa'a manawa. 2. *Nomination.* Wae, ho'okohu.

appreciate. Ho'omaika'i.

approach. Ho'okokoke, hiki, hō'ea'ea.

appropriation. Ha'awina.

approval. Ho'āpono, 'ae.

approve. Ho'āpono, 'ae, 'āpono.

approximately. Kahi, kokoke.

April. 'Apelila.

arch. Pi'o, pāpi'o, hoaka. *Arch of a foot,* poho wāwae. *Arch of a rainbow,* pi'o ke ānuenue.

arena. Kahua, pā.

argue. Ho'opa'apa'a, paio, pāku'iku'i.

argument. Paio, pa'apa'a, ho'opa'apa'a.

argumentative. Wahapa'a, puni ho'opa'apa'a.

arithmetic. Huina helu, helu, 'alimakika.

arm. 1. *Anatomy.* Lima; kālele (*as of a chair*); *upper part of arm,* uluna. *Arm below elbow,* kū'aulima. 2. *To supply arms.* Ho'olako i nā mea kaua.

armed forces. Pū'ali koa.

armpit. Pō'ae'ae, kīpō'ae'ae, napo'o.

arms. 1. *Anatomy.* Nā lima. 2. *War.* Lako kaua.

army. Pū'ali, kaua, pū'ulu, pū'ulu kaua.

around. Puni, kēlā wahi kēia wahi. *To go around,* ka'apuni, po'ai, kalawai. "*Around the island*" *hula step,* ka'apuni.

arrange. Ho'onoho, ho'onohonoho, ho'onoho papa, ho'oponopono, kūkulu papa, haku.

arrest. *Seize.* Hopu, hopuna.

arrive. Hō'ea, hiki, kū, kau.

arrow. Pua, pua pana.

arrowroot. Pia.

art. Hana no'eau.

artery. A'a.

article. 1. *Object.* Mea. 2. *Essay.* Mo'olelo.

artist. Kaha ki'i.

as. 1. *Resembling.* Me, like me. *As though,* mehe. *As follows,* penei, 'oia ho'i. *As if,* mehe mea lā. *As far as,* ā, ā hiki i. 2. *When.* I ka manawa, i, i . . . ka hana. 3. *See* because.

ascend. Pi'i.

ash. Lehu, pa'u ahi.

ashamed. Hilahila.

ashes. Lehu, lehu ahi, lehu ane.

ash tray. Pā lehu.

aside. Ma ka 'ao'ao, ma kahi ka'awale. *To set aside,* ho-'oka'awale.

ask. 1. *To question.* Nīnau, ui. *To ask insistently,* koi. 2. *To request.* Noi, nonoi. 3. *To invite.* Kono.

asleep. Hiamoe. *Fast asleep,* pa-

'uhia i ka hiamoe, hiamoe
pa'a loa.
assemble. 1. *To meet.* Hui pū,
anaina, 'ākoakoa, ho'ākoakoa.
2. *To collect.* Hō'ili'ili, hō-
'ulu'ulu.
assets. Waiwai.
assist. Kōkua, kāko'o.
assistant. Hope, kōkua.
association. Launa 'ana, pilina;
'ahahui; hui.
asthma. Hānō.
astonished. Pū'iwa, ha'oha'o,
kāhāhā.
at. Ma, i, iā. *Look at him,*
nānā iāia.
athlete. Mea i ma'ama'ahia i nā
pā'ani ho'oikaika kino.
athletic contest. Ho'okūkū ho-
'oikaika kino.
athletic field. Kahua pā'ani.
atmosphere. Lewa.
atomic. 'Akomika.
attach. Ho'opili, ho'opa'a.
attack. Ho'oūka kaua, pu'e, po-
'ipū, po'i pō, lele, ku'ia, li-
manui.
attempt. Ho'ā'o.
attention. Nānā, maliu. *To pay
attention,* nānā, maliu, ho-
'omaopopo.
attentive. Ho'olohe, ho'olono,
lohe pono.
attorney. Loio.

attract. 'Ume, ala'ume, hōnēnē, kā'ana.
attractive. 1. *As a magnet.* 'Ume.
2. *As a person or scene.* Hie,
makahehi, ma'ema'e.
audience. Anaina.
August. 'Aukake.
aunt. Makuahine, makuahine
hanauna, 'anakē.
Australia. 'Aukekulelia.
authentic. 'Oiā'i'o.
author. Mea kākau, kākau mo-
'olelo, haku mo'olelo.
auto license. Laikini ka'a 'okomopila.
automobile. Ka'a, ka'a 'okomopila, otomobila.
avenue. Alanui ākea.
avoid. 'Alo, hō'alo, kē, ka-
'akepa.
awake. Ala, makalahia. *To
awaken from sleep,* lana ka
hiamoe.
awaken. Ala, ho'āla, ho'ālahia.
away. Aku, 'ē, ma kahi 'ē, lilo.
Go away! Hele ma kahi 'ē!
Hele pēlā.
awe. 'E'ehia, ano, ho'āno.
awful. Weliweli.
awhile. Manawa pōkole, li'uli'u
iki.
awkward. Hemahema, pāhemahema, hāwāwā.
axe. See adze.

B

b. *No Hawaiian term.*
baby. Keiki, pēpē, kama.
bachelor. Wahine 'ole, kanaka
i male 'ole.
back. 1. *Anatomy.* Kua. **2.** *Behind.* Hope, muli. *At the
back,* i hope, mahope.
backbone. Iwikuamo'o, kuamo'o.
backward. I hope. *To go backward,* emi hope, emi kua,
pēki.
bacon. 'I'o pua'a uahi.
bad. Maikai 'ole, 'ino, kolohe.
Too bad! Minamina noho'i!

Aloha 'ino! Auwē! *Bad luck,*
pō'ino, pakalaki.
bag. 'Eke, 'eke'eke.
baggage. Ukana, 'ope'ope.
bait. Maunu.
bake. Kālua, ho'omo'a, 'oma,
ho'o'oma, puhi, ho'olua.
balance. 1. *Weigh.* Kaulike, ana
paona, paona, paona kaulike.
2. *Remainder.* Koena, koehonua.
bald. 'Ōhule.
ball. 1. *Sphere.* Kinipōpō, pōpō
pōko'a, pōkā. *To play ball,*
kinipōpō, pā'ani kinipōpō. **2.**

Dance. 'Aha hulahula, anaina hulahula.

balloon. Pāluna.

balloonfish. 'O'opu-hue.

ballot. Pāloka. *To cast a ballot,* koho pāloka. *To count ballots,* helu pāloka.

bamboo. 'Ohe. *Bamboo pipes,* kā'eke'eke, pahūpahū. *Bamboo rattles,* pū'ili.

banana. Mai'a. *Banana blossoms and sheath,* pola. *Dry banana leaf,* lauhulu. *Banana bunch,* 'āhui mai'a. *Hand, as of banana,* 'ekā. *Banana stalk,* pū mai'a.

bandage. Wahī 'eha.

bang. Pohā (*as a gun*).

bank. 1. *Border.* Kapa, ka'e. 2. *Finance.* Panakō.

baptize. Papekema, papekiko.

bar. 1. *Barrier.* Kaola, lā'au kī, lā'au ke'a, paukū, pale. 2. *As of soap.* 'Aukā kopa. 3. *For drinking.* Wahi inu lama, pākaukau. 4. *Music.* Pale.

barbecue. Kō'ala.

barber. Kanaka 'ako lauoho.

bare. Kohana.

barefoot. Kāma'a 'ole.

barely. Wale nō.

bargain. Makepono, ho'ēmiemi i ke kumu kū'ai. *Bad bargain,* makehewa, pohō.

bark. 1. *Of a tree.* 'Ili, 'ili lā'au. **Outer bark,** 'ili luna. 2. *Of an animal.* Hae, 'aoa.

barracuda. Kākū.

barrel. Pahu, palala, palela. *Water barrel,* pahu wai.

base. Kumu, kahua, kū.

baseball. Kinipōpō. *To play baseball,* pā'ani kinipōpō.

bashful. Hilahila.

basic. Kumu, honua. *Basic knowledge,* 'ike kumu.

basin. 1. *Container.* Ipu, po'i, ipu holoi, po'i wai, pā holoi, pā kini. 2. *Land.* Poho 'āina, kīpoho.

basket. 'Eke, 'ie, hīna'i, hīna'i poepoe.

basketball. Kinipōpō hīna'i.

bass. 1. *Music.* Leo kāne, leo 'uwō. 2. *Fish.* 'O'opu-haole (*black bass*).

bastard. Keiki manuahi, keiki kāmeha'i.

baste. 1. *Sewing.* Ho'oholoholo, kāholo, 'ōmau. 2. *Cooking.* Ho'oma'ū.

bat. 1. *Mammal.* 'Ōpe'ape'a, pe'a, pe'ape'a. 2. *To strike.* Hili. 3. *Bat for ball.* Lā'au kinipōpō, lā'au pa'i kinipōpō.

bath. 'Au'au.

bathhouse. Hale 'au'au.

bathing suit. Lole 'au'au.

bathroom. Lumi 'au'au, lua. *See* toilet.

bathtub. Kapu 'au'au.

batter. 1. *As in baseball.* Mea hili kinipōpō. 2. *Cookery.* Mea'ono mo'a 'ole.

battery. 1. *Artillery.* Huina pū kuni ahi. 2. *Electric.* Pākali, iho uila. 3. *Assault.* Hō'eha 'ana.

battle. Kaua, ho'oūka kaua, paio.

battleship. Moku kaua, manuwā, pāpū lewa.

bay. Kū'ono, kai-kū'ono; Hono-, Hana- (*in place names only*).

be. *There is no verb "to be" in Hawaiian. The copula is omitted entirely in equational sentences, or may be represented by verb markers* (ua, e . . . ana, ke . . . nei, i, e) *or by the article* he. *I am well, l' was well,* ua maika'i au. *I will be well,* e maika'i ana au. *You are happy,* hau'oli 'oe. *This is a box,* he pahu kēia.

beach. Kahakai, kahaone, papa kea.

beacon. Lama kuhikuhi.

beak. Nuku, ihu.

beam. *Ray of light.* Kukuna.

bear. 1. *Carry.* Hāpai, hi'i, hali, pa'a; hā'awe (*on the back*). 2. *Reproduce.* Hānau, hāpai, hua, ho'ohua. 3. *Animal.* Pea.

beard. 'Umi'umi.

beast. Holoholona.

beat. 1. *Strike.* Pepehi, ku'i, pa'i, hahau, uhau, pā. *Beat, as the heart or pulse,* pana, 'api. 2. *Defeat.* Make, eo, lanakila, pio.

beautiful. Nani, u'i, maika'i, makalapua.

beautify. Ho'onani, ho'oū'i, ho-'ou'iu'i, ho'owehi, ho'ohiehie.

beauty. Nani; u'i (*youthful*).

because. No, no ka mea, ma, i, ma o, muli, mamuli.

beckon. Ani, pe'ahi.

become. Lilo, hele . . . a, ua, lawe.

becoming. 1. *Befitting.* Kūpono. 2. *Attractive.* Kohukohu, hiehie.

bed. Moe, moena, wahi moe.

bedroom. Lumi moe.

bed sheet. Uhi pela.

bedspread. Kapa moe (*general name*); hāli'i moe, uhi moe.

bedtime. Wā hiamoe, manawa moe.

bee. Meli, nalo-meli (*honeybee*).

beef. Pipi. *Beef meat,* 'i'o pipi.

beehive. Pahu meli, pūnana meli.

beer. Pia, bia.

beetle. Pu'u, ane.

before. Mua, 'ē, alia, i ka wā mamua.

beforehand. Mua, 'ē.

befriend. Ho'omakamaka, ho-'ohoaloha, ho'āikāne.

beg, beggar. Mākilo.

begin. Ho'omaka, ho'okumu. *To begin again,* ho'omaka hou.

beginner. Mea ho'omaka.

beginning. Ho'omaka 'ana, ma-ka, maka mua, kinohi, kumu.

behave. Hana, noho. *Behave well,* noho pono.

behind. Hope, muli, ma ke kua; mahope (*referring to both time and place*); i hope (*does not refer to time*).

being. Mea (*person, thing*); kanaka (*human*).

believe. Mana'o'i'o, hilina'i.

bell. Pele.

belly. 'Ōpū, hakualo.

belong. No, na, kuleana. *This belongs to me,* na'u kēia, no'u kēia.

belonging. Kā, kō, na, no. *Belonging to that place,* no laila.

beloved. Aloha 'ia, mea aloha, milimili.

below. Lalo, i lalo, malalo, iho.

belt. Kuapo, 'ili kuapo, kuapo 'ōpū.

bench. Noho, noho lō'ihi, papa noho.

bend. Pelu, ho'opi'o, ho'oke'e, ho'okeke'e.

beneath. Lalo, malalo, i lalo.

benefit. Pono, maika'i.

Bermuda grass. Mānienie-haole.

berry. Hua li'ili'i.

beside. Ma, ma ka 'ao'ao.

besides. Koe, ho'i, kekahi, kahi. *Besides that,* koe kēlā.

best. 'Oi, 'oi loa, maika'i a'e, po'okela, kilohana. *Maui is the best,* Maui nō ka 'oi.

bet. Pili, piliwaiwai.

betray. Kumakaia.

better. Maika'i a'e, aho, ahona, ho'okā'oi; polapola (*of health*). *That is better,* e aho ia.

between. Waena, mawaena, i waena.

beverage. Meainu. *Cold beverage,* meainu ho'ohu'ihu'i.

beware. Akahele, mālama, ao.

bewilder. Ho'opohihihi, ho-'opōna'ana'a, ho'opāha'oha'o.

beyond. Waho, 'ō. *Far beyond,* ma'ō loa aku.

Bible. Paipala, Baibala. *Holy Bible,* Paipala Hemolele.

bicycle. Paikikala, ka'a paikikala, ka'a hehi wāwae.

big. Nui, nunui.

bill. Pila; kāki (*charge*); palapala (*document*). *Bill of sale,* palapala kū'ai.

billiards. Pahupahu, pilioki.

billow. 'Ale.

bind. See tie.

bird. Manu.

birdhouse. Hale manu.

bird's-nest fern. 'Ekaha.

birth. Hānau, hanauna, ho'ohānau.

birth certificate. Palapala hānau.

birth control. Kaupalena hānau.

birthday. Lā hānau, lā piha makahiki. *Happy birthday*, hau'oli lā hānau.

birthmark. Ila.

birthplace. 'Āina hānau, one hānau.

biscuit. Pelena.

bishop. Pihopa.

Bishop Museum. Hale Hō'ike'ike o Kamehameha.

bitch. 'Īlio wahine.

bite. Nahu, nanahu, 'aki, 'a'aki, 'akina.

bits. Li'ili'i, oka, hunahuna, hunehune.

bitter. 'Awa, 'awa'awa.

black. 'Ele'ele, 'ele, pō'ele, pā'ele, uliuli, hiwa, hiwa pa'a.

blackboard. Papa-'ele'ele.

black eye. Maka uli.

blame. 'Āhewa, 'imi hala, ho-'āhewa, ho'ohewa, kāpilipili.

blanket. Kapa moe, huluhulu, kapa huluhulu.

bleach. Ho'oke'oke'o, pūkai, kuakea, ho'okuakea, ho'oheu.

bleed. Kahe koko.

bless. Ho'omaika'i, ho'opōmaika'i, mōlia.

blind. Makapō, maka'alā. *Blind in one eye*, makapa'a.

blink. 'I'imo, 'ōnini, ho'olili, ha-'alili.

blister. Pō'olopū, hō'olopū, 'olopū, 'ōwela.

block. 1. *Obstruct*. 'Āke'ake'a, ke'ake'a, ke'a, pa'a. 2. *Piece of wood*. Paukū wahie, palaka.

blonde. Oho hākeakea, lauoho melemele.

blood. Koko. *Flow of blood*, kahe koko, he'e koko.

blossom. Pua.

blow. 1. *As air current*. Puhi, pā, papā, pā makani (*wind*).

2. *Strike*. Haua, hāuna, hahau, hauhauna, uhau.

blowhole. Lua puhi, puhi.

blue. *No exact equivalent:* uli, uliuli (*of deep sea*); polū (*as of clothes, eyes*). *Blue eyes*, maka 'ālohilohi, maka polū.

blunder. Lalau, hewa, kīna-'una'u.

blunt. Kūmūmū, mūmū.

blush. Pi'i ka 'ula.

board. 1. *Lumber*. Papa, papa lā'au, laupapa. *Rough, unfinished board*, papa huluhulu. *Ironing board*, papa 'aiana. 2. *To go on board*. Kau 'e'e. *To board a ship*, 'e'e moku. 3. *To feed*. Hānai, 'ai. 4. *Council*. Papa, ke'ena.

boarding school. Kula hānai, kula noho pa'a.

Board of Education. Papa Ho-'ona'auao.

Board of Health. Papa Ola.

Board of Supervisors. Papa Luna Kia'i.

boast. Kaena, ha'anui, liki, ha-'akei.

boat. Moku. *Rowboat*, wa'apā. *Steamboat*, mokuahi.

body. Kino.

body hair. Hulu, huluhulu.

body surfing. He'e umauma, kaha nalu.

boil. 1. *As water*. Paila, kupa, lapalapa. 2. *Carbuncle*. Ma'i hēhē, makalau; maka pala, palapū (*ready to burst*).

bold. Koa, maka koa, wiwo 'ole, 'a'a, maha'oi.

bomb. Pōkā pahū.

bone. Iwi.

bonefish. 'Ō'io.

bonito. Kawakawa.

bonus. Uku makana, uku keu.

booby. *Bird.* 'Ā, 'a'a.

book. Puke.

bookstore. Hale kū'ai puke.

border. Palena, lihi, nihi, kapa, pe'a, ka'e.

boring. *Uninteresting.* Hoihoi 'ole, manakā, ho'omanakā.

born. Hānau, loa'a.

borrow. Hōʻaiʻē, nonoi no ka manawa.

boss. Luna, haku hana, poki. *To boss,* noho haku.

bossy. Hoʻohaku, kuhikuhi, kuhilani.

both. Lāua ʻelua, nā mea ʻelua. *Both you and I,* ʻo kāua pū.

bother. Pilikia, hoʻopilikia, hana luhi, hoʻoluhi.

bottle. ʻŌmole, hue wai. *Nursing bottle,* ʻōmole hānai waiū.

bottom. Kumu, mole, kō lalo loa, papakū, kāhi malalo.

"bottoms up." Huli pau; ʻōkole maluna (*vulgar*).

boundary. Palena, mokuna, ʻaoʻao, kapa, lihi. *Land boundary,* palena ʻāina.

bow. 1. *Obeisance.* Kūlou, kūnou, kimo poʻo. **2.** *Forward part of vessel.* Ihu, ihu waʻa. **3.** *Weapon.* Pana, pana ʻiole, kīkoʻo.

bowels. 1. *Evacuation.* Kiʻo, kākā, pākiʻo; hana lepo (*euphemism*). *See* **excrement. 2.** *Innards.* Naʻau, ʻōpū.

bowl. 1. *Container.* ʻUmeke, ipu, pola. **2.** *Game.* ʻUlu maika, maika, paheʻe ʻulu. *Bowling ball,* ʻulu, puʻupā.

box. 1. *Receptacle.* Pahu. **2.** *Fight.* Kuʻikuʻi, kuʻikuʻi puʻupuʻu, mokomoko.

boxfish. Makukana, pahu.

boy. Keiki, keiki kāne, kama kāne. *Oh boy!* Auwē!

bracelet. Kūpeʻe, kūpeʻe lima, apo, apo lima.

brag. Kaena, akena, haʻakoi, hoʻokelakela.

braid. Hilo, hili, pahili, ulana.

brain. Lolo, lolo poʻo.

branch. Lālā, mana, ʻohā.

branches. Manamana.

brand. Kuni, hao.

brandy. Palani.

brass. Keleawe.

brave. Koa, hoʻokoa, wiwo ʻole.

bread. Palaoa, pelena.

breadfruit. ʻUlu.

break. *There is no general term;* the main usages follow. **1.** *As a stick or bones broken in two.* Haʻi, hahaʻi, uhaʻi, haki, hakihaki, uhaki; *break easily,* haʻi wale. **2.** *As a flat surface split or broken into pieces.* Wāhi, wāwahi wāhia, ʻulupā. **3.** *As a string that is severed.* Moku, momoku, mokumoku. **4.** *As a dish.* Nahā. **5.** *General.* Hoʻopilikia (*damage*); *break open or burst,* pohā, pakū; *break, as waves,* poʻi, haki; *break, as law,* wāwahi, pale, haʻihaʻi. *To break and enter a house,* wāwahi hale.

breakfast. ʻAina kakahiaka.

breast. Ū, waiū.

breath. Hanu, aho, ea, eaea.

breathe. Hanu, aho.

breeze. Ahe, aheahe makani, ani, aniani, makani aniani.

brick. Uwinihapa.

bride. Wahine male hou, wahine mare.

bridegroom. Kāne male hou, kāne mare.

bridge. Uwapo.

brief. 1. *Short.* Pōkole, muku. **2.** *Summary.* Palapala hoʻopokole ʻia.

bright. ʻAlohi, ʻālohilohi, kōnane, ʻōlino, laʻelaʻe.

bring. Lawe mai, hō mai.

brisk. Makaʻala, ʻeleu, māmā.

Britain. Pelekane, Pelekania.

broad. Laulā, ākea.

broadcast. Hoʻolele leo, hoʻolaha.

broaden. Hoʻolaulā.

broil. Pūlehu (*on coals*); lāwalu (*in leaves*).

broom. Pūlumi.

brother. Kaikuaʻana, kuaʻana (*older sibling of same sex*); kaikaina, kaina (*younger sibling of same sex*); kaikunāne, kunāne (*of a female*).

brother-in-law. Kaikoʻeke, koʻeke (*of a male*); kāne.

brown. *No exact Hawaiian equivalent;* uliuli, kamaʻehu.

bruise. Pohole, hoʻopohole, māhole, mōhole.
brush. 1. *Instrument.* Palaki,
hulu. *Scrubbing brush,* palaki ʻānai. *Scrubbing or painting brush,* huluʻānai. *Hairbrush,* palaki lauoho. *To
brush,* palaki. 2. *To brush
aside.* Pale, palepale.
bubble. Huʻa.
bucket. Pākeke. *See* **pail.**
bud. Liko, ʻōpuʻu. *To bud,*
ʻōmamaka.
buds. Makamaka; makalau (*fig.,
many offspring*).
bug. Mū, puʻu.
bugle. Pū.
build. Kūkulu, hana, kāpili.
building. Hale.
bull. Pipi kāne, pipi laho, pipi
pulu, pulu.
bullet. Pōkā, pōhaku waikī.
bump. Puʻu, ʻanapuʻu, ʻōhū.
bunch. ʻĀhui (*as of bananas*);
hui, huihui, huhui.
bundle. Pūʻolo, ʻope, ʻopeʻope.
bur. Kukū.
burden. Luhi; hāʻawe, hōʻawe,
ʻawe (*carried on back*); amo,
ʻauamo (*carried on shoulders*).
bureau. 1. *Office.* Keʻena, ʻoihana, māhele, pulo. 2. *Chest
of drawers.* Pahu ʻume.

burglary. Wāwahi hale ʻaihue.
burial. Kanu, kanu ʻana.
burn. ʻĀ, ʻaʻā, hōʻā, puhi, kuni,
puhi ahi.
burned. Pau ahi, wela, welawela, pāpaʻa, kunia.
burst. Pahū, pakū, pohā, pūhā.
bury. Kanu.
bus. Kaʻa ʻōhua.
bush. 1. *Shrub.* Lāʻau liʻiliʻi,
lāʻau haʻahaʻa. 2. *Vegetation.*
Nahele.
business. ʻOihana, hana, kuleana. *To transact business,*
hoʻoholo i ka hana.
busy. Paʻahana, paʻa i ka hana,
lilo, limahana.
but. Akā, naʻe, aia naʻe, eia (nō)
naʻe, koe, koe kēia.
butter. Waiūpaka, paka.
butterfly. Pulelehua, lepelepe-o-
Hina.
butterflyfish. Kīkākapu.
buttocks. Lemu, ʻōkole, pāpākole, ʻelemu, hope.
button. Pihi.
buy. Kūʻai, kūʻai mai.
by. E, na, ma, i. *By me,* naʻu.
By him, her, it, nāna. *By you,*
nāu.
by-and-by. Mahope, mamuli,
auaneʻi.

C

c. *No Hawaiian term.*
cabbage. Kāpiki, kākipi.
cabinet. 1. *Furniture.* Waihona,
pahu waihona. 2. *Political.*
ʻAha kuhina.
cactus. Pā-nini, pā-pipi.
café. Hale ʻaina.
cage. Pahu manu, pahu holoholona.
cake. Meaʻono. *Chinese meat
cake,* pepeiao. *Chinese pork
cake,* meaʻono puaʻa. *Flour
cake,* paʻi palaoa. *Pound
cake,* meaʻono paona.
calabash. ʻUmeke, ipu, pā ipu,

hōkeo, hue, ōpū-hue, ipu
pāwehe.
calendar. ʻAlemanaka, kalēna-
kalio.
calf. 1. *Animal.* Pipi keiki. 2.
Anatomy. ʻOlo, ʻoloʻolo wāwae, ʻolo wae.
California. Kaleponi.
call. 1. *To speak out.* Hea, kāhea. 2. *To give a name.* Kapa.
3. *To visit.* Kipa.
calm. Mālie, laʻi, hālaʻi, kālaʻe,
mālaʻe, malino, manino, linolino.
calmed. Laʻi, mālie, nā.

camera. Pahu-pa'i-ki'i.

camp. Kahua. *To make a camp, to camp,* ho'okahua, ho'omoana.

campground. Kahua ho'omoana.

can. 1. *Able.* Hiki. 2. *Tin.* Kini.

Canada. Kanaka, Kanada.

canal. Alawai, 'auwai, 'auwaha, kōwā, kanela.

cancel. Ho'opau, kāpae.

candidate. Moho.

candle. Ihoiho, ihoiho kukui.

candlenut. Kukui.

candy. Kanakē.

cane. 1. *See* sugarcane. 2. *Staff.* Ko'oko'o.

cannery. Hale ho'okomo kini. *Pineapple cannery,* hale hana hala-kahiki.

cannon. Pū kuni ahi. *Cannonball,* pōkā pū kuni ahi.

canoe. Wa'a.

canoe bailer. Kā.

canoe man. Mea wa'a.

canoe paddler. Hoe wa'a.

canoe race. Heihei wa'a.

can opener. Mea wehe kini.

can't. 'A'ole hiki, hiki 'ole. *I can't go,* 'a'ole hiki ia'u ke hele.

canvas. Kapolena.

cap. Kapu, pāpale kapu.

cape. 1. *Geographical.* Lae, 'ōlae, 'oi'oina. 2. *Garment.* Kīhei, 'ahu, kīpuka, koloka. *Feather cape,* 'ahu'ula.

Cape gooseberry. Pohā, pa'ina.

capital. 1. *City.* Kapikala. 2. *Wealth.* Kumu waiwai, kumupa'a.

captain. Kāpena, luna kaua, kāpena ali'ikoa.

captive. Pio.

capture. Lawe pio, hopu.

car. Ka'a. *To ride in a car,* kau ka'a, holo ka'a. *To drive a car,* kalaiwa ka'a. *To get in a car,* kau i ke ka'a. *To get out of a car,* lele mai ke ka'a.

carbon paper. Pepa kope.

card. Pepa.

cards. Nā pepa, pepa hahau (*playing*).

care. *To care for.* Mālama, nānā. *Well cared for,* mālama pono 'ia.

career. 'Oihana.

carefree. 'A'ohe no'ono'o, 'a'ohe ho'okaumaha, 'a'ohe pīhoihoi.

careful. Akahele, nānā pono, mālama pono.

carefully. Pono, nihi, aka-.

careless. Kāpulu, palaka, kiko-'olā, ho'oponopono 'ole, ho-'ohemahema.

caretaker. Kahu.

carfare. Uku ka'a.

cargo. Ukana.

carnation. Ponimō'ī.

carpenter. Kamanā.

carpet. Moena weleweka, kāpeka.

carrot. Kāloke.

carry. Lawe, hāpai, hali.

cart. Ka'a, ka'a huila lua.

carve. Kālai, kalakalai, ku'ikepa (*as wood*); 'oki'oki (*as meat*).

case. 1. *Container.* Pahu, wahī, poho. 2. *Court case.* Hihia, hihia kalaima, hihia waiwai. 3. *Situation.* Kūlana.

cash. Kālā kū'ike.

cash payment. Uku kū'ike.

casket. Pahu, pahu kupapa'u.

cast. 1. *To throw.* Ho'olei, nou, kiola. 2. *To cast for fish.* Kākele, kā'ili, hī, ho'okelekele.

cat. Pōpoki, 'owau, 'oau.

catalog. Puke nānā mea kū'ai, puke hō'ike hana.

catch. Hopu (*grab*); 'apo (*as a ball*); 'apo'apo; hei (*in a net*); loa'a, ho'opa'a.

caterpillar. Pe'elua, 'enuhe, nuhe, 'anuhe, poko.

Catholic. Kakōlika, Kakōlika Loma (*Roman*). *Catholic religion,* ho'omana Pope.

Catholicism. Kakōlika, Ho-'omana Palani.

cat's cradle. Hei.

cattle. Pipi; pū'ā pipi, kumu pipi (*herd*).

Caucasian. Haole. *See* white man.

caught. Hopu 'ia, 'apo 'ia; mau (*snagged, as a fish or hook*).

cautious. Akahele, ho'okanaha'i.

cave. Ana, lua, pao.

cavity. Po'o, napo'o, 'āpo'opo'o. *Tooth cavity,* puka niho.

cease. Pau, ho'opau, oki, ho'ōki, waiho.

ceiling. Kaupaku.

celebrate. Ho'olaule'a, hau'oli, ho'okelakela.

celebration. Ho'olaule'a; hana ho'ohiwahiwa (*as to honor an individual*).

cement. Kameki, kimeki, palaina kimeki. *To smooth fresh cement with a trowel,* palaina.

cemetery. Ilina, pā ilina, pā kupapa'u. *Plot in a cemetery,* pā ilina.

cent. Keneka. *Ten cents,* kenikeni.

center. Waena, waenakonu, konuwaena, kikowaena.

central. Waena; kikowaena (*telephone operator*).

ceremony. Hana ho'ohanohano. *Religious ceremony,* hana pili haipule.

cereus. Pā-pipi-pua.

certain. 1. *Particular.* Kekahi. 2. *Positive.* Maopopo loa.

certainly. Hiki, hiki nō, 'a 'oia, pēlā nō, 'oiā'i'o, pēlā 'i'o nō. *Certainly not!* 'A'ole loa!

certificate. Palapala, palapala hō'oia, palapala hō'ike. *Birth certificate,* palapala hānau.

chain. Kaula, kaula hao. *Watch chain,* kaula uwaki.

chair. Noho. *Kinds:* noho ali'i (*throne*); noho huila (*wheel*); noho 'ie (*wicker*); noho kū (*straight*); noho moe (*divan*); noho 'opi'opi (*folding*); noho paipai (*rocking*).

chairman. Luna ho'omalu, ali'i ho'omalu.

chalk. Poho.

challenge. 'A'a.

champion. Mea lanakila, po'okela, pūkaua.

chance. Manawa (*opportunity*). *Take a chance,* ho'ā'o.

change. 1. *Transformation.* Loli, ho'olilo, ho'ololi, huli. 2. *Money.* Kenikeni; wāhi (*to change a bill*).

chant. Oli (*not for dancing*); hula (*for dancing*); mele (*general term*).

chapter. Mokuna.

character. 1. *Nature.* 'Ano. 2. *Symbol.* Hō'ailona.

charcoal. Lānahu, nānahu.

charge. 1. *Levy a price.* Ho'oūku, uku. 2. *Defer payment.* Hō'ai'ē, kāki, 'auhau. 3. *Accusation.* 'Ōlelo ho'āhewa, 'āhewa.

charity. Aloha, manawale'a.

charming. Māhie, ho'omāhie, ho'opunihei.

chase. Alualu, hahai, uhai, 'āha'i.

chat. Kama'ilio, keaka.

cheap. Emi, makepono.

cheat. 'Āpuka, pākaha, kikiki, kolohe, 'aihue, ho'opunipuni.

check. 1. *Bank.* Pila kīko'o, pepa kīko'o, palapala kīko'o. 2. *To restrain.* Ke'ake'a, kāohi, ho'ālia. 3. *To mark.* Kaha. 4. *To verify.* Nānā pono i nā hewa, ho'oiā'i'o.

checkerboard. Papa kōnane, papamū.

checkers. Kōnane.

check mark. Kaha.

cheek. Papālina.

cheer. 1. *Encourage.* Ho'olana, ho'opaipai. 2. *Shout.* Ho'ōho.

cheerful. Hoihoi, hau'oli mau, ho'olana.

cheers. Hipahipa, hulō, ho'ōho hau'oli.

cheese. Waiūpa'a, waiūpaka pa'a.

cherish. Pūlama, ho'oheno; ha'aheo (*with pride*).

chest. 1. *Anatomy.* Umauma,

houpo, ke'apa'a. **2.** *Container.* Pahu, holowa'a.

chew. Mama (*without swallowing*); nau (*with closed mouth*).

chicken. Moa.

chicken pox. Ma'i pu'upu'u li-'ili'i, 'ulāli'i.

chief. Ali'i, lani.

chief of police. Luna māka'i.

child. Keiki.

childbirth. Hānau, ho'ohānau.

childhood. Wā kamali'i, wā li-'ili'i, wā 'u'uku.

childish. Ho'okamali'i.

childless. Kama 'ole, keiki 'ole, lālā 'ole.

children. Kamali'i.

chili pepper. Nioi.

chilly. Hu'ihu'i, lī, ko'eko'e, make anu, anuanu.

chin. 'Auwae.

China. 1. *The country.* Pākē, 'Āina Pākē. **2.** (*Not cap.*) *Crockery.* Pā a me nā pola like 'ole.

Chinese. Pākē.

Chinese New Year. Konohī.

chisel. Pao, kila, ko'i pāhoa.

chocolate. Kokoleka.

choice. 1. *Selection.* Koho, wae 'ana. **2.** *Of high quality.* Laha 'ole, mea laha 'ole, hiwa.

choir. Papa hīmeni.

choke. 'Umi, laoa, pu'ua, kalea.

choking. 'Umina.

choose. Koho, ho'okoho, wae, ho'owae, waewae.

chop. Kua, kākā, 'oki'oki, 'āpahu, pokepoke.

chopsticks. Lā'au 'ai, lā'au lālau mea'ai.

chorus. Hui, mele hui.

Christ. Kristo. *Jesus Christ,* Iesu Kristo.

Christian. Kalīkiano, Kristiano, Kilīkiano, Kiritiano.

Christianity. Ho'omana Kalīkiano.

Christmas. Kalīkimaka, Kalīkamaka.

church. Hale pule, luakini, pule.

Church of Jesus Christ of Latter-Day Saints. Ho'omana o Iesu Kristo o nā Po'e Ho'āno o nā Lā Hope Nei.

cigar. Kīkā.

cigarette. Kikaliki.

circle. Apo, pō'ai, pōhai, ho-'owiliwili.

circuit court. 'Aha ka'apuni, 'aha ho'okolokolo ka'apuni.

circular. Poepoe.

circulate. Ho'olaha, ho'olaulaha, wiliau.

circumcise. Kahe, kahe ule, 'oki poepoe.

citizen. Kupa, maka'āinana.

city. Kūlanakauhale. *"City of refuge,"* pu'uhonua.

claim. Palapala ho'opi'i; kuleana (*for land*).

clam. 'Ōlepe, pāpaua, paua.

clan. 'Ohana nui, 'ohana holo-'oko'a, 'alaea.

clap. Pa'i, pa'ipa'i, pa'ipa'i lima; ku'i (*as of thunder*).

class. Papa. *Chiefly class,* papa ali'i.

classify. Ho'onohonoho, ho'onohonoho papa, kūkulu papa.

classmate. Hoa kula.

claw. Miki'ao, mānea, mai'ao, māi'u'u.

clay. Pālolo, lepo kāwili, lepo mānoanoa.

clean. Ma'ema'e. *To clean,* ho-'oma'ema'e, holoi, ho'oholoi.

clear. Mōakaaka, akaaka, akāka, māla'e, kāla'e, mālamalama.

clerk. Kākau'ōlelo, kupakako.

clever. Akamai, no'eau, loea.

cliff. Pali, palipa'a.

climb. Pi'i.

cling. Pili, pili pū.

clock. Uwaki. *Alarm clock,* uwaki ho'āla.

close. 1. *Near.* Kokoke, pili. **2.** *To shut.* Ho'opa'a, pani, panipani, panikū, 'ūpiki. **3.** *To finish.* Ho'opau. *Close-out sale,* kū'ai ho'opau.

closed. Pa'a.

closet. Waihona, ke'ena waiho.

cloth. Lole.

clothe. 'A'ahu, hō'a'ahu, ho-'okomo lole.

clothes. Lole, 'a'ahu, kapa komo, lole komo.

clothesline. Kaula kaula'i lole.

clothing store. Hale kū'ai lole.

cloud. Ao; 'ōpua (*banks, billows*).

cloudburst. Ua lanipili.

cloudless. Kaula'ela'e, māla'e, pa'ihi.

cloudy. 'Ōmalumalu, 'omamalu.

club. 1. *Organization.* Hui, 'ahahui. 2. *Weapon.* Lā'au, lā'au pālau, lā'au māka'i, pālau, newa.

clumsy. Hemahema, pepe'ekue, hāwāwā.

cluster. 'Āhui, huihui.

coal. Lānaha, nānahu pikimana.

coarse. Mānoanoa.

coast. Kapakai.

Coast Guard. Kia'i Kai.

coat. Kuka, 'ahu.

cobweb. Pūnāwelewele.

cock. Moa kāne.

cockfighting. Hakakā a moa, hākā moa, ho'ohākā moa.

cockroach. 'Elelū.

cocktail. Lama ho'ohuihui 'ia, lama pa'ipa'i.

cocoa. Kōkō.

coconut. Niu.

coffee. Kope.

coffee grounds. Oka kope.

coffin. Pahu, pahu kupapa'u.

cold. 1. *Not warm.* Anu, anuanu; ko'eko'e, hu'ihu'i (*chilly*). 2. *Disease.* Anu. *Head cold,* hanu pa'a, punia. *To have a cold,* anu. *To catch a cold,* loa'a i ke anu.

collar. 'Ā'ī kala, kala.

collarbone. Iwilei.

collect. 'Ohi, ho'ākoakoa, ho-'āhu, hō'ili, hō'ili'ili. *To collect taxes,* 'ohi 'auhau.

collection. Ho'āhu, hō'ili'ili; lūlū (*church*).

college. Kulanui.

colony. Panalā'au.

color. Waiho'olu'u, kala.

column. Kolamu.

comb. Kahi.

combat. Paio, kaua paio, hakakā.

come. Hele mai; mai (*in commands*); hiki mai; haele mai; uhaele mai (*plural*).

comfort. 'Olu, hō'olu, maha, ho'onā.

comfortable. 'Olu'olu, hō'olu, mōhalu, mōhaluhalu.

comma. Koma.

command. Kauoha, kēnā, ho-'oūna.

commandment. 'Ōlelokauoha. *Ten Commandments,* nā kānāwai he 'umi.

commendation. Ho'omaika'i. *Letter of commendation,* palapala ho'omaika'i.

commerce. 'Oihana kālepa.

commission. Komikina (*board*).

commissioner. Komikina, luna.

committee. Kōmike.

common. Hana mau, ma'amau, laha, lauākea. *Not common,* laha 'ole.

commoner. Maka'āinana, noa, noanoa.

communion. Komunio. *Holy Communion,* 'Aha'aina a ka Haku.

community. Wahi noho like o ka po'e, kūlanakauhale, kaiāulu, po'e.

companion. Hoa.

company. Hui, 'ahahui.

compare. Ho'ōhālikelike, ho-'okūkū.

compass. Pānānā.

compete. Ho'okūkū.

complain. Ho'ohalahala, namunamu, 'ōhumu, 'ōhumuhumu.

complete. Piha pono, pau pono, ho'opau, ho'opa'a, ho'okō pono, holo'oko'a.

compose. Haku, haku mele (*song or chant*); haku mo-'olelo (*story*).

conceal. Hūnā, pe'e, ho'onalo.

conceited. Ho'okano, ho'oki-'eki'e, hō'oio, ho'okelakela.

conch shell. Pū, 'olē; 'olē'olē

(*small*). Conch horn, pū'olē-'olē.

conduct. 1. *Deportment.* Hana, 'ano o ka hana 'ana, noho 'ana, kūlana. **2.** *To lead.* Alaka'i, ho'okele, mālama, lawelawe.

confess. Mihi, hō'ike i ka hana i hana 'ia.

confuse. Ho'opohihihi, ho'ohui-kau.

confused. Huikau, pohihihi, pōna'ana'a.

confusion. Huikau, haunāele, pōha'aha'a, pi'oloke.

congratulate, congratulations. Ho'omaika'i.

Congregational. Kalawina.

congress. 'Aha'ōlelo lāhui (*as of the United States*).

connect. Ho'oku'i, ho'ohui.

conquer. Lanakila, lawe pio, na'i.

conqueror. Na'i.

conquest. Lanakila, lawe pio 'ana.

consent. 'Ae, 'āpono, ho'āpono.

consequence. Hopena, hope.

consider. No'ono'o pono, mana'o.

constant. Mau, kūpa'a.

constellation. Huihui.

constipation. Kukae-pa'a, lepo pa'a.

constitution. *Document.* Kumukānāwai.

consul. Kanikela, kanikele.

consult. Kūkā, kūkākūkā, 'ōlelo kūkā.

consume. 'Ai, ho'opau, luku, kemu, hamu.

contagious. Lele.

container. Ipu, pū'olo, po'i kā, poho.

contempt. Ho'owahāwahā.

contest. Ho'okūkū, ho'opāpā, pāpā; kahului (*athletic*).

continue. Ho'omau.

contract. 1. *Agreement.* 'Aelike, kepa, palapala 'aelike, ukupau, ho'oholo. **2.** *Shrink.* Mimiki, ho'ohāiki.

contrast. Ho'ohālike, ho'ohālikelike; 'oko'a (*noun*).

control. Kāohi.

convention. 'Aha, 'ahahui, hō-'ike.

conversation. Kama'ilio 'ana, pāpā'ōlelo, kūka'i kama'ilio.

converse. Kama'ilio, wala'au, kamakama'ilio, pāpā'ōlelo.

convict. 1. *Find guilty.* 'Āhewa, ho'āhewa. **2.** *Prisoner.* Pa-'ahao.

convinced. Mana'opa'a, ho'okū-'i'o, ho'omaopopo.

cook. Ho'omo'a, kuke; 'ōlala, lala (*over a fire*); kahu, kahuna (*at an oven*); kahu 'ai, kahūmu 'ai (*taro or vegetable food*). *See* **bake, boil, broil, roast.**

cooked. Mo'a; pāpa'a, pāpa'apū (*to a crisp*); māhinu (*under-done*); mo'a le'a (*thoroughly*).

cooky. Mea'ono, mea'ono-kuki.

cool. 'Olu'olu (*pleasantly*); hu-'ihu'i (*chilly*); ma'ū (*damp*).

cooled. Ma'alili; ma'ū'ū; kōani-ani (*by a breeze*).

cooperate. Ho'olaulima, kōkua, huki like, kāko'o, alu, alu like, hana like.

cooperation. Laulima, kōkua.

copra. Niu malo'o.

copy. Ho'ohālike; kope, kopena, mea like, kākau kope, lua, ponokope.

copyright. Palapala ho'okule-ana.

coral. Puna, ko'a, ko'ako'a.

cord. Aho, kaula; piko (*umbilical*).

cork. 'Umoki, 'omo, pani, pani 'ōmole (*stopper*).

corn. Kūlina; kūlina 'ono (*sweet*); kūlina, mānoanoa ka 'ili (*as on a toe*).

corner. Huina; kū'ono (*inside*); kihi (*outside*); kohe (*mat*); huina alanui (*street*); hio.

cornstarch. Pia kūlina.

corpse. Kupapa'u, kino wailua, kino make, heana.

corral. Pā.

correct. Pololei, pono. *To correct,* hoʻopololei, hoʻopono, hoʻoponopono, hoʻomaikaʻi.

correspond. *Write letters.* Launa palapala, kūkaʻi leka, hololeka.

cost. Kumu kūʻai, kumu lilo.

costly. Pipiʻi, nui ka hoʻolilo, waiwai.

costume. ʻAʻahu, lole.

cot. Moe ʻopiʻopi, moe ʻuʻuku.

cottage. Hale ʻuʻuku.

cotton. Pulu, pulupulu, maʻo.

couch. Hikieʻe (*large*); pūneʻe (*movable*); kokī, noho moe.

cough. Kunu, ʻehē, ʻahē, ʻahēʻahē.

council. ʻAha kūkā, pūkuʻi.

count. 1. *Number.* Helu, heluhelu, heluna. 2. *Title of nobility.* Kauna.

countrified. Kuaʻāina, hoʻokuaʻāina, pilikua.

country. ʻĀina (*land*); kuaʻāina (*as distinct from the city*); kahiki (*any foreign*).

county. Kalana.

couple. Lua, paʻa, papa lua.

courage. Koa, wiwo ʻole.

course. Ala, alanui, kahua. *Of course,* ʻoia hoʻi.

court. 1. *Legal.* ʻAha. 2. *Royal.* Aloaliʻi. 3. *To woo.* Hoʻoipo, hoʻoipoipo. 4. *See* courtyard.

courthouse. Hale hoʻokolokolo.

courtship. Hoʻoipoipo ʻana.

courtyard. Pā, kahua.

cousin. Hoahānau, kaukini.

cousin-in-law. Kaikoʻeke (*of same sex*).

cover. Uhi, pani, pale, wahī.

cow. Pipi wahine, pipi waiū.

coward. Hōhē, hoʻohē, makaʻu wale.

cowboy. Paniolo.

cowry shell. Leho.

crab. Pāpaʻi (*general name*). *Common kinds:* ʻaʻama, ʻelemihi, ʻalamihi, ʻōhiki, unauna, ʻalaʻeke, moʻala, kūhonu.

crack. 1. *Aperture.* Māwae. 2. *Noise.* ʻUʻina (*as a gun*); koʻele (*as thunder*); kohā, hoʻokani (*as a whip*); pāpaʻaʻina (*as joints*).

cracked. Nahā, naka, makili, ʻowā.

cracker. Pelena.

cradle. Moe luliluli, moe paipai.

cramp. Huki, lāʻau, ʻūmiʻi, wāwae huki.

cramped. ʻŌpili, pipiki, muikiiki, pilikia.

crane. 1. *Bird.* Manu-ʻū. 2. *Machine.* Kewe, hāpuku.

crank. Wili, kūʻau wili. *Hand crank,* wili lima.

cranky. ʻAʻaka, kekē, kekē niho, ʻekeʻeke, hoʻokeʻeke.

crash. 1. *Hit.* Hoʻokuʻi. 2. *Sound* Pohā, pahū.

crater. Lua, lua pele.

crawl. Kolo.

crazy. Pupule, hehena, hewahewa.

cream. Kalima, kalima waiū; kalima hamo (*face*).

create. Hana, hoʻokumu.

creation. Kumulipo, kumu honua.

creature. Mea ola (*living*); holoholona (*animal*).

credit. Hōʻaiʻē (*debt*); hua, heluna (*as for a university course*).

creep. Kolo.

crevally. Ulua.

crib. Moe kamaliʻi.

crime. Kalaima, hewa.

criminal. Kanaka hana, kalaima.

cripple. ʻOʻopa, hapakuʻe, kīnā.

crisscross. Kaha peʻa, ʻolokeʻa, hōʻolokeʻa, kaupeʻa, kahahiō (*mark*).

criticize. Loiloi, kē (*often constructively*); hoʻohalahala (*faultfinding*).

crook. 1. *Bend.* Kīkeʻe, keʻe, lanahua, hoʻokekeʻe. 2. *Cheat.* Kolohe.

crooked. Kapakahi, kekeʻe, kīkeʻekeʻe, hapakuʻe, nanahū, keʻe.

crop. 1. *Harvest.* Mea hoʻoūlu. 2. *Of a bird.* ʻŌpū.

cross. 1. *Of disposition.* 'A'aka, nauki, ka'e, kekē niho, niha. **2.** *Overlap.* Ke'a, pe'a. **3.** *As a street.* Hele ma kēlā 'ao'ao.

crossroads. Huina, huina alanui.

crotch. Kumuhele, mana; kapakapa (*human*).

crouch. 'Ōku'u.

crow. 1. *Bird.* 'Alalā. **2.** *Sound.* 'O'ō, kokō, kani.

crowd. Lehulehu, pihana kanaka, anaina, pū'ulu.

crowded. Pa'apū, pihaku'i.

crown. Kalaunu, kolona, pāpale ali'i, lei ali'i.

crown flower. Pua-kalaunu.

crucifix. Ke'a.

crucify. Kaulia i ke ke'a, mākia.

crude. 1. *Harsh.* Lula 'ole, ho-'oku'iku'i, hanahihi. **2.** *Raw.* Maka.

cruel. Loko'ino, māino, hana 'ino, ho'omāinoino.

crumb. Huna. *Bread crumb,* huna palaoa.

crush. Lomi, ho'oūpē, ho'opē, ho'omaūi, 'ōpā, pākī.

crust. Pāpa'a.

crutch. Ko'oko'o kālele.

cry. Uwē (*weep*); kani, oho, 'uwā (*call out*); puoho (*in alarm*); olo, pihe, kāhea, pū-'alalā.

crybaby. Uwē wale.

cucumber. Ka'ukama.

cue. 1. *Billiards.* Lā'au pahupahu. **2.** *Reminder.* Kumu ho'omana'o, 'ōlelo ho'omana'o.

cultivate. Mahi.

cunning. Ma'alea, 'āpiki.

cup. Pola, ipu, kī'aha, kī'o'e.

cupboard. Pahu pā, waihona pā ipu, waihona ipu.

cup-of-gold. Ipu-kula.

curb. 1. *Street curb.* Ka'e. **2.** *To restrain.* Kāohi.

cure. Ho'ōla, lapa'au, ho'opolapola.

cured. Ola loa (*completely*).

curiosity. Nīele.

curious. 1. *Strange.* 'Ano 'ē, kupanaha, kupaianaha. **2.** *Inquisitive.* Nīele.

curl. Milo. *To curl, as hair,* ho'omimilo.

curly. Pi'ipi'i (*as hair*).

currency. Kālā, kālā aupuni.

current. 1. *Moving matter.* Au (*in the sea*); kai holo, wai kō. **2.** *Contemporary.* O kēia au, o kēia manawa.

curse. Kūamuamu, amu, 'ānai, 'ōlelo hō'ino.

curtain. Pākū, pale, pālulu, pālulu 'ao'ao. *Window curtain,* pākū pukaaniani.

curved. Pi'o, kiwi, pāuma, kākiwi, kihikihi.

cushion. Kūkini, uluna.

customary. Ma'amau, pa'a mau, kūmau, kuluma, laha.

customer. Mea kū'ai mai.

customs. Kuke, dute. *Customs duty,* kuke.

cut. 'Oki, hō'oki, moku, mō, mokumoku, momoku, mokuhia, kālai, kaha; kua (*as a tree*); pa'ipa'i (*as a plant or the hair*). *Cut off,* mu'umu'u, 'akumu, po'omuku. *Cut into pieces,* ma'oki, ho'omākoli, 'oki'oki, paukū. *Cut in short pieces,* 'āpoke, pokepoke. *Cut in half,* pahupū. *To cut cards,* 'oki pu'u pepa. *To cut stone,* kālai pōhaku.

cycle. 1. *Period.* Au, wā. **2.** *Wheel.* Huila.

D

d. *No Hawaiian term.*

dagger. Pāhoa, pahi 'ō, pīkoi lua.

daily. I kēlā me kēia lā; puka lā (*as a newspaper*).

dairy. Hale 'uwī waiū, hui 'uwī waiū, wahi mālama pipi waiū.

dam. Pani wai, kaupale, māno.

damage. Pohō, pō'ino, hō'ino-'ino, ho'o'ino. *To damage,* hō'ino.

damages. Uku pohō.

damn. Hō'ino wale, kūamuamu.

damp. Ma'ū.

dampen. Ho'oma'ū, ho'omā'ū'ū.

dance. Hula; hulahula (*ballroom dance*).

dancing school. Kula a'o hulahula.

danger. Mea pō'ino, maka'u.

dangerous. Maka'u loa, weliweli 'ia, pō'ino.

dare. 'A'a, ho'ohoa.

dark. Pō'ele, pō'ele'ele, 'ele'ele, pā'ele, uli, uliuli, āuli, hāuli, hāuliuli, lāuli, māuli, pouli, polohiwa, 'āhiwa, pōuliuli, pō; māku'e (*any dark color*). *Dark-complexioned,* 'ili uliuli, 'ili pala uli, 'ili māku'e, 'ili kou, pā'ele; pōpolo (*slang*). *To become dark,* hō'ele'ele.

darkness. Pō'ele'ele.

darling. Makamae, hiwahiwa, milimili, lei.

dart. *Spear.* Ihe, ihe 'ō, kao.

dash. *Run.* Holo māmā, heihei.

date. 1. *Time.* Manawa, lā, makahiki. 2. *Fruit.* Hua pāma. 3. *Engagement.* Ho'opa'a manawa no ka launa pū.

daughter. Kaikamahine.

daughter-in-law. Hūnōna wahine.

dawn. Ao, wana'ao, kaiao, moku ka pawa.

day. Lā, ao. *Weekday,* lā noa. *Day of worship,* lā ho'āno. *School day,* lā kula. *Workday,* lā hana.

dead. Make, make loa, moelepo. *Dead body,* kino make, kino kupapa'u.

deadline. Kaupalena.

deadly. Make.

deaf. Kuli, ho'okuli, pepeiao kuli.

deaf-mute. Leo pa'a, a'alolo kuli. *Deaf-mutes,* po'e kuli a 'ā'ā.

deal. 1. *Apportion.* Māhele, hā-'awi, ha'awina (*as cards*). 2. *Agreement.* 'Aelike. 3. *Act.* Hana, ho'ohana.

dear. 1. *Beloved.* Aloha. 2. *Exclamation.* Auwē! 3. *Costly.* Pipi'i.

death. Make, make loa. *His death,* kona make.

debit. Ka 'ao'ao 'ai'ē (*in bookkeeping*); pōkole ke kālā (*shortage of funds*).

debt. 'Ai'ē.

decay. Palahō, palahū; popopo (*wood*).

deceitful. Ho'opunipuni, 'āpiki, wahahe'e, waha wale, haku 'epa.

December. Kēkēmapa, Lēkēmapa, Kekemaba.

decide. Ho'oholo, holo mana'o, koho.

decision. Ho'oholo, 'ōleloho-'oholo, mana'o ho'oholo.

deck. 1. *Platform.* 'Oneki, papahele. 2. *Of cards.* Pu'u pepa. 3. *Adorn.* Wehi, ho-'ohiluhilu, ho'owehiwehi, ho-'onani.

declaration. Kuahaua, ha'ina.

declare. Ha'i, ho'olaha, wahi, 'ī, 'ōlelo, hō'ike.

decline. 1. *Descending slope.* 'Aui, 'auina. 2. *Refuse.* Hō-'ole.

decorate. Wehi, wehiwehi, ho-'owehi, ho'owehiwehi, ho-'oūluwehi, ho'oūluwehiwehi, ho'oūlumāhiehie, kauluwehi, ho'ohiwahiwa, ho'okāhiko, ho'ohiluhilu, pāpahi, ho-'onani.

decrease. Emi, ho'oli'ili'i, koi'i.

dedicate. Ho'ola'a, ho'omāhanahana.

deed. 1. *Act.* Hana. 2. *Document.* Palapala, palapala ho-'olilo, palapala kila, hō'oiā-'i'o, kila.

deep. Hohonu, kūhohonu; kūlipo (*as a cave*).

defeat. Make, ho'opio, holopapa, hō'auhe'e, lilo, hā'ule.

defect. Kīnā, kīna'u.

defend. Pale, kūpale, ālai; 'ōlelo pale, ho'opale (*in court*).

define. Wehewehe 'ano, wehewehe pono.

definite. Pa'a, maopopo, kā'oko'a.

deformed. Pepe'e, kīnā, hapaku'e, ku'e.

degree. Kekele.

deify. Ho'ākua, ho'omanamana.

dejected. Kaumaha, pilihua, pū, noho pū, kukule.

delay. Lohi, kali, ho'okali, 'apa. *Without delay*, 'emo 'ole.

delegate. 'Elele.

delicate. Lahi, lahilahi, lālahi, pīlahi, hunehune, palupalu.

delicious. 'Ono, mikomiko. *Very delicious*, 'ono loa.

delight. Hau'oli, 'oli'oli, hau'oli'oli, hoihoi, ho'ohoihoi, puni.

delighted. Ohohia, kamahoi, hia'ai, hia'ai'ono.

delightful. Māhie, ho'omāhie, ho'ohie, le'a.

deliver. Hā'awi, lawe. *To deliver a child*, pale, pale keiki, ho'ohānau.

demand. Koi, kauoha.

democracy. Aupuni a ka lehulehu.

Democrat. Kemokalaka.

demolish. Wāwahi, ho'ohiolo, ku'i palu, nāhāhā.

Denmark. Kenemaka, Denemaka.

dense. Pa'apū, lanipō, pōpō uahi.

dentist. Kauka niho.

deny. Hō'ole, 'ole, ho'onele.

depart. Hele i kahi 'ē, ha'alele, waiho.

department. Mahele, ke'ena, 'oihana.

Department of Instruction. 'Oihana Ho'ona'auao.

Department of Water Supply. 'Oihana Wai.

depend. Kauka'i, kauko'o, kālele. *That depends on you*, aia nō ia iā'oe.

deposit. Ho'okomo; uku ho-

'opa'a (*as on a purchase*). *Deposit money in the bank*, ho'okomo i ke kālā i ka panakō.

depressed. **1.** *Sad.* Kaumaha, lu'ulu'u. **2.** *See* **sunken.**

depth. Hohonu.

descend. Iho, hele iho, ho'oihona, hele i lalo.

descendant. Mamo, pua, mo'opuna, keiki pulapula.

describe. Hō'ike 'ano, ha'i 'ano, ho'ākaaka.

desert. *Abandon.* Ha'alele; mahuka (*flee*).

design. Lau, ana, ki'i.

desire. Makemake, 'i'ini, 'ano'i, hia, make, ake, puni, 'upu.

desk. Pākaukau, pākaukau hana.

despair. Hā'ule ka mana'olana, ku'ihē ka na'au.

despise. Ho'okae, ho'owahāwahā.

dessert. Mea'ai momona.

destroy. Luku, ho'opau, hana make. *Destroy completely*, luku ho'opapau, ho'opau, ku'ikē. *Destroy by fire or lava*, lauahi, pau ahi, he'a.

destruction. Luku, lukuna, make.

detective. Māka'ikiu, makākiu.

determine. Holo mana'o, holo, ho'oholo, mana'o pa'a.

detour. Ala kāpae.

develop. Ho'omōhala, hana (*as a photograph*); ho'okino (*as an infant*).

developed. Mōhala, mohahala, mōhalahala, mōhola.

devil. Kiapolō, kepolō, akua.

devoted. Aloha, la'a, la'ahia, puni, lilo; pili aloha (*loving*); ho'opapau.

dew. Kēhau, hau.

diagonal. Lala, ka'akepa, hiō.

diagram. Ki'i.

dial. Wili (*as on a telephone*).

diamond. Kaimana.

Diamond Head. Kaimana Hila, Lē'ahi.

diaper. Kaiapa.

diarrhea. Hī, palahī.

dictionary. Puke wehewehe ʻōlelo.

did. *See* **do.** *The one who did,* ka mea i, ka i. *He did go,* ua hele nō ʻoia.

die. Make, make loa (*contrasted to* make, *which may mean "defeated, faint"*).

diet. Meaʻai e pono ai ke kino.

difference. Mea ʻokoʻa.

different. ʻOkoʻa, ʻē, ʻē aʻe, ʻano ʻē, like ʻole.

difficult. Paʻakikī, hana nui.

difficulties. He mau pilikia, hihia.

dig. ʻEli.

digging stick. ʻŌʻō; ʻōʻō hao (*iron*).

dignified. Hanohano, kūoʻo, kei, ʻihi, keha.

dignity. Hanohano, kapukapu, hie, hiehie, keha.

diligent. Huli hana, hana mau, paʻahana.

dillydally. Hoʻolohi, loloiāhili, lōiele, hōʻapaʻapa.

dim. Poahi, kōliʻuliʻu, palaweka, lipo, ʻāhiahia.

dime. Kenikeni.

diminish. Emi, hoʻēmi, hoʻoiki.

dining room. Lumi ʻaina.

dining table. Papa ʻaina.

dinner. ʻAina ahiahi, papa ʻaina, pāʻina. *Dinner party,* ʻahaʻaina.

dip. 1. *To plunge or immerse.* Kūpenu, hoʻoluʻu, luʻu. 2. *Depression.* Hālua.

diploma. Palapala. *High school diploma,* palapala puka, palapala hoʻomaikaʻi. *University diploma,* palapala hōʻoia kulanui.

direct. 1. *Oversee.* Alakaʻi, kuhikuhi, kaʻi. 2. *Straight.* pololei.

direction. 1. *Compass direction.* ʻAoʻao. 2. *See* **direct, 1.** *Wrong directions,* kuhi hewa.

directory. Papa kuhikuhi, puke inoa.

dirge. Kanikau, mele kanikau, hoʻouwēuwē, ʻuhane.

dirt. Lepo, lepo hānai, ʻeka.

disagree. Kūʻēʻē, hukihuki, kūlikeʻole, lōkahiʻole.

disagreement. Kūʻēʻē, mokuāhana.

disappear. Nalo, nalowale, nalohia, pio, hanini.

disappointment. Hoka, mokuāhua, homa.

disapprove. ʻĀpono ʻole, hoʻāhewa.

disaster. Pōpilikia, pōʻino, ulia, weliweli.

disbelieve. Hilinaʻi ʻole, manaʻoʻiʻo ʻole.

discard. Kiloi, kiola, hoʻolei, kāpae, haʻalele.

discharge. 1. *Dismiss.* Hoʻokuʻu, hoʻopau, kipaku. 2. *See* **unload.** 3. *Flow.* Hoʻokahe, walewale, walewalena; heheʻe (*as of pus*). 4. *Fire, as a gun.* Kī pū.

discomfort. ʻOluʻolu ʻole, noʻonoʻo ʻihaʻiha, ʻīnea, ʻihaʻiha.

disconnect. Hoʻokaʻawale, hoʻohemo, kala.

discount. Uku hoʻēmi, hoʻēmi.

discouraged. Pauaho.

discover. ʻImi a loaʻa, ʻike mua, loaʻa, hōʻike.

discuss. ʻŌlelo kūkā, kūkā, kūkākūkā, hoʻokamaʻilio.

disease. Maʻi.

disgrace. Waia, hoʻohilahila, ʻālina.

disguise. Hoʻomeamea, hoʻokohukohu, hoʻonalonalo i ke kūlana, hūnā.

disgusting. Hoʻopailua, kāpulu, luaʻikū.

dish. Pā, ipu. *Glass dish,* pā aniani. *Iron dish or pan,* pā hao. *Paper dish,* pā pepa.

dishcloth. Kāwele pā. *To wipe or dry with a dishcloth,* kāwele.

dishonest. Hoʻopono ʻole, pono ʻole, ʻāpiki, paukeʻe, ʻapakeʻe.

dislike. Makemake ʻole, hoihoi ʻole.

dismiss. Hoʻokuʻu, kuʻu, hoʻopau, waiho.

disobey. Hoʻolohe ʻole, pale ʻōlelo, hoʻokuli.

disorder. Mōkākī, kīpalalē, hōkai.

display. Hōʻike, hōʻikeʻike, hoʻokahakaha, hoʻokelakela.

disposition. ʻAno, loko, manawa, naʻau, ʻōpū.

dispute. Hoʻopaʻapaʻa, hakakā ʻōlelo.

disregard. Nānā ʻole.

dissatisfied. Kūhalahala, hoʻohalahala, loiloi.

dissipate. ʻUhaʻuha.

dissolve. Hoʻoheheʻe.

distance. Mamao, lōʻihi.

distant. Mamao, lilo loa, haʻalilo.

distinction. Kaulana, hanohano, poʻokela.

distinguished. Hanohano, kūlana hiehie.

distress. Pilikia, pōpilikia, pōʻino, hoʻopōʻino, ʻīnea, hoʻīnea, ʻeha, hōʻehaʻeha.

distribute. Hoʻomāhelehele, hoʻolaha.

district. ʻĀpana, ʻokana, moku, mokuʻāina.

disturb. Hoʻoluhi, hoʻopilikia.

disturbance. Haunāele, uluaōʻa.

disturbed. Hoʻoluhi ʻia, pono ʻole ka manaʻo, pīhoihoi, piʻoloke.

ditch. ʻAuwaha, hā, ʻāwaʻa. *Water ditch,* ʻauwai.

dive. Luʻu.

divide. Māhele, puʻunaue, ʻokiʻoki, helehele, kāʻana. *To divide equally,* kaʻi like; hoʻokāʻana.

divination. Hailona, puʻuone.

divine. Akua, hoʻākua, ʻano akua, hoʻāno.

diving board. Papa lele kawa.

division. 1. *Section.* Māhele, pale, mokuna. 2. *Arithmetic.* Puʻunaue.

divorce. ʻOki, hōʻoki, ʻoki male.

dizzy. Pōniu, pōniuniu, niniu, niua.

do. Hana, lawelawe; hoʻokō (*complete*). There is no Hawaiian equivalent for the English auxiliary. *Do you like this?* Makemake anei ʻoe i kēia? *Yes, I do,* ʻAe, makemake nō. *See* **done.**

dock. Uwapo.

doctor. Kauka.

document. Palapala.

dodge. ʻAlo, ʻaloʻalo, hōʻalo, hoʻohala.

dog. ʻĪlio.

doll. Kiʻi, kiʻi pēpē.

dollar. Kālā.

dolphin. Mahimahi.

donate. Hāʻawi wale, makana, hāʻawi manawaleʻa.

donation. Lūlū, haʻawina, makana.

done. Hana ʻia, pau. *See* **do.**

donkey. Kēkake, ʻēkake.

do-nothing. Palaualelo, kūhana ʻole, lemukū.

don't. 1. *Negative command.* Mai, uoki. 2. *Negative.* ʻAʻole.

door. Puka, puka hale, puka komo, ʻīpuka.

doorway. Puka komo.

dormitory. Hale moe.

dot. Kiko, pōhaka.

dotted. Kikokiko.

double. Pālua, pāpālua, hoʻopālua, lua like, lua, kaulua.

doubt. Kānalua.

dough. Palaoa hoʻowali ʻia, pelena moʻa ʻole.

dove. Manukū, manu-nūnū, nūnū, kuhukulū.

down. 1. *Below.* Lalo, i lalo iho. *See* **fall.** 2. *Feathers.* Heu, heuheu, ʻae, ʻae moa, hulu weuweu.

down payment. Uku hoʻopaʻa.

downpour. Loku, ua lanipili, hoʻolokuloku, haʻalokuloku.

doze. Moe hoʻolana.

dozen. Kākini, ʻumi kūmālua, ʻumi kumamālua.

draft. 1. *Current of air.* Hihio, mōhio. *See* **gust.** 2. *Money order.* Palapala kīkoʻo, pepa kīkoʻo, pila kīkoʻo.

drag. Kauwŏ, alakŏ.

dragged. Kō.

dragonfly. Pinao. *Larvae of dragonfly*, lohelohe.

draw. 1. *Sketch.* Kaha. 2. *Pull, extract.* 'Ume, huki, 'u'u. 3. *Tie.* Pa'i, pa'i wale, pa'i a pa'i.

drawer. Pahu 'ume.

drawing. 1. *Picture.* Ki'i, ki'i i kaha 'ia, kahana. 2. *Pulling.* 'Ume 'ana, kō.

dreadful. Weliweli, māna'ona'o.

dream. Moe'uhane.

dregs. Oka, ko'ana, ki'o, mākū.

drenched. Pulu pē, pē.

dress. 1. *Garment.* Lole, 'a'ahu. *To dress*, komo, komo lole. 2. *To wrap a wound.* Wahī. 3. *As a fowl.* Unuunu (*pluck*); kua'i (*disembowel*).

dried. Malo'o.

drift. Lana wale, lana hele.

drill. 1. *Tool.* Nao wili, wili, kāhei, 'ōmilo. 2. *Military.* Paikau. 3. *Practice.* Ho'oma-'ama'a.

drink. 1. *Verb.* Inu, inumia, pā. 2. *Noun.* Meainu.

drip. Kulu, kulukulu.

drive. 1. *As cattle.* Ho'ohuli, hō'ā. 2. *To drive away.* Kipaku, ho'okuke. 3. *As a car.* Kalaiwa, ho'okele. 4. *As nails.* Kākia, mākia, kīpou.

driver. Kalaiwa, ho'okele ka'a.

drool. Hā'ae, kahe ka hā'ae.

droop. Luhe, loha, ho'olo'u.

drop. 1. *Trickle.* Kulu, kahe, mākili. 2. *Let fall.* Hā'ule,

hā'ule'ule, hā'ulehia, ho'ohā-'ule.

drought. Wā malo'o.

drown. Piholo, ho'opiholo, ho-'opalemo.

drowsy. Maka hiamoe, kulu, kulu hiamoe.

drug. Lā'au 'ona, lā'au ho'omalule kino, lā'au ho'oonoenoe, lā'au ho'ohiamoe, lā'au moe, mea 'ona.

drum. Pahu, ipu.

drunk. 'Ona.

dry. Malo'o.

dual. Pālua.

duck. 1. *Bird.* Kakā (*domesticated*), koloa (*Hawaiian*). 2. *To plunge or bow.* 'A!u, luma'i, lu'u.

dues. Uku kūmau.

dull. 1. *Not sharp.* Kūmūmū, mūmū. 2. *Stupid.* Lolohi, le-'ale'a 'ole, hoihoi 'ole, maluhi.

dumb. Leo pa'a, mūmule, 'ā'ā. *Struck dumb*, hakanū.

dust. Ehu lepo, kuehu, ehu, 'ehu, uahi, lelehuna, lepo 'ae'ae.

dusty. Ehu, ehu lepo, 'e'a.

duty. 1. *Obligation.* Pono, hana, māhelehana. 2. *Customs.* Kuke.

dwelling. Nohona, noho 'ana. *Dwelling house*, hale noho. *Dwelling place*, wahi noho, kahi noho.

dye. Wai, waiho'olu'u, wai 'ele, wai 'ele'ele.

dynamite. Kianapauka.

dysentery. Hī, kulu.

E

e. 'Ē.

each. Kēlā mea kēia mea, pākahi.

ear. Pepeiao.

early. Koke, mua, hiki mua, miki'ala.

earn. Loa'a.

earring. Kulapepeiao.

earth. 1. *World.* Ao, honua, 'āina. 2. *Dirt.* Lepo.

earthquake. 'Ōla'i, nāueue.

ease. Maha, nanea, pu'uho-'omaha.

easily. Hikiwale, wale, ma'alahi.

east. Hikina.

Easter. Ka lā i ala hou ai ka Haku (*Protestant*); Pakoa (*Catholic*).

easy. Hikiwale, ma'alahi.

eat. 'Ai, 'ai iho, amu.

eavesdrop. Ho'olohelohe 'ōlelo, ho'olono.

ebb. Emi.

eccentric. 'Ano 'ē.

echo. Kūpina'i, nakulu, papā, hāku'i.

eclipse. Pouli.

economical. Makauli'i, mina-mina, pākiko.

Eden. 'Ēkena, Edena. *Garden of Eden*, Kīhāpai o 'Ēkena, mahina'ai ma 'Ēkena.

edge. Ka'e, kapa, kihi, lihi, nihi, niao, maka, kūkulu, hu'a, pe'a.

edit. Ho'oponopono.

edition. Pa'i 'ana, ho'opuka 'ana.

editor. Luna ho'oponopono.

educate. Ho'ona'auao.

education. A'o palapala, ho'ona-'auao.

eel. Puhi.

effort. Ho'ā'o, ho'āho.

egg. Hua, huamoa (*chicken*).

egg plant. Laho-pipi.

eight. 'Ewalu, walu, 'awalu.

eighteen. 'Umi kūmāwalu, 'umi kumamāwalu.

eighty. Kanawalu.

eighty-one. Kanawalu kūmā-kahi, kanawalu kumamākahi.

either. kekahi.

elbow. Ku'eku'e, ku'eku'e lima, ku'e lima.

elder. Kahiko a'e; kaikua'ana (*sibling of the same sex*); lunakahiko (*church*).

elderly. 'Āo'o, o'o, makule.

elect. Koho, ho'okoho, wae.

election. Koho, koho pāloka.

electric, electricity. Uila, uwila.

elephant. 'Elepane, 'elepani.

elevate. Hāpai, ho'oki'eki'e, hō-'iu.

elevator. 'Eleweka.

eleven. 'Umi kūmākahi, 'umi kumamākahi.

else. 'Ē a'e.

elsewhere. Ma kahi 'ē, 'ē.

embarrass. Ho'ohilahila.

embarrassed. Hilahila.

embassy. Nohona kuhina.

emblem. Ho'ailona.

embrace. Pū'ili, pūliki, 'āpona, kūwili, apo.

embroider. Humulau, 'ōni'o-ni'o.

emerge. Puka, pua.

emergency. Ulia pōpilikia, pili-kia kūhewa.

emotion. *No general term, but emotions may be described by descriptive words following* pu'uwai, na'au, *or* pi'i ka, *as* pu'uwai hau'oli, *happiness*, pi'i ka huhū, *to be angry*.

emphasize. Ho'oko'iko'i, kālele leo, kālele mana'o.

employ. Ho'ohana (*use*); ho-'olimalima, hai (*hire*).

employed. Pa'a i ka hana.

employee. Po'e hana, limahana.

employer. Haku, haku hana.

employment. Hana, 'oihana, ho'ohana.

empty. Haka, hakahaka, 'olo-haka, ukana 'ole.

encircle. Pō'ai, anapuni, 'ai-puni, ka'apuni.

enclose. Puni, ka'apuni, ho'o-komo.

enclosure. Pā.

encourage. Ho'opaipai, ho'oi-kaika, hō'ikaika, ho'olana, hō'eu.

end. Pau 'ana, panina, hope. *To end*, ho'opau, ho'ōki.

endearing. Ho'ālohaloha.

ending. Hopena, 'okina, panina.

endless. Pau 'ole, mau loa.

endure. Ho'omanawanui, mau, 'alo, ō.

enemy. Hoa paio, hoa kaua, 'enemi.

energetic. 'Eleu, mikimiki, hō-'ele'eleu.

enforce. Ho'okō, ho'one'e ika-ika, ho'oholo.

engaged. 1. *Occupied*. Pa'a, lilo.

2. *Betrothed.* Palau, ho'opalau.

engine. 'Enikini, mīkini.

engineer. Wilikī.

England. Pelekane, 'Enelani.

English. Pelekane. *English language.* 'Ōlelo Pelekane, 'ōlelo haole.

engrave. Kaha, kālai.

enjoy. Luana, walea, nanea, hoihoi, 'oli'oli, le'a.

enjoyment. 'Oli'oli, hau'oli, hoihoi.

enlarge. Ho'onui, ho'omāhua, ho'omāhuahua; ho'olele (*as a picture*).

enough. Lawa, nui, lawa puni, ka'aka'alawa.

ensnare. Ho'opunihei, hei, ho'oheihei.

entangled. Hihia, kāhihi, hihipe'a, hakakē.

enter. Komo, ho'okomo.

entertain. Ho'okipa, ho'ohale kipa, ho'ole'ale'a, ho'ohau'oli.

entertaining. Hoihoi.

entertainment. Mea ho'ohau'oli, hō'ike'ike ho'ohau'oli.

enthusiasm. 'Oli'oli nui, ohohia.

entire. Holo'oko'a, kā'oko'a.

entirely. Holo'oko'a, apau, pū, 'oko'a, pau.

entrance. *Opening.* Komo 'ana, puka, 'īpuka, nuku.

envelope. Wahī, wahī leka.

envy. Lili, hūwā.

epidemic. Ma'i laulā, ma'i ahulau, ma'i pālahalaha.

equal. Like, like ālike, lua, kaulike, pa'i.

equator. Pō'ai-waena-honua, ke alanui a ke ku'uku'u.

equip. Ho'olako, ho'olawa.

-er (*Agent*). **1.** *Agent in Hawaiian same as act performed. See* **driver, leader, paddler.** **2.** Mea, kanaka. *See* **actor, rider, translator.**

era. Wā, paukū manawa, au.

erase. Holoi.

erect. Kū, kūkulu.

error. Hewa, hala, pa'ewa.

eruption. Lua'i pele, hū ka pele.

escape. Pakele.

escort. Hele pū, 'alo, ukali, ho'oholoholo.

establish. Ho'okahua, ho'okumu, ho'okū.

establishment. Hale 'oihana (*business*); kūkulu 'ana.

estate. **1.** *Property.* Waiwai, kuleana, ho'olina. **2.** *Position.* Kūlana.

eternal. Mau loa, i ka wā pau 'ole, manawakolu.

eucalyptus. Pale-piwa.

Europe. 'Eulopa, Europa.

Europeanized. Ho'ohaole 'ia.

evening. Ahiahi. *Good evening,* aloha ahiahi.

ever. Mau. *Forever and ever,* a mau loa aku.

every. Kēlā . . . kēia, apau.

everyone. Ka po'e apau, pau apau.

everything. Nā mea apau, pauloa, kēlā mea kēia mea.

everywhere. Ma nā wahi apau, mai 'ō a 'ō, holopuni.

evidence. 'Ōlelo, hō'ike, 'ōlelo a nā hō'ike.

evil. Loko 'ino, lawehala, 'ino.

exactly. Pono, pono'ī.

exaggerate. Ho'onui, ho'onuinui, ho'onui 'ōlelo.

examination. Ha'awina hō'ike, nīnau hō'ike.

example. Mea ho'ohālikelike, hō'ike, 'ano, kumu ho'ohālike.

excel. Kela, ho'okela, po'okela, 'oi, hō'oi, pākela.

excellence. Maika'i loa, pono loa, kūpono.

excellent. Kilohana, maika'i.

except. Koe.

excess. Pākela, koe, kaulele.

exchange. Kūka'i, ku'aku'ai, pāna'i, ho'ololi.

excite. Ho'opīhoihoi, hō'eu'eu, ho'olalelale.

exclaim. Ho'ōho, 'ū, āhē.

excrement. Kūkae, kae; lepo, hana lepo (*euphemism*).

excuse. **1.** *Pretext.* 'Ōlelo hō-'alo'alo. **2.** *Pardon.* Kala, huikala, mihi, ho'oku'u. *Excuse me,* kala mai ia'u.

exercise. Ho'oikaika kino (*bodily*); ho'ohana; ha'awina ho-'oma'ama'a (*lesson*).

exhale. Hanu, hanu i waho, hā.

exhausted. Paupauaho, mālo'elo'e; piula (*slang*).

exhibit. Hō'ike, hō'ike'ike.

exist. Kū, ō, ola.

exit. Puka 'ana, pukana, 'īpuka.

expand. Ho'onui, ho'omāhua, ho'omāhuahua.

expect. Mahu'i, kuhi, mana'olana.

expel. Kipaku, ho'okuke, paku, lua'i.

expense. Ho'olilo, lilo.

expensive. Pipi'i, pi'i, nui ka ho'olilo.

experience. 'Ike.

expert. Kahuna; akamai, 'ailolo, lolo, no'eau, loea, mākaukau.

explain. Wehewehe, ho'ākaaka, hō'ike; ho'omōakaaka, ho'omāla'e (*clearly*).

explode. Ho'opahū, pahū.

explore. 'Imi loa, huli.

expose. Hō'ike ākea, ho'owaiho, waiho wale.

express. **1.** *To state.* Ho'opuka, ha'i, ho'ākaaka, hō'ike. **2.** *To extract.* 'Uwī, 'ūpī (*by squeezing*).

expression. Māpuna leo, māpuna 'ōlelo.

extend. Ho'oloa, ho'olō'ihi, kīko'o.

exterior. Waho.

extinguish. Ho'omake, ho'opio, kinai (*as a fire*).

extra. Keu, 'oi, hou, kaulele.

extraordinary. Kupaianaha, kupanaha, mea 'ē.

extravagant. 'Uha'uha, 'uha, 'uha 'ai, māunauna.

extreme. Wēlau, 'ēlau, welelau, palena, 'oi loa aku.

eye. Maka.

eyeball. 'Ōnohi, haku 'ōnohi, pona.

eyebrow. Ku'emaka, ku'eku'emaka, hulu ku'emaka.

eyeglasses. Makaaniani.

eyelashes. Lihilihi.

eyelid. 'Ūpo'i maka, kuapo'imaka, lihilihi.

eyesight. 'Ike maka.

eye socket. Pona, naho, lua maka.

F

f. *No Hawaiian term.*

face. Maka, helehelena, alo. *To face,* huli. *Face to face,* he alo a he alo.

fact. Mea kū'i'o, mea 'oiā'i'o.

factory. Hale hana.

faculty. *Academic.* 'Āuna kumu kula, pū'ulu kumu kula.

fade. Mae, ho'omae (*as flowers*); hehe'e (*as clothes*); hākea, hākeakea, kuakea, ākeakea (*as in the sun*).

fail. Pohō; holo le'a 'ole (*as in business*); hā'ule (*as in school*); emi mau ke olakino (*in health*).

faint. **1.** *Lose consciousness.*

Ma'ule, ho'oma'ule, make. **2.** *Weak, dizzy.* Makapōuli, maka pōniuniu, 'ona'ona. **3.** *Difficult to see.* Aneane, 'āwe'awe'a, 'ehu, pōehiehi.

fair. **1.** *Just.* Kūpono, pono, kaulike. **2.** *Complexion.* 'Ili kea, 'ili mā'ila. **3.** *Exhibit.* Pea, hō'ike'ike. **3.** *Somewhat good.* 'Ano maika'i.

faith. Mana'o'i'o, paulele.

fall. **1.** *From a height.* Hā'ule (*a solid object*); helelei, helele'i, ho'ohelele'i (*as leaves, rain*). **2.** *Topple.* Hina. **3.** *Autumn. No Hawaiian word; terms some-*

times used: hā'ule lau, la'a make, la'a 'ula.

false. Ho'opunipuni, wahahe'e.

familiar. Kama'āina, walea, ma'a, ma'ama'ahia, 'ike.

family. 'Ohana.

famine. Wī, pōloli.

famous. Kaulana.

fan. Pe'ahi.

fancy. Mana'o ulu wale, moemoeā.

far. Mamao, lilo loa.

fare. 1. *Pay.* Uku. 2. *Happen.* 'Ano, holo. 3. *Food.* 'Ai.

farewell. Aloha.

farm. Mahi'ai, mahi, mahina'ai.

farmer. Mahi'ai.

farther. Mamao a'e, mamao aku, mamao mai, ma'ō aku.

fascinate. Ho'opunihei, ho'oheihei, punihei.

fast. 1. *Quick.* 'Āwīwī, wikiwiki, māmā, holo, ala-, alamimo, alapine, alawiki. 2. *Fixed.* Pa'a. 3. *Not eat.* Ho'okē 'ai.

fasten. Ho'opa'a, hana pa'a.

fat. 1. *As a human.* Momona. 2. *Animal fat, food.* Momona (*uncooked*); kelekele (*cooked*).

father. Makua kāne, makua.

father-in-law. Makuahūnōwai kāne.

fatherland. 'Āina makua.

fathom. Anana.

fatigue. Māluhiluhi, luhi.

fault. Hewa, hala, ke'e, kīnā.

favor. Hana lokomaika'i; kako'o, makemake (*prefer*).

favorite. Punahele, milimili.

fear. Maka'u, weli, weliweli, 'e'ehia.

fearless. Maka'u 'ole, wiwo 'ole, koa.

feast. 'Aha'aina, lū'au.

feather. Hulu.

feather cloak. 'Ahu'ula.

feather helmet. Mahiole.

feather standard. Kāhili.

features. Hi'ohi'ona, helehelena (*human*).

February. Pepeluali, Feberuari.

fee. Uku.

feeble. Nāwaliwali, hapauea, nāwali, palupalu.

feed. Hānai, hānai 'ai, hō'ai, hō'omā'ona:

feel. 1. *Grope, touch.* Hāhā, hāhā hele, hāpapa, ho'opāpā, pā. 2. *As emotion.* 'Ike, lohe, komo. *Feel angry,* pi'i ka huhū, pi'i ka 'ena.

feelings. Na'au, loko.

feet. *See* foot.

fellow. Hoa, kōko'olua.

fellow worker. Hoa hana, hoa pa'ahana.

female. Wahine.

fence. 1. *Barrier.* Pā. *Wooden fence,* pā lā'au. 2. *With swords or sticks.* Kākā pahi, kākā lā'au.

fern. Kupukupu. *Common kinds include:* 'ama'u, 'āma'uma'u; hāpu'u (*tree fern*).

ferry. Moku halihali, wa'apā.

fertile. Momona; hānau, hānau kama (*person*).

fertilize. Ho'opulu, ho'omomona, kīpulu.

festival. Ho'olaule'a, manawa ho'olaule'a.

festive. Hiwahiwa, ulumāhiehie, ho'owehiwehi.

fetch. Ki'i, lawe.

fever. Piwa, ma'i-kuni.

few. Kaka'ikahi, wahi, kekahi, 'u'uku, li'ili'i.

fiddle. Pila.

field. Kīhāpai, kula.

fierce. Hae, ho'oweliweli.

fiery. 'Ā, ahi.

fifteen. 'Umi kūmālima, 'umi kumamālima.

fifth. Lima, hapalima.

fifty. Kanalima.

fifty-one. Kanalima kūmākahi, kanalima kumamākahi.

fig. Piku.

fight. Hakakā, paio, kaua; mokomoko (*general hand-to-hand, including wrestling and boxing*); pā'ume'ume.

fighter. Pūkaua, koa.

figure. 1. *Number.* Huahelu,

helu, hua. 2. *Human figure.*
Kino.

Fiji. Pīkī.

file. 1. *Rasp.* Apuapu, waiehu,
waiahu. 2. *Row.* Lālani. 3.
Collection. Waihona (palapala).

Filipino. Pilipino.

fill. Hoʻopiha.

film. Pepa paʻi kiʻi (*photo-
graphic*).

filth. Lepo, pelapela, ʻeka, ʻeka-
ʻeka, mea ʻino, moka, hau-
kaʻe.

fin. Lā.

final. Hope, hope loa, pau,
panina.

finance. ʻOihana kālā, ʻoihana
ʻimi kālā.

find. Loaʻa.

fine. 1. *Minute.* Hune, hunehune; makaliʻi (*as mats,
mesh*); nāwele, māhune, ʻae-
ʻae, puehu, liliʻi. 2. *Excellent.*
Maikaʻi nō, maikaʻi loa, pono.
3. *Penalty.* Uku hoʻopaʻi, uku.

finger. Manamana lima.

fingernail. Mikiʻao, maiʻao.

finish. Hoʻopau, oki, hoʻōki;
panina (*noun*); kaekae (*rub
smooth*).

finished. Pau, paʻa, kūpau.

fire. Ahi; pau ahi (*incendiary*).

firecracker. Pahūpahū.

fire department. ʻOihana kinai
ahi.

fire engine. Kaʻa kinai ahi,
kaʻa pauahi, kaʻa wai.

fireplace. Kapuahi.

fire-plow. ʻAunaki.

fireproof. Pale ahi.

fire station. Hale kinai ahi.

firewood. Wahie.

firm. 1. *Solid.* Paʻa, kūpaʻa,
ʻonipaʻa. 2. *See* **company.**

first. Mua, mua loa, ʻakahi...
ā. *First time,* maka mua, malihini, ʻakahi nō...ā. *First
child,* hiapo.

fish. Iʻa. *To fish,* lawaiʻa.

fisherman. Lawaiʻa.

fishhook. Makau; lou (*any
kind of a hook*).

fishing grounds. Koʻa, kai
lawaiʻa, kaʻakaʻa.

fishing pole. Mākoi, koi, mō-
koi.

fishline. Aho.

fish net. ʻUpena.

fishpond. Loko iʻa, loko kuapā.

fist. Puʻupuʻu lima, puʻu, puʻu
lima, puʻupuʻu.

fit. 1. *Suitable.* Kohu, kū, kūpono; komo (*as a garment*).
2. *Seizure.* Huki, maʻihuki,
ʻapoʻapo. 3. *To join.* Hoʻokuʻi,
pānaʻi.

five. Lima, ʻelima, ʻalima.

five cents. ʻElima keneka, ha-
paʻumi.

fix. Hoʻopaʻa, kāpili hou, hana
a maikaʻi, hoʻonipaʻa.

flabby. ʻAluʻalu, nenelu.

flag. Hae, lepa.

flagpole. Pahu hae, kia hae.

flame. Ula ahi, ula, lapa ahi.

flap. 1. *Motion.* ʻUpaʻi, ʻōpa-
ʻipaʻi, kūlepe, hulei. 2. *End.*
Pola (*as of a* malo).

flash. ʻŌlapa, lapa.

flashlight. Kukui paʻa lima.

flat. Pālahalaha.

flatter. Hoʻomalimali.

flavor. ʻOno, hōʻonoʻono.

flea. ʻUku-lele.

flee. Heʻe, ʻauheʻe, mahuka.

fleet. 1. *Naval.* ʻAu moku, ʻau
waʻa, ulu moku, ulu waʻa.
2. *Swift.* Holo.

flesh. ʻIʻo.

flesh food. Iʻa.

flight. Lele.

fling. Kā, hiu, hoʻolei. *See*
throw.

flirt. Hoʻohaʻi, hoʻohaʻi wale,
hoʻohaʻilua.

float. 1. *Not sink.* Lana. 2. *Of
a net.* Mouo, pīkoi, ou. 3. *Of
a fishhook.* Kōheoheo. 4. *See*
outrigger float.

flock. Pūʻā, ʻāuna, hoʻāuna, ulu.

flood. Wai hālana, wai piʻi.

floor. Papahele, papa keʻehina,
papa.

flounder. *The fish.* Pāki'i, moe-one.

flour. Palaoa maka.

flow. Kahe. *Flow swiftly,* kikī, kīpalalē.

flower. Pua.

flu. Palū.

fluent. Poeko, mākaukau i ka 'ōlelo, 'ōlelo pahe'e.

fluid. Wai, hehe'e.

flush. 1. *Show red.* Pi'i ka 'ula, nono'ula, 'āpane. 2. *To wash out.* Ho'oholo i ka wai. 3. *In poker.* Palaki.

flute. 'Ohe-kani, puhi 'ohe, 'ohe puluka, puluka.

flutter. Kōwelo, kapalili, kolili, welo, konikoni.

fly. 1. *As a bird.* Lele. 2. *Insect.* Nalo.

flycatcher. 'Elepaio.

flying fish. Mālolo.

foam. Hu'a, 'ehu.

foetus. 'Alu'alu.

fog. 'Ohu, noe, ua ñoe, uhiwai.

fold. 'Opi, pelu, 'opi'opi, pelupelu, 'ōwili.

folding chair. Noho 'opi'opi.

follow. Hahai, ukali, alualu, ma'awe, kaukolu. *As follows,* penei.

fond. Puni, laka, aloha.

fontanel. Manawa.

food. 'Ai, mea'ai.

fool. 1. *Simpleton.* Hūpō, wa'awa'a; pulu '(Eng.). 2. *To deceive.* Ho'opuni wale, ho'owalewale.

foot. 1. *Anatomical.* Wāwae. 2. *Twelve inches.* Kapua'i.

football. Kinipōpō peku.

for. No, na, i, iā. *For me,* no'u, na'u.

forbid. Pāpā, ho'okapu, hō'ole.

force. 1. *Strength.* Ikaika. 2. *To use force.* Ha'akoi, pu'e, pu'e wale, hao, hu'e.

forecast. Wānana.

forehead. Lae.

foreign. Mai ka 'āina 'ē mai, 'ē, haole.

foreigner. Kanaka 'ē, haole, mea mai ka 'āina 'ē.

foreman. Luna, luna hana, luna nui.

foremost. Mua loa, po'okela.

forest. Ulu lā'au, nahele.

forever. Mau loa, i ka wā pau 'ole, kau a kau.

forget. Poina.

forgive. Kala, huikala.

forgotten. Nalo, nalowale, nalohia, poina, poina 'ia.

fork. Mana (*branch*); 'ō (*for eating*).

form. Kino (*figure*); 'ano (*style*).

former. Mua, kēlā.

fort. Pāpū, hale pūkaua, pu'ukaua, hale kaua.

forth. I mua, aku. *And so forth,* a pēlā aku, a pēlā wale aku.

fortress. Pāpū.

fortunate. Pōmaika'i, ahona.

forty. Kanahā.

forty-one. Kanahā kūmākahi, kanahā kumamākahi.

forty thousand. Kanahā kaukani, kini.

forward. Mua, i mua.

foster. Hānai, ho'omakua, hi'i, mālama, kōkua.

foul. 1. *Filthy.* 'Eka, kelo, 'ino-'ino. 2. *In sports.* Pā'ani hewa.

found. Ho'okahua (*establish*); kūkulu (*as a society*); ho-'okumu. *See* find.

foundation. Kahua, kumu, papa, mole, kumupa'a. *House foundation,* kahua hale.

four. 'Ehā, hā, 'ahā, kāuna.

four hundred. 'Ehā haneli, lau.

four o'clock. Hola 'ehā; nani-ahiahi, pua-ahiahi (*the flower*).

fourteen. 'Umi kūmāhā, 'umi kumamāhā.

fourth. Hā, hapahā.

Fourth of July. Lā 'Ehā o Iulai, Pokiulai.

four thousand. 'Ehā kaukani, mano.

fowl. Moa, manu.

fraction. Hakina; 'ano pili, hapa.

fracture. Ha'i.

fragile. Haki wale, palupalu, 'ūpalu, palahē.

fragrance. 'A'ala, onaona, paoa, kūpaoa, māpu, moani.

frail. Nāwaliwali, palupalu.

frame. Haka kaula'i, hakakū (for drying); lā'au (picture frame); kū (of a bed).

France. Palani, Farani.

free. 1. State, condition. Kū-'oko'a, kuakahi; manuahi, manawale'a (gratis); ka'awale (as time). 2. To free. Ho-'oku'u, ho'oku'u la'ela'e, kala, weke; ho'ohemo.

freedom. Kū'oko'a.

freight. Ukana.

freighter. Moku lawe ukana.

frequent. Mau, pinepine, mau-mau, alapine.

fresh. Hou; maka, makamaka hou (as fish).

freshman. Haumāna komo hou.

fret. 1. Complain. Nē, ho-'onē. 2. Of ukulele. Wā.

friction. 1. Rubbing. 'Ānai. 2. Disagreement. Hukihuki, kū-'ē.

Friday. Pō'alima.

fried. Palai.

friend. Hoaloha, makamaka (o-class); aikāne (a-class); hoa.

friendly. Ho'ālohaloha, ho'oho-aloha, laulauna, maka launa.

friendship. Pilialoha, maka-maka ola, laule'a.

frigatebird. 'Iwa.

fright. Pū'iwa, hopohopo, ma-ka'u, puoho, hikilele.

frighten. Ho'omaka'u, ho'oweli.

frog. Poloka, lana.

from. Mai, mai...mai, no. From Honolulu, mai Hono-lulu, mai Honolulu mai; no Honolulu (in sense of "na-tive of").

front. Alo, mua.

frown. Ho'oku'emaka, pupuku, ho'oku'eku'emaka.

fruit. Hua, hua'ai.

fruitful. Hua nui, huahua, mo-mona.

fry. 1. Cook. Palai. 2. Small fish: Pua, pua 'i'i.

frying pan. Pā palai.

fuel. Wahie.

full. Piha; poepoe (as the moon); mā'ona, piha ka 'ōpū, (from eating). Com-pletely full, piha pono. Full-blooded, piha.

full-grown. Makua.

fun. Le'ale'a, ho'ole'ale'a.

funds. Kālā. Out of funds, 'a-'ohe kālā; puki, poloke (slang).

funeral. Ho'olewa.

funny. Ho'omāke'aka, kū i ka 'aka, ho'okolohe.

fur. Hulu, huluhulu, huhulu, hulu kupu, 'ili holoholona.

furious. Hae, pi'i ka huhū wela loa.

furnish. Ho'olako. Well-fur-nished, lako.

furniture. Lako hale, pono hale.

furthermore. Koe kēia, eia hou ho'i, eia nō na'e, aia na'e.

future. Mua, ka wā mahope.

G

g. No Hawaiian term.

gain. Loa'a, puka.

gale. Makani nui, kelawini.

gallon. Kālani.

gamble. Piliwaiwai.

game. Pa'ani, mea pa'ani, kemu, ho'okūkū. See **baseball, bas-ketball, checkers, football, hide-and-seek, jacks, mar-bles, swing, top, tug-of-war, wrestling.**

gannet. Ka'upu.

garage. Hale kaʻa.

garbage. ʻŌpala.

garden. Māla, māla pua, māla ʻai, mahi, mahinaʻai, kīhāpai, pā kanu, ulu kanu, ulu pua, waena.

gardenia. Kiele, nāʻū, nānū.

garlic. ʻAkaʻakai-pilau, ʻaka-ʻakai-pūpū, kālika.

garment. ʻAʻahu, lole komo.

gas. 1. *A fluid, vapor.* Ea, eaʻaʻā. 2. *Of the stomach.* ʻŌpihapiha.

gasoline. Kakalina, ʻailaea, ʻailea.

gasp. Paʻa ka hanu, hanu paʻa, pauaho, paupauaho.

gate. Puka, puka pā, ʻīpuka, pani, pani puka.

gather. 1. *Collect.* ʻOhi (*pick*); hoʻāhu, hōʻiliʻili (*collect*); ʻako (*as papayas, seaweed*). 2. *Assemble.* Hoʻākoakoa.

gay. Hauʻoli, ʻoliʻoli, leʻaleʻa.

gem. Pōhaku makamae.

genealogy. Kūʻauhau, moʻo kū-ʻauhau, moʻo aliʻi, moʻo kupuna.

general. 1. *Army.* ʻAlihikaua, pūkaua, kenelala. 2. *Widespread.* Laulaha, laulā, laha.

generation. Hanauna.

generous. Manawaleʻa, puʻuwai aloha, lokomaikaʻi.

genital. Maʻi, piko.

genital chant. Mele maʻi.

gentle. Akahai, mālie, laka, waipahē.

gentleman. Keōnimana.

genuine. Maoli, ʻiʻo.

geography. Hōʻike honua.

germ. Mū, ʻeleao, ʻanoʻano.

Germany. Kelemania.

gesture. Kuhi, ani ka lima.

get. Loaʻa, kiʻi, hoʻokiʻikiʻi, pā.

ghost. Lapu, akua lapu, akua, ʻuhane.

giant. Pilikua.

gift. Makana, haʻawina.

gin. Kini.

ginger. ʻAwapuhi.

girdle. Kāʻai.

girl. Kaikamahine.

give. Hāʻawi, hō.

glad. Hauʻoli, lauleʻa.

glance. ʻAlawa, ʻalaʻalawa, kilohi, leha, maka leha, maka lena, kokoe maka.

glare. Maka weli, ʻaʻā maka.

glass. Aniani, kīʻaha (*for drinking*).

glasses. *Spectacles.* Makaaniani.

gleam. ʻAnapa, ʻōlino, huali.

glide. Kīkaha.

glimpse. ʻIke mahuʻi, ʻike lihi, ʻaweʻaweʻa.

glitter. ʻĀlohi, ʻālohilohi, ʻanapa.

globe. Paʻa poepoe, poepoe, hulipoepoe, poepoe honua.

gloom. Pōuliuli, pouli, ʻomamalu.

glorify. Hoʻonani, hoʻohanohano, hoʻokapukapu.

glory. Hanohano, nani, kei.

glottal stop. ʻOkina, ʻuʻina.

glove. Mikini lima, miki lima.

glow. ʻEna, ʻenaʻena, ʻaʻā.

glue. Kolū, mea hoʻopipili.

go. Hele, hele aku, haele, uhaele, uhele. *Go down,* iho, hele iho; napoʻo (*as the sun*). *Go up,* piʻi, piʻi aku.

goal. Pahu; kumu (*objective*).

goat. Kao.

goatfish. Weke, kūmū, moano.

goby. ʻOʻopu.

god. Akua; Makua (*in Christian prayers*). *Stone fishing god,* kūʻula. *Family or personal god,* ʻaumakua.

gold. Kula, gula.

goldfish. Iʻa-ʻulaʻula.

golf. Kolepa, golepa.

gone. Nalowale, lilo, hele i kahi ʻē.

good. Maikaʻi.

good-bye. Aloha; a hui hou aku (*lit., until meet again*).

good evening. Aloha ahiahi.

good-for-nothing. Lapuwale, mea waiwai ʻole.

Good Friday. Pōʻalima Hemolele, Pōʻalima Maikaʻi.

good-looking. Maikaʻi, maikaʻi ke nānā aku; kūmū (*slang*).

good morning. Aloha kakahi-aka.

good-natured. Waipahē, 'olu-'olu.

goodness. Pono, maika'i, hemo-lele; kā, auwē (exclamation).

goods. Waiwai, pono, mea.

good will. Lokomaika'i.

goose. Nēnē.

gooseberry. Pohā, pa'ina.

gooseflesh. 'Okala, 'ōkakala, lī ka 'ili, lī ka 'i'o.

gospel. 'Euanelio.

gossip. Holoholo'ōlelo, lawe 'ōlelo, 'imi 'ōlelo, ho'owā, hauwala'au.

got. Loa'a.

gourd. Ipu, hue, pōhue, 'umeke pōhue.

govern. Ho'omalu, noho au-puni, noho ali'i.

government. Aupuni.

governor. Kia'āina.

grab. Kā'ili, 'apo.

grace. Aloha (mercy, compassion); lokomaika'i (kindness); pule ho'omaika'i i ka papa-'aina (before a meal); kalakia (Catholic). To ask grace, pule ho'omaika'i.

grade. 1. Rank, class. Kūlana, papa, 'ano. Sixth grade, papa 'eono. 2. Evaluation. Heluna, kaha. 3. To level. Hō'iliwai.

graduate. Puka, ho'opuka.

graft. Verb. Pāku'i, pāna'i, ho-'opili.

grain. 1. Small particle. Huna. 2. In wood, stone. 'I'o, wai, nao.

grammar. Pili'ōlelo, hō'ike'ōlelo.

grand. Maika'i loa (fine); hano-hano (glorious); nui (large, important).

grandchild. Mo'opuna.

grandfather. Kupuna kāne, tūtū, kūkū, kūkū kāne.

grandmother. Kupuna wahine, tūtū, kūkū, kūkū wahine.

grandparent. Kupuna.

granny. Tūtū, kūkū.

grasp. Hopu, 'apo, hao, lālau.

grass. Mau'u, weuweu.

grasshopper. 'Ūhini, 'ūhini-ake-lika.

grateful. Ho'omaika'i.

gratitude. Ho'omaika'i, mahalo.

grave. 1. Burial. Hē, lua ku-papa'u. 2. Serious. Ko'iko'i.

gravel. 'Ili'ili makali'i.

gravestone. Kia ho'omana'o.

graveyard. Pā ilina, pā kupa-pa'u.

gravy. Kai, kai penu, kai liko-liko.

gray. 'Āhinahina, hinahina; hi-na, po'o hina (of hair).

grease. 'Aila, 'aila hamo, hinu, 'ōhinu.

great. Nui, nunui. Very great, nui loa, 'oi aku ka nui.

greatest. Nui, po'okela, heke, hapa nui, hapa loa.

Greece. Helene.

greed. 'Ālunu, 'ānunu, nunu.

green. 'Ōma'oma'o, 'ōma'o, ma-'oma'o, ma'o, uliuli (vegetation); maka (as fruit).

greenery. Lau nahele, lau ho-'ohiwahiwa (for decorations).

green rose. Loke-lau.

greens. Lau; lau 'ai 'ia (edible).

greet. Aloha, aloha aku. Old forms: weli, welina, 'ano'ai.

greeting. Aloha.

grief. Kaumaha, kani'uhū, kū-makena, 'ū.

grill. Hao manamana, hao haka-haka.

grin. 'Ōlē'olē (widemouthed, as of an idol). See smile.

grind. Wili, 'uwī, ho'okala, 'ānai.

groan. Nā, 'ū, uhū, kani'ū.

groceries. Mea'ai.

grocery store. Hale kū'ai mea-'ai.

groin. Kumu 'ūhā; pani kai (sea wall).

grope. Hāhā.

ground. 1. Earth. Lepo, honua. 2. See grind.

group. Pū'ulu, 'ao'ao.

grove. Ulu, ulu lā'au, maha lā-'au, moku lā'au, nahele. Co-conut grove, ulu niu.

grow. Ulu, ho'oūlu, kupu.

growl. Nunulu, hae.

grudge. Mauhala, 'au'a. *To bear a grudge,* ho'omauhala, manawahūwā.

grumble. 'Ōhumu, 'ōhumuhumu, namunamu, kunukunu, 'ōhalahala.

grunt. Hū.

guard. Kia'i, mea kia'i, māka'i, maka'ina, pale.

guardian. Kahu.

guava. Kuawa.

guess. Koho, koho wale, mahu'i.

guest. Malihini kipa, mea i kono 'ia. *My guest,* ka'u malihini.

guide. Alaka'i, hō'ike.

guilty. Hewa. *To find guilty,* ho'āhewa.

guitar. Kīkā. *To play the guitar,* ho'okani kīkā.

gulch. Awāwa, kahawai, 'oawa.

gulp. Ale, alapoho, moni.

gum. Kamu (*for chewing*); pīlali (*from kukui tree*).

gums. 'I'o pale niho.

gun. Pū.

gunpowder. Pauka kī pū.

gush. 1. *Of water.* Huahua'i, hua'ina, hū, hūlani. 2. *Of speech.* Pua'ohi, waha kale, 'ohi.

gust. Kokololio, makani pūkīkī.

guts. Na'au.

gutter. 'Auwaha (*ditch*); 'alu (*ravine*); pulumi (*as on a house*).

H

h. Hē.

habit. Hana ma'a, 'ao'ao.

habitual. Ma'amau.

hag. Luahine pī'alu, luahine 'ālu'a.

hair. Lauoho, oho (*head*); hulu, huluhulu, huhula (*body*).

hairbrush. Palaki lauoho.

haircut. 'Oki ('ako) i ka lauoho.

hairy. Huluhulu, 'ōhuluhulu.

half. Hapa lua. *Half dollar,* hapa lua.

hall. Holo, hale. *Meeting hall,* hālau, ke'ena hālāwai.

halloo. 'Ō, oho; ūi, hūi (*modern*).

halt. Kū.

ham. Pua'a hame, 'ūhā pua'a, hame, 'ūhā hame.

hamburger. 'I'o pipi i wili 'ia.

hammer. Hāmale. *To hammer,* ku'i, hāmale.

hammerhead shark. Manōkihikihi.

hand. Lima; manamana, lima kuhikuhi (*of a clock*); 'ekā, ke'a (*of bananas*); ha'awina (*of cards*). *To hand,* hā-

guitar. Kīkā. *To play the guitar,* ho'okani kīkā.

'awi; hō mai (*towards speaker*).

handbag. 'Eke'eke pa'a lima, 'eke pa'a lima.

handbook. Puke lawe lima.

handful. Piha lima, poho lima, haona lima.

handkerchief. Hainakā, hinakā. *Paper handkerchief,* hainakā pepa.

handle. 1. *Verb.* Lawelawe, limalima, lole, lapulapu, mili. 2. *Noun.* 'Au, kū'au, pa'a lima, kano, kau; kākai (*as of a bucket*). *Axe handle,* 'au ko'i.

handmade. Hana lima.

handshake. Lūlū lima.

handsome. U'i, nohea, maika'i.

hand wrestling. Uma, pāuma, huinalima.

handwriting. Kākau lima, lima kākau, pūlima kākau, pūlima.

handy. Mākaukau, loea, no'eau.

hang. Ho'olewalewa, lewalewa, lewa, kau.

hanging. Kālewa, kūlewa, kaulia, kauna, uleule.

happen. 1. *Occur.* Hana, lo-'ohia. *What happened?* He aha ka mea i hana 'ia? I aha 'ia? 2. *By chance.* Kupu wale, hiki honua.

happiness. Hau'oli, 'oli'oli, laule'a, hoihoi. *To cause happiness,* ho'ohau'oli.

happy. See **happiness.** *Happy birthday,* hau'oli lā hānau; hānau (*in toasts*). *Happy New Year,* Hau'oli Makahiki Hou, Hapenūia.

harbor. Awa, awa kū moku.

hard. 1. *Not soft.* 'O'ole'a, pa'a. 2. *Difficult.* Pa'akikī, hana nui.

hardhearted. Loko 'ino, mākonā, laukona.

hardly. 'Ane'ane, kokoke.

hardship. Pōpilikia, 'īnea, ho-'īnea.

harelip. 'ūlepe.

harm. Ho'opōpilikia, ho'opō-'ino, ho'opilikia, ho'o'ino, 'ino, pō'ino.

harmony. 1. *Agreement.* Lōkahi, like ka nohona. 2. *Musical.* Ka hui maika'i 'ana o nā leo mele.

harp. Hapa.

harpoon. 'Ō; 'ō koholā (*for whales*); hāpuna.

harsh. 'O'ole'a, kakanai'i.

harvest. Loa'a, wā 'ohi (*season*). *To harvest,* 'ohi.

hasten. Ho'ohikiwawe, 'āwīwī, māmā, wiki, wikiwiki.

hat. Pāpale.

hatch. Kiko, ho'okiko, kiko ka hua.

hate. 'Ino, mana'o 'ino, pu-'uwai 'ele'ele, inaina. *Full of hate,* makawela.

haul. Kauwō, huki, lawe.

haughty. Ho'okano, hukikū, ha-'akei, ha'aheo.

have. 1. *To possess.* No word in Hawaiian; commonly expressed by he followed by a possessive: *I have a car, I had a car,* he ka'a ko'u. 2.

Necessity. Pono. *I have to go,* pono au e hele. 3. *Verb auxiliary.* Ua *or* unexpressed. *I have gone,* ua hele au; hele au.

Hawaiian. Hawai'i. *Hawaiian person,* Hawai'i, kanaka Hawai'i.

Hawaiian Islands. Kō Hawai'i Pae 'Āina.

hawk. 'Io.

he. 'Oia, ia, 'oia nei, 'oia ala.

head. Po'o. *Human head,* po'o kanaka.

headache. 'Eha ke po'o, nahoa; nalulu (*dull*); po'o hua'i (*splitting*).

headman. Ali'i, po'o, luna; konohiki (*of an ahupua'a*).

headquarters. Kikowaena.

headstrong. Po'o pa'akikī, uhu, ho'ohuki, ho'ohuhuki, hukihuki.

heal. Lapa'au, ola, ho'ōla; kōhi (*as a wound*); pāla'au (*as with herbs*).

health. Olakino, ola pono, ola. *Good health,* olakino maika'i.

health certificate. Palapala hō-'ike olakino.

heap. Pu'u ahu, kuāhua, āhua, kuapapa, anu'a, nu'a, ho'onu'a.

hear. Lohe, ho'olono.

heart. Pu'uwai; iho (*as of celery, core*); 'i'o (*as of wood, central part*); haka (*in deck of cards*). *Generous heart,* manawale'a, loko maika'i.

heart attack. Ma'i-hohola, ho-upo-'ume-pau, ma'i-'uhola; kauhola (*fatal*).

heartbreaking. Hō'eha'eha i ka na'au.

heartless. Laukōnā, loko 'ino, makonā.

heartsick. Māna'ona'o, hō'eha-'eha i ka pu'uwai.

heat. Wela, hahana, ikiiki, welawela, wewela, wāwena, 'āwela, 'ōwela. *In heat (of a bitch),* kahe.

heathen. Pekana.

heave. Ho'olei, pākī.

heaven. Lani, papa lani, lewa, aoūli.

heavenly. Lani.

heavy. Kaumaha, ko'iko'i.

hedge. Pā la'au, pā la'alā'au, pālulu lā'au.

heed. Maliu, ho'omaliu, ho'olohe, mālama.

heedless. Nānā 'ole, ho'olohe 'ole.

heel. Ku'eku'e wāwae (*human*); hila (*of a shoe*).

heiau. Heiau.

height. Ki'eki'e, ki'eki'ena, loa, lō'ihi, nu'u.

heir. Ho'oilina, ho'īlina.

hell. Kehena, lua ahi, ki'o ahi, pō.

Hello! Aloha! *See* **halloo.**

helmet. Mahiole; 'a'ahu a po'o (*head shield*).

help. Kōkua, lawelawe lima.

helpless. Nāwaliwali, kū nānā.

hem. Pelu.

hen. Moa wahine.

her. 1. *Possessive. Same as* **his.** 2. *Pronoun. Same as* **him.**

herb. Lau nahele, lā'au palupalu, la'alā'au, mau'u.

herd. Pū'ā, kumu. *Herd of cattle,* pū'ā pipi.

here. Ma'ane'i, eia, nei, i ne'i, ne'i, 'o ne'i, 'ane'i. *Here!* Eia! 'Ei'a!

hereditary. Mai na kūpuna mai, welo.

hermit crab. Unauna, pāpa'i-iwi-pūpū.

hero. Me'e, koa. *Youthful hero,* u'i.

heron. 'Auku'u.

hers. *Same as* **his.**

herself. *Same as* **himself.**

hesitate. Kali, kūnānā, kānalua, ho'ohākālia, ka'ulua.

hibiscus. Aloalo, koki'o.

Hibiscus tiliaceus. Hau.

hiccough. Mauli'awa.

hidden. Huna, nalowale, nalo-nalo, nalohia. *Hidden meaning, see* **meaning.**

hide. Hūnā, ho'ohūnā (*transitive*); pe'e (*oneself, intransitive*).

hide-and-seek. Pe'epe'e-kua, pe-'epe'e-akua, huape'epe'e.

high. Ki'eki'e.

higher. Ho'okela, 'oi aku ke ki'eki'e.

highest. Ki'eki'e loa.

high school. Kula ki'eki'e.

highway. Alanui, alaloa, ala hele.

hike. Hele wāwae.

hill. Pu'u, kuahiwi (*high*); pu'e (*as of sweet potatoes*).

hilly. 'Ōpalipali.

him. Ia. *To him,* iāia. *For him,* nona, nāna.

himself. 'Oia iho, 'oia pono'ī (*subject*); iāia iho (*object*). *For himself,* nona iho. *By himself,* nāna iho, 'oia ho-'okahi.

hinder. Ālai, ke'a, ke'ake'a, ho-'oke'a.

hinge. 'Ami; pu'u (*of pearl oyster*). *Door hinge,* 'ami puka.

hint. Ho'ohelehele 'ōlelo, ho-'ohele 'ōlelo.

hip. Kīkala, pāpākole.

hire. Limalima, ho'olimalima, hai.

his. 1. *Singular possessed object.* Kona (o-class); kāna (a-class). 2. *Plural possessed objects.* Ona (o-class); āna (a-class).

history. Mo'olelo, kuamo'o 'ō-lelo.

hit. Ku'i, ho'oku'i, pa'i, ho'opa'i, hahau, kū, ku'ia, kā, pā.

hive. Pūnana meli, pahu meli.

hoard. Ho'āhu, ho'olaholaho (*as a miser*).

hoarse. Hā, leo hā, hano, hanopilo.

hobby. Hana punahele, hana ho'onanea, hana ho'ohala manawa.

hog. Puaʻa.

hoist. Hāpai, huki i luna.

hold. 1. *Grip.* Paʻa, hoʻopaʻa. *Hold a note,* kō. 2. *Of a ship.* O lalo.

hole. Puka (*usually of a perforation*); lua (*with a bottom*); haka (*breach*). *Full of holes,* pukapuka, haka, hoʻohaka, lualua, hālua.

holiday. Lānui.

hollow. Pūhā (*as a log*); hakahaka, ʻolohaka (*as a surfboard*); poʻopoʻo, ʻāpoʻopoʻo, hālua, napoʻo, kānoa (*as in earth*); poho, pāiki, kaʻele, kāwaha, homa (*as of the hand or of a bowl*).

holy. Hemolele, hoʻāno, kapu, laʻa, laʻahia, ʻihiʻihi, kaneka, saneta. *Holy day,* lā hoʻāno.

Holy Communion. ʻAhaʻaina a ka Haku, ʻahaʻaina pelena.

Holy Ghost. ʻUhane Hemolele.

Holy Trinity. Akua kahikolu, Kolukahi Hemolele.

home. Home, kauhale.

homeland. One hānau, ʻāina hānau, kulaīwi.

homeless. Kuewa, lewa, home ʻole.

homely. Pupuka.

homesick. Aloha kaumaha i ka home.

homestead. ʻĀina hoʻokūʻonoʻono, home hoʻokūʻonoʻono. *To homestead,* hoʻokahua i ka ʻāina hoʻokūʻonoʻono.

homosexual. Māhū.

honest. Kūpono, pono.

honey. Meli, wai meli, wai pua, hone, pīlali.

honeybee. Nalo-meli.

honeycomb. Waihona meli.

honeycreeper. ʻIʻiwi, mamo, ʻōʻū, ʻakekeʻe, ʻapapane, ʻamakihi.

honeyeater. ʻŌʻō, ʻāʻā.

honeymoon. Mahina meli.

honk. Hoʻokani i ka ʻolē; unele (*of goose*).

Honolulu. Honolulu (*lit., sheltered bay*).

honor. Hoʻohanohano, hoʻonani, hoʻohiwahiwa.

hoof. Maiʻao holoholona, mānea, māiʻuʻu.

hook. Lou, loulou, kīlou (*as on a door*); kēlou, huka.

hoop. ʻApo, kuapo, hupa.

hoot. Keʻu, keʻu (*as owl*).

hop. Lele, lelele.

hope. Manaʻolana, ʻupu, lana ka manaʻo.

horizon. Hālāwai, pōʻailani, kumulani, ʻalihi, ʻalihilani.

horizontal. ʻIliwai, moe.

horn. 1. *On animal.* Kiwi, hao, pepeiaohao; kākala (*as of fish or caterpillar*). 2. *Wind instrument.* Pū, pū puhi.

hornet. Hope-ʻō, kopena, naloʻaki, nalo-hope-ʻeha.

horrible. Weliweli, mānaʻonaʻo, ʻino loa.

hors d'oeuvre. Pūpū, hōʻonoʻono ʻai.

horse. Lio. *Race horse,* lio heihei. *Pack horse,* lio lawe ukana.

horseback. Kau lio. *To ride horseback,* kau lio, holo lio.

horseshoe. Kāmaʻa hao, kapuaʻihao lio. *Horseshoe pitching,* kiolaola lio.

hose. 1. *See* stocking. 2. *Conveyor.* ʻIli. *Water hose,* ʻiliwai. *To hose,* kikī wai.

hospitable. Hoʻokipa aloha, hoʻohale kipa, heahea, makamaka nui.

hospital. Hale maʻi, haukapila.

hospitality. Hoʻokipa.

host. 1. *As at a party.* Haku hale, mea hoʻokipa, ka mea nāna ka ʻahaʻaina, ka mea nona ka hale. 2. *Crowd.* Lehulehu.

hostess. Haku hale wahine.

hostile. Kūʻē, paio, kamaniha, hoʻokamaniha, ʻāniha, loko ʻino.

hot. Wela, hahana; ikiiki (*stifling*); wewela, welawela, ʻāwela.

hotel. Hōkele.

hour. Hola.

house. Hale, kauhale.

housefly. Nalo.

household. 'Ohana (*family*); kauhale (*houses occupied by a family*).

housekeeper. Mālama hale, kahu mālama hale.

House of Representatives. Hale o nā Lunamaka'āinana.

housewife. Wahine o ka hale.

how. Pehea, pehea lā. *How?* Pehea? *How are you?* Pehea 'oe?

however. Akā, koe kēia, eia na'e.

hug. Apo, pūliki.

huge. Nui loa, nui hewahewa.

hula. Hula. *Kinds:* 'ōlapa, 'ulī-'ulī, pa'i umauma, 'ili'ili, *and others.*

hula studio. Ke'ena a'o hula.

human. Kanaka.

humane. Lokomaika'i, kū'ē i ka ho'omāinoino.

humanity. Lāhui kānaka.

humble. Ha'aha'a, ho'oha-'aha'a, pē, pēpē, ūpē. *See* **modest.**

humid. Kawaū, ma'ū; ikiiki (*and hot*).

humiliate. Ho'ohilahila, ho-'oha'aha'a.

humility. Ha'aha'a. *See* **humble.**

humor. Ho'omāke'aka, piha 'eu.

hunchback. Kuapu'u.

hundred. Hanele, haneri.

hungry. Pōloli, make'ai.

hunt. Hahai, 'imi, hahai holoholona.

hurricane. Makani pāhili, makani uluulu, makani hele uluulu.

hurry. 'Āwīwī, 'āwiki, wiki, ho-'owiki, wikiwiki, alawiki, elewiki.

hurt. 'Eha, hō'eha, 'ino, māino.

husband. Kāne, pilikua.

husk. Pulu. *To husk,* wehe i ka pulu.

hut. Pupupu hale, pāpa'i, hale kāpi'o 'ili lā'au.

hymn. Hīmeni, leo ho'onani, mele haipule, mele ho'omaika'i.

hyphen. Kiko moe, kahamoe.

hypocrite. Ho'okamani, kanale'o, hūpō kaliko.

I

i. 1. *The letter.* 'Ī. 2. (*Cap.*) *Pronoun.* Au, wau, 'o wau, 'o au.

ice. Hau.

icebox. Pahu hau.

ice cream. Haukalima, 'aikalima.

iced. Hau. *Iced beverage,* meainu ho'ohu'ihu'i.

ice water. Wai hau.

idea. Mana'o; mana'o 'ino (*evil*); mana'o nui (*important*).

ideal. Kūpono ma nā 'ano apau (*perfect*); mea i kuko 'ia, mea i mana'o nui 'ia (*thing desired*).

identical. Like loa, kūlike.

identify. Hō'oia, ho'omaopopo.

idiom. 'Ikeoma.

idiot. Lōlō, hūpō, hepa.

idol. Ki'i akua.

if. Inā, aia nō, i, ke.

ignite. Ho'ā, hō'a'ā.

ignorance. Na'aupō; pō, pouli.

ignore. Nānā 'ole, kāpae 'ōlelo, huli kua.

ill. Ma'i, 'ōma'ima'i.

illegal. Kū 'ole i ke kānāwai, mawaho o ke kānāwai.

illegitimate. Manuahi, po'o 'ole, mawaho o ke kānāwai.

ill-feeling. Mana'o 'ino, 'ōpū kopekope.

illness. Ma'i, nāwaliwali.

illustrate. Kaha ki'i; ho'ohālikelike (*exemplify*).

image. Ki'i, akua, ki'i akua.

imagination. No'ono'o ulu wale, mana'o ulu wale.

imitate. Ho'opili.

immediate. Koke, hikiwawe, wawe.

immediately. Koke, manawa 'ole, 'emo 'ole, 'ānō.

immense. Nui loa, nui hewa-hewa.

immigrant. 'E'e moku.

immortal. Ola mau, make 'ole.

immovable. Kūpa'a, 'onipa'a.

impatient. Nauki, kū'aki, pau-aho wale, ahonui 'ole.

imperfect. Kīnā, hemahema, 'a'ole i ponopono loa, pa'ewa, 'ewa.

impertinent. Maha'oi, ho'oma-'oi, kiko'olā.

import. 1. *Bring in.* Ho'okomo. *See* imports. 2. *Meaning.* Mana'o nui.

importance. Waiwai, 'ano nui.

important. Nui, 'ano nui.

imports. Waiwai ho'opae mai, waiwai komo.

impossible. Hiki 'ole.

impression. 'Ikena, pa'i 'ana, mō'ali.

imprison. Ho'opa'ahao.

improper. Kohu 'ole, kūpono 'ole.

improve. Holomua, ho'omaika'i, ho'onui aku ka maika'i.

impulse. Mana'o ulu wale, no-'ono'o ulu wale.

impure. Paumā'ele, haumia, kele.

in. I, ma, i loko, maloko, i luna, maluna.

in-. 'Ole.

inability. Hiki 'ole.

inaccurate. Hewa, 'apake'e, hape.

inactive. Noho wale, noho hana 'ole.

inaugurate. Poni, ho'oponi, ho-'okumu.

incapable. Mākaukau 'ole, he-mahema.

incest. Moe 'ohana pili pono'ī.

inch. 'Iniha.

incident. Hanāna, mea hiki wale mai, hana.

incline. Pi'ina, ihona, hiō.

include. Helu, ho'okomo pū, ho'ohui pū, pau pū, a me.

income. Kālā loa'a mai.

income tax. 'Auhau maluna o ka loa'a.

incoming. Komo mai ana.

incompetent. Mākaukau 'ole, hemahema, hāwāwā.

incomplete. 'A'ole piha pono, hapapū, kīhapa.

incorrect. Pololei 'ole, pa'ewa, hewa, hape, 'ewa, kuhihewa.

increase. Ho'onui, ho'omāhua-hua, ulu, ho'olaha.

indeed. pēlā nō, pēlā 'i'o, ho'i, noho'i.

indefinite. Maopopo 'ole, aka-aka 'ole.

independence. Kū'oko'a, ea.

index. Papa kuhikuhi, papa hō-'ike.

indicate. Kuhikuhi, hō'ike.

indifference. Ho'omaopopo 'ole, palaka, nānā 'ole.

indirect. Hiliau, lauwili.

indistinct. 1. *Of vision.* Pāpa-laweka, palaweka, poehi, pō-wehiwehi. 2. *Of speech.* Aka-aka 'ole, huikau ka leo, 'olē, nei, hepa.

individual. Kanaka.

industrious. Pa'ahana, lawe-hana, limahana.

inexperienced. 'Akahi akahi, hemahema, ma'a 'ole, hāwā-wā.

infancy. Wā li'ili'i, wā 'u'uku, manawaea.

infant. Pēpē, keiki, kamali'i.

infanticide. 'Umi keiki.

infantry. Pū'ali kaua ka'i wā-wae, koa hele wāwae.

infection. Ma'i lele, ma'i laha, 'a'ai.

inferior. 'A'ohe maika'i loa, ha-'aha'a, emi iho.

inflate. Ho'ohū, hō'olopū, ho-'opuhalu.

influence. Ho'ohuli mana'o, ho-'ololi.

influenza. Palū.

inform. Hō'ike, ha'i, ho'omaopopo.

information. 'Ike, hō'ike.

infrequent. Kaka'ikahi, no ka manawa.

-ing. Ana, 'ana. *His going,* kāna hele 'ana.

ingratitude. 'Awahua, ho'omaika'i 'ole.

inhabit. Noho.

inhale. Hanu, hanu i loko.

inherit. Ili.

inheritance. Ho'oilina, hō'ilina, waiwai ho'oilina, ili.

initiate. Ho'omaka, ho'okumu; ho'olilo i lālā (*to membership*).

injection. Hoene, pahu kui (*hypodermic*).

injure. 'Ino, ho'o'ino, hana 'ino, ho'opō'ino.

injustice. Kaulike 'ole, pololei 'ole, hana pono 'ole.

ink. 'Inika.

inland. Uka, mauka, i uka; wao.

in-laws. 'Ohana pili ma ka male 'ana.

inn. Hōkele, hale kipa, hale ho-'okipa.

innocent. Hala 'ole, hewa 'ole.

innumerable. Hiki 'ole ke helu, nui hewahewa, lehulehu, kinikini, kini lau a mano.

in order to. E, i, no, i hiki ai ke.

inquire. Nīnau.

inquisitive. Nīele.

insane. Pupule, ulala, hehena, lōlō.

insect. Mea kolo, holoholona lele; mū (*destructive*); huhu (*wood-boring*).

insecure. Pa'a 'ole ke kahua.

insert. Ho'okomo, 'ōkomo, ho'ō, 'ō'ō, hō'o'ō.

inside. Loko, i.

insignificant. Mea 'ole.

insist. Koi, ho'olā'au, ho'opa'a, ha'akoi.

inspect. Nānā, māka'i.

inspire. Ulu, ho'oūlu, ho'olalelale.

installment. 1. *Payment.* Uku mähele. 2. *Portion.* Māhele, hapa, 'āpana.

instance. Mea ho'ohālike. *For instance,* penei; e la'a me kēia.

instant. Manawa pōkole loa. *Instant coffee,* kope hikiwawe.

instead. Ma kahi o.

instinct. 'Ike hānau.

institution. Hui ho'ohana 'imi na'auao (*scholarly*); hui, hale.

instruction. A'o, 'ōlelo a'o, a'o palapala, kuhikuhina.

instrument. Mea pa'ahana; pila (*musical*).

insult. Hō'ino, kūamuamu.

insurance. Ho'opa'a, 'inikua.

intelligent. Na'auao.

intercourse. Launa 'ana. *See* sexual intercourse.

interest. 1. *Concern.* Hoihoi, kuleana, pili laulā (*broad, general*). 2. *On principal.* Kuwala, puka, puka o ke kālā, uku pane'e.

interfere. 'Āke'ake'a, kakekake, komo kuleana 'ole, hōkake.

interior. Loko, wālua.

interisland. Pili 'āina.

intermarry. Male 'ohana, male no iā loko iho.

intermediate. Mawaena.

internal. Kō loko.

international. O nā 'āina 'ē, kō nā 'āina like 'ole.

interpret. Unuhi, unuhi 'ōlelo, ho'omāhele, māhele 'ōlelo.

interrupt. Kahamaha.

intersection. Huina.

interview. Kūkā kama'ilio.

intestines. Na'au; na'ana'au (*small*); uha (*large*).

intimate. Pili koke.

into. I loko.

intoxicated. 'Ona.

introduce. Ho'ohui, ho'olauna (*as people*); ho'okomo.

intrude. Komo wale, komo hewa, kipa wale.

invalid. 1. *Ill.* Mea nāwaliwali,

mea 'ōma'ima'i. 2. *Not valid.*
Mana 'ole, waiwai 'ole.

invent. Hakuwale.

inventory. Helu, helu waiwai.

investigate. Kolokolo, ho'okolokolo, noi'i.

investment. Waiwai no ka ho-
'opukapuka 'ana.

invisible. 'Ike maka 'ole 'ia,
po'o huna.

invitation. Kono, palapala kono
(*written*).

invite. Kono.

involuntary. Me ka 'ae 'ole.

involve. Hihia, kūhihi, kāwili
kā'ekā.

Irish potato. 'Uala-kahiki.

iron. Hao; pāpa'a hao (*scrap*);
'aiana (*for pressing clothes*).

irregular. E like 'ole me ka mea
mau, loli ke kūlana, pololei
'ole.

irrigate. Ho'okahekahe wai, kau
wai, ho'oma'ū, hanawai.

irritable. Nauki, 'a'aka, huhū
koke.

irritate. Ho'oukiuki, ho'oūluhua.

is. *See* be.

island. Moku, mokupuni, moku-
'āina, 'ailana.

islands. Pae 'āina. *Hawaiian
Islands,* kō Hawai'i pae 'āina.

isn't. 'A'ole. *Isn't it?* 'A'ole anei?

isolate. Ho'oka'awale.

issue. 1. *Offspring.* Pua, keiki.
2. *Put or come out.* Puka, ho-
'opuka, pukana.

it. Ia, 'oia, kēlā; akua (*in game
of tag*). *This word is frequently omitted. It is said,* ua
'ōlelo 'ia.

itch. Mane'o.

item. 'Ikamu.

its. *Same as* **his.**

itself. 'Oia nō, 'oia iho, 'oia
pono'ī.

ivory. Palaoa (*whale tooth*);
niho 'elepani.

J

j. *No Hawaiian term.*

jack. 1. *A fish.* Ulua. 2. *In deck
of cards.* Keaka.

jackass. *Same as* **donkey.**

jacket. Lakeke.

jackknife. Pahi pelu.

jacks. Kimo (*game*).

jagged. Nihoniho, nihoa.

jail. Hale pa'ahao. *To jail,* ho-
'opa'ahao.

jam. Kele (*jelly*).

janitor. Kahu mālama a ho'oma-
'ema'e hale.

January. Iānuali, Ianuari.

Japan. Iāpana, 'Āina Kēpanī.

jar. *Noun.* 'Ōmole waha nui;
poho aniani (*glass*).

jasmine. Pīkake.

jaw. Ā, papa niho; papa 'auwae
(*lower jaw*).

jealous. Lili, nini, 'ōpū nini,
manawahūwā.

Jehovah. Iēhowa, Iehova.

jelly. Kele.

jerk. Huki 'ino.

Jesus. Iesu.

jet. Kī.

Jew. Kiu, Iukaio.

jewelry. Lako kula, mea ho-
'onani kino.

jiggle. Hō'oni'oni, 'oni'oni.

jingle. Kanikani. *Jingle bells,*
kani nā pele.

job. 'Oihana, hana.

join. Pili, pili pū, hui, ku'i,
kāpili.

joined. Ku'i, hui 'ia, huihui.

joint. 1. *Anatomical.* Ku'eku'e,
'ami ho'oku'i, 'ami, ha'i. 2.
United. Hui 'ia.

joke. 'Ōlelo pā'ani, ho'opā'ani.

jolly. Le'ale'a, laupa'apa'ani.

journal. Mo'olelo, puke ho-
'omana'o.

journey. Huaka'i.

joy. Hau'oli, 'oli, le'a.

judge. Luna kānāwai (*noun*);
ho'okolokolo (*verb*).

judgment. 'Ōleloho'oholo, 'ōle-

loho'okō, 'ōlelo-kū-pa'a, ho-
'oholo.
juice. Wai.
July. Iulai.
jump. Lele, lelele.
June. Iune.
jungle. Wao nahele, uluaō'a.
junior. 'Ōpio. *Charles, junior,*
Kale, 'ōpio.

jury. Kiule, kiure. *Grand jury,*
kiule nui.
just. 1. *Fair.* Pono, kūpono,
kaulike, na'au pono. **2.** *Recently.* 'Akahi, 'ānō iho nei. **3.**
See almost.
justice. Kaulike.
juvenile. 'Ōpio, 'ōpiopio.

K

k. Kē.
kava. 'Awa.
keep. Mālama, pa'a. *To keep
still,* noho mālie.
keepsake. Mea ho'omana'o.
kerosene. 'Ailahonua, 'aila māhu.
kettle. Ipu hao, kikila.
key. Kī.
kick. Peku, pekuna.
kidneys. Pu'upa'a, kōnāhua.
kill. Pepehi ā make, ho'omake,
make, hana make.
kin. 'Ohana, pili koko, pilikana.
kind. 1. *Sort.* 'Ano, kaina. **2.**
Not cruel. 'Olu'olu, lokomaika'i, aloha, na'au ali'i.
kindergarten. Kula kamali'i.
kindling. Pulu, pulupulu ahi,
pula, mea hō'ā'ā ahi.
king. Mō'ī, ali'i kāne, kini.
kinship. Pili 'ohana.
kiss. Honi.
kitchen. Lumi kuke.

kite. Lupe, pe'a.
knapsack. 'Eke lawe ukana, 'eke
hā'awe.
knead. Kūpele, ho'opele, pele,
poho, 'ōpā, ka'awili.
knee. Kuli.
kneel. Kukuli.
knife. Pahi.
knit. Kā, ulana.
knob. Pōheo, pōheoheo, heo,
heoheo, pu'u, 'āpua.
knock. Kīkēkē.
knot. 1. *Tied.* Hīpu'u, kīpu'u,
nīpu'u. **2.** *In a tree.* Kīnā o
ka lā'au. **3.** *Nautical.* Mile-
loa.
know. 'Ike.
knowledge. 'Ike, na'auao, pa'a
na'au.
knuckle. Ku'eku'e, 'ōku'eku'e,
pu'upu'u, pu'u, 'ōpu'upu'u;
pu'upu'u lima *(of hands).*
Korea. Kōlea, Korea.

L

l. Lā.
labor. Hana, limahana, lawehana, luhi.
laboratory. Ke'ena hana, ke'ena
'imi na'auao.
laborer. Limahana, lawehana.
Fellow laborer, hoa lawehana.
labor pains. Nahu kuakoko,
nahunahu, hō'i'ī, kōhi.
lace. 1. *Needlework.* Lihilihi,

lihilihi hana lima. **2.** *Cord.*
Lī. *Shoelace,* lī kāma'a.
lacking. Nele, 'ole, hemahema.
lad. Keiki, keiki kāne.
ladder. Alapi'i, alahaka, haka.
lady. Wahine, haku wahine.
ladyfish. 'Ō'io.
lagoon. Kai kohola, loko kai,
kua'au.
lake. Loko, loko wai. *Salt lake,*
loko pa'akai.

lamb. Keiki hipa, hipa keiki, pua hipa.

lame. ʻOʻopa, kīʻopa, māʻuluʻulu.

lament. Uwē, uwē helu, makena, kanikau, kūmākena.

lamp. Kukui, ipukukui, kukui pōhaku.

lance. 1. *Spear.* Ihe pakelo. 2. *Surgical instrument.* Ā, ā ʻōʻō, koholua.

land. 1. *Ground.* ʻĀina, honua, one. 2. *Debark.* Pae, lele, hoʻili, hoʻoili.

landholder. Paʻa ʻāina.

landing. Paena, kāhonua.

landlady. Haku hale wahine.

landlord. Haku ʻāina, haku hale.

landmark. Hōʻailona ʻāina.

landscape. Hiʻohiʻona ʻāina, waihona ʻāina, ka moena ʻana o ka ʻāina.

land shell. Pūpū kuahiwi, hinihini, kāhuli.

landslide. Hāneʻe ka mauna, heheʻe, hiolo, holo, ʻaholo.

lane. Ala ʻololī.

language. ʻŌlelo.

lantana. Lākana.

lantern. Ipukukui hele pō, kukui hele pō, lamakū.

lap. 1. *Noun.* ʻŪhā. 2. *Verb.* Mē, palu, paluhia.

lard. ʻAila puaʻa.

large. Nui, nunui.

larger. Nui loa.

lash. *Tie.* Hāwele, hauhana, hauhoa.

lashing. Aho, aho kā, luʻukia.

last. 1. *Most recent.* Hope, muli, nei, aku nei. *Very last.* hope loa, muli hope; hopena, panina. 2. *To continue.* Kāmau, hoʻomau, mau.

late. Lohi, hope, mahope. *Late at night,* aumoe.

lately. Aʻe nei, ʻānō iho nei, ʻānō wale iho nei nō.

later. Mahope aku.

Latter-Day Saints. Poʻe Hoʻāno o nā Lā Hope Nei.

laugh. ʻAka, ʻakaʻaka.

laundry. Lole lepo, lole holoi, lole pia (*with starch*), lole wai (*without starch*). *Laundry room,* lumi holoi.

lava. ʻĀ, ʻaʻā, ʻā pele (*rough lava*); pāhoehoe (*smooth lava*); ʻalā (*water-worn*).

law. Kānāwai. *Code of law,* kumukānāwai. *Lawmaking body,* ʻahaʻōlelo kau kānāwai.

lawn. Pā mauʻu.

lawsuit. Hoʻopiʻi, hihia ma ke kānāwai.

lawyer. Loio.

lay. Waiho, moe, hoʻomoe. *To lay eggs,* hānau i ka hua, hāʻule hua.

lazy. Molowā; palaualelo (*and verbose*).

lead. 1. *Mineral.* Kēpau, kēpau pōkā. 2. *To guide.* Alakaʻi, kaʻi, kaʻikaʻi.

leader. Alakaʻi, mua, aliʻi, luna.

leaf. Lau; lā- (*in contractions, as* lāʻalo *taro leaf;* lāʻī *ti leaf;* lāʻie ʻie *leaf;* lāʻō *sugarcane leaf*).

leak. Kulu, kulukulu, liu, nō.

lean. 1. *Thin.* Wīwī, ʻōlala, ʻāʻaua, ʻaua. 2. *As meat.* Pākā, pākaʻa, kōkaʻa. *Lean beef,* ʻiʻo pipi momona ʻole. 3. *Incline.* Hiō, hiōhiō, pahiō, kahiō.

leap. Lele.

learn. Aʻo, hoʻopaʻa, ʻimi naʻauao.

lease. Hoʻolimalima, palapala hoʻolimalima.

leash. Kaula paʻa lima.

leather. ʻIli, ʻili holoholona, ʻili pipi.

leave. *Verb.* Hoʻi, haʻalele, waiho.

lecture. Haʻiʻōlelo, haʻi aʻo.

ledge. Kaulu, kaulu ʻanuʻu, ʻanuʻu, kaola, lihi kaola, niao.

lee. Lulu. *Lee side of the island,* ʻaoʻao Kona o ka moku, lalo.

leeward. Lalo. *See* **lee.**

left. 1. *Direction.* Hema. 2. *Remaining.* Koe. 3. *Departed.* Haʻalele.

leg. Wāwae.

legal. Kū i ke kānāwai, pono i ke kānāwai, kau kānāwai, kānāwai.

legend. Moʻolelo, kaʻao.

legislature. ʻAhaʻōlelo, ʻahaʻōlelo kau kānāwai, ʻaha kau kānāwai. *Session of the legislature,* ʻaha kau kānāwai, kau ʻahaʻōlelo.

legitimate. Kū i ke kānāwai.

lei. Lei.

leisure. Manawa nanea, manawa walea, wā kaʻawale.

lemon. Lemi, kukane, lemona.

lemonade. Wai lemi.

lend. Hōʻaiʻē, hāʻawi no ka manawa, haʻawi ʻaiʻē.

length. Lōʻihi, loa, loloa, lau loa.

Lent. Kalema, Karema.

leprosy. Maʻi lēpela, lēpela, maʻi-Pākē, maʻi-aliʻi, maʻi-hoʻokaʻawale.

less. Hapa iki, hapa ʻuʻuku, emi iho, hapa.

lesson. Haʻawina.

lest. O.

let. ʻAe, hoʻokuʻu, e.

letter. 1. *Missive.* Leka. 2. *Character.* Hua palapala, hua, hua nui, hua iki, hua liʻi.

lettuce. Lekuke.

level. ʻIliwai, ʻiliwai like, pālahalaha. *Carpenter's level,* ʻiliwai.

lever. Une.

levy. Kau, hoʻoūku, ʻauhau.

liar. Wahaheʻe, hoʻopunipuni.

libel. Laipila.

liberal. Ākea, laulā, lipelala.

liberty. Kūʻokoʻa.

librarian. Kahu puke, mea mālama puke, mea mālama waihona puke, mālama waihona puke.

library. Hale waihona puke, waihona puke.

lice. ʻUku, ona.

license. Laikini, palapala ʻae.

lick. Palu.

lid. Pani, poʻi, uhi, ʻomo.

lie. 1. *Recline.* Moe, hina moe.

2. *Falsify.* Hoʻopunipuni, wahaheʻe, waha wale.

lieutenant. Lukānela.

life. Ola (*as opposed to death*); nohona, noho ʻana (*way of life*).

lifeguard. Kiaʻi ola.

life insurance. ʻInikua ola.

lifesaving. Hoʻopakele ola.

lifetime. Ka wā e ola ana.

lift. *Verb.* Hāpai.

light. 1. *Illumination.* Ao, lama, malama, kukui. 2. *Ignite.* Hōʻā, hōʻaʻā. 3. *Not heavy.* Māmā.

lighthouse. Hale ipukukui.

lightning. Uila. *Flash of lightning,* lapa uila.

like. 1. *As.* Ā, me, like me, kū, kohu, mehe, mehe mea, pe, hele ā, laʻa. *Like this,* penei, pe kēia, pēia, ʻano like me kēia, e laʻa me kēia. 2. *Wish, to be fond of.* Makemake, mamake, puni, ʻiʻini, ʻono (*food*).

likeness. Kohu, kohu like, ʻano, kiʻi, aka, lua.

lily. Lilia.

limb. Lālā, mana.

lime. 1. *Fruit.* Lemi. 2. *Calcium oxide.* Puna.

limestone. Hauone, paʻakea, pāpaʻakea, pōhā kea.

limit. Palena, kaupale, ʻoki. *To limit,* kaupalena.

limp. 1. *Verb.* ʻOʻopa, ʻopa, māʻopaʻopa, hakiʻopa, kīʻopa, ʻoʻi. 2. *Adjective.* Malule, nāwali, nāwaliwali.

limpet. ʻOpihi.

line. 1. *Cordage.* Kaula, aho. 2. *Geometric.* Lālani, laina, kaha. 3. *To cover.* Pale.

lineage. Lālani ʻohana, kūʻauhau, welo, ēwe.

linen. Lilina, pulu, pulupulu, olonā.

linger. Kali, ʻapa.

link. Paukū, loulou, hoʻohui, hoʻokuʻi. *Link of chain,* paukū kaula hao.

lion. Liona.

lip. Lehe, lehelehe.

liquid. Wai, 'ae.

liquor. Wai; wai 'ona (*intoxicating*).

list. Helu, papa helu. *List of names*, papa inoa.

listen. Lohe, ho'olohe, ho'olono.

literature. Mo'olelo; palapala (*written only*).

litter. 1. *Trash.* 'Ōpala, mōkākī, ho'ōpala. 2. *Stretcher.* Mānele.

little. Iki, li'i, lili'i, li'ili'i.

live. 1. *Exist.* Ola. 2. *Dwell.* Noho.

livelihood. Ola, pono.

lively. 'Eleu, 'eu'eu.

liver. Ake, akepa'a. *Raw liver*, ake maka.

livestock. Holoholona hānai (i ka mahina'ai).

living. Nohona, 'ao'ao (*way of life*); ola (*life*).

living room. Lumi ho'okipa.

lizard. Mo'o, mo'o kiha.

load. Hā'awe. *To load*, ho'okaumaha, ho'īli, ho'oili, ho'oūka, ho'oūkana.

loaf. 1. *Noun.* 'Omo'omo. *Loaf of bread*, 'omo'omo palaoa, pa'i pelena. 2. *Verb.* Noho hana 'ole, ho'ohala manawa, ho'onanea.

loafer. Palaualelo, molowā.

loan. Hā'awi no ka manawa, hō'ai'ē.

lobby. 1. *Foyer.* Lumi ho'okipa. 2. *Political.* Hana ho'opaipai, paipai.

lobster. Ula.

local. Kūloko, kō laila, ne'i, one'i. *Local people*, kō 'one'i po'e.

location. Kahua, wahi, kāhi.

lock. Kī, laka.

locomotive. Ka'aahi.

locust. 'Ūhini.

lodge. 1. *House.* Hale. 2. *Fraternal or secret society.* Hui malū.

log. 1. *As of wood.* Paukū kumulā'au, kua lā'au. 2. *Ship's record.* Mo'olelo.

loincloth. Malo.

loiter. Kali.

lone. Ho'okahi, kaukahi, noho ho'okahi.

loneliness. Mehameha.

long. Loa, loloa (*usually spatially*); lō'ihi; kō (*as a sound*).

long for. See want.

long rice. Laiki loloa.

look. Nānā, kilo.

lookout. Wahi nānā, wahi kia'i, 'ale'o.

loose. Hemo, puhemo, 'alu'alu, hō'alu'alu, pū'alu.

lopsided. Kapakahi.

lord. Haku.

lose. Nalo, nalowale, ho'olilo.

loss. Emi, pohō; pohō ma'ū (*complete*).

lost. Lilo; lilo loa (*permanently*); nalo, nalowale, nalohia.

lot. 1. *Quantity.* Nui, nui 'ino, nui loa. 2. *Land.* Pā, pā hale. 3. *Chance.* Hailona.

loud. Wā, hana kuli, kulikuli (*too loud*).

loudspeaker. Ho'onui leo, ho'onui i ka leo.

lounge. 1. *See* couch. 2. *Parlor.* Lumi ho'oluana, lumi ho'okipa. 3. *Relax.* Ho'onanea, hō'olu'olu i ke kino.

louse. 'Uku, 'uku li'i, ona; 'uku-po'o (*head louse*); 'uku-kapa (*body louse*).

love. Aloha, 'ano'i, nipo, kāunu, ho'oipoipo, ho'oheno, puni.

love affair. Pili ho'oipoipo.

lovely. Nohea, onaona.

lover. Ipo.

low. Lalo, ha'a, ha'aha'a, pē, pēpē, emi; pāpapa (*as a reef*).

lower. Lalo, lalo iho, emi, ho'oha'aha'a; ku'u (*as a net*); ho'ēmi, emiemi, ho'ēmiemi (*price*).

loyal. Kūpa'a, ho'okūpa'a.

luck. Pōmaika'i, laki. *Bad luck*, pō'ino, pakalaki, moe wa'a. *Out of luck*, pohō.

lucky. Laki, pōmaika'i.

luggage. Ukana, ukana pilikino.

lukewarm. Mūhea, 'ala'alae, 'ano 'ōwelawela.

lullaby. Mele ho'ohiamoe keiki, mele ho'onānā keiki, mele ho'oluluhi.

lumber. Papa, papa lā'au, laupapa.

lump. Pu'u, haku, huku.

lunatic. Hehena.

lunch. 'Aina awakea.

lung. Akemāmā, akemakani.

lure. 1. Attract. 'Ume, makaki'i (with the eyes); ho'ōnaona. 2. See fishhook.

luscious. 'Ono.

lush. Uluwehi, uluwehiwehi, ulu nui.

lust. Kuko, 'a'ako, 'ako.

Lutheran. Lukelano.

luxury. Mea e ho'ohiwahiwa ai ka noho 'ana, lako loa.

M

m. Mū.

machine. Mīkini.

mad. 1. Insane. Hehena, pupule. 2. Angry. Huhū.

madam. Makame.

magazine. Puke heluhelu.

maggot. Ilo.

magic. Ho'okalakupua.

magnet. Makēneki, hao makēneki.

magnificent. Hanohano, nani loa, hīhīmanu.

magnify. Ho'onui.

maid. Wahine lawelawe, kauwā wahine.

maidenhair fern. 'Iwa'iwa.

mail. Leka.

maile. Maile.

main. 'Ano nui, hapa nui.

mainland. 'Āina makua, 'āina nui, loko. To go to the mainland, hele i loko.

majestic. Kilakila.

majority. Hapa nui, hapa loa.

make. Hana.

male. Kāne.

mama. Māmā. See mother.

man. Kanaka, kāne.

manage. Ho'oponopono, ho'oholo, ho'ohele, ho'ohana.

manager. Haku nui, luna ho'ohana.

mango. Manakō.

mangrove. Kukuna-o-ka-lā.

manioc. Manioka.

mankind. Lāhui kanaka.

manners. Lula, loina, 'ano launa.

man-of-war. Manuwā. See Portuguese man-of-war.

manta ray. Hāhālua.

manual. 1. Directory. Kumu, a'o, manuale. 2. By hand. Hana lima.

manure. Kūkae.

many. Nui, nunui, lau, mano, manomano, lehu, lehulehu, kini.

map. Palapala'āina.

marbles. Kinikini. To shoot, as marbles, pana.

march. 1. Action. Naue, ka'i huaka'i. 2. Month. (Cap.) Malaki.

marine. 1. Of the sea. Kai. 2. Military. Koa malina.

mark. Kaha, kahakaha, kiko, kākau, kākau kaha.

market. Mākeke.

marriage. Male 'ana, moe, noho pū 'ana, ho'āo.

marigold. 'Ōkole-'oi'oi.

marlin. A'u.

marry. Male, moe, ho'āo, noho.

marvelous. Kupaianaha, kupanaha, kamaha'o.

masculine. Kāne, ho'okāne.

mask. Makaki'i, po'oki'i, uhi maka.

mass. 1. Quantity. Pu'u, nu'a, anu'a, ahu. 2. Ritual. Meka, pule meka.

massacre. Luku.

massage. Lomi, lomilomi, kōkō, kaomi.

master. Haku, kahu.

mat. Moena.

match. 1. *Contest.* Hoʻokūkū. 2. *Equal.* Lua, kohu like. 3. *For starting fire.* Kūkaepele.

mate. 1. *Companion.* Hoa, kōkoʻolua. 2. *Of ships.* Mālama moku.

mathematics. Makemakikia.

matter. 1. *Thing.* Mea; kumuhana (*topic*). 2. *To be important.* ʻAno nui, manaʻo nui.

mattress. Pela, pela moe.

mature. Makua, kanaka makua, oʻo.

may. 1. *See* **can.** 2. *See* **maybe.** 3. *Month.* (*Cap.*) Mei.

maybe. Paha; pēlā paha, malia paha.

mayor. Meia.

me. Aʻu, iaʻu, i oʻu. *To me,* iaʻu, i oʻu.

meal. ʻAina, pāʻina.

mean. 1. *Cruel.* Mākonā, hoʻomainoino. 2. *Average.* Waena. 3. *Signify.* Manaʻo.

meaning. Manaʻo, manaʻo nui, ʻano. *See* **hidden.**

meantime. Ia wā nō, ia manawa.

measles. ʻUlāliʻi.

measure. Ana, hoʻāna.

meat. ʻIʻo, ʻiʻo holoholona, iʻa.

medal. Mekala.

medical. Lāʻau, kauka.

medicine. Lāʻau, lāʻau lapaʻau, wai lāʻau.

medium. 1. *Intermediate.* Waena. 2. *Spiritualist.* Haka.

meek. Akahai, haʻahaʻa.

meet. Hui, hālāwai.

meeting. ʻAha, hālāwai.

melody. Leo, melokia.

melon. Ipu.

melt. Heheʻe, kahe.

member. Lālā (*as of a society*).

memorize. Hoʻopaʻanaʻau, hoʻopaʻa.

memory. Hoʻomanaʻo ʻana.

men. Kānaka.

mend. Hono, pāhonohono, poho, hana hou, kāpili.

menstruate. Hanawai, kahe, peʻa.

mentality. Waihona noʻonoʻo.

mention. Haʻi, ʻōlelo, hoʻopuka.

merchant. Kālepa.

mercy. Aloha.

merry. Leʻaleʻa, ʻoliʻoli, ʻakaʻaka; mele (*as in Merry Christmas*).

merry-go-round. Lio lāʻau.

mesh. Maka, maka ʻupena.

mess. Mōkākī.

message. ʻŌlelo hoʻoūna ʻia.

messenger. ʻElele.

meteor. Hōkū-lele.

meter. 1. *Distance.* Mika, mekele. 2. *For measuring.* Ana.

method. ʻAno hana, papa hana.

Mexico. Mekiko.

microphone. Mea hoʻolele leo.

microscope. ʻOhe nānā, ʻohe hoʻonui ʻike.

midday. Awakea.

middle. Waena, waenakonu.

midnight. Aumoe.

midrib. Nīʻau (*coconut frond*).

midway. Mawaena, waenakonu.

mighty. Ikaika loa, mana loa.

mildew. Auloli, kūkaeloli.

mile. Mile (*statute*); mile-loa (*nautical*).

military forces. ʻOihana koa.

milk. Waiū.

milkfish. Awa.

milk shake. Waiū luliluli.

Milky Way. Hōkū-noho-aupuni, Iʻa.

mill. Wili, hale wili. *Sugar mill,* wili kō.

million. Miliona.

mimic. Hoʻopili.

mind. 1. *Intellect.* Manaʻo, waihona noʻonoʻa, naʻau. 2. *Obey.* Lohe. 3. *Heed.* Mālama, maliu.

mine. 1. *Possessive.* Koʻu, kaʻu, kuʻu, oʻu, aʻu, noʻu, naʻu. *See* **my.** 2. *Pit.* Lua, lua ʻeli waiwai. 3. *Military.* Pōkā pahū kai.

minimum. Hapa ʻuʻuku loa, haʻahaʻa.

minister. 1. *Priest.* Kahuna, kahuna pule, kahu. 2. *Statesman.* Kuhina.

minor. 1. *Small.* 'U'uku iho. 2. *Underage.* O'o 'ole.

minority. Hapa iki, hapa 'u'uku.

minute. Minuke.

miraculous. Mana, ho'okalakupua, kupaianaha.

mirror. Aniani, aniani kilohi; aniani pa'a lima (*hand*).

miscarriage. He'e wale, poholo.

mischief. Kolohe, 'eu.

miser. Pī, puni kālā.

misery. Pō'ino oki loa.

misfortune. Pō'ino, pōpilikia.

misprint. Pa'i hewa.

mispronounce. Hewa ka hopuna, pa'ewa ka hopuna.

miss. 1. *Fail to hit.* Hala, hewa. 2. *Perceive absence.* Ha'o. 3. *Nostalgia.* Ha'o wale, minamina. 4. *Unmarried woman.* Wahine male 'ole. *No equivalent to the title.*

missing. Nalowale, nalo.

missionary. Mikanele, mikionele.

mist. Uhiwai, noe, 'ohu, ehu (*in approximate order of decreasing denseness*).

mistake. Hewa, kuhihewa, pa-'ewa, lalau; kīna'u (*flaw*).

mister. *See* Mr.

mite. Ona, ane.

mix. Ho'ohui, ho'owali (*as poi, dough*).

mix up, mix-up. Huikau, ho-'ohuikau.

moan. 'Ū, 'uhū, 'uhū'uhū, kani'ū.

mob. Uluaō'a, po'e ho'ohaunāele.

model. Ana, ana ho'ohālike.

modern. No kēia au.

modest. Akahai, ha'aha'a, pē, na'au pē. *See* humble.

moist. Ma'ū, mā'ū'ū, ko'ū, pa'ū, līhau.

molasses. Malakeke.

moment. Manawa iki. *Wait a moment,* kali iki, eia iho.

Monday. Pō'akahi.

money. Kālā, moni.

mongoose. 'Iole-manakuke, manakuke.

monkey. Keko, mākinikā.

monkeypod. 'Ōhai.

mons pubis. Hene, hehe, pu-'ukole.

month. Mahina, malama.

monthly. Kēlā mahina kēia mahina, puka mahina.

moon. Mahina.

moonlight. Mālamalama o ka mahina.

mop. Lā'au holoi papahele, kāwele wai.

moral. Pono.

more. Hou, keu.

moreover. Kekahi, eia kekahi, eia hou, koe kēia.

Morinda citrifolia. Noni.

Mormon. Molemona.

morning. Kakahiaka. *See* good morning.

morning-glory. Koali.

Morning Star. Hōkū-ao, Hōkū-loa.

mortgage. Molaki.

mosquito. Makika.

mosquito net. Pākū makika.

moss. Limu.

most. Hapa nui, nui, hapa loa, loa.

moth. Pulelehua; mū (*clothes moth*).

mother. Makuahine, māmā.

mother-in-law. Makuahūnōwai wahine.

Mother's Day. Lā o nā mākuahine.

Mother Hubbard. Holokū.

mother tongue. 'Ōlelo makua.

motion. 1. *Movement.* 'Oni, au, ne'e mōkio. 2. *Parliamentary.* Noi. *To second a motion,* kōkua.

motor. Mīkini.

motorcycle. Mokokaikala, ka'a mokokaikala.

motto. Mākia.

mound. Ahu, āhua, pu'u.

mount. Pi'i, 'e'e, hō'e'e, kau.

mountain. Mauna, kuahiwi.

mountain apple. 'Ōhi'a-'ai.

mourn. Kanikau, uwē, 'ū.

mouse. 'Iole.

mousetrap. 'Ūmi'i 'iole.

mouth. Waha.

move. Ne'e, ho'one'e, naue; ka'i hele (*in line or succession, or as in checkers*).

movement. Au, 'oni, ne'ena.

movie. Ki'i 'oni'oni.

mow. 'Oki.

Mr. *No term today; formerly, but not used commonly:* Mī, Mika.

Mrs. *No term today; formerly, but not used commonly:* wahine.

much. Nui. *Very much,* nui 'ino, nui hewahewa, nui loa, kai! *How much?* 'Ehia?

mucus. Hūpē, 'ūpē, hākelo, wale.

mud. Kelekele, pālolo, lepo 'ūkele.

mudhen. 'Alae, nūkea, koki.

mulberry. Wauke.

mule. Hoki, miula, piula.

mullet. 'Ama'ama.

multiplication. Ho'onui.

multiply. Ho'omāhuahua, ho'onui.

mumble. Namunamu, kolokolo.

mumps. 'Auwae-pahāha, 'ā'ī-pahāha.

murder. Pepehi kanaka.

murmur. Nē, hamumu, hē.

muscle. 'I'o, 'i'o huki, olonā.

museum. Hale hō'ike'ike.

mushroom. Kūkaelio, māmalu.

mushroom coral. Ko'a-kohe, 'āko'ako'a-kohe.

music. Mele (*vocal*); pila ho-'okani (*instrumental*).

musician. Mea ho'okani pila (*player*); mea hīmeni, pu-'ukani (*singer*); haku mele (*composer*).

must. Pono.

mustache. 'Umi'umi.

mute. Mumule. *Deaf mute,* kanaka kuli a 'ā'ā.

mutiny. 'Olohani, mokuāhana, kipi i luna o ka moku.

mutter. Namunamu.

mutton. 'I'o hipa. *Leg of mutton,* 'ūhā hipa.

mutual. Like, kaulike, pāna'i like.

my. 1. *Singular possessed object.* Ko'u, ka'u, ku'u. 2. *Plural possessed object.* O'u, a'u.

mynah. Piha-'ekelo.

myself. 'O wau nō, 'o wau pono'ī, 'o wau iho nō.

mystery. Pohihihi, kumulipo, mikelio.

myth. Mo'olelo.

N

n. Nū.

nail. 1. *Carpenter's.* Kui, kui nao, kui hao. 2. *Human.* Mai'ao, miki'ao.

naked. Kohana.

name. 1. *Noun.* Inoa. 2. *Verb.* Hea, hea inoa, kapa, kāhea.

name chant. Inoa, mele inoa.

namely. 'Oia ho'i.

nap. Hiamoe iki.

napkin. Kāwele. *Paper napkin,* kāwele pepa. *Sanitary napkin,* mea hume.

narcotic. Lā'au ho'ohiamoe, lā-'au moe, lā'au ho'omalule kino.

narrow. Lā'iki, hāiki, ho'ohāiki.

nasty. Pelapela, hauka'e.

nation, national. Aupuni, lāhui.

native. Kama'āina, maoli, 'ōiwi, kupa, keiki papa.

natural. Kūpono.

nature. 'Ano (*kind*). *There is no single Hawaiian word for the physical universe.*

naughty. Kolohe, 'eu, 'āpiki.

nausea. Pailua, papailua, liliha.

nauseating. Ho'opailua.

navel. Piko.

navy. 'Oihana moku.

near. Kokoke.

neat. Maiau, 'auli'i; mikioi (*in craftsmanship*).

necessary. Pono, kūpono.

eck. 'Ā'ī; waha (*of a dress*).

ecklace. Lei.

ecktie. Lei 'ā'ī.

eed. 1. *Necessity.* Pono. **2.** *To lack.* Nele, hemahema.

eedle. Kui, kui kele, kui humuhumu, mānai.

eedlefish. 'Aha, 'aha-mele, 'aha'aha.

egative. 1. *Negate.* 'Ole, hō-'ole. **2.** *Of a picture.* Aka ki'i.

eglect. Mālama 'ole, waiho wale, ho'opalaleha, ho'ohemahema.

Negro. Pā'ele; pōpolo (*slang*); nekelo.

eighbor. Hoa noho, hoalauna.

either. 'A'ole, 'a'ole ho'i.

ephew. Keiki.

erve. A'a, a'alolo, a'alolo lohe.

ervous. Pīhoihoi wale, ha'alulu o loko.

est. Pūnana.

et. 'Upena; kōkō, 'a'aha (*carrying net*).

eutral. Kā'oko'a.

ever. 'A'ole, 'a'ole loa.

evertheless. Akā, akā ho'i, na'e.

ew. Hou, meahou, 'ano hou, malihini.

ewcomer. Malihini.

ews. Meahou, nūhou, nū, lono.

ewspaper. Nūpepa.

New Testament. Kauoha Hou.

New York. Nuiōka.

New Zealand. Nukīlani.

ext. A'e, hope, hiki. *Next week,* kēia pule a'e.

ibble. Nalinali, 'a'aki, nome.

ice. 'Auli'i; 'olu'olu (*pleasant*); maika'i.

ickel. Hapa'umi.

ickname. Inoa kapakapa.

iece. Kaikamahine.

ight. Pō. *Last night,* i ka pō nei.

ight-blooming cereus. Pā-nini-o-ka-Punahou.

ightgown. Mu'umu'u moe pō, lole moe pō.

ightmare. Moehewa, moe 'ino.

nimble. 'Eleu, miki, māmā.

nine. Iwa, 'eiwa, 'aīwa.

nineteen. 'Umi kūmāiwa, 'umi kumamāiwa.

ninety. Kanaīwa.

ninety-one. Kanaīwa kūmākahi, kanaīwa kumamākahi.

nipple. Maka waiū, maka.

nit. Liha, lia.

no. 'A'ole, 'a'ohe.

nobody. 'A'ohe mea, 'a'ohe kanaka.

noddy tern. Noio kōhā.

noise. Hana kuli, kulikuli, wā, wawā, kani.

nominate. Koho, wae, waiho inoa.

none. 'A'ohe mea, 'a'ohe, 'a'ole.

nonsense. 'Ano 'ole, kohu 'ole.

noon. Awakea, kau ka lā i ka lolo.

normal. Kūlike me ke 'ano mau, 'ano mau.

north. 'Ākau.

North America. 'Amelika-'Ākau.

northeast. Hikina 'ākau.

North Pole. Wēlau-'ākau.

North Star. Kio-pa'a, Hōkū-pa'a.

northwest. Komohana 'ākau, noweke.

nose. Ihu.

nose flute. Hano, kōheoheo.

nostril. Pukaihu.

not. 'A'ole, 'ole, 'a'ohe.

notched. Nihoniho, nihoa, pū-'ali.

note. 1. *Letter.* Leka pōkole, 'ōlelo ho'omana'o. **2.** *Financial.* Palapala 'ai'ē, pila hō-'ai'ē. **3.** *Musical.* Leo mele, hua, hua mele.

notebook. Kālana kākau.

nothing. 'Ole, mea 'ole, 'a'ohe mea, nele.

notice. Hō'ike. *To notice,* nānā.

notify. Hō'ike.

nourish. Hānai.

novel. 1. *Story.* Ka'ao. **2.** *Strange, new.* 'Ano 'ē.

November. Nowemapa.

novice. 'Akahi akahi, ma'a 'ole.

now. I kēia manawa, 'ānō.

nuisance. Pilikia, mea ho'opilikia wale, ho'oluhi.

numb. Lōlō, mā'e'ele.

number. Helu, heluna, nui (*quantity*); huahelu (*numeral*).

numerous. Lau, ho'olau, mano, manoa, lehu, lehulehu, kinikini, kini lau.

nun. Wilikina, nuna.

nurse. Kahu ma'i, kahu mālama ma'i.

nut. Kukui-haole.

O

o. 'Ō.

oar. Hoe.

oarsman. Mea hoe wa'a, hoe wa'a.

oath. 1. *In court.* Ho'ohiki, 'ōlelo ho'ohiki, 'ōlelo pa'a. **2.** *See* **swear.**

obedient, obey. Ho'olono, ho'olohe.

obituary. Mo'olelo o ka mea 'akahi nō a make.

object. 1. *Thing.* Mea. **2.** *Purpose.* Kumu, mea. **3.** *See* **oppose.**

obligation. 'Ai'ē (*debt*).

obscene. Pelapela, haumia, ho'ohilahila.

obscure. Poahi, poehi, powehi, pohihihi.

observe. Nānā, nānā pono, hākilo, haka pono.

obstacle. Ālaina, mea ala'alai, mea ke'ake'a.

obstetrician. Kauka ho'ohānau.

obstinate. Pa'akikī, 'o'ole'a, pa'a loa, po'o pa'a.

obstruct. Alai, ke'a ho'oke'a, ho'okāpae.

obtain. Loa'a.

obvious. Maopopo le'a, aniani, mōakaaka.

occasion. Wā, hanana.

occupation. 'Oihana, hana.

occupy. Noho (*as a house*).

occur. Kupu, hiki mai.

ocean. Moana, kai.

o'clock. Hola.

October. 'Okakopa.

octopus. He'e.

odd. 'Ano 'ē (*unusual*); pa'ewa (*uneven*).

odor. *See* **smell.**

of. O, a, kō, kā.

off. Mai (*from*); 'ē (*away*).

offend. Ho'ohuhū, ho'onāukiuki.

offense. Hewa, hala, lawehala.

offer. Hā'awi, hō.

offering. Mōhai. *Church offering,* lūlū, ho'okupu, mahina hou.

office. 1. Position. 'Oihana, hana. **2.** *Room.* Ke'ena, ke'ena hana.

officer. Ali'i, luna.

offspring. Keiki, hānau, pua, hua.

often. Pinepine.

oh. Auwē, kā, 'ā.

oil. 'Aila, hinu.

oilfish. Walu.

oily. Hinuhinu, kūhinu, kelekele, 'ūkele, liliha.

ointment. Mea hamo, 'aila hamo, lā'au hamo, hinu.

O.K. Hiki, hiki nō, pololei.

old. Kahiko (*usually not of people*); o'o, 'elemakule, luahine.

old age. Wā 'elemakule, wā luahine.

older. Mua, hiapo (*of children in a family*), makua.

old-fashioned. Ho'okahiko, 'ano o ke au kahiko.

old man. 'Elemakule.

Old Testament. Kauoha Kahiko.

old woman. Luahine.

oleander. 'Oliana, 'oliwa, nohomālie.

olive. 'Oliva.

omelet. Hua pākā, hua palai i ka'awili 'ia.

omen. 'Ōuli, hō'ailona.

omit. Waiho, kāpae, holoi.

on. I, ma, maluna o.

once. Hoʻokahi wā, kekahi wā, pākahi, ʻekahi, ʻakahi, kuakahi.

one. ʻEkahi, ʻakahi (*counting in a series*); hoʻokahi, kahi, kekahi; hapa- (*in fractions: one-eighth,* hapawalu).

onion. ʻAkaʻakai.

only. Wale nō, wale.

onward. I mua.

open. 1. *State of being open, as a door.* Hāmama, makili, mikili, nakili, hoʻomakili (*as a crack*). **2.** *As a flower.* Mōhala, mōhalu. **3.** *Verb, transitive (as a door, package).* Wehe, weke, ʻuwehe.

openhearted. Puʻuwai hāmama.

opening. Puka, wehena, wehe ʻana, waha, hoʻowaha, mōhala, ʻīpuka.

opera. Keaka mele.

operate. ʻOki, kaha (*surgically*).

opinion. Manaʻo.

opponent. Hoa paio, mea kūē, ʻaoʻao kūʻē.

opportunity. Manawa kūpono.

oppose. Kūʻē, ālai, keʻakeʻa, pākuʻi, kē.

opposite. Kūʻē, ʻēʻē.

oppress. Hoʻoluʻuluʻu, hoʻoluhi hewa, hoʻokaumaha, hoʻokoʻikoʻi.

optimism. Hoihoi mau, hoʻohoihoi mau.

or. Aiʻole, a . . . paha.

oral. Haʻi waha, waha, ʻōlelo.

orange. *The fruit or tree.* ʻAlani.

orchard. Māla lāʻau huaʻai, kīhāpai.

orchestra. Hui hoʻokani pila.

orchid. ʻOkika.

order. 1. *Command.* Kauoha, kēnā. **2.** *Arrangement.* Hoʻonohonoho ʻana, papa, noho papa.

ordinary. Maʻamau, laha, mea loaʻa wale, aʻe nei.

organ. 1. *Musical instrument.* ʻOkana. **2.** *Part of body.* Māhele. *Internal organs,* loko.

organization. Hui, ʻahahui.

origin. Kinohi, hoʻomaka ʻana, kumu.

ornament. Wehi, kāhiko, kīnohi, hoʻokāhiko.

orphan. Keiki makua ʻole.

other. Kekahi, ʻē aʻe, ʻē.

otherwise. Akā naʻe, ma kekahi ʻano ʻē aʻe.

ouch. Auwē, auwī.

ought. Pono.

ounce. ʻAunaki.

our. Kō kāua, kā kāua, kō māua, kā māua, kō kākou, kā kākou, kō mākou, kā mākou, o kāua, a kāua, o māua, a māua, o kākou, a kākou, o mākou, a mākou.

ours. No kāua, no māua, no kākou, no mākou, na kāua, na māua, na kākou, na mākou.

out. Waho, i waho, mawaho; pio (*extinguished*).

outcast. Kauwā.

outcry. Oho.

outdoors. O waho.

outhouse. Wahi hoʻopau pilikia, hale liʻiliʻi, lua liʻiliʻi, lua, hale lua.

outrigger boom. ʻIako.

outrigger canoe. Waʻa.

outrigger float. Ama.

outside. Waho, i waho, mawaho, kō waho, kūwaho.

outsider. Kanaka ʻē, kanaka o waho.

outstanding. Poʻokela, kau i ka wēkiu, kūlana kiʻekiʻe.

oven. Imu, umu, ʻoma.

over. 1. *Above.* Luna, i luna, maluna. **2.** *Completed.* Pau. **3.** *Again.* Hou.

overcast. ʻŌmalumalu, ʻomamalu, hoʻōmalumalu.

overcome. 1. *To defeat.* Lanakila, hoʻopio. **2.** *Defeated.* Pio, puni. **3.** *Possessed, as by fear, passion, joy, or grief.* Loʻohia, ilihia.

overcooked. Moʻa loa.

overeat. Pākela 'ai.
overflow. Hū, hālana, hanini, ho'ohanini, pi'ipi'i.
overload. Ho'oūka nui, ho'olu-'ulu'u loa.
overseer. Luna, luna hana, luna kia'i, haku, haku hana.
overshadow. Ho'omalumalu, ho'oūmalu.
oversized. Nui loa, nui maluna o ka mea ma'amau.

oversleep. Hiamoe loa, moe loa.
overthrow. Kahuli, ho'okahuli, hiolo, ho'ohiolo.
overtime pay. Uku kaulele.
overwhelm. Po'ipū, popo'i, uhi.
owe. 'Ai'ē.
owl. Pueo.
own. Pono'ī (self); kuleana (ownership).
owner. Haku, mea, 'ona.
oyster. 'Ōlepe.

P

p. Pī.
Pacific. Pākīpika, Moana Pā-kīpika.
pack. Ho'okomo (as a trunk); 'awe, hā'awe (carry).
package. Pū'olo.
paddle. Hoe.
paddler. Hoe wa'a.
page. 'Ao'ao.
paid. Ka'a.
pail. Pela, kini, kini pela, pā-keke.
pain. 'Eha; hu'i (in tooth, bones); nalulu (dull, in stomach, head); 'ūmi'i (inside).
paint. Pena.
painter. Kaha ki'i (artist); mea pena (as of houses).
pair. Pa'a, kaulua.
pajamas. Lole wāwae moe pō.
palace. Hale ali'i.
pale. Hākea.
pali. See cliff.
palm. 1. Tree. Pāma, pālama; niu (coconut). 2. Of hand. Poho, poho lima.
pan. Pā.
pancake. Palaoa palai.
pandanus. Hala.
panic. Maka'u kūhewa, haunā-ele.
pansy. Po'o-kanaka, pāneki.
pantry. Lumi waiho pā.
pants. Lole wāwae.
papa. Pāpā.
papaya. Mīkana, hē'ī, papaia.

paper. Pepa.
parade. Huaka'i, ka'i huaka'i; paikau (as of military).
paradise. Palekaiko.
paragraph. Paukū, palekalapa.
parallel. Kaulike, moe like, 'ili-wai like.
paralysis. Lōlō, ma'i lōlō.
parasite. 1. Plant. Lā'au kumu 'ole. 2. Person. Kū 'īpuka hale, kūkake, lelewa, ho'opi-limea'ai.
parched. Malo'o loa.
pardon. Kala, huikala.
parent. Makua.
Paris. Palika, Parisa.
park. 1. Recreation area. Pāka. 2. To station. Ho'okū, kūkulu.
parlor. Lumi ho'okipa.
parrot. Manu-aloha.
parrotfish. Uhu.
part. Portion. Māhele, mokuna, hapa, 'āpana.
particle. Huna, māhune, pula, lihi.
particular. 1. Special. Nō. 2. Fussy. 'Ano waewae, 'eke-'eke, kamalani.
partition. Pale, kaupale, pākū.
partner. Hoa, hoa hana, kōko'o, pakanā.
party. 1. Group. 'Aha, pū'ulu, 'ao'ao (political). 2. Festivity. Ho'olaule'a (large), pā'ina (dinner or supper). 3. Person. Kanaka, mea, po'e.
pass. 1. Movement. Mā'alo, kā-

'alo, 'aui, kaha (*pass by*), holo.
2. *Permission.* Palapala ho-
'oku'u.

passenger. 'Ōhua.

passion. Ko'iko'i, konikoni, kāunu. *The Passion of Christ,*
ka 'Eha'eha o ka Haku.

passion fruit. Liliko'i, lemi-wai,
lemona, pohāpohā.

passover. Pakoa, mōliaola.

passport. Palapala ho'āpono,
palapala kuhikuhi, palapala
'ae e holo.

past. Hala, ka'a i hope.

paste. Ho'opipili, mea ho'opipili.

pastime. Ho'ohala manawa, hana ho'ohala manawa.

pastor. Kahuna pule, kahu.

pastry. Mea'ono.

pasture. Kula, pā holoholona,
kula holoholona.

patch. 1. *On clothes.* Poho. 2.
Garden. Mahi, māla.

paternal. Makua kāne, ma ka
'ao'ao o ka makua kāne.

path. Ala.

patience. Ahonui, 'ōpū ahonui,
ho'omanawanui.

patient. Ma'i, mea ma'i.

patriotism. Aloha 'āina.

pattern. Ana, ana ho'ohālike.

pause. Ho'omaha.

pavement. Kīpapa, paepae, kī-
paepae.

paw. Wāwae, kapua'i.

pawnshop. Hale hō'ai'ē.

pay. Uku, ho'oka'a.

peace. Malu, maluhia, la'i.

peach. Piki.

peacock. Pīkake.

peak. Pu'u 'oi'oi, pu'u, wēkiu,
'oi'oina.

peanut. Pineki.

pear. Pea.

pearl. Momi.

pearl shell. Pā, uhi, kea.

pebble. 'Ili'ili.

pebble hula. Hula 'ili'ili.

peculiar. *Unusual.* 'E, 'ē'ē, 'ano
'ē, 'e'epa.

pedal. Hehi wāwae.

pedestrian. Kanaka hele wāwae.

peel. Ma'ihi; koli (*pare*).

peeved. Ukiuki, nuha.

Pele's hair. Lauoho o Pele.

Pele's tears. Waimaka o Pele.

pelt. 1. *Skin.* 'Ili. 2. *To throw,*
hit. Pehi, pehia, nou.

pen. 1. *Enclosure.* Pā. 2. *Writ-*
ing instrument. Peni kila.

penalty. Ho'opa'i, uku hala.

pencil. Penikala, peni.

penetrate. Komo.

penis. Ule.

penknife. Pahi pelu.

pen name. Inoa kapakapa.

penny. Keneka, keneta.

pension. Uku ho'omau, ha'awina ho'omau.

people. Po'e, lāhui, lāhui kanaka, kānaka.

pepper. Pepa, nīoi.

percent. Pakeneka.

perfect. Hemolele, kīnā 'ole,
pono loa.

perform. Lawelawe, hana, ho-
'okō.

perfume. Lūkini, wai lūkini, wai
'ala, wai hō'a'ala.

perhaps. Paha, pēlā paha, malia, malia paha.

period. 1. *Punctuation.* Kiko.
2. *Time.* Wā, manawa, au.

permanent. Pa'a, loa, mau, mau
loa.

permission. 'Ae.

persecute. Ho'omāino, ho'omāinoino, māino, hō'ino.

persevere. Noke, ho'omanawanui, ho'omau.

persist. Ho'omau, ho'opa'a, noke.

person. Kanaka, mea, kama.

personal. Pilikino, kino, pono'ī.

perspiration. Hou.

persuade. Koi, mali.

pessimist. Kūlana hoihoi 'ole.

pet. 1. *Favorite.* Punahele, milimili. 2. *To caress.* Hamoha-
mo.

petal. Lihilihi.

petition. Palapala noi, palapala
ho'opi'i.

petrel. 'Ua'u, 'ou, 'ou'ou, 'akē-
'akē, lupe'akeke.

petroglyph. Ki'i pōhaku.
petticoat. Palekoki.
pharmacy. Hale kū'ai lā'au.
Philippines. 'Āina Pilipino.
phonograph. Pahu 'ōlelo, pono-
karapa. *Phonograph record,*
pā, pā ho'okani.
photograph. Ki'i. *To photograph,* pa'i ki'i.
physical. Kino, pilikino.
physician. Kauka, kauka lapa-
'au, kahuna lapa'au.
piano. Piano.
pick. 'Ohi, 'ako (*gather*); wae,
koho (*select*).
pickaxe. Kipikua.
pickle. Pīkala.
picnic. Pikiniki.
picture. Ki'i.
pidgin English. 'Ōlelo pa'i 'ai,
namu pa'i 'ai.
pie. Pai. *Apple pie,* pai 'āpala.
piece. 'Āpana, paukū, māmala,
māhele, poke.
pieces. Okaoka (*small, as
broken glass*); 'āpa'apana
(*larger*); momoku (*severed
objects*); māhele.
pier. Uwapo, uapo.
pierce. 'Ō, hou, pahu, 'ō'ō.
pig. Pua'a.
pigeon. Nūnū, manukū.
pile. Ahu, pu'u, āhua.
pill. Huaale.
pillow. Uluna, 'aki, 'ope'ope.
pilot. Pailaka.
pimple. Pu'u. *Pimples,* huehue.
Pimpled, hāpu'upu'u, kukuku,
pu'upu'u.
pin. Kui, pine, mākia, hākia,
kākia, 'ō. *Safety pin,* pine
kaiapa.
pinch. 'Iniki, 'ūmi'i, 'ini'iniki.
pineapple. Hala-kahiki, hala-'ai.
Pineapple cannery, hale hana
hala-kahiki.
pine tree. Lā'au paina, paina.
pink. *Color.* 'Ākala.
pinkeye. Maka 'ula'ula.
pint. Paina.
pipe. 'Ohe, paipu. *Tobacco pipe,*
ipu paka. *Water pipe,* hā wai,
'ohe-wai.

Piper methysticum. *See* kava.
pistol. Pū, pūpanapana.
pit. Lua.
pitch. 1. *Throw.* Nou, ho'olei.
2. *Motion of a vessel.* Luli,
kulana. 3. *Resin.* Hū lā'au,
kēpau. 4. *Music.* Kī, ki'ina o
ka leo, kani.
pitcher. 1. *Vessel.* Pika, kī'aha,
kī'aha 'o'oma. 2. *Thrower.*
Nou, mea nou.
pity. Aloha, aloha menemene,
mokuāhua.
place. 1. *Locality.* Wahi, kāhi,
kaha, kauwahi. 2. *To put.*
Kau.
plain. 1. *Level land.* 'Āina pālahalaha, kula, 'āina pāpū. 2.
Clear. Moakaaka. 3. *Simple.*
'A'ohe i ho'onani 'ia (*un-
adorned*); u'i 'ole (*not beautiful*).
plait. Ulana.
plan. Ho'olālā, kālai, ana. *To
draw plans,* kaha ki'i.
planet. Hōkū hele, hōkū 'ae'a,
hōkū lewa.
plant. Lā'au, mea ulu, lau nahele. *To plant,* kanu.
plantain. Mai'a.
plantation. Mahi, māla, māla
'ai. *Sugar plantation,* mahi
kō.
plaster. Puna, hamo puna.
plastic. *Malleable.* 'Ūlina.
plate. Pā. *Paper plate,* pā pepa.
platform. Kahua, haka, paepae.
platter. Pā pālahalaha.
play. 1. *Recreation.* Pā'ani. 2.
Play music. Ho'okani, ho'o-
kani pila. 3. *Drama.* Hana
keaka.
playful. Piha 'eu.
playground. Kahua, kahua pā-
'ani.
playing cards. Pepa, pepa pā-
'ani, pepa hahau.
playmate. Hoa pā'ani.
pleasant. 'Olu'olu, wai'olu.
please. Hō'olu, hō'olu'olu, ho-
'ole'a, ho'ohoihoi; 'olu'olu
(*command*). *Please come,* e
'olu'olu 'oe, e hele mai.

pleasing. Hia'ai, le'a, wai'olu.

pleasure. Le'ale'a, 'oli'oli, hoihoi.

Pleiades. Makali'i, Nā-huihui.

plenty. Lawa pono, nui, lako.

pliers. 'Ūpā 'ūmi'i.

plot. 1. *Conspiracy.* Kipi, 'ōhumu, 'ōhumu kipi. 2. *Plot of story.* Kahua o ka mo'olelo.

plover. Kōlea.

plow. 'Ō'ō hao, 'ō'ō palau, 'ō'ō hou, palau.

pluck. Unuunu (*as fowl*), 'ako (*as flowers*).

plug. Pani, 'umoki.

plumber. Palama.

plumeria. Melia.

plump. Pu'ipu'i, nepunepu.

plunder. Waiwai pio, waiwai hao. *To plunder,* hao, pōwā.

plunge. Lu'u.

plural. Helu nui.

plus. A me.

P.M. 'Auinalā (*afternoon*); ahiahi (*evening*); pō (*night*).

pneumonia. Numonia.

pocket. Pākeke, pa'eke, 'eke-'eke, 'eke.

poem. Mele.

poet. Haku mele.

poi. Poi, 'ai.

poinciana. 'Ōhai-'ula.

point. Kiko (*dot*); lae (*of land*); wēlau, 'ēlau, welelau (*tip*); maka, 'oi'oina.

poison. Lā'au make.

poke. 'Ō'ō, hou, 'o'e.

poker. 1. *Implement.* Ulu ahi, 'ō'ōahi. 2. *Card game.* Konoki.

pole. Pou, lā'au.

police. Māka'i. *Chief of police,* luna māka'i.

policy. 1. *Plan.* Mana'o ho'okō, kahua, papa hana. 2. *Document.* Palapala.

polish. 'Ānai, ho'ohinuhinu.

polite. 'Olu'olu, waipahē, waipehē.

politician. Loea kālai'āina.

politics. Kālai'āina, polokika.

pollute. Ho'ohaumia, ho'opaumā'ele, ho'opelapela.

Polynesia. Polenekia.

pond. Loko. *Freshwater pond,* loko wai.

pony. Pone, lio 'u'uku.

pool. 1. *Pond.* Ki'o wai. 2. *The game.* Pahupahu.

poor. 1. *Impoverished.* 'Ilihune. 2. *Quality.* 'Ino'ino, pono 'ole.

popcorn. Kūlina pohāpohā.

pope. Pope.

popular. Makemake nui 'ia, nui nā makamaka.

population. Heluna kānaka, po'e, lehulehu, kānaka.

porch. Lānai.

pork. Pua'a, 'i'o pua'a.

porpoise. Nai'a.

port. Awa.

porter. Hali ukana, kanaka hali ukana.

portion. 'Āpana, māhele, kuleana, ha'awina.

Portuguese. Pukikī.

Portuguese man-of-war. Pa'imalau.

position. Kūlana.

possible. Hiki.

post. 1. *Pole.* Pou, kia. 2. *To deposit.* Ho'oūna; ho'okomo (*as mail*); kū (*as a bond*). 3. *Military.* See fort.

postage. Uku leka. *Postage stamp,* po'oleka.

postcard. Pepa po'oleka.

postman. Lawe leka.

postmaster. Luna leka.

post office. Hale leka.

postpone. Ho'opane'e.

pot. Ipu.

potato. 'Uala-kahiki (*Irish*). *See sweet potato.*

poultry. Nā manu 'ai 'ia e like me ka moa.

pound. 1. *With hammer.* Ku'i. 2. *Unit of weight or currency.* Paona.

pounder. Mea ku'i. *Poi pounder,* pōhaku ku'i 'ai.

pour. Ninini.

powder. Pauka, paoka, pouka, paula.

power. Mana, lima ikaika.

practice. 1. *Train.* Ho'oma-
'ama'a. 2. *See* procedure.

praise. Mahalo, ho'omaika'i,
ho'onani.

pray, prayer. Pule.

preach. Ha'i'ōlelo, ha'i 'euanelio.

preacher. Kahuna pule, kahu.

precaution. Hana ho'omākaukau mamua o ka pōpilikia.

precede. Hele mamua.

precious. Makamae, hiwahiwa.

precise. Kūlike loa.

predict. Wānana.

pregnant. Hāpai.

prejudice. Mana'o kū'ē, ho-
'okae.

premature. 'Ē, mamua o ka wā
kūpono.

preparation. Mākaukau, ho-
'omākaukau 'ana.

prescription. Kuhikuhi.

present. 1. *Now.* 'Ānō, kēia
manawa. 2. *At hand.* Ma-
'ane'i; eia (*as response to
roll call*). 3. *Gift.* Makana.
4. *To present.* Hā'awi, waiho.

president. Pelekikena.

press. 1. *Exert pressure.* Kaomi; 'aiana (*as clothes*). 2.
Printing press. Pa'i palapala,
papa pa'i.

pretend. Ho'omeamea, ho'oko-
hukohu, ho'okamani.

pretty. 1. *Attractive.* Nani, maika'i, u'i, nohea. 2. *Some-
what.* 'Ano.

prevent. Kāohi, pale, ke'ake'a.

previous. Mua, mamua a'e.

price. Kumu kū'ai, kālā.

pride. Ha'aheo.

priest. Kahuna.

prime minister. Kuhina nui.

prince. Keiki ali'i, kamāli'i
kāne.

princess. Kamāli'i wahine.

principal. 1. *Main, head.* Nui,
mua, po'o. *School principal,*
po'o kumu. 2. *Capital sum.*
Kumupa'a.

print. Pa'i, kākau, kākau kaha.

print shop. Hale pa'i.

prison. Hale pa'ahao.

private. Pilikino, pono'ī.

prize. Makana, uku.

prized. Makamae.

probably. Paha, pēlā paha,
malia.

problem. Pilikia, hihia.

procedure. Hana 'ana, lawelawe 'ana.

proceed. Hele mua, holo mua.

procession. Huaka'i, ka'i huaka'i.

proclaim. kūkala.

profession. 'Oihana.

professor. Polopeka.

profit. Loa'a, puka, waiwai ho-
'opuka.

profound. Hohonu, kūli'u.

program. Papa kuhikuhi.

progress. Holomua, holo i mua.

prohibit. Pāpā, ho'okapu.

project. *Plan.* Papa hana.

prominent. 'Oi, ki'eki'e.

promise. 'Ōlelo-pa'a, 'ōlelo-ho-
'ohiki.

promote. Ho'opi'i.

prompt. Hikiwawe.

pronounce. Ho'opuka.

pronunciation. Hopuna, hopuna'ōlelo.

proof. Hō'oiā'i'o.

proofread. Heluhelu ho'oponopono.

propaganda. Ho'olaha mana'o.

proper. Kūpono, kū, pono.

property. Waiwai, pono, kuleana.

prophecy. Wānana.

prophet. Kāula, makāula.

propose. Ho'olale, noi.

prosecute. Ho'opi'i.

prostitute. Wahine ho'okamakama, wahine laikini.

protect. Ho'omalu, ho'omāmalu,
ho'omaluhia.

protest. Kū'ē, ho'ohalahala.

Protestant. Hō'olepope.

proud. Ho'okano, ha'aheo, ha-
'akei.

prove. Hō'oiā'i'o.

proverb. 'Ōlelo no'eau 'ōlelo
akamai.

provide. Ho'olako, ho'onoho.

provoke. Ho'oukiuki, ho'onā-ukiuki, ho'ohae.
prune. Puluna.
Psalm. Halelū.
public. Lehulehu, ākea.
publicity. Ho'olaha, ho'olaulaha.
publish. Pa'i, ho'olaha.
pudding. Pūkini.
puddle. Ki'o wai.
Puerto Rican. Pokoliko.
pull. Huki.
pulse. Pana.
pumice. 'Ana, 'ana ōla'i.
pump. Pauma.
pumpkin. Pala'ai, ipu-pū.
punch. 1. *Strike.* Ku'i. **2.** *Beverage.* Meainu ho'ohuihui, wai hua'ai.

punctuation. Kiko.
puncture. Puka.
punish. Ho'opa'i.
pupil. 1. *Scholar.* Haumāna. **2.** *Of eye.* 'Ōnohi maka.
purchase. Mea kū'ai. *To purchase,* kū'ai.
pure. Ma'ema'e.
purify. Ho'oma'ema'e.
purple. Poni, māku'e.
purpose. Kumu.
purse. 'Eke'eke, 'eke'eke pa'a lima.
push. Pahu. *Push along,* ne'e, pane'e.
put. Kau, waiho.
puzzled. Kāhāhā, kūnānā, ha-'oha'o.

Q

q. *No Hawaiian term.*
quail. Manu-kapalulu.
quake. Ha'alulu, naue. *See* earthquake.
qualified. Mākaukau, kūpono.
quality. 'Ano, kūlana.
quantity. Nui.
quarantine. Ho'omalu ma'i.
quarrel. Ho'opa'apa'a, paio.
quarry. Lua 'eli pōhaku.
quart. Kuaka.
quarter. Hapahā.
queen. Mō'ī wahine, ali'i wahine, kuini.
queer. 'Ano 'ē.
question. Nīnau, ui.
question mark. Kiko nīnau.

questionnaire. Palapala nina-ninau, mea ho'opihapiha, pa'i hakahaka.
quick. 'Āwīwī, koke, māmā, wiki, wikiwiki, wawe, hiki-wawe, 'eleu, 'emo 'ole, ala-wiki.
quiet. Mālie, ho'omālie, hilu, wailana, malu, maluhia, ho-'omalu, ho'ola'i, la'i. *Be quiet!* Kulikuli! Hāmau *(polite)*!
quilt. Kapa kuiki.
quit. Ha'alele, waiho.
quite. 'Ano, wale, nō.
quiz. Hō'ike pōkole.
quota. Māhele.

R

r. *No Hawaiian term.*
rabbit. Lāpaki, 'iole lāpaki.
race. 1. *People.* Lāhui. **2.** *Contest.* Heihei.
race prejudice. Ho'okae 'ili.
radiant. Mālamalama, 'ālohi-lohi, 'ōlinolino.
radio. Radio.
radio broadcast. Ho'olele leo.

rafter. Kua, o'a.
rag. Welu.
rage. Huhū loa, pi'i ka huhū wela loa, inaina.
raid. Pākaha.
railing. Pale.
railroad. Ala hao, ka'aahi.
rain. Ua.
rainbow. Ānuenue.

raincoat. Kukaua, kukaweke, kuka'aila.

raindrops. Paka ua.

raise. 1. *Lift.* Hāpai, pai. 2. *Bring up a child.* Hānai, luhi.

raisin. Huawaina malo'o.

rake. Kope, 'ō'ō kope.

ram. 1. *Sheep.* Hipa kāne. 2. *Shove.* Hou, pahu.

ramble. 'Auana, 'ae'a.

ranch. Wahi hānai holoholona.

rancher. Kahu pipi (*cattle*).

rank. Kūlana, papa.

ransom. Ho'ōla pāna'i, uku pāna'i, kū'ai ho'ōla.

rape. Pu'e, pu'e wale.

rare. 1. *Infrequent.* Kaka'ikahi. 2. *Underdone.* Mo'a iki, mo'a kolekole (*as of meats*).

rascal. Kolohe, kupu'eu, 'āpiki.

rash. 1. *Bold.* 'A'a makehewa. 2. *Of skin.* 'Ōhune.

raspberry. 'Ākala, kala.

rat. 'Iole.

rather. 1. *Somewhat.* 'Ano. 2. *Prefer.* 'Oi aku ka makemake.

ration. Hā'awi kaupalena, kaupalena ō.

rattle. Ko'ele, nakeke.

rattles. Pū'ili (*bamboo*); 'ulī'ulī (*gourd*).

ravine. Kahawai, awaawa, awāwa.

raw. Maka, makamaka; kolekole (*as meat or a wound*).

ray. 1. *As of the sun, or spoke.* Kukuna, wana. 2. *Fish* Hīhīmanu, hailepo, hāhālua. *See* sting ray.

razor. Pahi 'umi'umi.

reach. *Arrive at.* Hiki, kū, loa'a.

read. Heluhelu.

ready. Mākaukau.

real. Maoli, 'oiā'i'o, pono'ī.

real estate. Waiwai pa'a.

realize. Ho'omaopopo.

really. 'Ā 'oia, oia, 'i'o.

rear. 1. *Back.* Hope. 2. *Raise, as a child.* Hānai. 3. *As a horse.* 'Owala.

reason. Kumu, mea, kuleana.

reasonable. 1. *Sensible.* Kau- like ka no'ono'o. 2. *Not expensive.* Makepono.

rebel. Kipi.

recede. Emi, ho'i i hope.

receipt. Palapala ho'oka'a.

receive. Loa'a mai.

recent. Hou.

receptacle. Waihona.

reception. Kipa 'ana.

receptionist. Mea ho'okipa.

recess. Ho'omalolo.

recipe. Lula no ke kuke 'ana.

recite. Ha'i walewaha mai.

reckless. Nānā 'ole i ka pono, ho'oponopono 'ole.

recline. Kāmoe, momoe.

recognize. Ho'omaopopo, 'ike.

recommendation. Kāko'o (*support*).

record. 1. *Account.* Mo'olelo. 2. *Phonograph.* Pā, pā ho'okani.

recorder. Mīkini 'apo leo, kākau mo'olelo, kākau hana.

recover. Ola, ola hou, ola loa.

recreation. Mea ho'onanea, mea le'ale'a. *Board of Parks and Recreation.* papa o nā pāka a me nā hana ho'onanea.

rectum. 'Ōkole, 'amo, 'amo hulu.

red. 'Ula, 'ula'ula, wena. **Red Cross.** Hui Ke'a 'Ula'ula, Ke'a 'Ula'ula.

redeem. Uku pāna'i.

red-eyed. Mākole.

red-hot. 'Ena, 'ena'ena.

red snapper. 'Ula'ula, ko'i.

reduce. Ho'ēmi, ho'o'u'uku.

reef. Kohola.

reel. 1. *Whirl.* Kunewa, newa, kāhulihuli. 2. *Spool.* Pōka'a; mīkini ho'owili lawai'a (*fishing*).

refer. Pili, waiho.

referee. 'Uao.

reflection. Aka, wai aka, no'ono'o.

reform. Ho'opololei, ho'ohuli.

refrain. 1. *Abstain.* Ho'ōki. 2. *Song.* Puana.

refreshment. Mea'ai māmā.

refrigerator. Pahu hau.

refuge. Pu'uhonua.

refund. Uku pāna'i.

refuse. 1. *Deny.* Hō'ole, kē. **2.** *See* rubbish.

regain. Loa'a hou.

regal. Ali'i, ho'āli'i, lani, 'ihi-'ihi.

regards. Aloha, mahalo.

register. Kākau ho'opa'a, kākau inoa, papa inoa.

regret. Mihi.

regular. Ma'amau.

regulation. Lula, kānāwai.

rehearsal. Ho'oma'ama'a.

reign. Noho ali'i, noho aupuni, noho, 'ai, kū, ho'omalu.

reins. Kaula waha, laina kaula waha, 'ili.

reject. Hō'ole, ha'alele.

rejoice. 'Oli, hau'oli, 'oli'oli.

related. Pili 'ohana.

relationship. Pili, pilina, pili-kana.

relative. 'Ohana, pili koko.

relax. Ku'u aku, ho'onanea, lu-ana.

release. Kala, ku'u, ho'oku'u.

relief. Kōkua.

religion. Ho'omana.

religious. Haipule.

relish. Pūpū, mea hō'ono'ono. *To relish,* 'ono.

rely. Paulele, hilina'i.

remain. Koe, noho loa, waiho.

remarkable. Kamaha'o, kupai-anaha, kupanaha.

remedy. Lā'au (*medicine*).

remember. Ho'omana'o, ho-'omaopopo.

remnant. Koena.

remind. Ho'omana'o mai, ho-'omaopopo, ho'āla mana'o.

remote. Mamao.

remove. Lawe i kahi 'ē, lawe aku, kāpae.

renew. Hana hou, ho'omau hou, ho'omaka hou.

rent. Ho'olimalima.

reorganize. Ho'onohonoho hou, ho'oponopono hou.

repair. Pāhonohono, kāpili, hana hou.

repeat. 'Ōlelo hou, hana hou.

repent. Mihi.

replace. Pani, pani hakahaka.

report. Hō'ike, palapala hō'ike; lono (*news*).

reporter. Kākau nūpepa, 'aha-'ilono.

representative. Lunamaka'āina-na.

reptile. Mo'o, naheka.

republic. Aupuni pelekikena, lepupalika.

Republican. Lepupalika, Repu-balika.

reputation. Kūlana.

request. Noi, nonoi.

requirement. Koi.

rescue. Ho'opakele, ho'opale-kana.

research. 'Imi i ke kumu; huli puke (*literary*).

resemble. Kohu like, kohu, like, kū, kūlike, ho'ohālikelike.

resent. Ukiuki, mauhala.

reserve. Ho'oka'awale, ho'opa'a, mālama.

reservoir. Luawai, luawai ho-'oki'o.

residence. Hale noho, kāhi noho, nohona.

resign. Ha'alele, waiho.

resist. Kū'ē, pale, kipi, 'alo, hō'o'ole'a.

resolution. 'Ōlelo ho'oholo.

resources. Kumu waiwai.

respect. Mahalo, 'ihi, hō'ihi.

respectfully. Me ka mahalo, me ka pono.

responsibility. Kuleana, kuleana hana, ko'iko'i.

rest. 1. *Stop work.* Maha, ho-'omaha, mahana. **2.** *Placed on.* Kau. **3.** *Remainder.* Koe, koena.

restaurant. Hale 'aina.

resting place. O'io'ina, pu'uho-'omaha, moena.

restless. Pīhole, hī'ō, ulukū.

restrain. Kāohi.

rest room. Lumi ho'omaha.

result. Hopena, hope, hua.

resurrection. Ola hou, ala hou, kū hou 'ana.

retail. Kūʻai liʻiliʻi.

retarded. Lohi, lohiʻau.

retire. Hoʻomaha loa.

retreat. Neʻehope, hoʻi hope, kuemi.

return. Hoʻi hou, hoʻihoʻi.

reveal. Hōʻike, hōʻike ā maka.

Revelations. Hōʻike ʻAna (Biblical).

revenge. Hoʻopaʻi, pānaʻi, hoʻopānaʻi, uku.

reverend. Kahu.

reverent. Hāipule, manaʻo haipule, manaʻo hoʻoʻihiʻihi.

reverse. Huli, lole, hoʻi i hope.

review. Hoʻomaʻamaʻa hou.

revise. Hoʻoponopono hou, hoʻololi hou.

revive. Ola hou, hoʻōla hou, hoʻāla hou, hoʻūlu hou.

revolt. Kipi, hoʻokipi.

revolting. Hoʻopailua, liliha.

revolution. Hōʻauhuli ʻana, kipi ʻana.

revolve. Kaʻa, kaʻapuni, kakaʻa.

revolver. Pū panapana.

reward. Makana, uku, uku pānaʻi.

rheumatism. Lumakika.

rhythm. Pana o ka mele, pā.

rib. Iwi ʻaoʻao (human); nīʻau (of coconut leaf or umbrella).

ribbon. Lipine. Typewriter ribbon, lipine kikokiko.

rice. Laiki.

rich. 1. Wealthy. Waiwai, lako, kūʻonoʻono. **2.** Of food. Liliha, momona, kelekele.

rid. Hoʻokaʻawale aku, kipaku, hoʻopau.

riddle. Nane, ʻōlelo nane, nane huna.

ride. Holo, holoholo, kau.

rider. Holo lio, kau lio (horseback).

ridge. Kualapa, kualono, lapa.

ridgepole. Kaupoku, kauhuhu.

ridicule. Hoʻohenehene, henehene, hoʻowahāwahā, pāhenehene, hōʻakaʻaka.

ridiculous. Kohu ʻole, kū i ka pāhenehene.

rifle. Pū laipala, pū laipela.

right. 1. Direction, ʻĀkau. **2.** Correct. Pololei, pono, hoʻoponopono. **3.** Privilege. Kuleana.

righteous. Pono.

rim. Lihi, nihi, kaʻe, huʻa.

rind. ʻIli, ʻaluʻalu.

ring. 1. Jewelry. Komo, apo. **2.** Circle. Pōʻai, pōʻaha, lina. **3.** To sound. Kani, hoʻokani, kakani.

rinse. Mūmū (mouth); kaka (fish, clothing).

riot. Haunāele, anaina hoʻohaunāele.

rip. Nahae, nohae.

ripe. Pala.

ripple. ʻAle, ʻaleʻale, holu, lapalapa.

rise. 1. To rise up. Ala, piʻi, aea, ea, kau, hoʻāla. **2.** An incline. Piʻina, alana, kiʻekiʻena.

risk. Makaʻu, ʻaʻa, hoʻāʻo me ka nānā ʻole.

ritual. See ceremony.

rival. Hoa paio, hoa pāonioni.

river. Kahawai, muliwai, wai.

roach. ʻElelū.

road. Ala, alanui, ala hele.

roar. Wawā, wā, hoʻowā, uwō, halulu, nākolokolo.

roast. ʻOma, loke, ʻōhinu.

rob. ʻAihue, pōwā.

robe. ʻAʻahu, lole hoʻoluʻeluʻe.

rock. 1. Stone. Pōhaku, ʻā, ʻalā. **2.** Motion. Kulana, hoʻoluli, naue, hoʻonaue, kāhulihuli, paipai.

rocket. Kao lele.

rocking chair. Noho paipai.

rocky. Nui ka pōhaku, pōhaku.

roll. 1. Turn. Kakaʻa, kaʻa. **2.** Bundle. Lola, ʻōwili, ʻapā, pōkaʻa. **3.** Bread. Palaoa liʻiliʻi.

roll call. Hea inoa.

Roman Catholic. Kakōlika Loma.

romance. 1. Novel. Kaʻao. **2.** Love affair. Pili hoʻoipoipo.

roof. Kaupoku, kaupaku.

roofing. Pili.

room. 1. Part of a house. Lumi, keʻena. **2.** Space. Hakahaka.

roommate. Hoa lumi.

rooster. Moa kāne.

root. 1. *Of plant.* A'a, mole, weli. **2.** *Source.* Kumu, mole. **3.** *Dig.* 'Eku, naku, haunaku, peu.

rope. Kaula.

rosary. Lōkālio, kolona, lei kolona.

rose. Loke, loke-lani; roselani (*a red rose*).

rotate. Ka'apuni, ka'a, pōniu.

rotten. Pilau, palahū, 'ino'ino, palahō, popopo.

rough. 1. *As terrain.* Ho'olua, 'ālualua, mālualua, lualua. **2.** *As cloth or skin.* 'Ōkala, kala, kākala, pākala. **3.** *As sea or wind.* Pikipiki'ō, 'ālo'alo'a, lo-'alo'a. **4.** *Manner.* 'Ōkalakala, kākala, kalakala.

round. Poepoe, popohe, kūpoepoe.

roundabout. Ho'olalau, lauwili.

roundup. Ho'ohuli pipi, ho'ā pipi.

route. Ala hele.

row. 1. *Paddle.* Hoe. **2.** *Line.* Pae, lālani, laina.

rowboat. Wa'apā.

royal. Ali'i, lani.

rub. 1. *Friction.* 'Ānai, kuai kuolo, hoana. **2.** *Massage.* Lomi, kōmi, kaomi.

rubber. Laholio.

rubbish. 'Ōpala.

rudder. Hoe uli.

rudderfish. Nenue.

rude. Kiko'olā.

rug. *See* **carpet.**

ruin. 'Ino'ino, pilikia, hō'ino, mā'ino'ino.

rule. 1. *A regulation.* Lula, loina, kānāwai. **2.** *To govern.* Noho ali'i, kū, 'ai, noho aupuni.

ruler. 1. *Leader.* Ali'i. **2.** *Measuring stick.* Lula.

rum. Lama, rama.

rumble. Halalū, nāku'i, nākolo, kamumu, kani.

rumor. Lono wale.

run. 1. *Move swiftly.* Holo, hoholo, ho'oholo, ka'aholo. **2.** *Manage.* Ho'oholo, ka'a.

runner. 1. *Messenger.* Kūkini. **2.** *Of a vine.* 'Awe'awe, hā-'awe'awe; kāili, kālī (*sweet potato*).

rupture. Pu'ulele, laho he'e.

rural. Kua'āina.

rush. Holo 'ino, holo 'āwīwī, lele'ino, auau, pūlale.

Russia. Lukia, Rusia.

rust. Kūkaehao, lepohao.

rustic. Kua'āina.

rye. Lai, rai.

S

s. *No Hawaiian term.*

-s. *The plural is shown in Hawaiian by the particles* nā *and* mau *before nouns, or by the zero-class possessives.*

-'s. *Same as* **of.**

Sabbath. Kāpaki, Sabati.

sack. 'Eke, 'eke'eke.

sacrament. Kakelema, kakelemeneka (*Catholic*); kino o ka Haku (*other churches*).

sacred. Kapu, la'a, ano, 'ihi.

sacrifice. Mōhai, kaumaha, hai.

sad. Kaumaha, lu'ulu'u.

safe. 1. *Not in danger.* Palekana, malu. **2.** *Depository.* Pahu hao, pahu kālā.

sail. 1. *Verb.* Holo, ho'oholo, kele, ho'okele, holomoku. **2.** *Noun.* Lā, pe'a.

sailfish. A'u.

sailing vessel. Moku pe'a.

sailor. Kelamoku, kela, holomoku, luina, 'aukai.

saint. Kaneka, Saneta, Kana.

salad. Lau 'ai 'ia.

salary. Uku hana.

sale. Kūʻai aku, kūʻai hoʻolilo, kūʻai hoʻēmi.

salesman. Kanaka kūʻai aku, kālepa.

saliva. Kuha, hāʻae, ʻae, wale wai.

salmon. Kāmano.

salt. Paʻakai. *To salt*, kāpī, kōpī, hoʻomiko. *Ocherous earth used to color and flavor salt*, ʻalaea. *Salt thus treated*, paʻakai ʻulaʻula.

salutation. Aloha, welina, weli, ʻanoʻai.

salvation. Ola, ola mau loa.

Salvation Army. Pūʻali Hoʻōla.

same. Like, like pū, kohu like, hoʻokahi. *Same as ever*, ʻoia mau nō. *The same father*, hoʻokahi nō makua kāne.

Samoa. Kāmoa.

sanctuary. Wahi hoʻāno.

sand. One.

sandal. Kāmaʻa hāwele, kāmaʻa hakahaka, pale wāwae.

sandalwood. ʻIliahi.

sandbar. Puʻeone.

sand crab. ʻOhiki.

sandpaper. Pepa kalakala.

sandpiper. Upupā, ʻuliuli.

sandwich. Nā palaoa me nā mea hōʻonoʻono i waena.

sandy. Oneone.

San Francisco. Kapalakiko.

sap. Kohu, wai, wale, wale hau, wai lāʻau.

sarcastic. Kikoʻolā, pākīkē.

sardine. Makalē.

sarong. Pāʻū, kīkepa.

sash. Kāʻai, kāʻei.

Satan. Kākana, Satana.

satin. Pāhoehoe.

satisfactory. Pono, kūpono.

Saturday. Pōʻaono.

sauce. Kai.

saucepan. Pā hoʻolapalapa, ipu hao.

saucer. Pā liʻiliʻi.

sausage. Naʻaukake.

savage. Hihiu loa, mākaha.

save. 1. *As a life*. Ola, hoʻōla, hoʻopakele. *God save the king*,

ola ka mōʻī i ke Akua. 2. *Keep*. Mālama, pūlama, hoʻoili.

saving. *Thrifty*. Makauliʻi, minamina.

savings bank. Panakō hoʻāhu.

savior. Hoʻōla, palekana.

saw. 1. *Tool*. Pahi olo, olo. 2. *Same as* see. *I saw*, ua ʻike au.

say. ʻŌlelo, haʻi, ʻī, wahi a, pēlā, mea mai.

saying. ʻŌlelo noʻeau.

Scaevola sp. Naupaka.

scale. 1. *Measure*. Alapiʻi. 2. *Fish*. Unahi. *To scale*, unaunahi.

scales. *Balance*. Kau paona, paona, ana paona.

scalp. ʻIli poʻo. *To scalp*, lole.

scandal. Hana i wā ʻia.

scar. ʻĀlina, linalina.

scarce. Kakaʻikahi, pānoanoa.

scarf. Lei ʻāʻī.

scarlet fever. Pīwa ʻulaʻula.

scatter. Hoʻopuehu, lū, lūlū.

sceptical. Hilinaʻi ʻole, hoʻomahuakala.

schedule. Papa kuhikuhi, papa hōʻike.

scholarship. 1. *Pursuit of knowledge*. Hana ʻimi naʻauao. 2. *Student aid*. Waihona kōkua hoʻonaʻauao.

school. 1. *Educational*. Kula. 2. *Of fish*. Iʻa kū, kū.

schoolhouse. Hale kula.

schooner. Moku, moku kia lua, kuna.

science. Akeakamai, hana ʻimi naʻauao, huli kanaka.

scissors. ʻŪpā.

scold. Nuku, keʻu, hoʻokekē niho, huhū.

scorch. Kuni, pāpaʻa wela, eina, pāwela.

score. Helu, ʻai.

scorpion. Moʻo-niho-ʻawa.

Scotch. Kekokia.

scoundrel. Lapuwale, puʻuwai ʻeleʻele.

scour. Kuai, ʻānai, kuolo.

scowl. Hoʻokuʻekuʻemaka.

scramble. Ho'ohuikau. *Scrambled eggs,* hua kai, hua pākā.

scrap. Huna, hakina, hunahuna, 'āpana li'ili'i.

scrape. Wa'u, wawa'u, wa'uwa'u, koe, kūai, kahi.

scratch. Walu, wawalu; helu (*as a hen*).

scream. 'Alalā, pū'alalā.

screen. Pākū, pālulu, ālai, ānai.

screw. Kui nao.

screwdriver. Kui kala, kala.

Scriptures. Palapala Hemolele.

scrotum. Laho.

scum. Hu'a, hu'ahu'a.

sea. Kai, moana.

sea area. Kai.

seacoast. Kahakai.

sea cucumber. Loli.

sea gull. Nēnē-'au-kai.

seal. 1. *Emblem.* Kila. 2. *Mammal.* 'Īlio-holo-i-kauaua.

seam. Ku'ina, ku'i, humu, humuna.

search. 'Imi, huli, 'imina, hulina.

seashell. Pūpū.

seashore. Kahakai, kapa kai.

seasick. Poluea, luea, ho'opapailua, 'ōlanalana.

season. 1. *Time.* Kau, wā, manawa. 2. *Impart taste.* Hō'ono, ho'omiko.

seat. Noho, nohona, ho'onoho.

sea urchin. Wana, 'ina, hā'uke.

seaward. Makai, i kai, o kai.

seaweed. Limu. *Kinds:* kala, kohu, līpoa, 'a'ala-'ula, 'ele-'ele, līpe'e, līpe'epe'e, manauea, līpa'akai, pakele-a-wa'a.

second. Lua, kualua; kekona (*time unit*).

secret. Mea huna, huna malū.

secretary. 1. *Clerical aid.* Kākau 'ōlelo. 2. *High official.* Kuhina.

secretary of interior. Kuhina kalai'āina.

secretary of state. Kuhina moku'āina.

secret service. 'Oihana kiu.

section. Paukū, moku, mokuna, 'āpana, māhele.

secure. Pa'a.

seduce. Ho'owalewale hewa, alaka'i hewa, pu'e.

see. 'Ike, nānā.

seed. 'Ano'ano, hua.

seek. 'Imi, huli.

seen. 'Ike 'ia, kūmaka.

seer. Kāula, kilo, kuhikuhipu'uone, nānā ao, 'imi loa.

segregate. Ho'oka'awale.

seine. Hukilau, lau, 'upena kō lau.

seize. Hopu, 'apo, lālau, kā'ili.

seldom. Kaka'ikahi.

select. Koho, wae, 'ohi.

self. Iho, kino, pono'ī, 'ōiwi.

selfish. 'Au'a, no'ono'o iāia wale iho nō.

sell. Kū'ai aku, kālepa, ho'olilo.

semen. Keakea.

semester. Kau.

senate. 'Aha kenekoa.

senator. Kenekoa.

send. Ho'oūna, kēnā, ki'i, kauoha.

senior. Mua, makua, hele mua, hānau mua.

sennit. 'Aha.

sense. 1. *Faculty.* 'Ike. *Sense of taste,* 'ike i ka 'ono. 2. *Meaning.* Mana'o nui.

sensitive. 1. *Perceptive.* 'Ike ho'omaopopo. 2. *As to criticism.* 'Eha wale, ku'ia wale.

sensitive plant. Pua-hilahila.

sentence. Māmala'ōlelo (*words*), 'ōlelo ho'opa'i (*penalty*).

separate. 1. *Adjective.* Ka'awale, kau 'oko'a. 2. *Verb.* Ho'oka'awale.

September. Kepakemapa.

sergeant. Kakiana.

series. Māhele, mo'o.

serious. Kūo'o.

sermon. Ha'i'ōlelo, ha'i a'o.

servant. Kanaka hana, kanaka lawelawe, wahine hana.

serve. Lawelawe.

service. Lawelawe. *Church service,* hālāwai haipule. *Military service,* 'oihana koa.

session. Kau.

set. Kau, ho'onoho, ho'omoe, ku'u.

settle. Kau, mākū, ko'ana.

settlement. Kauhale.

seven. Hiku, 'ehiku, 'ahiku.

seventeen. 'Umi kūmāhiku, 'umi kumamāhiku.

Seventh-day Adventist. Ho-'omana Pō'aōno.

seventy. Kanahiku.

seventy-one. Kanahiku kūmā-kahi, kanahiku kumamākahi.

sever. 'Oki, moku.

several. Kekahi, kekahi mau.

severe. 'O'olea, ko'iko'i.

sew. Humuhumu, hono, ku'i.

sewer. 'Auwai, kua, hā wai.

sewing machine. Mīkini humu-humu.

sex. *No Hawaiian term. Masculine sex,* keka kāne. *Feminine sex,* keka wahine.

sexual intercourse. Ai, ei, hana ma'i, moe, pi'i, panipani, aina.

shade. Malu, māmalu.

shadow. Aka, huaka, 'ūmalu.

shady. Malumalu.

shake. Naue, nāueue, lūlū, hō-'oni, ho'oluliluli.

shall. E . . . ana, e.

shallow. Pāpa'u, hāpapa.

shame. Hilahila, waia.

shampoo. Holoi lauoho.

shape. 'Ano, hō'omo'omo.

share. Māhele, pu'u; kea (*stocks*).

shark. Manō, lālākea, niuhi.

sharp. 'Oi, 'āwini, 'oi'oi.

sharpen. Ho'okala.

shatter. Wāwahi, nahā, nāhāhā, kā.

shave. Kahi.

shawl. Kīhei.

she. *Same as* he.

shearwater. 'Ua'u-kani, hō'io.

shed. 1. *Building.* Hale ho'āhu, hale pupupu, hale kāmala. 2. *Throw off.* Helele'i, ho'oma-lule.

sheep. Hipa.

sheet. Lau, papa. *Sheet of paper,* 'āpana pepa. *Bed sheet,* uhi pela, hāli'i moe.

shelf. Haka, haka kau, papa.

shell. Pūpū, iwi.

shelter. Wahi lulu, wahi ho-'omalu, hale pupupu.

shepherd. Kahu hipa.

sheriff. Māka'i nui, ilāmuku.

shield. Pālulu, pale.

shiftless. 'Ae'a.

shin. Lapawāwae.

shine. Hulali, liko, 'ānapanapa, 'ālohi.

ship. Moku.

shipmate. Hoa wa'a, hoa holo-moku.

shipwreck. Ili (*go aground*), nāhāhā (*broken to bits*).

shirt. Pālule, 'ahu.

shiver. Ha'ukeke, naka, hulilī.

shoal. Hāpapa.

shock. Puoho, hikilele, ho'olele hauli, loa'a i ka uila.

shoe. Kāma'a. *Pair of shoes,* pa'a kāma'a.

shoelace. Lī kāma'a.

shoot. 1. *Discharge.* Pana, kī. *Shoot with bow and arrow,* pana pua, pāpua. 2. *Sprout.* Keiki, 'ao, 'ohā.

shooting star. Hōkū-lele.

shop. Hale kū'ai (*store*); hale 'oihana (*workshop*).

shopping. Kū'ai hele, māka'ika'i hale kū'ai.

shore. kahakai, kapa kai, kai, 'ae kai.

short. Pōkole, 'ekeke'i, mū-'ekeke'i.

shorten. Ho'opōkole.

shorthand. Kākau 'ōlelo pōkole.

shorts. Lole wāwae 'ekeke'i.

shot. Pōkā.

shotgun. Pū kī lū.

shot-put. Maika.

should. Pono e, pono ke.

shoulder. Po'ohiwi, hokua.

shoulder blade. Hoehoe, iwi hoehoe.

shout. 'Uwā, ho'ōho, kani ka pihe.

shove. Pahu, kē, hou, kula'i.

shovel. Kopalā.

show. 1. *Demonstrate.* Hō'ike,

kuhikuhi. **2.** *Performance.*
Hana keaka.

shower. Kuaua, ua naulu, naulu,
kualau.

shriek. Pū'alalā, alawī.

shrimp. 'Ōpae.

shrine. Heiau, haiau, ahu, ko'a,
kū'ula.

shrink. Miki, ho'ohāiki.

shudder. Mania, menene, liha,
liliha.

shut. Pani.

shutter. 'Ōlepelepe, 'ope'ape'a.

shy. Hilahila, 'ena.

sick. Ma'i.

sickle. Pahi kākiwi, pahi keke'e.

sickly. 'Ōma'ima'i, ma'ima'i.

side. 'Ao'ao, kūkulu, paia, kapa.

sideburns. 'Umi'umi pēheuheu.

sidewalk. Ala hele wāwae.

sieve. Kānana, kālana.

sigh. Nui ka hanu, nū, nā'ū, 'ū,
'uhū.

sight. Nānaina, maka, hi'ohi-
'ona.

sign. Hō'ailona, 'ōuli; papa hō-
'ike (*as for a store*).

signal. Hō'ailona, pe'ahi.

signature. Kākau inoa, pūlima.

signboard. Papa hō'ike.

silent. Hāmau, leo 'ole.

silk. Kilika, kalika.

silly. Kohu 'ole, 'ūlala.

silver. Kālā ke'oke'o, kālā.

silversword. Hinahina, 'āhinahina, iliau.

similar. Kohu like, 'ano like,
like pū.

simple. Ma'alahi.

sin. Lawehala, hala, hewa.

since. 1. *After.* Mahope mai. **2.**
Because. No ka mea.

sincere. 'Oiā'i'o. *I am, yours
sincerely,* 'o au nō me ka
'oiā'i'o.

sing. Mele, hīmeni, kani.

singer. Pu'ukani, mea mele.

single. 1. *One only.* Ho'okahi,
kahi. **2.** *Unmarried.* Male
'ole.

sink. 1. *Descend.* Palemo, piholo. **2.** *Basin.* Kāhi holoi
pā.

sinker. Kēpau.

sip. Mūkī, mūkīkī.

sir. *No modern word; in old
days as term of address:* e
ku'u haku, e ku'u lani, *O my
lord,* O my royal one. Dear
Sir (*in letters*), aloha 'oe.

Sirius. 'A'ā.

sisal. Malina.

sister. 1. *Sibling.* Kaikua'ana
(*older, of a female*); kaikaina
(*younger, of a female*); kaikuahine (*of a male*); tita
(*slang*). *Terms of address are
frequently* kua'ana, kaina,
kuahine. **2.** *Nun.* Nuna, wilikina.

sister-in-law. Wahine, wahine
makua, wahine 'opio (*of a
male*); kaiko'eke (*of a female*); punalua.

sit. Noho.

site. Kahua, wahi, kūlana.

sitting hula. Hula noho.

situation. Kūlana.

six. Ono, 'eono, 'aōno.

sixteen. 'Umi kūmāono, 'umi
kumamāono.

sixty. Kanaōno.

sixty-one. Kanaōno kūmākahi,
kanaōno kumamākahi.

size. Nui.

skate. Holo pahe'e.

skeleton. Kino iwi, iwi kanaka.

sketch. Ki'i, kaha.

skid. Pahe'e.

skilled. No'eau, loea, mākaukau, akamai, 'ailolo, lolo,
'ōlohe. *Skilled labor,* hana
lima 'ike.

skin. 'Ili.

skip. Lelele, lele.

skipjack. Aku.

skirt. Palekoki.

skull. Iwi po'o, po'o kanaka,
pūniu.

skunk. 'Īlio hohono.

sky. Lani.

slack. 'Alu'alu.

slack key. Kī hō'alu.

slacks. Lole wāwae.

slander. Holoholo'ōlelo, 'aki,
ho'omā'ino'ino.

slang. 'Ōlelo 'eu ho'ohaku wale.

slant. Hiō. *Slant eyes,* maka lilio.

slap. Pa'i, ho'opa'i.

slave. Kauwā.

sled. Hōlua, papa hōlua, ka'a holo hau.

sleep. Moe, hiamoe.

sleepless. Hia'ā, makahia, makalahia.

sleepy. Maka hiamoe.

sleeve. Lima.

slender. Wīwī.

slice. Poke, 'āpana, kaha, pāpa'a.

slide. He'e, pahe'e, holo.

slime. Wale, walewale.

sling. Ma'a.

slip. 1. *Slide.* He'e, pahe'e, pakika, paholo. **2.** *Scion.* Lālā ho'oūlu. **3.** *Garment.* Mu'umu'u.

slipknot. Pikoholo.

slipper. Kāma'a pale wāwae, pale wāwae.

slippery. Pahale, pakika, pakelo.

slope. Ihona, lapa, papali.

slow. Lohi.

sly. Ma'alea.

small. Iki, li'i, li'ili'i, 'uku, 'u-'uku.

smallpox. Ma'i-pu'upu'u-li'ili'i.

smart. 1. *Intelligent.* Akamai. **2.** *Pain.* Lili'u, welawela.

smash. Nahā, ho'onahā, palahē.

smell. *Transitive verb.* Honi, honihoni. *See* **fragrant, stench.**

smile. Mino'aka.

smoke. Uahi. *To smoke tobacco,* puhi paka.

smooth. Malino, pahe'e.

smuggle. Ho'opae malū.

snack. 'Ai māmā, pūpū.

snail. Kama-loli, hīhī-wai, wī, pūpū.

snake. Naheka, nahesa.

snap. 1. *Break.* Ha'i, haki, uhaki, kepa. **2.** *Bite.* 'Aki, hae.

snapper. 'Ula'ula, 'ōpakapaka.

snare. Hei, ahele, pahele, 'ūpiki, hihi.

snarl. 1. *Growl, snap.* Nunulu, nanā, kekē niho. **2.** *Tangle.* Hihia.

snatch. Kā'ili, kā'ili'ili, po'i.

sneeze. Kihe.

snore. Nonō, hohō, 'olā'olā ka ihu.

snow. Hau, hau kea.

so. 1. *Similar.* Penei, pēlā. *That's so,* pēlā nō; 'oiā'i'o kā ho'i. *So do I,* 'o au pū. *Maybe so,* pēlā paha. **2.** *Therefore.* No laila.

soak. Ho'oma'ū, ho'opa'ū.

soap. Kopa; kopa pauka (*powdered soap*), kopa holoi (*wash soap*).

soar. Kīkaha, lele ho'olahalaha, kaulele.

society. 1. *Club.* 'Ahahui, hui, hui malū, kalapu. **2.** *Companionship.* Launa 'ana.

soft. Palupalu, palu, nahe, nahenahe, hone.

soil. 1. *Noun.* Lepo. **2.** *Verb.* Ho'olepo.

soldier. Koa, pū'ali.

solid. Pa'a, pa'apū.

solitary. Mehameha, kakahi.

solution. 1. *Explanation.* Ha'ina, wehewehe 'ana, wehena, loa'a. **2.** *Liquid.* Wai pa'ipa'i.

some. Kekahi, wahi.

someone. Kekahi kanaka. *Someone else,* ha'i.

somersault. Kuwala, 'owala.

something. Kekahi mea.

sometime. Kekahi manawa.

somewhat. 'Ano, 'ō-.

son. Keiki kāne.

song. Mele, hīmeni.

son-in-law. Hūnōna kāne.

soon. Koke, auane'i, koe, eia aku.

soothsayer. Kilo lani, kuhikuhipu'uone, ha'i 'ōuli.

sorcerer. Kahuna, kahuna 'anā'anā, kahuna ho'opi-'opi'o.

sorcery. Hana kahuna, 'anā-'anā, ho'oūnauna, ho'opi-

'opi'o, kuni, hana aloha, kala aloha.

sore. 'Eha.

sorrow. Kaumaha.

sorry. Kaumaha, minamina.

sort. 1. *Kind.* 'Ano. 2. *Select.* Wae, māwae, ho'oka'awale.

soul. 'Uhane.

sound. Leo, kani, pā, papā, wawā, 'uwā, walo, puwō.

soup. Kai, kupa.

sour. 'Awa, 'awa'awa, mala, malaia, mulemule, 'ī'ī.

source. Kumu, mole.

south. Hema.

South America. 'Amelika-hema.

southeast. Hikina hema.

Southern Cross. Hōkū-ke'a, Newa.

south pole. Wēlau-hema.

southwest. Komohana hema.

souvenir. Mea ho'omana'o.

space. Lewa, haka.

spade. 'Ō'ō, peki.

Spain. Kepania, Sepania.

Spaniard. Paniolo.

spare. 1. *Save.* Ola, ho'ōla, kāpae. 2. *Extra.* Keu, koe.

spareribs. Iwi 'ao'ao.

spark. Hunaahi.

sparkle. 'Ā, hulali, hulili.

sparrow. Manu-li'ili'i.

speak. 'Ōlelo, wala'au.

speaker. Ha'i'ōlelo, luna ho-'omalu.

spear. Ihe, ihe pahe'e, pololū.

special. Mea i wae 'ia, kūikawā.

species. Lāhui.

speckled. Kikokiko, pulepule.

spectacles. Makaaniani.

speech. 'Ōlelo, ha'i'ōlelo.

speed. 'Āwīwī, māmā, wiki-wiki.

spell. Pela, kepela.

spend. Ho'olilo, ho'omāuna.

spider. Lanalana, nananana, ku'uku'u, pūnāwelewele.

spider web. Hihi punawele-wele, 'upena nananana.

spill. Hanini, nini.

spin. Niniu, ho'oniniu.

spine. Iwikuamo'o, kuamo'o.

spirit. 'Uhane, wailua, akua.

spirits. Wai 'ona.

spiritual. Pili 'uhane, mana, lani.

spit. *Expectorate.* Kuha, pu-puhi.

spite. Na'au kopekope, mau-hala. *In spite of,* i loko o.

splash. Pakī.

splendor. Nani, nani kamaha'o.

splinter. Māmala.

split. Wahī.

spoil. 1. *Decay.* Pilau, pilapilau, 'ino, mā'ino'ino. 2. *Pamper.* Pai, mailani, pailani, ho-'okamalani. 3. *Booty.* Wai-wai kaua, loa'a.

spool. Pōka'a.

spoon. Puna.

sport. Mea pā'ani.

spot. Kiko.

spotted. Kikokiko, pākikokiko, panini'o, kīnohi, pulepule.

sprain. Maūi, 'anu'u.

spray. 'Ehu, ehu, ehu kai, huna kai, hune kai.

spread. Hāli'i, laha.

spring. 1. *Water source.* Puna, kumu wai, māpuna. 2. *Season. No Hawaiian word; terms sometimes used:* ku-pulau, la'a ulu. 3. *Coil.* Pi-lina.

sprinkle. 1. *Scatter.* Pīpī, kā-pīpī, kūpīpī. 2. *Rain.* Ua kilikili, ua kilikilihune.

sprout. Kupu.

spry. 'Eleu.

spy. Kiu.

squander. 'Uha'uha, ho'omā-unauna, lū.

square. Huinahā, huinahā kau-like, kuea.

squash. Pū, ipu-pū, pala'ai.

squat. 'Ōku'u.

squeak. 'Uwī'uwī, kakani.

squeeze. 'Uwī, 'ōpā, kaomi, lomi, 'ūmi'i.

squid. He'e, mūhe'e. *See* octo-pus.

squint. Pipī, pipipi, maka pili.

squirm. Pīhole, hole, laumilo.

squirrelfish. 'Ū'ū, ala'ihi.

squirt. Pakī, 'ūpī, kī.

stab. Hou, 'ō.

stadium. Kahua pā'ani.

stage. Kahua.

stagger. Kunewa, kūnewanewa.

staghorn fern. Uluhe.

stain. Kohu, kāpala, hauka'e, kīkohu, palahe'a.

stairs. Alapi'i, 'anu'u.

stake. 1. *Staff*. Pahu. 2. *Wager*. Pili.

stalk. *Stem*. Hā, 'au, kū'au, ko'o.

stamp. 1. *Postage*. Po'oleka. 2. *Imprint*. Hō'ailona pa'i.

stand. 1. *Upright position*. Kū, kukū, kūlia. 2. *Table*. Pākaukau.

stanza. Paukū.

star. Hōkū.

starboard. 'Ao'ao 'ākau.

starch. Pia.

stare. Nānā pono, haka pono, hō'a'ā maka.

starfish. Pe'a, pe'ape'a, 'ōpe-'ape'a, hōkū-kai.

start. Ho'omaka, maka hou.

startle. Ho'opū'iwa.

starve. Make pōloli, ho'ōki 'ai.

state. 1. *Condition*. 'Ano, kūlana, kū. 2. *Political unit*. Moku'āina. 3. *To say*. Ha'i, ha'i mana'o.

statement. 'Ōlelo ha'ina. *Bank statement*, hō'ike panakō.

station. Hale ho'olulu. *Stations of the cross*, alanui o ke ke'a.

stationary. Pa'a, mau.

stationery. Kālana, kānana.

statue. Ki'i, ki'i kālai 'ia.

stay. Noho, kū.

steadfast. Kūpa'a, 'onipa'a, pa'a.

steak. Pipi kō'ala, pipi palai.

steal. 'Aihue.

steam. Māhu.

steam bath. Pūlo'ulo'u.

steamship. Mokuahi, mokumāhu.

steel. Kila.

steep. Kūnihinihi, kūnihi, kū, laumania.

steeple. Pū'o'a.

steer. 1. *To direct*. Uli, ho'o-

kele, kia. 2. *Male bovine*. Pipi po'a.

stem. *Same as* stalk.

stench. Pilau, pilapilau, 'ōhonohono, hohono, 'ōpilopilo, hauna, maea.

stenographer. Kākau 'ōlelo pōkole.

step. 1. *Foot movement*. Ke'ehi, ka'i, ne'e. 2. *On stairway*. Alapi'i, 'anu'u.

stepfather. Makua kāne kōlea.

stepmother. Makuahine kōlea.

sterile. Pā, hua 'ole.

stevedore. Po'olā.

stew. Kupa, kū.

steward. Kuene, 'ā'īpu'upu'u, pu'ukū, kanaka lawelawe.

stewardess. Wahine lawelawe, kuene wahine.

stick. 1. *Wood*. Lā'au. *See* digging stick. 2. *To adhere*. Pili.

sticky. Pipili, ho'opili.

stiff. 'O'ole'a, mālo'elo'e, 'ainā, mākū.

stiff neck. 'Ā'īkū, 'ā'ī 'o'ole'a, 'ā'ī uaua.

stifle. 'Umi, 'u'umi.

still. 1. *Motionless, silent*. Mālie, lana, wailana, ho'omalu. 2. *Yet*. Na'e, koe, ā hiki i kēia wā. 3. *Distilling apparatus*. Ipu hao puhi 'ōkolehao.

stilts, stilt (*bird*). Kukuluāe'o, āe'o.

stimulant. Mea ho'oikaika, mea ho'opaipai.

stimulate. Ho'oūlu, ho'oikaika, hō'eu'eu, ho'opaipai, ho'olalelale.

sting. Kiki, kui, 'ō, 'o'oi.

sting ray. Hīhīmanu, lupe.

stingy. Pī, 'au'a.

stir. 'Oni, kāwili.

stirrup. Ke'ehi, 'ili ke'ehi, hao ke'ehi.

stitch. Humu, ku'i, hono.

stocking. Kākini.

stomach. 'Ōpū.

stone. Pōhaku, 'ili'ili, 'alā, 'a'ā, pāhoehoe. *Precious stone*, pōhaku makamae.

stool. Noho li'ili'i, paepae.

stoop. Kūlou, kūnou.

stop. *Cease.* Ho'opau; ho'oku'u (*disperse*); waiho (*leave off*); kū (*as a car*). *Stop it!* Uoki! *Stop the car,* ho'okū i ke ka'a.

stopper. 'Umoki, popo'i, mea ho'opa'a, pani.

store. 1. *Noun.* Hale kū'ai. 2. *Verb.* Hō'ili'ili, ho'āhu.

storehouse. Hale ho'āhu, hale ahu waiwai, hale ukana.

stork. Kikonia, pia.

storm. 'Ino.

story. 1. *Narrative.* Mo'olelo, ka'ao. 2. *See* lie, 2. 3. *Floor.* Papahele, papa.

stout. Pu'ipu'i, poupou.

stove. Kapuahi.

straight. Pololei; kālole (*as hair*).

straighten. Ho'opololei.

strain. 1. *Filter.* Kānana, kālana. 2. *Exert.* Ho'oikaika, kōhi.

strait. Kōwā, kaikōwā.

strand. *Fiber.* Ma'awe, awe, mō'ali.

stranded. Ili.

strange. 'E, 'ano 'ē, mea 'ē, kupaianaha, kupanaha, ha-'oha'o.

stranger. Malihini, kanaka 'ē, mea 'ē.

strangle. 'Umi, 'u'umi, kā'awe.

strap. Kaula 'ili.

straw. Mau'u malu.

strawberry. 'Ōhelo-papa.

stray. 'Auwana, 'ae'a, holoholo.

streak. Wana, no'a.

streaked. Mā'oki'oki, ni'o, kāni'o, 'āwe'awe'a.

stream. *Same as* river.

street. Alanui.

strength. Ikaika.

stress. Ko'iko'i, ho'okālele; kālele mana'o; kālele leo (diacritical mark).

stretch. Kīko'oko'o.

stretcher. Manele, moe ho'olewa.

strike. 1. *Hit.* Ku'i, pepehi,

hau, hahau, uhau, kā. 2. *Work stoppage.* 'Olohani.

string. Kaula, aho, 'aha.

string figure. Hei.

stripe. Kaha.

striped. 'Ōni'oni'o, kahakaha.

stroke. 1. *Blow.* Hāuna, pā. *Breast stroke in swimming,* 'au umauma. 2. *To touch lightly.* Kahi, hamo. 3. *Sudden attack.* Huki, kūhewa, ulupō.

strong. Ikaika, mahi, wīkani, lawakua, ho'olehua.

stuck. Pa'a.

struggle. Paio, 'a'ume'ume.

stubborn. Pa'akikī, po'o pa'a, lae pa'a, kananuha.

student. Haumāna.

studious. Ho'opa'a ha'awina, puni ho'opa'a ha'awina.

study. Ho'opa'a ha'awina.

stumble. Ku'ia ka wāwae, 'ōkupe.

stump. 'Ōmuku.

stupid. Hūpō, wa'awa'a, na-'aupō.

stutter. 'Ū'ū, mā'ū'ū, 'ā'ā.

stylish. Kū i ke kaila, kū i ke paikini.

subject. 1. *Citizen.* Maka'āinana, kanaka. 2. *Topic.* Kumuhana, kumumana'o.

subscribe. Kākau inoa.

subtract. Ho'olawe.

suburb. Hu'a.

succeed. 1. *Accomplish.* Holomua, holopono, kō, loa'a. 2. *Follow.* Ukali, pani, hahai.

such. Like.

suck. Omo, omōmo, mūkī.

suddenly. 'Emo 'ole, hikiwawe.

sue. Ho'opi'i.

suffer. 'Eha'eha.

sugar. Kōpa'a.

sugarcane. Kō.

sugar mill. Wili kō, hale wili kō.

sugar plantation. Mahi kō.

suggest. Ho'opuka mana'o, ho-'olale.

suit. 1. *Clothing.* Pa'a lole. 2. *Court action.* Ho'opi'i, hihia.

suitable. Kūpono, kū, kohu.

suitcase. Paiki.

summer. Kau, kau wela.

summit. Wēkiu, piko, poʻo.

summon. Kiʻi, kēnā, kāhea, ka-uoha.

sun. Lā.

sunburned. Pāpaʻa lā.

Sunday. Lāpule.

Sunday school. Kula Kāpaki.

sunken. Poʻopoʻo, kapoʻo.

sunrise. Pukana lā, puka ʻana o ka lā.

sunset. Napoʻo ʻana o ka lā.

sunshine. Pā ʻana a ka lā.

superintendent. Haku hana, luna nui. *School superintendent,* kahu kula nui.

supermarket. Mākeke nui.

supervisor. Luna, luna hoʻoponopono, luna kiaʻi.

supper. ʻAina ahiahi, pāʻina ahiahi.

supplies. Lako, ukana, pono.

support. Kākoʻo, kōkua.

suppose. Mahuʻi, kuhi, manaʻo.

suppress. Kaomi.

Supreme Court. ʻAha Hoʻokolokolo Kiʻekiʻe.

sure. ʻOiāʻiʻo. *See also* **certain, 2.**

surf. Nalu. *To surf,* heʻe nalu.

surface. ʻIli, ʻiliwai, papa.

surfboard. Papa heʻe nalu.

surgeon. Kauka kaha.

surgeonfish. Kala, ʻapi, kole, palani.

surprise. Pūʻiwa, hoʻopūʻiwa, hoʻohaʻohaʻo.

surrender. Hāʻawipio, hāʻulepio.

surround. Kaʻapuni, hoʻopuni.

survey. Ana.

suspect. Hoʻohuoi, mahuʻi.

swallow. 1. *Ingest.* Ale; moni. **2.** *Bird.* Manu-ʻioʻio, kualo.

swamp. Pohō, naele, kele.

swear. 1. *Vow.* Hoʻohiki. **2.** *See* **curse.**

sweat. Hou.

sweater. Kueka.

sweep. Pūlumi, kāhili.

sweet. Momona.

sweetheart. Ipo, aloha, huapala, hoa.

sweet potato. ʻUala.

swelling. Pehu, hū.

swift. *Same as* **fast, 1.**

swim. ʻAu.

swing. Lele, lele koali, kālewa.

sword. Pahi kaua.

swordfish. Aʻu.

symbol. Hōʻailona.

sympathy. Aloha menemene.

syphilis. Kaokao.

T

t. *No Hawaiian term.*

table. Pākaukau.

tablecloth. Uhi pākaukau, pale pākaukau.

tablet. Kālana kākau.

taboo. Kapu.

tag. 1. *Game.* ʻIo, pio. **2.** *Symbol, label.* Hōʻailona, mekala (*as for a dog*).

Tahiti. Kahiki.

tail. Huelo (*of animal*); hiʻu (*of fish and other sealife*); puapua, pupua (*of birds*); pola (*of a kite*).

tailor. Kela, kela lole.

take. Lawe, lawe aku, hopu, loaʻa. *Take off,* kala, wehe, unuhi, hoʻohemo.

tale. Moʻolelo, kaʻao.

talk. ʻŌlelo, kamaʻilio; walaʻau (*colloquial*).

talkative. Walaʻau wale, ʻama.

tall. Loa, loloa (*as a person*); kiʻekiʻe (*as a hill*).

tame. Laka, hoʻolaka.

tangle. Hihia, hoʻohei, kāhihi.

tank. Pahu.

tanned. Pāpaʻa lā.

tapa. Kapa.

tapioca. Kapioka.

tar. Kā, kēpau.

tardy. Lohi, liʻu.

target. Māka, hōʻailona.

taro. Kalo.

tart. 1. *Pie.* Pai. **2.** *Sour.* ʻAwaʻawa.

taste. *Verb.* Hoʻāʻo.

tasteless. Koʻekoʻe, hūkākai.

tasty. ʻOno.

tattoo. Kākau.

tavern. Hale inu lama.

tax. ʻAuhau.

taxi. Kaʻa hoʻolimalima, kaʻa ʻōhua.

tea. Kī.

teach. Aʻo, kula.

teacher. Kumu, kumu aʻo, kumu kula.

teacup. Kīʻaha kī, pola kī.

teahouse. Hale inu kī.

teakettle. Ipu kī (*common term*), kikila kī.

team. Hui, ʻaoʻao.

teapot. Ipu kī, kikila kī.

tear. 1. *Weeping.* Waimaka. **2.** *Sunder.* Hae, nahae, haehae.

tease. Hoʻohenehene, hoʻohene, hoʻohaehae.

teeth. Niho.

teetotaler. Hōʻole lama.

telegram. Kelekalama.

telephone. Kelepona. *To telephone,* kelepona, kāhea.

telescope. ʻOhe nānā, aniani hoʻonui ʻike.

tell. Haʻi, haʻina, hōʻike, ʻōlelo.

temper. Naʻau, ʻano, ʻano o ka naʻau.

temperature. Anu, wela.

temple. 1. *Edifice.* Luakini, heiau. **2.** *Anatomical.* Maha.

temporary. Kūikawā, no ka manawa pōkole.

tempt. Hoʻowalewale.

ten. ʻUmi.

tenant. Hoaʻāina, mea hoʻolimalima.

tender. Palupalu (*as meat*).

tennis. Kenika.

tent. Hale lole, hale peʻa.

tentacle. ʻAwe.

tenure. Kuleana.

term. 1. *Period of time.* Kau, māhele manawa, wā. **2.** *Expression.* Inoa, huaʻōlelo.

terminal. *Station.* Hale hoʻolulu.

terminate. Hoʻopau, hoʻōki.

termite. Naonao-lele, huhu.

tern. Noio, ʻekiʻeki.

terrible. Weliweli, kau ka weli.

terrify. Hoʻoweli, hoʻoweliweli, hoʻomakaʻu.

territory. Kelikoli.

test. Hōʻike.

testament. Kauoha. *Last will and testament,* palapala kauoha, palapala hoʻoilina. *Old Testament,* Kauoha Kahiko. *New Testament,* Kauoha hou.

testicles. Hua, huahua, laho.

testify. Hōʻike, haʻi manaʻo.

than. Mamua o.

thank. Mahalo, hoʻomaikaʻi.

Thanksgiving Day. Lā Hoʻomaikaʻi.

that. Kēlā, lā (*at a distance*); kēnā, nā (*near the person addressed*); ia, ua . . . lā. *That way,* pēlā. *Is that so?* Pēlā anei?

thatch. Ako, pili.

the. Ka, ke (*singular*); nā (*plural*).

theater. Keaka.

their. Kō lāua, kā lāua, kō lākou, kā lākou, o lāua, o lākou, a lākou.

theirs. No lāua, no lākou, na lāua, na lākou.

them. Iā lāua, iā lākou.

then. A laila, malaila, i laila.

therefore. No laila, no ia mea.

thermometer. Kelemomeka, ana wela, mea ana wela.

these. Kēia mau, ua . . . nei.

they. Lāua, lākou.

thick. Mānoanoa.

thicket. ʻŌpū nahelehele.

thief. ʻAihue.

thigh. ʻŪhā.

thighbone. Iwi hilo.

thimble. Komo, komo humuhumu.

thimbleberries. ʻĀkala.

thin. 1. *As the body.* Wīwī, emi. **2.** *As cloth, paper.* Lahi, lahilahi.

thing. Mea.

think. Manaʻo, noʻonoʻo.

third. Hapakolu, kolu.

thirst. Make wai.

thirteen. ʻUmi kūmākolu, ʻumi kamamākolu.

thirtieth. Kanakolu.

thirty-one. Kanakolu kūmākahi.

this. Kēia, ia, ʻoia nei.

thorn. Kukū, ʻoiʻoi, kākala.

thorough. Pau pono, piha pono.

those. Kēlā mau, ua . . . lā.

thou. ʻOe.

though. I loko o. *As though.* Mehe.

thought. Manaʻo, noʻonoʻo.

thousand. Kaukani.

thread. Lopi.

threadfish. Moi.

threat. ʻŌlelo hoʻoweliweli.

three. Kolu, ʻekolu, ʻakolu.

three-fourths. ʻEkolu hapahā.

thrifty. Makauliʻi.

thrill. Kapalili ka houpo.

throat. Puʻu, puʻumoni.

throb. Koni, konikoni, kapalili.

throne. Noho aliʻi.

through. 1. *Finished.* Pau. 2. *In.* Ma, ma loko o.

throw. Nou, hoʻolei, pehi, lū.

thrush. Kāmaʻo, ʻōmaʻo, ʻāmaui.

thumb. Manamana lima nui.

thunder. Hekili.

Thursday. Pōʻahā.

thus. Pēlā, pēia, pe, penei.

ti. Kī.

ticket. Kikiki, likiki.

tickle. Hoʻomāneʻoneʻo.

ticklish. Maneʻo.

tidal wave. Kai ʻeʻe.

tide. Au, kai. *Low tide,* kai make, kai maloʻo. *Rising tide,* kai piʻi, kai ea. *High tide,* kai nui, kai piha.

tie. 1. *To bind.* Hīkiʻi, nīkiʻi, hākiʻi, nākiʻi, mūkiʻi, lawa, hele, hoʻopaʻa, hoa, lī, paʻi, hīpuʻu. 2. *A draw.* Paʻi, paʻi wale, paʻi ā paʻi.

tight. Pili pono, likiliki.

till. *See* until.

time. Wā, manawa, au; hola (*o'clock*).

timekeeper. Kiko manawa.

timetable. Papa kuhikihi, papa hōʻike.

timid. Makaʻu, hilahila, hoʻopē.

tin. Kini, keleawe, piula.

tinkle. Kani, wī, ō.

tiny. ʻUʻuku, ʻuku liʻi.

tip. 1. *Top.* Wēkiu, wēlau, ʻēlau. 2. *To tilt.* Kāhulihuli. 3. *Gratuity.* Uku lawelawe.

tired. Luhi, māluhiluhi.

title. 1. *Rank.* Kūlana. 2. *Right.* Kuleana. 3. *Heading.* ʻInoa, poʻo.

to. I, iā, iō; ā, ā hiki i.

toad. Poloka.

toast. 1. *Bread.* Palaoa hoʻopāpaʻa. 2. *Drinking.* Inu hoʻomaikaʻi.

tobacco. Paka.

today. Kēia lā.

toe. Manamana wāwae.

toenail. Maiʻao, manea o ka manamana wāwae.

together. Pū.

toilet. Lua, wahi hoʻopau pilikia.

toilet paper. Pepa hāleu.

tolerant. Manaʻo laulā.

tomato. ʻŌhiʻa, ʻōhiʻa-haole, kamako.

tomb. Hale kupapaʻu, lua kupapaʻu, ilina.

tomorrow. ʻApōpō.

ton. Kana, kona.

tone. Leo, kani o ka leo.

tongue. Alelo, elelo.

tonight. Kēia pō.

too. 1. *Also.* Kekahi, hoʻi. *Me too,* ʻo au pū. 2. *Excessive.* Loa, nui loa, keu.

tool. Mea hana, mea paʻahana.

tooth. Niho.

toothache. Niho huʻi.

toothbrush. Palaki niho.

toothpick. Lāʻau ʻōhikihiki niho.

top. 1. *Uppermost.* Wēkiu, wēlau. 2. *Toy.* Hū, ʻōniu, ʻōkaʻa.

topic. *See* subject, 2.

torch. Lama, lamakū.

torment. Hōʻehaʻeha.

torture. Hoʻomāinoino.

toss. Hoʻolei, kiola.

total. Huina, huina helu, heluna.

touch. Pā, hoʻopā, pili.

tough. Paʻakikī, māuaua, uaua.

tour. Kaʻapuni, kaʻahele. *Tour group,* poʻe mākaʻikaʻi like.

tourists. Poʻe mākaʻikaʻi, malihini mākaʻikaʻi, malihini.

towel. Kāwele.

tower. ʻAleʻo, pūʻoʻa.

town. Kūlanakauhale, kaona.

toy. Mea pāʻani, milimili.

track. Meheu, kapuaʻi, mōʻali.

trade. 1. *Barter.* Kālepa. 2. *Occupation.* ʻOihana, ʻoihana hana lima.

tradition. Moʻolelo.

traffic. Neʻe ʻana i ke alahele.

tragic. Kaumaha loa.

trail. Ala, ala hele.

train. 1. *Teach.* Aʻo, hoʻomaʻamaʻa. 2. *See* railroad.

trait. Welo, ēwe.

traitor. Kumakaia.

transfer. Hoʻolilo, hoʻīli.

transform. Loli.

translate. Unuhi, unuhi ʻōlelo.

translator. Mea unuhi, unuhi ʻōlelo.

transport. Halihali, lawe.

trap. ʻŪmiʻi, ʻūpiki, pahele.

trash. ʻŌpala.

travel. Kaʻahele, kaʻapuni, huakaʻi hele, huakaʻi.

tray. Pā halihali.

treachery. Kumakaia, ʻāpiki, ʻūpiki.

tread. Hehi, hehihehi, keʻehi.

treason. Kipi.

treasure. Mea makamae.

treasurer. Puʻukū.

treasury. Waihona, waihona waiwai.

treat. 1. *Attend to.* Lapaʻau, hana. 2. *Pleasure.* Mea e hoihoi ai, mea hoʻohauʻoli. *My treat,* naʻu e uku.

treaty. Palapala ʻaelike.

tree. Lāʻau, kumulāʻau, kumu.

tremble. Haʻalulu, kapalili.

trepang. Loli.

trespass. Komohewa, komo wale, ʻaeʻa, kahakū, ʻaʻe kū.

trial. Hoʻokolokolo.

triangle. Huinakolu.

tribe. Lāhui.

tribute. Hoʻokupu, uku, ʻauhau.

trick. Hana maʻalea, ʻāpiki, hana kolohe.

trickle. Kahe, kulu.

Tridacna. ʻŌlepe-nui.

trifle. Mea ʻole, mea iki.

triggerfish. Humuhumu.

trinity. Kahikolu.

trio. Pūkolu.

trip. 1. *Voyage.* Huakaʻi. 2. *Stumble.* ʻŌkupe.

triple. Kaukolu.

trite. Pākūwā.

triumph. Lanakila.

troll. *Verb.* Hī. *To troll for bonito,* hī aku.

troops. Pūʻali koa.

trophy. Hōʻailona lanakila.

tropicbird. Koaʻe.

trouble. Pilikia, pōpilikia.

trough. Holowaʻa.

troupe. Hui. *Hula troupe,* pā hula.

trousers. Lole wāwae.

truck. Kalaka.

true. ʻOiāʻiʻo.

trumpet. Pū, pū hoʻokani.

trumpetfish. Nūnū, nuhu.

trunkfish. Pahu, moa, moamoa.

trust. Hilinaʻi, kālele, paulele.

trustee. Kahu waiwai.

truth. ʻOiāʻiʻo.

try. Hoʻāʻo.

tub. Kapu.

tuber. Hua.

tuberculosis. Maʻi-ʻai-ake, akepau, hōkiʻi.

tuberose. Kupaloke.

Tuesday. Pōʻalua.

tug-of-war. Hukihuki, pāʻumeʻume.

tuna. ʻAhi, aku, kawakawa, hiʻu-wīwī.

tune. Leo, leo mele.

tunnel. Ana puka, lua pao, alapao.

turn. 1. *Move.* Huli; kā (*to turn a jump rope*). 2. *Time.* Manawa. *My turn,* koʻu manawa.

turtle. Honu.

turtledove. Kuhukukū.

tusk. Niho, ku‘i.

twelve. ‘Umi kūmālua, ‘umi kumamālua.

twenty. Iwakālua.

twenty-one. Iwākalua kūmākahi, iwakālua kumamākahi.

twice. Pālua, lua, ‘elua, ‘alua, ‘elua manawa.

twilight. Mōlehu.

twin. Māhoe, māhana.

twinkle. ‘Imo, ‘amo.

twist. Wili, ka‘awili, lauwili, milo.

two. Lua, ‘elua, ‘alua. ,

type. 1. *Kind.* ‘Ano. 2. *Print.* Hua, hua ho‘onoho. *To type,* kikokiko.

typewriter. Mīkini kikokiko hua.

typhoid. Pīwa-ho‘onāwaliwali.

typist. Kokokiko hua.

U

u. ‘Ū.

ugly. Pupuka.

ukulele. ‘Ukulele.

ulcer. Pūhā, pūhō, hēhē. *Stomach ulcer,* ‘ōpū pūhā.

umbilical cord. Piko.

umbrella. Māmalu, loulu.

umpire. ‘Uao.

un-. ‘Ole, hiki ‘ole.

unanimous. Mana‘o lōkahi.

unbelieving. Hilina‘i ‘ole, maloka.

uncertain. Kānalua, kūlanalana, kūnānā.

uncle. Makuakāne, ‘anakala.

unclean. Ma‘ema‘e ‘ole, haumia, kāpulu, hawa, pe‘a.

uncomfortable. ‘Olu‘olu ‘ole, ho‘o‘iha‘iha.

uncomplaining. Leo ‘ole, ho‘ohalahala ‘ole.

unconditional. Kaupalena ‘ole ‘ia.

unconscious. Pau ka ‘ike, pau ka lohe.

unconstitutional. Kū‘ē kumukānāwai.

under. Lalo, malalo, i lalo.

underdrawers. Palema‘i.

underline. Kaha lalo.

underneath. Malalo iho.

undershirt. Pale‘ili.

understand. Maopopo, ho‘omaopopo. *I understand,* maopopo ia‘u; ho‘omaopopo au.

undertaker. Kanaka ho‘olewa

undress. Wehe i ka ‘a‘ahu.

unethical. Kū ‘ole i nā lula maika‘i.

unfaithful. Kūpa‘a ‘ole, no‘ono‘o ‘ole i ka pono.

unfasten. Wehe, ho‘ohemo.

unfold. Lole.

unfortunate. Pō‘ino, pōpilikia.

unfriendly. Laulauna ‘ole.

unhappy. Kaumaha.

uniform. 1. *Dress.* Makalike, pa‘a lole makalike. 2. *Similar.* Kohu like, like.

unimportant. Mea ‘ole.

union. Hui, pilina; uniona (*labor*).

unique. Lua ‘ole, laha ‘ole.

unite. Hui, hui pū, pili pū, kāpili, ho‘ohui.

united. Hui pū ‘ia, huihui, hui kahi.

United Nations. Nā Lāhui Hui Pū ‘Ia.

United States of America. ‘Amelika-hui, ‘Amelika-huipū-‘ia.

unity. Lōkahi, ku‘ikahi.

universe. Ao holo‘oko‘a.

university. Kulanui.

unless. Ke ‘ole, ina ‘a‘ole.

unlimited. Palena ‘ole, kaupalena ‘ole ‘ia.

unload. Wehewehe i ka ukana.

unlock. Wehe me ke kī.

unlucky. Pakalaki, pōmaika‘i ‘ole.

unnecessary. Ho‘opaumanawa, waiwai ‘ole, makehewa.

unpleasant. Hoihoi ‘ole.

unprepared. Mākaukau ʻole, hemahema.

unskilled. Pāhemahema, hemahema.

unsteady. Luliluli, kāhulihuli, kūlanalana.

unsuccessful. Pohō, holo pono ʻole.

unsuitable. Koho ʻole, kūpono ʻole.

untidy. Mōkākī, kāpulu.

untie. Wehe, ʻuwehe, kala.

until. Ā, ā hiki i.

unusual. Mea ʻē, ʻano ʻē, ʻē, ʻike nui ʻole ʻia.

up. Luna, i luna, maluna.

upland. Uka.

upper. Luna, maluna aʻe.

upright. 1. *Erect*. Kū, kūpono. 2. *Moral*. Naʻau pono.

upset. 1. *Capsize*. Hoʻokahuli, kahuli. 2. *Worried*. Pīhoihoi ka manaʻo.

upside down. Hulihia.

upstairs. Papahele o luna.

urge. Koi, haʻakoi, pai, hoʻopai, lale.

urgent. Koʻikoʻi, hiki ʻole ke kāpae.

urinate. Mimi.

us. Iā kāua, iā māua (*dual*); iā kākou, iā mākou (*plural*).

use. 1. *Value*. Waiwai, pono. 2. *Utilize*. Hoʻohana.

used to. Maʻa, maʻamaʻa, maʻamaʻahia.

useful. Waiwai, mea kōkua.

useless. Waiwai ʻole, makehewa, ʻole wale.

usual. Maʻamau, mea mau.

V

v. *No Hawaiian term.*

vacant. Haka, hakahaka.

vacation. Wā hoʻomaha, hoʻomahana.

vaccinate. ʻŌ.

vacuum cleaner. Mīkini hoʻomaʻemaʻe hale.

vagabond. Kanaka ʻaeʻa, kuewa, lewa.

vagina. Kohe, peo.

vain. 1. *Proud*. Hoʻokano, hoʻokela, hoʻokiʻekiʻe. 2. *Without results*. Pohō, makehewa.

valley. Awaawa.

valuable. Waiwai, makamae.

vanish. Nalowale.

variety. ʻAno.

vast. Nui ʻino, nui loa.

vault. Waihona, keʻena.

veal. ʻIʻo pipi.

vegetable. *No Hawaiian equivalent; early Hawaiians distinguished* poi (ʻai, poi) *and accompaniments to* poi (iʻa, ʻīnaʻi). *Nearest equivalents to English term:* mea ulu, mea kanu, meaʻai launahele.

vehicle. Kaʻa, waʻa.

vein. Aʻa koko, aʻa.

velvet. Weleweka.

Venus. Hōkū-ao, Hōkū-loa, Mānalo.

verb. Haʻina.

verify. Hōʻoia, hōʻoiāʻiʻo.

verse. Laina, lālani (*line*); paukū, ʻoki (*stanza*).

very. Loa, nō, wale, maoli, ʻino.

vessel. 1. *Container*. Ipu, ʻumeke, hue. 2. *Ship*. Moku.

veteran. Koa kahiko.

veterinary. Kauka holoholona.

veto. Hōʻole, wiko.

vice. Hewa, hala, ʻino, hana haumia.

vice-. Hope, pani. *Vice-president,* hope pelekikena.

victim. Luaahi, pio, heana.

victory. Lanakila, eo.

view. ʻIkena, nānaina.

village. Kūlanakauhale, kauhale.

vine. Lāʻau hihi.

vinegar. Pinjka, wineka.

violet. Waioleka.

violin. Pila, waiolina.

virgin. Pu'upa'a (female); ulepa'a (male).

virile. Ke'a, pūkonakona.

virtue. Hemolele, pono.

vision. Haili moe, hihi'o, 'ike, akakū.

visit. Māka'ika'i, kipa, launa.

visitor. Mea māka'ika'i, mea kipa.

visitors bureau. Pulo ho'okipa malihini.

vocabulary. Papa 'ōlelo (list); huina 'ōlelo (word totality).

voice. Leo.

volcanic. Pele, 'a'ā pele.

volcano. Lua pele, pele, ahi 'ai honua.

volume. 1. Quantity. Nui. 2. Book. Puke, helu.

volunteer. 'A'a.

vomit. Lua'i, pua'i.

vote. Koho pāloka.

vowel. Hua palapala leo kahi.

voyage. Huaka'i, holokai.

W

w. Wē.

wages. Uku, uku hana.

wagon. Ka'a.

wail. Uwē, uwē helu, 'alalā, kanikau.

wait. Kali, alia. Wait on tables, lawelawe.

waiter. Kuene.

wake. Awaken. Ala, ho'āla.

walk. Hele wāwae, hele.

wall. Pā; paia (of houses).

wallpaper. Pepa hale.

wander. 'Auana, ki'ihele, lalau, 'ae'a, kuewa.

want. 1. Desire. Makemake; mamake (colloquial). 2. Lack. Nele, hemahema.

war. Kaua. Civil war, kaua kūloko. Revolutionary war, kaua hulihia.

wardrobe. Nā 'a'ahu apau (clothes); ke'ena waihona 'a'ahu (clothes closet).

warehouse. Hale ukana, hale ho'āhu.

warm. Mahana, pumehana.

warning. A'o 'ana, hō'ike pilikia.

warrant. Palapala.

warrior. Koa, pū'ali.

warship. Moku kaua, manuwā.

was. No equivalent; see be, ua.

wash. Holoi.

washcloth. Kāwele holoi.

washing machine. Mīkini holoi.

Washington. Wakinekona, Wasinetona.

wasp. Hope-'ō, kopena.

waste. Ho'omāunauna, 'uha-'uha.

wastebasket. 'Ie 'ōpala.

watch. 1. Observe. Kia'i, nānā pono, kilo. 2. Timepiece. Uwaki, uaki. Wrist watch, uwaki pūlima.

watchful. Maka'ala, miki.

watchman. Kia'i, kū uwaki.

water. Wai (fresh). To water, ninini wai, ho'okahe wai. Spring water, wai puna, wai māpuna.

water bottle. Hue wai, ipu wai, 'ōmole wai.

watercress. Lēkō.

waterfall. Wailele.

water hole. Lua wai, ki'o wai.

watermelon. Ipu, ipu-haole.

waterproof. Komo 'ole ka wai.

waterspout. Waipu'ilani.

wave. 1. Of the ocean. Nalu, 'ale. 2. Motion. Ani, pe'ahi, welo, kālepa.

way. 1. Route. Ala, ala hele, alanui. 2. Manner, custom. 'Ano. That way, pēlā. This way, penei.

we. Kāua (dual, inclusive), kākou (plural, inclusive), māua (dual exclusive), mākou (plural, exclusive).

weak. Nāwaliwali; lahilahi (*as coffee*).

wealth. Waiwai, lako, loaʻa.

weapon. Mea-kaua, mea make, mea pepehi kanaka.

wear. Komo, ʻaʻahu.

weary. Luhi, māluhiluhi, paʻa luhi, pauaho.

weather. Ke ʻano o ka manawa.

wedding. Male ʻana. *Wedding feast*, ʻahaʻaina male.

Wednesday. Pōʻakolu.

weed. Nahele, nāhelehele. *To weed*, waele.

week. Pule. *Next week*, kēia pule aʻe. *Last week*, kēlā pule aku nei.

weekday. Lā noa.

weekly. I kēlā me kēia pule.

weep. Uwē.

weigh. Kau paona, ana kaumaha.

weight. Kaumaha, ana kaumaha, paona.

weird. Ano, ʻeʻehia, aīwaīwa.

welcome. Heahea. *There is no equivalent to the English. One may say* komo mai. *You are welcome*, he mea ʻole, he mea iki (*modern*).

welfare. Pono, pōmaikaʻi. *Public welfare*, pono o ka lehulehu. *Spiritual welfare*, pono ʻuhane.

well. 1. *Good.* Maikaʻi, pono. **2.** *Source of water.* Luawai, wai ʻeli. *Artesian well*, luawai aniani.

well-being. Ola kino, pono.

were. *No equivalent; see* be.

west. Komohana.

wet. Pulu, pulu pē, maʻū, ʻelo.

whale. Koholā, palaoa.

whale tooth. Niho palaoa.

whaling. ʻŌ koholā.

wharf. Uwapo.

what. 1. *Interrogative.* Aha. *What is that?* He aha kēlā? **2.** *Relative pronoun.* Mea.

whatsoever. Nā mea like ʻole.

wheat. Huika, huapalaoa.

wheel. Huila.

when. 1. *Declarative past.* I ka manawa . . . i, i ka wā . . . i. **2.** *Declarative future.* I ka manawa . . . e, i ka wā . . . e, ke. **3.** *Interrogative future.* Āhea? I ka manawa hea . . . e? **4.** *Interrogative past.* Ināhea? I ka manawa hea . . . i? I ka wā hea . . . i?

where. 1. *Declarative.* Kahi. **2.** *Interrogative.* Ai hea? I hea? Aia i hea? ʻAuhea?

whether. Inā.

whetstone. Hoana.

which. 1. *Declarative.* Ka mea i, ka i (*past*); ka mea e, ke (*future*). **2.** *Interrogative.* Hea? Ka mea hea?

while. ʻOiai, ʻoi, i ka manawa, i ka wā, i.

whip. Hahau, hau, uhau.

whirlpool. Wiliwai, mimilo.

whiskers. ʻUmiʻumi.

whiskey. Wekeke, waikeke.

whisper. Hāwanawana.

whistle. Hōkio, hōkiokio, pio.

white. Keʻokeʻo, kea; hina (*of hair*).

white man. Haole, ʻilipuakea.

whitewash. Paʻi puna, puna, hamo puna.

whitish. Haʻakea.

whittle. Kalakalai, kolikoli.

who. 1. *Declarative.* I, e, nāna. **2.** *Interrogative.* Wai? ʻO wai? Iā wai?

whole. Holoʻokoʻa, okoʻa, paʻa.

wholesale. Kūʻai nui, kūkaʻa.

whom. Iā wai.

whose. 1. *Declarative.* Nona, nāna. **2.** *Interrogative.* Na wai? No wai?

why. 1. *Declarative.* Ke kumu, ka mea. **2.** *Interrogative.* Aha, hea; no ke aha?

wick. ʻUwiki.

wicked. ʻIno, hana ʻino, ʻaiā.

wide. Laulā, ākea.

widow. Wahine kāne make.

widower. Kāne wahine make.

wife. Wahine, wahine male.

wig. Lauoho kuʻi.

wiggle. ʻOniʻoni.

wild. ʻĀhiu, hihiu, ñae.

wilderness. Wao akua, wao nahele.
will. 1. *Testament.* Kauoha,
palapala hoʻoilina. **2.** *Desire.*
Makemake, manaʻo. **3.** *Verb
markers.* E . . . ana.
wilt. Mae.
win. Lanakila, eo, loaʻa, puka.
wind. 1. *Air movement.* Makani. **2.** *To twist.* Wili, wini,
pōkaʻa, kaʻa.
windbreak. Kūmakani, pālulu.
windmill. Wili makani.
window. Pukaaniani, puka hale.
windshield. Pale makani, pālulu.
windward. ʻAoʻao Koʻolau, ʻao-
ʻao makani, naʻe.
wine. Waina.
wing. ʻĒheu.
wink. ʻImo, ʻamo.
winter. Hoʻoilo.
wipe. Kāwele, holoi, hāleu.
wire. Uwea.
wisdom. Naʻauao, akamai.
wish. Makemake, ake, ʻiʻini.
witchcraft. Hana mana, hoʻokalakupua.
with. Me.
withdraw. Emi hope, hoʻi, unuhi.
withhold. ʻAuʻa, lauʻauʻa.
without. Nele, ʻole.
witness. Hōʻike.
woe. Pōpilikia nui, kaumaha
nui.
wolf. ʻĪlio hae, lupo.
woman. Wahine.
womb. Pūʻao, ʻōpū.
women. Wāhine.
wonder. Kāhāhā, pāhaʻohaʻo.
wonderful. Kupaianaha, kupanaha, kamahaʻo.
woo. Hoʻoipo, hoʻonipo.

wood. Lāʻau.
wood borer. Huhu-pao-lāʻau.
wool. Hulu, pili.
woolen. Huluhulu.
word. ʻŌlelo, huaʻōlelo, hua.
work. Hana.
worker. Kanaka hana, limahana, paʻahana.
workshop. Keʻena hana, hale
hana.
world. Ao, honua.
world war. Kaua honua.
worm. Koʻe, ilo.
wormy. Iloilo, huhuhu.
worried. Pīhoihoi, pono ʻole ka
manaʻo.
worry. Hoʻopīhoihoi, pīhoihoi
o ka naʻau.
worse. ʻOi aku ka ʻino.
worship. Hoʻomana, haipule,
pule.
worth. Waiwai, waiwai ʻiʻo.
worthless. Lapuwale.
worthy. Kūpono, pono.
wound. Palapū, ʻeha.
wrap. 1. *Bind.* Wahī. **2.** *Garment.* ʻAʻahu, kuka.
wrasses. Hīnālea, ʻaʻawa, ʻōpule.
wrath. Inaina.
wreath. Lei.
wreck. Wāwahi, hoʻopōʻino.
See **shipwreck.**
wrench. *Tool.* Wili, hao wili.
wrestling. Hākōkō, uma.
wretch. Lapuwale.
wretched. Kaumaha, luʻuluʻu.
wrinkle. Minomino, ʻaluʻalu.
wrist. Pūlima.
write. Kākau, kākau lima.
writer. Mea kākau.
writing. Palapala, kākau.
wrong. Hewa, pono ʻole, ʻola-
lau.

Y

y. *No Hawaiian term.*
yacht. Moku peʻa.
yam. Uhi.
yard. 1. *Unit of measure.* Iā,
iwilei. **2.** *Enclosure.* Pā.

year. Makahiki. *New Year,*
Makahiki Hou. *Happy New
Year.* Hauʻoli Makahiki Hou.
yellow. Melemele, ʻōlenalena.
yes. ʻAe, ʻē, ō, eō.

yesterday. Nehinei, inehinei.

yet. 1. *Still.* Koe, na'e. **2.** *See* **but.**

you. 'Oe (*singular*), 'olua (*dual*), 'oukou (*plural*).

young. 'Ōpio, 'ōpiopio.

your. 1. *Singular possessed object, singular.* Kou (*o-class*); kāu (*a-class*); kō (*neutral class*). **2.** *Singular possessed object, dual.* Kō 'olua (*o-class*), kā 'olua (*a-class*). **3.** *Singular possessed object, plural.* Kō 'oukou (*o-class*); kā 'oukou (*a-class*). *To show plural possessed objects, delete k- in all except the neutral class.*

yours. Nou, no 'olua, no 'oukou, nāu, na 'olua, na 'oukou.

Z

z. *No Hawaiian term.*

zero. 'Ole.

zigzag. Kīke'eke'e, kihikihi.

zoo. Kahua hō'ike'ike holoholona.

HAWAIIAN GIVEN NAMES FROM ENGLISH

A Christian name spelled with an initial vowel in Hawaiian is actually preceded by a glottal stop. These have been eliminated here in order to conform more closely with established orthography. Spellings with English letters follow spellings with Hawaiian letters. For substitutions of Hawaiian letters for English, see section 10 of the Grammar.

NAMES OF MEN

Aaron. Āʻālona, Aarona.
Abel. Apela, Abela.
Abelard. Apelaka, Abelada.
Abiah. Apia, Abia.
Abiathar. Apiakala, Apiekela, Abiatara.
Abihu. Apihu, Abihu.
Abijah. Apiʻia, Abiia.
Abinadab. Apinakapa, Abinadaba.
Abiram. Apilama, Abirama.
Abishai. Apikai, Abisai.
Abner. Apenela, Abenera.
Abraham. Apelahama, Aberahama.
Abram. Apelama, Aberama.
Absalom. Apekaloma, Abesaloma.
Adam. Akamu, Adamu.
Adonijah. Akoniʻia, Adoniia.
Adoniram. Akonilama, Adonirama.
Adrian. Akiliano, Adiriano.
Adriel. Akeliela, Aderiela.
Agrippa. Akelipa, Ageripa.
Ahab. Ahapa, Ahaba.
Ahasuerus. Ahakuelo, Ahasuero.
Ahaz. Ahaka, Ahaza.
Ahaziah. Ahakia, Ahazia.
Ahiah. Ahia.
Ahimelech. Ahimeleka.
Aladdin. Alakana, Aladana.
Alan. *Same as* **Allen.**

Alban. Alepana, Alebana.
Albert. Alapaki, Alabati.
Alberto. Alepako, Alebato.
Alex. Alika.
Alexander. Alekanekelo, Alekanedero.
Alexis. Aleki.
Alfred. Alepeleke, Aleferede, Alapai.
Allen. Alena.
Aloysius. Aloiki, Aloisi.
Alton. Alekona, Aletona.
Alvin. Alewina, Alevina.
Ambrose. Amapolokio, Amaborosio.
Amos. Amoka, Amosa.
Ananias. Anania.
Anastasius. Anakakio, Anatasio.
Andre. Anakalē, Anadare.
Andrew. Analū (*not Biblical*); Anekelea, Anederea (*Biblical*).
Andros. Anekaloka, Anedarosa.
Anselm. Anakelemo, Anaselemo.
Anthony. Akoni, Atoni; Anakoni, Anatoni (*Catholic*).
Antone. Akoni, Atoni.
Apollo. Apolo.
Appolyon. Apoluona.
Archibald. Ake.
Archie. Ake.
Ariel. Aliela, Ariela.

Armand. Amana; Alemana, Aremana.

Artemas. Alekema, Aretema.

Arthur. Aka, Ata.

Asa. Aka, Asa.

Aser. Akela, Asera.

Ashur. Akela, Asera.

Aubert. Aupeleke, Auberete.

Aubrey. Aupele, Aubere.

August. Aukake, Augate.

Augustine. Aukukino, Augutino.

Augustus. Aukukeko, Auguseto.

Aurelius. Aulelio, Aurelio.

Aymar. Aima.

Azariah. Akalia, Azaria.

Ballam. Pala'ama, Balaama.

Barnabas. Palenapa, Barenaba.

Barsabbas. Palekapa, Baresaba.

Bartholomew. Palekolomaio, Baretolomaio.

Bartimaeus. Pakimea, Batimea.

Basil. Pakile, Basile.

Belshazzar. Pelehakala, Belehazara.

Ben. Peni, Beni.

Benedict. Penekiko, Benedito.

Benjamin. Peni'amina, Beniamina.

Bernard. Pelenalako, Berenarado (*Catholic*); Pelenako (*not Catholic*).

Bethuel. Pekuela, Betuela.

Bill. Pila.

Bob. *Same as* **Robert.**

Bonaventure. Ponawenekula, Bonavenetura.

Boniface. Ponipake, Bonifake.

Boyd. Poe.

Bruce. Puluke, Buruse.

Bruno. Puluno, Buruno.

Caesar. Kaikala, Kaisara.

Caiaphas. Kai'apa.

Cain. Kaina.

Caius. Kaio.

Caleb. Kalepa, Kaleba.

Calvin. Kalawina, Kalavina.

Carrolus. Kalolo.

Casimir. Kasimilo.

Casper. Kakapa, Kasapa.

Cecil. Kekila, Kikila.

Cedric. Kekelika, Kederika.

Celestino. Kelekino, Keletino.

Cephas. Kepa.

Charles. Kale; Kalolo, Karolo (*Catholic*).

Christopher. Kilikikopa, Kirisitopa.

Chrysostom. Kalekokome, Karesotome.

Cicero. Kikelo, Sisero.

Clarence. Kalalena, Kalarena.

Claude. Kalauka, Kalauda.

Claudius. Kelaukio, Kelaudio.

Claus. Kalauka, Kalausa.

Clement. Kelemeneke, Kelemenete.

Clifton. Kalipekona, Kalifetona.

Clyde. Kalaila, Kalaida.

Constantine. Konekākino, Konesatino.

Cornelius. Kolenelio, Korenelio.

Crispus. Kelikepo, Kerisepo.

Cyprinus. Kipiliano, Kipiriano.

Cyril. Kilila, Kirila.

Cyrus. Kulo, Kuro.

Damasius. Kamakio, Damasio.

Dan. Kana, Dana.

Dana. Kana, Dana.

Daniel. Kaniela, Daniela.

Darius. Kāliu, Dariu.

David. Kāwika, Davida; Kewiki.

Demitrius. Kemikilio, Demitirio.

Dennis. Kenika, Denisa.

Dick. *Same as* **Richard.**

Dionisius. Kionikio, Dionisio.

Domingo. Kominiko, Dominigo.

Dominik. Kominiko, Dominiko.

Don. Kona, D'ona.

Douglas. Koukalaka, Dougalasa.

Dwight. Kuaika, Duaita.

Eben. Epena, Ebena.

Ebenezer. Epenekela, Ebenezera.

Edgar. Ekeka, Edega.

Edmond. Ekemona, Edemona; Ekumena, Edumena.
Edward. Ekewaka, Edewada; Ekualo, Eduaro (*Catholic*).
Edwin. Eluene, Ailuene.
Eleazar. Eleakala, Eleazara.
Eli. Eli.
Eliezer. Eliekera, Eliezera.
Elihu. Elihū.
Elijah. Elia.
Elisha. Elikai, Elisai.
Elmer. Elema.
Elroy. Eleloe, Eleroe.
Elton. Elekona, Eletona.
Emmanuel. Emanuela.
Enoch. Enoka.
Enos. Enoka, Enosa.
Ephraim. Epelaima, Eperaima.
Erasmus. Elamo, Eramo.
Erastus. Elakeko, Eraseto.
Eric. Elika, Erika.
Ernest. Eleneki, Ereneti; Eneki, Eṅeti.
Esau. Ekau, Esau.
Ethan. Ekana, Etana.
Eugene. Iukini, Iugini.
Eusebius. Eukepio, Eusebio.
Eustace. Eukakio, Eutakio.
Evaristus. Ewaliko, Evarito.
Ezekiel. Ekekiela, Ezekiela.
Ezra. Ekela, Ezera.
Fabian. Papiano, Fabiano.
Faustinus. Paukekino, Fausetino.
Felix. Pelike, Felike.
Ferdinand. Pelekinako, Feredinado.
Floyd. Poloika, Foloida.
Francis. Palakiko, Farakiko.
Francisco. *Same as* **Francis.**
Frank. Palani, Farani.
Franklin. Pelanekelina, Feranekelina.
Fred. Peleke, Ferede.
Frederick. *Same as* **Fred.**
Gabriel. Kapeliela, Gaberiela.
Gamaliel. Kamaliela, Gamaliela.

Gelasius. Kelakio, Gelasio.
Geoffrey. Keopele, Geofere.
George. Keoki, Geogi.
Gerald. Kelala, Gerala.
Gideon. Kileona, Kikeona, Gideona.
Gilbert. Kilipaki, Gilibati; Kilipeka, Gilibeta.
Gilmore. Kilemoa, Gilemoa.
Goliath. Kolia, Golia.
Gordon. Kolekona, Goredona.
Gregory. Kelekolio, Geregorio.
Gustav. Kukakawe, Gusatave.
Habakkuk. Hapakuka, Habakuka.
Haggai. Hakai, Hagai.
Ham. Hama.
Haman. Hamana.
Hannibal. Hanipala, Hanibala.
Hans. Haneke, Hanese.
Haran. Halana, Harana.
Harold. Halola, Harola.
Harry. Hale, Hare.
Hector. Hekekā, Heketa.
Henry. Henelē, Hanalē; Heneli, Heneri.
Herbert. Hapaki, Habati.
Herman. Helemano, Heremano.
Herod. Heloke, Herode.
Hezekiah. Hekekia, Hezekia; Hezekea.
Hilary. Hilalio, Hilario.
Hiram. Hailama, Hairama; Hilama; Hirama.
Homer. Hōmela, Homera.
Honorius. Honolio, Honorio.
Horace. Holeka, Horesa.
Horatio. Holakio.
Hosea. Hokea, Hosea.
Howard. Haoa.
Hubert. Hupeka, Hubeta.
Hugh. Hiu, Hiuwe.
Hugo. Huko, Hugo.
Humbert. Humepaka, Humebata; Humepeleka, Humebereta.
Ichabod. Ikapoka, Ikaboda.

Ignatius. Ikenaki, Igenati.
Innocent. Inokene.
Irving. *Same as* **Irwin.**
Irwin. Iwini, Ivini.
Isaac. Ika'aka, Isaaka (*Biblical*); Aikake (*not Biblical*).
Isaiah. Ikaia, Isaia.
Ishmael. Ikema'ela, Isemaela.
Isidore. Ikikolo, Isidoro.
Israel. Ikela'ela, Iseraela.
Ivan. Iwana, Ivana.
Ivanhoe. Iwanahō, Ivanaho.
Jack. Keaka.
Jacob. Iakopa, Iakoba.
Jael. Ia'ela.
James. Kimo; Iakopo, Iakobo.
Japheth. Iapeka, Iapeta.
Jason. Iakona, Iasona.
Jared. Ialeka, Iaredạ.
Jasper. Iakepa, Iasepa.
Jehu. Iehu.
Jephthah. Iepeka, Iepeta.
Jeremiah. Ielemia, Ieremia.
Jerome. Ielome, Ierome; Hieronimo (*Catholic*).
Jesse. Ieke, Iese.
Jesus. Ieku, Iesu.
Jethro. Iekelo, Ietero.
Jim. Kimo.
Joaquin. Iōkina; Wākina.
Job. Iopa, Ioba.
Joe. Keō.
Joel. Io'ela.
John. Keoni (*not Biblical*); Ioane (*Biblical*).
Jonah. Iona.
Jonathan. Ionakana, Ionatana.
Jose. Hokē, Hose.
Joseph. Iokepa, Iosepa; Iokewe, Ioseve (*Catholic*).
Joshua. Iokua, Iosua.
Josiah. Iokia, Iosia.
Jotham. Iokama.
Juan. Huanu.
Judah. Iuka, Iuda.
Jules. Kiule.
Julian. Kuliano.

Julius. Iulio.
Jupiter. Iupika, Iupita.
Justin. Iukekini, Iusetini.
Justinian. Kukiniano, Iutiniano.
Kelvin. Kelewina, Kelevina.
Kenneth. Keneke, Kenete; Keneki, Keneti.
Laban. Lapana, Labana.
Lamech. Lameka.
Lawrence. Lauleneke, Laurenete; Lowene.
Lazarus. Lakalo, Lazaro.
Lemuel. Lemuela.
Leo. Leone.
Leonard. Leonaka, Leonada.
Leopold. Leopolo.
Levi. Lewi, Liwai.
Liberius. Lipelio, Liberio.
Libert. Lipeleko, Libereto.
Linus. Lino.
Lionel. Laionela.
Lloyd. Loeka, Loeda.
Lorenzo. Loleneko, Lorenezo.
Lorin. Lolina.
Lot. Loka, Lota.
Louis. Lui.
Lucifer. Lukipela, Lukipera.
Lucius. Lukio.
Luke. Luka.
Luther. Lukela, Lutera.
Mahlon. Mahelona.
Malachi. Malaki.
Malcolm. Malakoma.
Manasseh. Manake, Manase.
Manoah. Manoa.
Manuel. Manuela.
Marcellus. Malakelo.
Marion. Maliona, Mariona.
Mark. Maleko, Mareko.
Matthew. Makaio, Mataio.
Matthias. Makia, Matia.
Maximus. Makimo.
Melchizedek. Melekikekeka, Melekizedeka.
Melvin. Melewina, Melevina.
Mephibosheth. Mepipokeka, Mepiboseta.

Methuselah. Mekukala, Metusala.
Micah. Mika.
Michael. Mikaʻele, Mikala.
Michal. Mikala.
Michelle. Mikala.
Miguel. Mikuela, Miguela.
Mike. *Same as* **Michael.**
Mohammed. Mohameka, Mohameda.
Mordecai. Molekekai, Moredekai.
Moses. Moke, Mose.
Naaman. Naʻamana.
Nabal. Napala, Nabala.
Nahor. Nahola, Nahora.
Napoleon. Napoliana, Napoliona.
Nathan. Nakana, Natana.
Nathaniel. Nakanaʻela.
Nebuchadnezzar. Nepukaneka, Nebukaneza; Nebukadeneza.
Ned. Neki, Nedi.
Nehemiah. Nehemia.
Nero. Nelo, Nero.
Nicholas. Nikolao; Nikolo.
Nicodemus. Nikokemo, Nikodemo.
Noah. Noa.
Noel. Noela.
Norbert. Nolepeleko, Norebereto.
Norman. Nolemana, Noremana; Nōmana.
Obadiah. Opakia, Obadia.
Obed. Opeka, Obeda.
Oliver. Oliwa, Oliva.
Oscar. Oka.
Oswald. Okewoleka, Osewoleda.
Patrick. Pakelika, Paterika.
Paul. Paulo.
Pedro. Pekelo, Petero.
Percy. Peleki, Peresi.
Peter. Pekelo, Petero; Pika (*not Biblical*).
Philemon. Pilemona, Filemona.
Phillip. Pilipo.

Phineas. Pinehaka, Pinehasa.
Pilate. Pilako, Pilato.
Pius. Pio.
Polycarp. Polikape.
Pomponius. Pomeponio.
Potiphar. Pokipala, Potipara.
Ptolemy. Petolomai.
Quentin. Kuenekina, Kuenetina.
Ralph. Lalepa, Ralepa.
Raphael. Lapaʻela, Rafaela; Lapaʻele, Rafaele.
Ray. Lei, Rei.
Raymond. Leimana; Remone.
Rechab. Lekapa, Rekaba.
Reginald. Lekinala, Reginala.
Rehoboam. Lehopoama, Rehoboama.
Reuben. Leʻupena, Reubena.
Reuel. Leuela, Reuela.
Richard. Likeke, Rikeke.
Robert. Lopaka, Robata.
Robin. Lopine, Robine.
Rodney. Lokenē, Rodene.
Roger. Lōkela, Rogera.
Roland. Lolana, Rolana.
Rolin. Lolina, Rolina.
Romeo. Lomiō, Romio.
Romulus. Lomulu, Romulu.
Rufus. Lupe, Rufe; Rupo.
Rupert. Lupeko, Rupeto.
Salathiel. Kalakiela, Salatiela.
Samson. Kamekona, Samesona.
Samuel. Kamuela, Samuela.
Saul. Kaulo, Saulo.
Sebastian. Kepakiano, Sebatiano; Pakiana.
Sergius. Kelekio, Seregio.
Seth. Keka, Seta.
Shadrach. Kakelaka, Saderaka.
Shem. Kema, Sema.
Sidney. Kikinē; Kikanē.
Silas. Kila, Sila.
Simeon. Kimeona, Simeona.
Simon. Kimona, Simona.
Simplicius. Kimipilikio, Simipilikio.
Socrates. Kokalakē, Sokarate.

Solomon. Kolomona, Solomona.

Stanislaus. Kanilao, Tanilao.

Stanley. Kanalē, Sanale.

Stephen. Kepano, Tepano (*Catholic*); Kekepana, Setepana (*Protestant*).

Steven. Kiwini, Tivini.

Tarzan. Kakana.

Ted. *Same as* **Theodore.**

Tertius. Kelekio, Teretio.

Thaddeus. Kakaio, Tadaio.

Theodore. Keokolo, Teodoro (*Catholic*); Keokoa, Teodoa.

Theophilus. Keopilo, Teopilo.

Thomas. Koma, Toma; Kamaki.

Timothy. Kimokeo, Timoteo.

Titus. Kiko, Tito.

Tobias. Kopia, Tobia.

Tom. Koma, Toma. *Tom Thumb,* Koma Kamu.

Ulrich. Ulaliko, Ulariko.

Ulysses, Uleki, Ulesi.

Uriah. Ulia, Uria.

Uriel. Uliela, Uriela.

Valentine. Walenekino, Valenetino; Walekino, Walakino.

Valerian. Waleliano, Valeriano.

Vernon. Wenona, Venona.

Victor. Wikoli, Vitori.

Victorinus. Wikolino, Vitorino.

Vincent. Winikeneke, Vinikeneke.

Virgil. Wilikilia, Virigilia.

Waldemar. Waledema.

Walter. Walaka, Walata.

Warren. Walena, Warena.

Wilbert. Wilipaki, Wilibati.

Wilford. Wilepoka, Wilefoda.

Wilfred. Wilipeleke, Wiliferede.

Wilhelm. Wilehailama.

Willard. Wilika, Wilida.

William. Wiliama, Uilama.

Willie. Wile.

Wilmore. Wilemoa.

Winfred. Winipeleke, Winiferede.

Zacchaeus. Kakaio, Zakaio.

Zacharias. Kakalia, Zakaria.

Zadok. Kakoka, Zadoka.

Zebedee. Kepekaio, Zebedaio.

Zebulun. Kepuluna, Zebuluna.

Zedekiah. Kekekia, Zedekia.

Zepherin. Kepelino, Zeferino; Kepilino.

Zerubabel. Kelupapela, Zerubabela.

Zorobabel. Kolopapela, Zorobabela.

NAMES OF WOMEN

Abbie. Apī.

Abigail. Apika'ila, Abigaila.

Abishag. Apikaka, Abisaga.

Ada. Aka.

Adelaide. Akelaika, Adelaida.

Adeline. Akelina, Adelina.

Adella. Akela, Adela.

Agatha. Akaka, Agata.

Agnes. Akeneki, Ageneti.

Ahinoam. Ahinoama.

Ailene. Ailina.

Alberta. Alepeka, Alebeta.

Alethia. Alekia, Aletia.

Alexandria. Alekanekalia, Alekanedaria.

Alexandrina. Alekanekelina, Alekanederina.

Alice. Aleka, Alesa.

Alma. Alema.

Almira. Alamila, Alamira.

Alvina. Alawina, Alavina.

Amanda. Amanaka, Amanada.

Amelia. Amelia.

Amy. Eme.

Anastasia. Anakakia, Anatasia.

Andrea. Anakalia, Anadaria.

Angela. Ānela.
Anita. Anika, Anita.
Anitra. Anikala, Anitara.
Ann. Ana.
Anna. Ana.
Annabelle. Anapela, Anabela.
Annette. Aneka, Aneta.
Annie. Ane.
Antoinette. Anakonia, Anatonia.
Antonia. *Same as* **Antoinette.**
Arabella. Alapela, Arabela.
Asenath. Akenaka, Asenata.
Athalia. Akalia, Atalia.
Audrey. Aukele, Audere.
Augusta. Aukaka, Augata.
Aurelia. Aulelia, Aurelia.
Aurora. Alola, Arora.
Barbara. Palapala, Barabara.
Bathsheba. Pakekepa, Bateseba.
Beatrice. Peakalika, Beatarisa;
    Piakilika, Biatirisa.
Becky. Peke.
Bella. Pela, Bela.
Belle. *Same as* **Bella.**
Bernadette. Pelenakeka, Berena-
    deta.
Bernadine. Pelenakino, Berena-
    dino.
Bernice. Berenike.
Bertha. Peleka, Bereta.
Beryl. Pelulo, Berulo.
Beth. *Same as* **Elizabeth.**
Betty. Peke.
Beulah. Peula, Beula.
Bilhah. Pileha, Bileha.
Bonnie. Poni.
Bridget. Pilikika, Birigita.
Carlotta. Kaloka, Kalota.
Carmelia. Kamelia; Komela,
    Pua-komela.
Carmen. Kalamela.
Carmilla. Kamila.
Carol. Kālola, Karola.
Caroline. Kalolaina, Karolaina;
    Kalalaina, Karalaina; Keala-
    laina.
Catherine. Kakalina, Katarina.

Cecelia. Kikilia, Sisilia; Kekilia,
    Sesilia.
Celestine. Kelekina, Keletina.
Celia. Kilia.
Charlotte. Halaki, Harati; Ka-
    loke, Kalote.
Chloe. Koloe.
Christina. Kilikina, Kiritina.
Christine. *Same as* **Christina.**
Christophine. Kilikipine, Kirisi-
    pine.
Cinderella. Kinikalela, Kinida-
    rela.
Clara. Kalala, Kalara.
Clarice. Kalalika, Kalarisa.
Claudia. Kalaukia, Kalaudia;
    Kelaukia, Kelaudia.
Claudine. Kalaukina, Kalaudina.
Cleopatra. Kaleopakala, Kaleo-
    patara.
Clotilda. Kelokilaka, Kelotilada.
Cobina. Kopina, Kobina.
Consuelo. Konokuelo, Kono-
    suelo.
Cordelia. Kokelia, Kodelia.
Corinne. Kolina, Korina.
Cornelia. Kolenelia, Korenelia.
Cynthia. Kinikia, Kinitia, Sini-
    tia.
Dagmar. Kakamā, Dagama.
Deborah. Kepola, Debora.
Delia. Kelia, Delia.
Deliah. *Same as* **Delia.**
Della. Kela, Dela.
Delphine. Kelepine, Delepine.
Denise. Kenike, Denise.
Diana. Kiana, Diana.
Dinah. Kina, Dina.
Dolores. Kololeke, Dolorese.
Dora. Kola.
Dorcas. Koleka, Doreka.
Doreen. Kōlina, Dorina.
Doris. Kolika, Dorisa.
Dorothy. Kolokea, Dorotea,
    Kōleka.
Drusilla. Kelaukila, Derausila.
Edith. Ekika, Edita.
Edna. Ekena, Edena.

Edwina. Eluina, Eluena.
Eilene. Ailina.
Elaine. Ileina.
Elberta. Elepeka, Elebeta.
Eleanor. Elenola, Elenora; Elenoa.
Eliza. Laika.
Elizabeth. Elikapeka, Elisabeta; Kapeka.
Ella. Ela.
Ellen. Elena.
Elmira. Elemila, Elemira.
Eloise. Eloika, Eloisa.
Elsie. Eleki, Elesi.
Elvira. Elewila, Elewira, Elevira.
Emelia. Emelia, Emalia.
Emily. Emelē.
Emma. Ema.
Emmaline. Emalaina.
Erica. Elika, Erika.
Ernestine. Elenekina, Erenetina.
Estelle. Ekekela, Esetela.
Esther. Ekekela, Esetera.
Ethel. Ekela, Etela.
Eugenia. Iukinia, Iuginia; Iukina, Iugina.
Eulalie. Ulalia; Iulalia.
Eunice. Eunike; Iunia.
Euphemia. Eupemia.
Eva. Iwa.
Evangeline. Ewanekelina, Evanegelina.
Eve. Ewa.
Evelyn. Ewalina, Evalina.
Faith. Mana'o'i'o.
Fanny. Pane, Fane.
Faustina. Paukekina, Fausetina.
Fidelia. Pikelia, Fidelia.
Flora. Polola, Folora.
Florence. Pololena, Folorena.
Florinda. Pelolina, Felorina.
Frances. Palakika, Farakika.
Freda. Pelika, Ferida.
Georgiana. Keokiana, Geogiana.
Georgina. Keokina, Geogina.
Gertrude. Kekaluka, Getaruda;

Kelekuluke, Gereturude (*Catholic*).
Gloria. Kololia, Goloria.
Hagar. Hakala, Hagara.
Hannah. Hana.
Harriet. Haliaka, Hariata.
Hazel. Hakela, Hazela.
Heidi. Heiki.
Helen. Helena, Helene, Helina.
Helena. Helena.
Henrietta. Heneliaka, Heneriata.
Hepzibah. Hepeziba.
Herodias. Helokia, Herodia.
Hester. Hekekela, Hesetera; Hekeka, Heseta.
Hettie. Heke, Hete; Heki, Heti.
Hilaria. Hilalia.
Hilda. Hileka, Hileda.
Hope. Mana'olana.
Hortense. Holekeneke, Horetenese.
Hulda. Huleka, Huleda.
Ida. Aika, Aida.
Ina. Aina.
Inez. Aineki, Ainesi.
Irene. Ailina, Airina.
Isabelle. Ikapela, Isabela.
Jane. Kini.
Janet. Ianeke, Ianete.
Jean. Kini.
Jennie. Kini.
Jerusha. Keluka, Kerusa.
Jezebel. Iezebela.
Joan. Iō'ana, Koana.
Johanna. Iō'ana, Koana.
Josephine. Iokepine, Iosepine.
Juanita. Wanika, Wanita.
Judith. Iukika, Iudita.
Julia. Iulia, Kulia.
Julianna. Kuliana.
Juliette. Kuliana.
June. Iune.
Juno. Iuno.
Justina. Iukikina, Iusitina.
Kate. Keke.
Katherine. *See* **Catherine.**
Kathleen. Kakalina, Katalina.

Katie. Keke, Kete.
Keturah. Kekula, Ketura.
Laura. Lala, Lara.
Leah. Lea.
Lena. Lina.
Leonora. Leonola, Leonora.
Letitia. Lekikia, Letitia.
Libbie. Lipe, Libe.
Liberta. Lipeka, Libeta.
Lillian. Liliana.
Lily. Lilia.
Lois. Loika, Loisa.
Lolita. Lolika, Lolita.
Loretta. Loleka, Loreta.
Lorraine. Loleina, Loreina.
Louisa. Luika, Luisa.
Louise. See Louisa.
Lucia. Lukia, Lusia.
Lucille. Lukila, Lusila.
Lucinda. Lukina, Lusina.
Lucy. Luke, Luse; Lukia.
Lydia. Lukia, Ludia; Lulia.
Mabel. Meipala, Meibala.
Madeline. Makelina, Madelina.
Malvina. Malawina, Malavina.
Mamie. Mame.
Marcella. Mākela, Masela.
Margaret. Makaleka, Magareta.
Marguerite. Makalika, Magarita.
Maria. Malaea, Maraea.
Marian. Maliana, Mariana.
Marianne. Same as Maryann.
Marie. Malia, Maria.
Marietta. Meliaka, Meriata; Maliaka, Mariata.
Marilda. Malilaka, Marilada.
Marilyn. Melelina, Merelina.
Marlene. Malina.
Martha. Maleka, Mareta (Biblical); Malaka, Marata (Catholic).
Martina. Malakina, Maratina.
Mary. Malia, Maria (Biblical); Mele, Mere.
Maryann. Meleana, Mereana.
May. Mei.
Maybelle. Meipela, Meibela.

Melissa. Melika, Melisa.
Mercedes. Mekeke, Mesede.
Michelle. Mikala.
Milcah. Mileka.
Mildred. Milikeleka, Milidereda.
Millicent. Milikena, Milisena.
Millie. Mile.
Minerva. Minewa, Mineva.
Minnie. Mine.
Miriam. Miliama, Miriama.
Mona. Mona.
Monica. Monika.
Muriel. Miuliela, Miuriela.
Myra. Maila, Maira.
Myrna. Milena, Mirena.
Myrtle. Makala, Matala.
Nancy. Naneki.
Nanette. Naneka, Naneta.
Naomi. Naomi.
Nathalie. Nakeli, Nateli.
Nell. Same as Nellie.
Nellie. Nele.
Nettie. Neki, Neti.
Nina. Nina.
Nora. Nola, Nora.
Noreen. Nolina, Norina.
Norma. Noma.
Olga. Oleka, Olega.
Olive. Oliwa, Oliva.
Olivia. Oliwia, Olivia.
Olympia. Olumepia.
Orpah. Orepa.
Orpha. Olepa, Orepa.
Pamela. Pamila.
Pansy. Pāneki.
Patience. Ahonui.
Patricia. Pakelekia, Paterekia.
Paulette. Poleke, Polete.
Pauline. Polina.
Pearl. Momi.
Persis. Peleki, Peresi.
Phillipa. Pilipa.
Philomena. Pilomena; Pilomina.
Phoebe. Pō'ipe.
Phyllis. Piliki.
Polly. Pole.
Portia. Polekia, Poretia.

Priscilla. Pelekila, Peresila; Peresekila.

Prudence. Pelukena, Perudena.

Rachel. Lāhela, Rahela.

Rahab. Lahapa, Rahaba.

Rebecca. Lepeka, Rebeka.

Reina. Leina.

Rena. Lina, Rina.

Rhoda. Loke, Rode.

Roberta. Lopeka, Robeta.

Romelia. Lomelia, Romelia.

Rosa. Loka, Rosa.

Rosabelle. Lokapela, Rosabela.

Rosalie. Lōkālia, Rosalia.

Rosamond. Lokamona, Rosamona.

Rose. Loke, Rose.

Roselind. Lokelina, Roselina.

Rosemary. Lokemele, Rosemere.

Rosina. Lokina.

Rowena. Lowena, Rowena.

Ruby. Lupe, Rube.

Ruth. Luka, Ruta.

Sally. Kāle, Sale.

Salome. Kalome, Salome.

Sarah. Kala, Sara; Kela, Sera.

Sarai. Kalai.

Selina. Kelina.

Serah. Sera.

Sibyl. Kipila, Sibila.

Sonya. Kōnia, Sonia.

Sophia. Kopia, Sofia; Kopaea, Sofaea.

Stephanie. Kekepania, Setepania.

Susan. Kukana, Susana.

Susannah. *Same as* **Susan.**

Susie. Kuke, Suse.

Sybil. Kepila, Sebila.

Sylvia. Kiliwia, Silivia.

Tabitha. Kapika, Tabita.

Tallulah. Kalula, Talula.

Tamar. Kamala, Tamara.

Theresa. Keleka, Teresa.

Therese. Kelekia, Teresia.

Thomasine. Komakina, Tomasina.

Tryphena. Kelupaina, Terupaina.

Ulrica. Ulalika, Ularika.

Ursula. Ulukula, Urusula.

Valeria. Walelia, Valeria.

Vera. Wila, Vira.

Verna. Welena, Verena.

Veronika. Walonika, Varonika, Walanika, Welonika.

Victoria. Wikolia, Vitoria.

Viola. Waiola.

Violet. Waioleka, Vaioleta.

Virginia. Wilikinia, Viriginia.

Vivian. Wiwiana, Viviana.

Wanda. Wanaka.

Wilhelmina. Wilemina.

Willa. Wīla.

Winifred. Winipeleke, Winiferede.

Yolanda. Iolana.

Yvonne. Iwone, Ivone.

Zenobia. Kenopia, Zenobia.

Zilpah. Kilepa, Zilepa.

Ziporah. Kipola, Zipora.

Grammar

1. OVERALL VIEW

Hawaiian grammar is complex and imperfectly studied; only salient features are discussed here.

The inventory of significant sounds in the language includes only eight consonants, five short vowels, and five long vowels. Certainly few if any other languages in the world have so meager a list.

Words in Hawaiian are of two main types, content words and particles. Content words may occur alone and usually have dictionary glosses. Students have most trouble with particles. Many are short (*ka, ke, na, nā, ua, e, i, iā, ʻo, no, nō*), but the functions are manifold. They are important, as they may indicate whether the nearby content words are nouns or verbs, whether action is completed or going on, whether a noun is subject, object, agent, possessor, or locative—the sort of grammatical information that in Latin and Greek is often given by inflected endings. Hawaiian has no tenses and no inflections.

If this be thought simple, one should examine Hawaiian pronouns, possessives, and demonstratives. They are more numerous than their English counterparts and have very explicit meanings that make the English ones seem crudely vague.

Another feature surprising to those whose linguistic sophistication is confined to European languages is that the Hawaiian language contains no verbs corresponding to English ʻto beʼ and ʻto haveʼ.

The common order of content words in sentences is:

Verb ± subject ± object or other prepositional phrase

Each of these slots may begin and close with particles, and be followed by qualifying content words. There are no words that serve only as qualifiers, in the manner of English adjectives and adverbs.

Another common type of sentence contains no verb at all:

"I am a man" is *he kāne au*, literally, ʻa man Iʼ.

2. PRONUNCIATION: AMPLIFICATION AND COMMENTARY

For the list of sounds in the Hawaiian language, and comments on stress, see the table on page ix.

By the term *aspiration* of *p* and *k* is meant that a puff of breath accompanies the release of these sounds, as occurs in initial *p* and *k* in English. In speaking Hawaiian one attempts to reduce the strength of the aspiration and to achieve the *p* in *spit* and the *k* in *skit*.

In the Ni'ihau dialect of Hawaiian and occasionally in chants, *k* is irregularly replaced by an unaspirated *t*.

Hawaiian diphthongs and single vowels need to be distinguished: *e* and *ei: ke* 'the', *kei* 'proud'; *o* and *ou: no* 'for', *nou* 'for you'. (The English speaker tends to say *kei* for *ke* and *nou* for *no*.)

Similarly, the speaker of English must learn to distinguish -*ae* and -*ai*, and -*ao* and -*au*. The following pairs are troublesome: *pae* 'row', *pai* 'to urge'; *mae* 'to wilt', *mai* 'hither'; *kao* 'dart', *kau* 'to place'; *pao* 'to scoop', *pau* 'finished'.

Diphthongs are *always* stressed on the first vowel unless the first vowel is long ('*āina* 'meal', '*ăina* 'land').

The presence or absence of glottal stops and macrons changes both pronunciation and meaning, as shown by the following groups of words conventionally spelled *pau, kau,* and *koi*:

pau 'finished'	*kau* 'to place'	*koi* 'to urge'
pa'u 'soot'	*ka'u* 'mine'	*ko'i* 'adze'
pa'ū 'moist'	*Ka'ū*, a place name	*kōī* 'shrill'
pā'ū 'sarong'		

The glottal stop also occurs nonsignificantly before vowels preceded by silence. A Hawaiian will greet a friend with the single word *Aloha!* The same word *within* an utterance will have no glottal stop: *ua aloha mai* 'did send greeting'. Such utterance-initial glottal stops do not influence meaning and are not written.

Other utterance-initial glottal stops persist in noninitial position and their occurrence does change meanings, as evidenced by the following pairs:

| *ai* 'sexual intercourse' | *ili* 'to inherit' | *ulu* 'to grow' |
| *'ai* 'to eat' | *'ili* 'skin' | *'ulu* 'breadfruit' |

| *ea* 'life' | *oli* 'chant' |
| *'ea*, turtle species | *'oli* 'joy' |

All monosyllabic content words bear macrons. Vowels marked with macrons are stressed regardless of position: *kū* 'standing', *wāhíne* 'women', *mō'í* 'king', *hòlokū* 'dress with a train'.

Spaces between words indicate boundaries of particles or content words, but do not necessarily mark pauses in pronunciation. The phrase *ka imu kī* 'the ti oven' is composed of three words, but in normal speech is pronounced as a single word (*kàimukí*).

COLLOQUIAL SPEECH

The orthography used in the Pocket Dictionary represents the slow speech of careful speakers. Normal fast speech differs in several ways. Some of them are:

(a) *Ai* assimilates to *ei*, and, less commonly, *au* to *ou*: *ikaika* 'strong' is usually *ikeika*; *kēlā mau mea* 'those things' is sometimes *kēlā mou mea*.

(b) Like vowels separated by a glottal stop reduce to glottal stop plus vowel: Hawai'i becomes Hawa'i; *pua'a* 'pig' becomes *pu'a*.

(c) *-aCo* (C = consonant) assimilates to *-a'a*: *'a'ole* 'not' becomes *'a'ale*; *ma'ona* 'full' becomes *ma'ana*; *mahope* 'afterwards' becomes *mahape*.

(d) Vowels before silence may be whispered or dropped; thus *Punalu'u*, a place name, becomes *Punalu'* (not *Punaluw*); *hele akula* 'went away' becomes *hele akul* or even *hele kū*.

3. VERBS AND VERB PHRASES

Verbs may be defined as content words that may be preceded by *verb-marking particles*. The most common of these particles are:

ua (verb), perfective aspect (completed action)
e (verb) *ana*, imperfective aspect (incomplete action)

ke (verb) *nei,* present
e (verb), imperative
*mai*₁ (verb), negative imperative

Ua indicates that the following verb represents a completed action, state of being, or newly arrived state ("inceptive"). The verb following *ua* is usually translated in English by present or past tense: *ua maika'i 'oia* 'he is well'; *ua hele 'oia* 'he went'.

E (verb) *ana* is incomplete action. *E hele ana au* may be translated, according to context, 'I was going, I am going, I will go', but never 'I went'. *Ke* (verb) *nei* indicates present continuing action, as the lover says in the famous love song, *Ke kali nei au* 'I am waiting'. The imperative is *e: E hele!* 'Go ahead!' The negative imperative is *mai: Mai hele!* 'Don't go!'

Ua and the imperative *e* are frequently omitted in colloquial speech if the context is clear.

The verb phrase is diagrammed in the lower portion of figure 1.

Most verbs may function also in other capacities. Very commonly they are used as nouns; that is, they follow noun markers such as articles (*ka, ke, he, nā*) and possessives. The situation is something like that of English 'love' and 'hope':

> Verb: *Ua aloha au iāia* 'I *love* her'
> Noun: *Ko'u aloha* 'my *love*'

> Verb: *Ua mana'olana lākou* 'they *hope*'
> Noun: *Kō lākou mana'olana* 'their *hope*'

Such words in Hawaiian are extremely numerous and impart great flexibility to the language. Besides functioning as both noun and verb, they may also qualify nouns and verbs:

> Verb: *Ua maika'i lākou* 'they [are] *well*'
> Verb qualifier: *Ua hana maika'i lākou* 'they work *well*'

> Noun: *Ka maika'i o ka 'āina* 'the *goodness* of the land'
> Noun qualifier: *He 'āina maika'i* 'a *good* land'

Most verbs may be followed by the particle *'ia,* which usually passivizes the verb, but sometimes marks the imperative. Thus *'ai 'ia ka poi* is usually 'the poi was eaten' but could also mean 'eat the poi!' Such forms in the Dic-

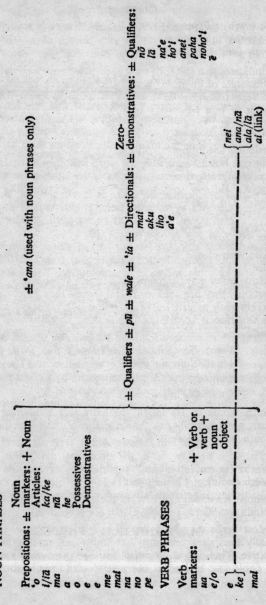

Figure 1. Hawaiian phrases.

tionary are labeled passive/imperative. There is a very restricted list of verbs that take also certain closely bound
suffixes with the same dual roles (*-a, -hia, -lia, -mia, -nia,
-na*).

Some verbs, called *loa'a*-type or stative, do not take *'ia*
or the suffixes just mentioned; they seem to be inherently
passive, as in the sentence *loa'a ka i'a iā Pua* 'the fish was
obtained by Pua'. But once a stative, not always a stative.
Statives, like most verbs, may take causative prefixes (*ho'o-,
hō'-, ho-, hō-*); they are then transitives rather than statives.

> Stative: *Pau ka hana iāia* 'the work was finished by him'
> Transitive: *Ho'opau 'oia i ka hana* 'he finished the work'

In the stative sentence the agent is marked by *iā*; in the
transitive sentence by *'o*. Some persons today rarely use the
stative construction. They might translate the stative sentence above as *pau 'oia ka hana*.

Repetition of an entire base or part of a base is common.
Such reduplication indicates repetition or frequency of action, and in some instances, a diminutive. Examples are
hoe 'paddle', *hoehoe* 'paddling on and on, several persons
paddling'; *puhi* 'to blow', *pupuhi* 'blowing frequently or for
a long time, several persons blowing'; *āhole*, adult stage of
a fish, *āholehole*, young stage of the same fish.

Verbs are commonly followed by particles termed directionals. They are *mai₂*, toward the speaker; *aku*, away from
the speaker; *iho* 'down'; and *a'e* 'up, adjacent'. They are
usually separated from the preceding verb by a slight pause:
thus, *manà'o iho* 'think', not *màna'óiho*.

Use of directionals is complicated. *Mai* may be used as
a complete sentence meaning 'come'; however, it never follows verb markers. On the other hand, *iho* may be used as
a verb 'to go down' and follows all the verb markers; it is
also used reflexively, as in the preceding paragraph. *A'e*
expresses comparative and superlative degrees: *maika'i*
'good', *maika'i a'e* 'better, best'.

For use of directionals after nouns, see section 4.

4. NOUNS AND NOUN PHRASES

Nouns are content words that may occur in noun phrases
consisting of optional preposition plus optional noun
marker plus noun. The noun markers include articles (sec-

tion 4), possessives (section 5), and demonstratives (section 5). The noun phrase is diagrammed in the upper part of figure 1.

PREPOSITIONS INTRODUCE NOUN PHRASES

The important prepositions, with examples, follow:

'o, subject marker: *Ua hele 'o Pua. Ua hele 'oia.* 'Pua went. She went.' (*'O* is used most commonly before names of persons and before the third person singular pronoun *ia* used as subject. Otherwise, the subject is commonly unmarked.)

i/iā, object marker, 'at (general locative)': *Ua nānā 'o Pua i ka hale* 'Pua looked at the house'. *Ua nānā 'o Pua iā Kimo* 'Pua looked at James'. *Ua nānā 'o Pua iāia* 'Pua looked at him'. *Ua noho i Maui* 'living at Maui'. (*Iā* precedes pronouns and names of people; otherwise *i* is used; occasionally *iā* precedes place names. In fast speech *i* is sometimes omitted.)

ma 'at, in (specific locative)': *Noho ma Kahuku i O'ahu* 'living at Kahuku on O'ahu'. (Note the contrast between *ma* and *i.*)

a 'of, acquired by': *Hale-a-ka-lā,* place name, literally 'house acquired by the sun'.

o 'of (inherited, spatial), in honor of': *Nā-iwi-o-Pele,* place name, literally 'the bones of Pele'. (The *a-o* distinction is discussed in section 5.)

e_1 'by': *'Ai 'ia e Pua* 'eaten by Pua'.

e_2, vocative: *E Pua, hele mai!* 'Pua, come here!'

me 'with, and, like, by means of': *Noho 'oia me Pua* 'he lived with Pua'. *Hele mai lāua, Pua me Kimo* 'the two came, Pua and Jim'. *Holo mehe lio* 'run like a horse'. *Kākau me kēia penikala* 'write with this pencil'.

mai_3 'from': *Mai Maui* 'from Maui'. *Mai Maui mai* 'here from Maui'. (The second *mai* is the directional particle.)

na 'for, by': *Na Pua ka puke* 'the book is by Pua'.

no 'for': *No Pua ka puke* 'the book is for (or about) Pua'. (*-a* and *-o* in these prepositions are similar to the *a* and *o* possessives. See section 5.)

pe 'like': *Pe kēia* 'like this'.

The prepositions *a, o, ma, na,* and *no* are usually short, but are automatically lengthened before long vowels and diphthongs: *nā lei a Lani* 'the leis (made) by Lani' and *nā lei ā Kū* 'the leis (made) by Kū'; *nā hale o ke ali'i* 'the houses of the chief' and *nā hale ō Maui* 'the houses of Maui'; *ma ka hale* 'at the house' and *mā laila* 'there'; *na Kimo* 'by James' and *nā lākou* 'by them'; *no Pua* 'for Pua' and *nō mākou* 'for us'. This lengthening is predictable and hence is not indicated in the spelling nor in the entries in the Pocket Dictionary.

ARTICLES MARK NOUNS

'*Ka* and its variant *ke* are usually called singular definite articles, commonly translated 'the'. *Ke* precedes nouns beginning with *a-, e-, o-,* and *k-,* and before some nouns beginning with the glottal stop and *p-; ka* occurs elsewhere (*ke aloha* 'the love', *ke ea* 'the life', *ke oho* 'the hair', *ke kanaka* 'the person', *ka hale* 'the house'; *ke 'ala,* 'the fragrance'· but *ka 'alā* 'the stone', *ke pā* 'the dish' but *ka pā* 'the fence'). The plural definite article is *nā* (*nā pua* 'the flowers'). In contrast to English usage, the articles precede abstract nouns (*maika'i ke aloha* 'love is good'). *He* is a singular indefinite article (*he pepa kēia* 'this is a paper'). *He* does *not* follow prepositions other than *me* (see the Pocket Dictionary for *mehe*). *He* coalesces with the negative '*a'ole* to '*a'ohe* 'to be or have none': '*a'ohe āna puke* 'he has no books', literally, 'to-be-none his (plural) book'.

The articles are omitted if the meaning is 'any, any whatsoever': *Lawe mai he puke* 'bring a book'. *Lawe mai i puke* 'bring any book'. *Hele mai nā kānaka* 'the people came'. *Hele mai kānaka* 'some people (any at all) came'.

Nouns classed as locatives (place words) occur most commonly without articles, as in noun phrases that may be schematized as follows:

$$
\left.\begin{array}{l} i \\ ma\text{-} \end{array}\right\} + \left\{\begin{array}{l} luna \text{ 'over, on top'} \\ lalo \text{ 'under'} \\ mua \text{ 'first, front'} \\ waena \text{ 'middle'} \\ hope \text{ 'after, last'} \\ loko \text{ 'in, inside'} \\ waho \text{ 'out, outside'} \\ kai \text{ 'seaward'} \\ uka \text{ 'inland'} \end{array}\right\} + o + \left\{\begin{array}{l} ka \\ ke \\ k\text{-word} \end{array}\right\} + \text{noun}
$$

Examples: *i luna o ka mauna* 'on top of the mountain', *maloko o ka hale* 'inside the house'.

Laila 'there' and names of people and places also occur without articles.

Ma- is written, by convention, joined to the locative (*i lalo o ka hale, malalo o ka hale* 'under the house').

Following articles, the locatives have somewhat different meanings:

> *ka luna* 'the foreman'
> *ka lalo* 'the bottom'
>
> *ka mua* 'the firstborn, first'
> *ka waena* 'the middle'
> *ka hope* 'the youngest, last'
>
> *ka loko* 'the inside, lake'
> *ka waho* 'the outside'
>
> *ke kai* 'the sea'
> *ka uka* 'the uplands'

The locatives are characterized by metonymy, that is, the use of one term to mean another—in this case the term for the container to mean the thing contained; for example, *waho* 'outside' also means 'the people who are outside'. Other nouns may also be personalized. *Wa'a* means both 'canoe' and 'people in the canoe, crew'.

COMPOUNDS

Compounds are indivisible sequences of content words whose total meaning is not readily apparent. *Na'auao* 'intelligent' is composed of the sequence *na'au* 'intestines' and *ao* 'daylight' and thus meets the test. It is a compound. *Kanaka akamai* 'smart man', however, is not. Another compound noun is *'ōkole'oi'oi* 'marigold' (literally 'jutting buttocks'). *Uluwehi* 'to be lush and beautiful, verdure' (literally 'decorative growth') is a compound verb-noun, but less obviously a compound. Compound verbs seem to be lacking, although verb + noun object is a common sequence that behaves like a single verb (*hoe wa'a mai!* 'canoe-paddle here!'

NOMINALIZATIONS

Some verbs are made into nouns by the addition of the particle *'ana* or the suffix *-na*. *'Ana* is probably productive (that is, it occurs with nearly any verb), but *-na* occurs only with a restricted list, as *kālai* 'to carve' and *kalaina* 'carved object' (the long vowel is shortened). Compare *ua maika'i kāna kālai 'ana* 'his carving (the act rather than the object) is good'.

DIRECTIONALS AFTER NOUNS

Use of the four directionals after verbs or as verbs was described in section 3.

Directionals also follow nouns. *Mai* and *iho* used alone have direction meanings similar to those when following verbs. *Mai Maui mai* 'from Maui this way, from Maui'. *Maluna iho* 'not quite on top, a little below the top'.

Aku and *a'e* also follow time words; *aku* expresses past or future time and *a'e* future time, the *aku* time being perhaps more distant than the *a'e* time. *Kēia* and *ia* meaning 'this' refer to the future; *kēlā* 'that' refers to the past.

this, future	*kēia* ⎫ *ia* ⎬ *pule aku nei* 'week after this'	*kēia pule a'e* 'next week (imminent)'
		'apōpō ā ia lā aku 'day after tomorrow'
that, past	*kēlā pule aku nei* 'last week'	

5. PERSON WORDS

Person words differ from other content words such as *hale* 'house' in that all of them (except the singular pronouns and the zero-demonstratives) are made up of at least two elements that cannot be used alone; that is, they do not contain bases. The three types of person words are pronouns, possessives, and demonstratives. In the following treatment of each of these types, identifiable elements are set off by hyphens.

PRONOUNS

The pronouns in Hawaiian may be tabulated as follows:

Person	Singular	Dual	Plural
1 inclusive		*kā-ua* 'we'	*kā-kou* 'we'
exclusive	*au* 'I', *a'u* 'me'	*mā-ua* 'we'	*mā-kou* 'we'
2	*'oe* 'you'	*'o-lua* 'you'	*'ou-kou* 'you'
3	*ia* 'he, she, it'	*lā-ua* 'they'	*lā-kou* 'they'

The elements set off by hyphens are easily labeled: *kā-*, inclusive; *mā-*, exclusive; *-ua/-lua*, dual; *-kou*, plural; *'o-/'ou-*, second person; *lā-*, third person.

With the inclusive pronouns, the person addressed is included. He is unequivocably excluded by the exclusive pronouns. The use of inclusive pronouns imparts a nuance of cosy intimacy that is completely lacking with the exclusive pronouns.

Aloha kā-ua 'may there be love between you and me'
Aloha kā-kou 'may there be love among all of us'

Hele kā-ua i Honolulu 'you and I are going to Honolulu'
Hele mā-ua i Honolulu 'someone else and I are going to Honolulu'

In English, 'we're going to the hula' is ambiguous. The addressee can't be sure that he's invited. Perhaps the speaker is going with someone else. But if the Hawaiian is used, *hele kā-kou i ka hula*, the addressee knows he is included because of the inclusive *kā-kou*.

The third person singular form when used as the subject is usually preceded by the subject marker *'o*, the sequence being written *'oia*; similarly, *ia* when preceded by the object marker *iā* is usually written *iāia*.

A few speakers pronounce the duals *kā-'ua mā-'ua, lā-'ua*, that is, with glottal stops.

POSSESSIVES

Possessives are of two types: *k*-possessives (those beginning with *k*-) and zero-possessives (without *k*-). The *k*- possessives are listed below.

Person	Singular	Dual	Plural
1 inclusive		$k\text{-}\frac{\bar{a}}{\bar{o}}$ *kā-ua* 'our'	$k\text{-}\frac{\bar{a}}{\bar{o}}$ *kā-kou* 'our'
exclusive	$k\text{-}\frac{a}{o}\text{-}'u$ 'my' *k-u-'u* 'my'	$k\text{-}\frac{\bar{a}}{\bar{o}}$ *mā-ua* 'our'	$k\text{-}\frac{\bar{a}}{\bar{o}}$ *mā-kou* 'our'
2	$k\text{-}\frac{\bar{a}}{\bar{o}}\text{-}u$ 'your' *k-o* 'your'	$k\text{-}\frac{\bar{a}}{\bar{o}}$ *'o-lua* 'your'	$k\text{-}\frac{\bar{a}}{\bar{o}}$ *'oukou* 'your'
3	$k\text{-}\frac{\bar{a}}{\bar{o}}\text{-}na$ 'his, her, its'	$k\text{-}\frac{\bar{a}}{\bar{o}}$ *lā-ua* 'their'	$k\text{-}\frac{\bar{a}}{\bar{o}}$ *lā-kou* 'their'

The English glosses do not indicate that the possessives are translated by English possessive pronouns as well as by English possessive adjectives: *k-o-'u hale* 'my house' and *k-o-'u kēlā* 'that is mine'.

The table becomes less formidable when it is noted that the dual and plural forms consist of *k-ā* or *k-ō* plus the standard pronoun forms.

The most salient feature shown in the table is that in nearly every position at least two forms occur: one with *ā* (or *a*) and another with *ō* (or *o*). This important distinction is discussed below.

The *a-* (or *ā-*) in the possessives is equatable with the possessive preposition *a* (section 4). Similarly, *-o* (or *-ō*) is equatable with the possessive prepositions treated in the same section. They will be referred to henceforth as *a-* and *o-*forms.

As suggested by Albert J. Schütz and William H. Wilson, the use of *a* or *o* depends less on the nature of the possessed object than on the *relationship* of possessed and possessor. *A* indicates *controlled or acquired by the possessor*; *o* the reverse. Thus *k-a-'u keiki* 'my child' and *k-o-'u kupuna* 'my grandparent': the possessor controls and possibly begets the child, not the grandparent.

A change of possessive marker may change the meaning: *k-ā-na lei* 'lei made by her (or him)', *k-o-na lei* 'lei given to her (or him)'; *k-ā-na mele* 'song composed by him (or her)', *k-o-na mele* 'song in his (or her) honor'; *k-ā-u aliʻi* 'your (subordinate) chief', *k-o-u aliʻi* 'your (inherited) chief'.

Some words nearly always take a single form. Small possessions, as book, pencil, breadfruit, take *a*. Body parts take *o* (one does not set out to acquire them). Certain important objects in the old culture ordinarily take *o:* land, house, canoe, superior chief, ancestors, gods. These are "wished" on one; everyone has an inalienable right to them.

Words indicating spatial relation commonly take *o: i loko o ka hale* 'inside of the house'. Clothing that one wears takes *o;* one is inside them. Similarly, a chair, horse, or automobile one sits on or in.

For interesting discussions of *a* and *o* see Alexander's Hawaiian grammar (pages 9–11), Biggs' treatment of Maori (pages 43–49), and an unpublished paper by William H. Wilson. (See References.)

Two forms in the table of possessives are without *ā/a* and *ō/o*. They are alternate forms, sometimes called neutral, in the first and second persons singular. The *a/o* distinction is not involved in these forms. *K-u-ʻu* usually contains a nuance of affection. Thus, *k-u-ʻu ipo* 'my sweetheart', but not *k-u-ʻu pākaukau* 'my table'. *K-o*, second person singular, is likewise neutral, but without any particular connotation. It is perhaps most common in highly colloquial speech.

The prepositions *na* and *no* contain the same *a* and *o*. Both mean 'for', but *na* is also agentive.

K-ā and *k-ō* also directly precede proper nouns, locatives, and article or possessive + noun sequences. *Ke keiki a Lani* 'Lani's child'. *K-ā Lani keiki* 'Lani's child'. Note that the focus is on the first noun.

Other examples: *Ka poʻe o uka* 'the *people* of the uplands'. *K-ō uka poʻe* 'the *upland* people'. *Ka ʻāina o ke aliʻi* 'the *land* of the chief'. *K-ō ke aliʻi ʻāina* 'the chief's land'. *Ka ʻāina o k-o-na aliʻi* 'the *land* of his chief'. *K-ō k-o-na aliʻi ʻāina* 'his chief's land'.

The zero-possessives are used as indication of plural possessed objects, especially after numerals and the negative *ʻaʻohe* 'to have none': *ʻElua a-ʻu puke* 'I have two books'.

'Ehia ā-u puke? 'how many books have you?' *'A'ohe ā-na puke* 'he has no books'. (In sentences bereft of numerals or negatives, the *k*-possessives are used, and the plural is shown by *mau*: *k-a-'u mau puke* 'my books'.)

DEMONSTRATIVES

The three types of demonstratives are listed below.

	Near speaker	Near addressee	Far	Interrogative
kē-demonstratives	*kē-ia* 'this'	*kē-nā* 'that'	*kē-lā* 'that'	
pē-demonstratives	*pe-nei*, *pē-ia* 'like this'	*pē-nā* 'like that'	*pē-lā* 'like that'	*pe-hea* 'how?'
zero-demonstratives	*ia* 'this' *nei* 'this, here, now'	*nā* 'that, there'	*lā, ala* 'there' *-lā* 'then'	

The *kē*-demonstratives, as well as the *k*-possessives and the articles *ka/ke*, may be called *k*-words. They fill the same positions in the noun phrase. All contain the same *k-*.

$$i\left\{\begin{array}{l} ka \\ k\text{-}o\text{-}'u \\ k\bar{e}\text{-}ia \end{array}\right\} hale \qquad \text{'in}\left\{\begin{array}{l} \text{the} \\ \text{my} \\ \text{this} \end{array}\right\}\text{house'}$$

The *kē*-demonstratives have a link, not indicated by the translations in the table, with pronouns in that they often substitute for pronouns.

Maika'i 'oia 'he is well'
Maika'i kē-ia 'this person is well; he (whom we have been discussing and who is nearby) is well'

The *pē*-demonstratives most commonly function as unmarked verbs: *pē-ia nō* 'just like this', *pe-hea 'oe?* 'how are you?'

Note that the glosses of the difficult zero-demonstratives are demonstrative, locative, and (except for *nā*) temporal ('now, then'). *Ia* seems to be in a class by itself in that its only meaning is demonstrative and that it commonly *precedes* nouns and may substitute for nouns: *Maika'i ia mea* 'this thing is good'. *He maika'i ia* 'this is good'. *Ia* seems less specifically near the speaker than *nei*. *Nei*, extremely common, has the three types of meanings, and after nouns often carries a nuance of affection: *Hawai'i nei* 'this (beloved) Hawai'i'. Its temporal meaning is fairly common but comes near the end of verb phrases; note the famous lover's *ke kali nei au* 'I am now waiting here'. *Lā/ala* occurs in positions similar to those of *nei* but becomes a clitic *-la* in its temporal role: *'Ai iho-la 'oia* 'he then ate'. *Nā* seems not to have temporal functions and usually follows nouns. Both *nei* and *nā* (but not *lā/ala*) occasionally precede nouns.

Another demonstrative, *ua₂*, is pedantically translated 'aforementioned' but merely indicates that the noun head has already been mentioned. The noun is nearly always followed by the zero-demonstratives *nei*, *nā*, or la: *ua kanaka nei* 'this person (we've been talking about)'.

6. TRANSFORMATIONS

The manipulations that a native speaker unconsciously performs in his language may be termed transformations. This is a vast subject. A Hawaiian transformational grammar is yet to be written. Only two types of transformations will be mentioned here: concatenations (combining of more than one sentence into a single sentence) and fronting. The processes include substitution, deletion, and transposition.

CONCATENATIONS

(a) Replacement of *ua* by *i* (verb) *ai*.

> ⎰*'Oia ka manawa* 'that's the time'
> ⎱*Ua hele mai ke ali'i* 'the chief came'

> *'Oia ka manawa i hele mai ai ke ali'i* 'that's the time the chief came'.

The *ai* at the end of the final verb phrase refers to the previous noun *manawa* 'time'. It is called by various writers relative, linking, resultative, and anaphoric, and somewhat corresponds to perhaps nonstandard English prepositions at the end of sentences such as "That's where it's at." "Where are you going to?" "What's he laughing for?"

(b) Deletion of *mea* and replacement of *ua* by *i* and deletion of the subject in the combined sentence.

> { *'O wau ka mea* 'I'm the person'
> { *Ua hele mai au* 'I came'
>
> *'O wau ka i hele mai* 'I'm the one who came'

(c) Replacement of *ua* by *i* and transposition of a pronoun (but rarely if ever a noun) subject.

> { *Ua hele au* 'I went'
> { *'A'ole* 'no'
>
> *'A'ole au i hele* 'I didn't go'
>
> { *Ua hele ke kanaka* 'the man went'
> { *'A'ole* 'no'
>
> *'A'ole i hele ke kanaka* 'the man didn't go'

FRONTING

A rule of Hawaiian syntax is that important things come first. Nouns, for example, are followed by qualifiers, not preceded by them, as in English. Alexander (page 28) lists five ways to translate the English sentence "I give this to you," by fronting the phrase in focus.

One example will be given here.

Usual order: *Ua makemake nui au i kēlāmea* 'I liked that thing very much'.

To emphasize the object: *Kēlā o'u mea i makemake nui 'ia* 'that's what I liked very much'.

Another example of fronting is given at the end of the discussion of *k*-possessives in section 5.

7. NUMERALS

The cardinal numbers below 10 are as follows: 1 *kahi*, 2 *lua*, 3 *kolu*, 4 *hā*, 5 *lima*, 6 *ono*, 7 *hiku*, 8 *walu*, 9 *iwa*.

These may be preceded by the general classifier *'e-* (or rarely *'a-*), usually separated by a slight pause (*'e íwa*, not *'éiwa*). *Kahi* 'one' is usually preceded by *ho'o-*. Numbers above 9 have no classifying particles: 10 *'umi*, 11 *'umi-kūmā-kahi*, 12 *'umi-kūmā-lua*, 20 *'iwakālua*, 21 *'iwakālua-kūmā-kahi*, 30 *kana-kolu*, 40 *kana-hā*, 50 *kana-lima*, 60 *kana-ono*, 70 *kana-hiku*, 80 *kana-walu*, 90 *kana-iwa*. In Biblical usage *-kūmā-* is replaced by *-kumamā-*.

Formerly the vague numbers *lau*, *mano*, *kini*, and *lehu* were used for large numbers, or for 400, 4,000, 40,000, and 400,000, respectively. Missionaries introduced the terms *hanele* 'hundred', *kaukani* 'thousand', and *miliona* 'million', all from English.

The numeral interrogative *-hia* is usually preceded by *'e-*. *'E-hia āu puke?* 'How many books have you?' *'E-lua a'u* 'I have two books'.

8. QUALIFYING PARTICLES

The qualifying particles may be listed in order of occurrence within the phrase. Those in group (a) below may precede *'ia*, the passive/imperative marker. Those in group (b) end the phrase; several of them may occur in the same phrase but in the sequence indicated in the list. This is shown in figure 1.

(a) *pū* 'together'
   wale 'so much, very, for no reason'
(b) *nō*, intensifier
   lā₂, dubitative
   na'e 'yet'
   ho'i, intensifier
   anei, interrogative
   paha 'maybe, perhaps'
   noho'i, mild intensifier
   ē, intensifier

Pū in group (a) may precede *wale*. Most of the particles in group (b) may follow *wale* or *nō*. Common sequences are *wale nō* 'only' (*'elua wale nō* 'just two'), *nō na'e* (*maika'i nō na'e* 'still pretty good'), *noho'i ē* (*auwe noho'i ē!* 'Oh my!').

9. CONJUNCTIONS

Particles called conjunctions sometimes introduce simple
sentences that have only one verb, and sometimes connect
two simple sentences into a sentence with more than one
verb. A few are listed here.

 ā 'and, until, similar unto, like'
 āhea 'when (interrogative future)'
 akā 'but'
 i/iā/iō 'when, at the time that, while'
 inā, i 'if'
 ināhea 'when (interrogative past)'
 kē 'when (future)'
 'oiai, 'oi 'while, at the time that'

10. LOANWORDS

Most of the hundreds of loanwords in Hawaiian are from
English. The replacement of English phonemes by Hawaiian ones is in the main regular.

English	Hawaiian
p, b, f	p
v, w	w
hw	hu
s, h, š	h
l, r	l
m	m
n, ng	n
t, d, Θ, đ, s, z,	
ž, tš, dž, k, g	k
y, i, ɩ	i
e, ɛ	e
æ, a, ɝ, ə, ʌ	a
ɔ, o ɝ	o
ʊ, u	u

Hawaiian adaptations of English words beginning with
a-, e-, and *o-* begin with glottal stops.

As there are no consonant clusters in Hawaiian, English
adjoining consonants are separated in Hawaiian by a vowel

(*pūlumi* 'broom', *palaki* 'brush'), or one of the English consonants is deleted (*kila* 'steel', *Kapalakiko* 'San Francisco'). A vowel is added in Hawaiian to every word taken from English ending in a consonant (*poloka* 'frog'). Similarly, an initial glottal stop is added to every English word beginning with a vowel (*'alimakika* 'arithmetic' and *'īnika* 'ink'). Some loanwords follow English spelling rather than English sounds (*koma* 'comma', *hīmeni* 'hymn', *liona* 'lion').

Bible translators introduced words from Hebrew (*mula* 'myrrh'), Greek (*hepekoma* 'week'), and Latin (*Kaikala* 'Caesar'). Words from Chinese include *Pākē* 'Chinese' (*pai-kei*), and *pakalana* 'Chinese violet' (*pak-lan*). From Portuguese is *pakaliao* 'codfish' (*bacalhau*). From Tahitian are *mano'i* 'perfume' and *Lalako'a* 'Rarotonga' (*Raroto'a*).

11. THE POLYNESIAN LANGUAGE FAMILY

A "language family" is assumed to be a group of languages that were once a single language spoken in a single place. This relationship is proved by the establishment of regular sound correspondences in present-day languages and dialects, and older ones if written records are available. These shifts are regular. For example, the sound *l*, as in Hawaiian *lani* 'sky', is always *l* (or *r* or glottal stop) in the daughter languages; ancient *k* is always *k* except in those languages in which it has been replaced by a glottal stop. The ancient language is not a real language, but rather something worked out by linguists. The words in this original or "proto" language are called *reconstructions*. Each manifestation of a reconstruction in a daughter language is called a *reflex*. The method used in deducing reconstructions requires seemingly endless comparison of reflexes in as many daughter languages and dialects as possible. This technique was first applied to French, Spanish, Latin, Greek, Sanskrit, and other languages having ancient writing. Polynesian languages were not written down until the last century, but nevertheless the method so laboriously worked out with written languages was found to be applicable by consideration of known approximate rates of language change. Polynesia proved to be an excellent field for comparative work because of the relatively simple phono-

logical system, and because the great distances between
island groups assured that resemblances between words
were not due to late intergroup borrowings, but to actual
inheritance from an ancestral tongue.

The following simplified Polynesian family tree is generally accepted today by archaeologists and linguists. It traces
Hawaiian-language ancestry back for at least two thousand
years to Proto East Polynesian (PEP), Proto Nuclear
Polynesian (PNP), and Proto Polynesian (PPN). The
dates are highly approximate.

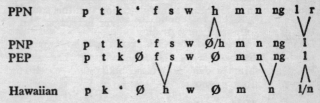

During these centuries the original PPN language under-
went reduction of consonants from 13 in PPN to 8 in Hawaiian (Ø in the following chart represents a complete
loss; *ng* is a velar nasal; the position of the Easter Island
language is not certain and is omitted from consideration):

PPN	p	t	k	'	f	s	w	h	m	n	ng	l	r
PNP	p	t	k	'	f	s	w	Ø/h	m	n	ng	l	
PEP	p	t	k	Ø	f	s	w	Ø	m	n	ng	l	
Hawaiian	p	k	'	Ø	h	w	Ø	m	n	l/n			

The five Polynesian vowels, in contrast to the consonants,
have remained fairly constant throughout history save for
assimilatory and dissimilatory changes. Long vowels, written with macrons in Hawaiian, are doubled in the reconstructions and in the other languages.

The following are the approximate numbers of reconstructions noted in the Pocket Dictionary: PEP 370, PNP
170, PPN 790. These totals will be significantly increased
when other Polynesian languages are studied. In general,
PEP reflexes have been noted only in Maori, Marquesan,
Rarotongan, Tahitian. and/or Tuamotuan besides Hawaiian. PNP reflexes were noted in East Futunan, Rennell-

ese/Bellonese, and/or Samoan. PPN reflexes were noted in Tongan.

The principal source for the reconstructions was Bruce Biggs' *Proto-Polynesian Wordlist*, a computerized summation of nine Polynesian languages. This list was supplemented by consultation of the following dictionaries: for PPN, Churchward; for PNP, Elbert, Milner; for PEP, Andrews and Andrews, Dordillon, Pukui and Elbert, Savage, Stimson and Marshall, Williams. Pawley's 1972 article was most useful, especially for analysis of affixes and pronouns.

Only the earliest form is given in the dictionary if the reflexes are regular. If PNP or PEP show innovations, these too are shown. An example is a word for 'priest':

Tongan *taula* } from PPN *taula*
Samoan *taula*

Maori *taaura* } from PEP *taaula*
Hawaiian *kāula*

The doubling of the first vowel in Maori and Hawaiian represents a PEP innovation, and is thus entered after Hawaiian *kāula*, in addition to the older PPN *taula*.

A few reconstructions in the dictionary contain a sound enclosed within parentheses as an indication that this sound occurs in some but not all of the daughter languages. An example is a word for neck:

Samoan -*'a'ii*   ⎫
Maori *kakii*   ⎬ from *kakii*
Rarotongan *kakii* ⎭

Hawaiian *'aa'ii*   } from *kaakii*
Tuamotuan *kaakii*

The reconstruction is PNP *ka(a)kii*.

Reconstructions with slight meaning discrepancies in the daughter languages are labeled 'probable' or 'possible' in the dictionary. Some Hawaiian reflexes do not perfectly reflect the reconstruction. These have not been analyzed.

If a selection of one of two possible ancestral sounds is not possible, both are entered in parentheses. This uncertainty exists in some instances for reflexes of PEP *f* and *s*, because they generally fall together in the PEP languages available for study.

What were the homelands of the three reconstructed languages? Archaeologists and linguists seem to agree that they may have been Tonga, Samoa, and probably the Marquesas Islands. Those accepting Marquesan origin believe that the first Hawaiians came from the South Marquesas rather than from the geographically closer North Marquesas. Linguistic evidence shows that of all the East Polynesian languages, only South Marquesan and Hawaiian coalesce earlier *n* and *ng* to *n*. Further, both South Marquesan and Hawaiian are replacing PEP *k* by a glottal stop (the South Marquesan change is incomplete; the Hawaiian change is almost complete; only a few double forms exist, as *haki* and *ha'i* 'to break' and *mukumuku* and *mu'umu'u* 'to cut'; *lōkihi* 'long', *kūlepe* 'hairlip', and *moko* 'lizard' are much less common today than *lō'ihi*, *'ūlepe*, and *mo'o*).

The reduction of consonant sounds in the history of the Polynesian languages has been mentioned. At the same time occurred a reduction of grammatical categories, especially in PNP. These losses may be summarized as follows: preposed subject pronouns, reduplicated possessives, *ma'a/mo'o* possessives, indefinite possessives, possessives of endearment, and reciprocal verb forms. Non-future PNP verb markers *kua, na, noko,* and *saa* were reduced to PEP *kua*.

The Polynesian languages, like all languages, constantly changed. Hawaiian, however, did stand as a conspicuous example of flourishing simplification.

SAMUEL H. ELBERT

References

Alexander, W. D. *A Short Synopsis of the Most Essential Points in Hawaiian Grammar.* Rutland, Vt.: Charles E. Tuttle Co., 1968. (First published in 1864.)

Andrews, Edmund, and Irene D. Andrews. *A Comparative Dictionary of the Tahitian Language. Tahitian-English with an English-Tahitian Finding List.* Chicago: The Chicago Academy of Sciences, 1944.

Biggs, Bruce. *Let's Learn Maori, a Guide to the Study of the Maori Language.* Wellington: A. H. and A. W. Reed, 1969.

——— "Proto Polynesian Wordlist, with Supporting Data from Nine Languages." Computer printout, University of Auckland, 1972.

Blixen, Olaf. "La Oclusión Glotica del Pascuense y Algunas Observaciones sobre la Posición del Pascuense dentro del Grupo de Lenguas Polenesias." *Moana* (Montevideo) 1 (5) (1972).

Churchward, C. Maxwell. *Tongan Dictionary (Tongan-English and English-Tongan).* London: Oxford University Press, 1959.

Dordillon, I.-R. *Grammaire et Dictionnaire de la Langue des Iles Marquises.* Paris: Imprimerie Berlin Frères, 1904.

Elbert, Samuel H. *Dictionary of the Language of Rennell and Bellona. Rennellese and Bellonese to English.* The University Press of Hawaii and the Danish National Museum, forthcoming.

Green, Roger C. Review of *Problems of Pre-Columbian Contacts,* edited by C. L. Riley, J. C. Kelly, C. W. Pennington, and R. L. Rands. *Journal of the Polynesian Society* 82 (1973):111.

Milner, G. B. *Samoan Dictionary. Samoan-English, En-*

glish-Samoan. London: Oxford University Press, 1966.

Pawley, Andrew. "On the Internal Relationships of Eastern Oceanic Languages." In *Studies in Oceanic Culture History,* vol. 3. Pacific Anthropological Records no. 13. Honolulu: Bernice P. Bishop Museum, 1972.

Pukui, Mary Kawena, and Samuel H. Elbert. *Hawaiian Dictionary.* Honolulu: University of Hawaii Press, 1971.

Savage, Stephen. *A Dictionary of the Maori Language of Rarotonga.* Wellington, N.Z.: Department of Island Territories, 1962.

Stimson, J. Frank, and Donald Stanley Marshall. *A Dictionary of Some Tuamotuan Dialects of the Polynesian Language.* The Hague: Martinus Nijhoff, 1964.

Williams, Herbert W. *A Dictionary of the Maori Language.* Wellington, N.Z.: W. A. G. Skinner, Government Printer, 1932. (First printed in 1844.)

Wilson, William H. "Possession in Hawaiian: -a- versus -o-." Unpublished manuscript, 1972. (In Sinclair Library, University of Hawaii.)